Alasdair MacIntyre's Engagement with Marxism

Historical Materialism Book Series

More than ten years after the collapse of the Berlin Wall and the disappearance of Marxism as a (supposed) state ideology, a need for a serious and long-term Marxist book publishing program has risen. Subjected to the whims of fashion, most contemporary publishers have abandoned any of the systematic production of Marxist theoretical work that they may have indulged in during the 1970s and early 1980s. The Historical Materialism book series addresses this great gap with original monographs, translated texts and reprints of "classics."

Haymarket Books is proud to be working with Brill Academic Publishers (http://www.brill.nl) and the journal *Historical Materialism* to republish the Historical Materialism book series in paperback editions. Current series titles include:

Alasdair MacIntyre's Engagement with Marxism: Selected Writings 1953–1974
Edited by Paul Blackledge and Neil Davidson

Althusser: The Detour of Theory, Gregory Elliott

Between Equal Rights: A Marxist Theory of International Law, China Miéville

The Capitalist Cycle, Pavel V. Maksakovsky, Translated with introduction and commentary by Richard B. Day

The Clash of Globalisations: Neo-Liberalism, the Third Way, and Anti-globalisation, Ray Kiely

Critical Companion to Contemporary Marxism, Edited by Jacques Bidet and Stathis Kouvelakis

Criticism of Heaven: On Marxism and Theology, Roland Boer

Exploring Marx's Capital: Philosophical, Economic, and Political Dimensions, Jacques Bidet

Following Marx: Method, Critique, and Crisis, Michael Lebowitz

The German Revolution: 1917–1923, Pierre Broué

Globalisation: A Systematic Marxian Account, Tony Smith

Impersonal Power: History and Theory of the Bourgeois State,
Heide Gerstenberger, translated by David Fernbach

Lenin Rediscovered: What Is to Be Done? *In Context,* Lars T. Lih

Making History: Agency, Structure, and Change in Social Theory, Alex Callinicos

Marxism and Ecological Economics: Toward a Red and Green Political Economy, Paul Burkett

A Marxist Philosophy of Language, Jean-Jacques Lecercle and Gregory Elliott

The Theory of Revolution in the Young Marx, Michael Löwy

Utopia Ltd.: Ideologies of Social Dreaming in England 1870–1900, Matthew Beaumont

Western Marxism and the Soviet Union: A Survey of Critical Theories and Debates Since 1917
Marcel van der Linden

Alasdair MacIntyre's Engagement with Marxism

Selected Writings 1953–1974

Edited by Paul Blackledge

and Neil Davidson

Haymarket Books
Chicago, Illinois

First published in 2005 by Brill Academic Publishers, The Netherlands

Published in paperback in 2009 by
Haymarket Books
P.O. Box 180165
Chicago, IL 60618
773-583-7884
www.haymarketbooks.org
ISBN: 978-1-608460-32-8

Trade distribution:
In the U.S., Consortium Book Sales, www.cbsd.com
In the UK, Turnaround Publisher Services, www.turnaround-psl.com
In Australia, Palgrave Macmillan, www.palgravemacmillan.com.au
In all other countries, Publishers Group Worldwide, www.pgw.com

Cover design by Ragina Johnson. Cover image by Natalia Goncharova, 1913.

Printed in the United States on recycled paper containing 100 percent post-consumer waste, in accordance with the guidelines of the Green Press Initiative, www.greenpressinitiative.org.

This book was published with the generous support of the Wallace Global Fund.

10 9 8 7 6 5 4 3 2 1

Library of Congress Cataloging-in-Publication Data is available.

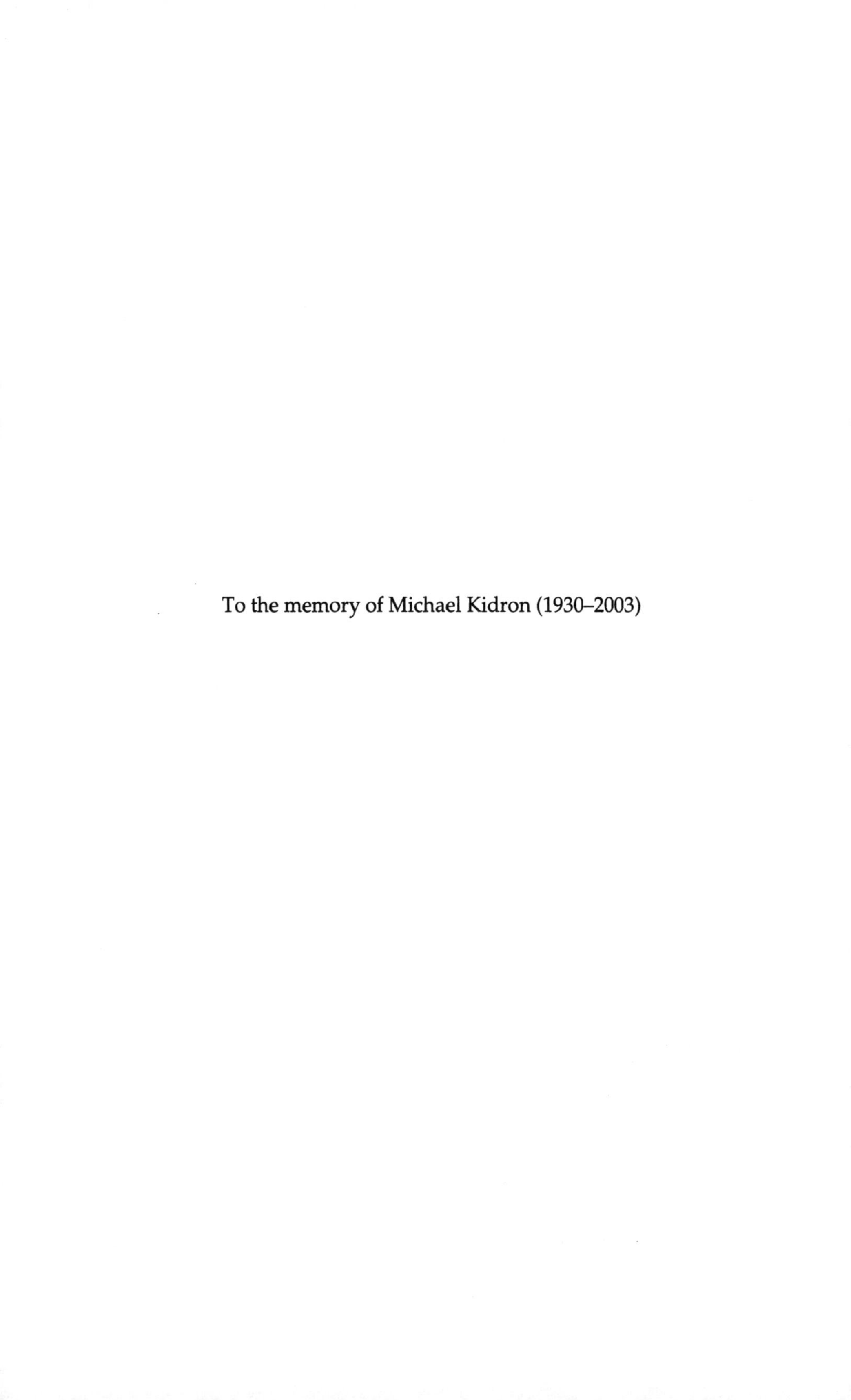

To the memory of Michael Kidron (1930–2003)

Contents

Acknowledgements

The book would not have been possible were it not for the kind help of Colin Barker, Alex Bavister-Gould, Ian Birchall, Sebastian Budgen, John Charlton, Mike Gonzalez, Kristyn Gorton, Chris Harman, Kelvin Knight, Jules Townsend, Cathy Watkins and Ben Watson. Johnny and Matthew Marsden once again proved inspirational. We would also like to thank the staff at the National Library of Scotland. Mostly, however, it is to Alasdair MacIntyre himself that we extend our gratitude for overcoming his initial doubts about this project, and giving us permission to republish these essays.

Introduction: the Unknown Alasdair MacIntyre

Paul Blackledge and Neil Davidson

Why read Alasdair MacIntyre's Marxist essays of the 1950s and 1960s in the early twenty-first century? Many would argue that the case made by MacIntyre in *After Virtue* and elsewhere for rejecting their arguments – that socialism no longer offers a realistic alternative to capitalism – has been vindicated by the collapse of the Soviet Bloc. Indeed, so prevalent is this opinion, that one form or another of liberalism has become almost absolutely dominant in recent discussions of political theory. However, despite the power of the contributions to contemporary political thought made by the likes of Rawls, Nozick, and Dworkin, in his mature work MacIntyre has convincingly shown that the arguments of these theorists rest upon various incommensurable preferences, and that the incommensurability of these preferences are rooted in forms of social practice associated with modern capitalism. If, in the mid-1960s, MacIntyre groped towards the conclusion that Marxism similarly expressed another set of incommensurable preferences, Kelvin Knight has convincingly argued against those who would portray MacIntyre's mature thought as a form of communitarian, that despite his rejection of certain elements of Marxism 'he has never abandoned Marx's idea of revolutionary practice'.[1] If this claim is reason enough to republish the essays below, we also intend to illuminate the strengths and weaknesses of the route through which MacIntyre moved towards, first, his break with Marx's politics and, second, his embrace of his mature politics. We publish these essays therefore with a view to providing both a standpoint from which the persuasiveness of his break with Marx can be adjudicated, and to suggest that his early Marxism might offer insights from

1 Knight 2007, p. 122.

the British New Left which speak to debates within the contemporary anti-capitalist movement.[2]

Throughout his career, MacIntyre has combined the view that ethical perspectives are rooted in specific social practices, with an argument that such practices are, in the modern world, irredeemably conflictual. If, in his mature thought, he has come to reject Marx's argument that the proletariat could develop social practices through which this tragic condition might be overcome, in the late 1950s and early 1960s he argued that while such forms of social practice could emerge, they would not do so as a mechanical consequence of the operation of the capitalist system. Accordingly, he insisted that socialists must necessarily play a pivotal role in the formation of proletarian class consciousness, and, indeed, that the most effective mechanism through which such a role might be executed was a revolutionary party. MacIntyre thus associated himself with the New Left's break with Stalinist crude economic determinism, but distanced himself from their rejection of 'Leninism'.[3] This movement entailed a critique of the dominant New-Left characterisation of Stalinism, and eventually to a break with Trotsky's classification of the Soviet social formation as a 'degenerate workers' state'. That MacIntyre had rejected this aspect of Trotskyism by around 1960 should warn us against too readily accepting his justification, as presented in *After Virtue*, for his break with Marxism: that 'a Marxist who took Trotsky's last writings with great seriousness would be forced into a pessimism quite alien to the Marxist tradition'.[4] For MacIntyre's mature period as a revolutionary socialist was predicated upon his acceptance of the proposition that, while Trotsky's perspectives for Russia had been refuted, a suitably revived Marxism need not share the weaknesses associated with orthodox Trotskyism. More problematic from our perspective is MacIntyre's argument, outlined in '*The Theses on Feuerbach*: A Road not Taken', that the modern proletariat is unable to embody the type of social practice imaged by Marx, and illustrated by Edward Thompson in his *The Making of the English Working Class*.[5] We suggest that, as an

---

[2] For a discussion of MacIntyre's contribution to historical materialism, see Blackledge 2005b and Blackledge 2006a, pp. 199–209.

[3] On MacIntyre's contribution to New and revolutionary Left debates on working class self-emancipation and socialist leadership see Blackledge 2007b. For a discussion of Lenin's politics that is indebted to MacIntyre see Blackledge 2005a.

[4] MacIntyre 1985, p. 262.

[5] MacIntyre 1998c, p. 231.

earlier articulation of this basic argument informed MacIntyre's slow break with Marxism though the 1960s and 1970s, it is incumbent upon Marxists to answer this charge if they are to salvage something positive from his engagement with Marxism in this period.

MacIntyre's contemporary reputation

Alasdair MacIntyre is best known today as the author of *After Virtue* and its sequels.[6] In these books, and in the numerous articles and interviews which complement them, MacIntyre has articulated what Knight has felicitously labelled a theory of 'revolutionary Aristotelianism'.[7] Whereas the importance of this contribution to political philosophy is not in doubt,[8] few of MacIntyre's interlocutors would profess an expert knowledge of his earlier Marxism, and fewer still have engaged with it. Indeed, the two collections published on his ideas, *After MacIntyre* and *Alasdair MacIntyre*, address his early Marxism only tangentially,[9] and while the monographs penned by Peter McMylor, Christopher Lutz and Thomas D'Andrea's do not share this failing, these books do not fully explore the relationship between the theoretical essays MacIntyre published for the New Left and the more directly political essays he wrote in this period.[10] In fact, McMylor and other commentators seem to be either unaware of the bulk of his early writings, or consider them unworthy of comment. This criticism is less applicable to Kelvin Knight's recent excellent study of MacIntyre's work, *Aristotelian Philosophy: Ethics and Politics from Aristotle to MacIntyre* (2007), but even Knight discusses only a fraction of the

[6] These include MacIntyre 1988; 1990; 1999.

[7] Knight 1996; Knight 2007. For MacIntyre's endorsement of this term, see MacIntyre 1998d, p. 235.

[8] This was, trivially, indicated by MacIntyre's pre-eminence in a poll of professional philosophers for *The Observer*, taken immediately after the publication of *Whose Justice? Which Rationality?*, see *Observer Magazine* 1989, pp. 10–11.

[9] Their bibliographies include only 'Notes from the Moral Wilderness'. See Horton and Mendus 1994, pp. 305–18; Murphy 2003, pp. 202–6.

[10] Of MacIntyre's essays published for and by the New and Trotskyist lefts, McMylor and D'Andrea discuss only 'Notes from the Moral Wilderness' and 'Breaking the Chain of Reason', while Lutz examines only the former of these essays. See McMylor 1994, pp. 202–3; D'Andrea 2006, p. 435; Lutz 2004, pp. 14–17. Each of these books ignores all articles or pamphlets published in or by *Universities and Left Review*, *Labour Review*, *New Left Review*, *International Socialism* and, more curiously, *The Listener*.

essays collected below.[11] Moreover, while Knight is to be congratulated for his inclusion of MacIntyre's 1958/9 essay, 'Notes From the Moral Wilderness', in his *The MacIntyre Reader* (1998), he tends to understate the power of this piece through his decision to locate it simply as a precursor to his later arguments, rather than as a key element of a more radical project.

One irony of the literature on MacIntyre is that the dismissive attitude towards his early Marxism, which is to be expected from those conservative thinkers who have praised his more recent critique of liberalism, is shared by many on the political Left. One reason for the distain shown to his work in these quarters can be traced to an understandable reaction on the part of many of his contemporaries in the New Left to MacIntyre's decision to publish some of his most important political essays of the 1960s in journals such as *Encounter* and *Survey*; whose relationship to the CIA's ideological role in the Cold War was even then something of an open secret. For instance, when the Socialist Society at the London School of Economics attempted to organise a series of Marxist lectures in 1965–6, problems arose when Isaac Deutscher did not want to appear on the same list as MacIntyre because the latter had criticised him on the pages of *Encounter*.[12] While this was embarrassing to MacIntyre's closest contemporary comrades in the International Socialism (IS) group,[13] the issue was neither raised within the organisation nor with MacIntyre individually. To the editors of *New Left Review*, by contrast, MacIntyre's decision to publish in *Encounter* was perceived as an act of renegacy which illuminated more general problems with his politics. For instance, in an early review of MacIntyre's *Marcuse* (1970), Robin Blackburn expressed a long standing animosity when he wrote that 'MacIntyre has for a long time specialized in doing hatchet jobs on such figures as Isaac Deutscher, C. Wright Mills, Georg Lukács and Herbert Marcuse, as well as purveying slanders on the Cuban, Chinese and Vietnamese revolutions.' Blackburn went on to argue that it was not only the 'miserable charlatan' MacIntyre who was at fault, but also the organisations which had harboured him: 'Perhaps older groups on the Left have indulged MacIntyre's political delinquency and intellectual bankruptcy in the past, but that was part

[11] Knight 2007. On MacIntyre's early Marxism see especially pp. 104–124.
[12] Harman, 2004: Harman was involved in organising the meetings.
[13] According to Harman IS's leading member, Tony Cliff, was privately furious with MacIntyre for publishing in *Encounter*.

of the traditional philistinism of the Left in this country.'[14] In 1972 another member of the *NLR* editorial team, Tariq Ali, advised his readers that an ironic 'look at the back copies of the *New Reasoner* provides an interesting insight into the workings of the *New Left* Mind'. Specifically, he recommend his readers 'read (for pure amusement)...an article by Alasdair MacIntyre entitled, "Notes from the Moral Wilderness"'.[15] Similarly, even at some distance removed from the heat of debate, *NLR* editor Perry Anderson summarily dismissed MacIntyre thus: he had entered the socialist movement 'fresh from providing books on Marxism for the Student Christian Movement' and subsequently 'ended up in the pages of *Encounter* and *Survey*'. Clearly, Anderson thought there was little more to be said for someone who had become a renegade from the socialist camp, other than that his work displayed 'a remarkable demonstration of ideological continuity' throughout his career.[16]

Anderson's comments on MacIntyre were written in the context of a discussion of Edward Thompson's deployment of MacIntyre's early ethical thought in support of his reinterpretation of historical materialism. For Thompson, the work of the young MacIntyre acted as a powerful Marxist humanist counter to Althusser's anti-humanism, which he associated with Perry Anderson specifically and the editorial board of *New Left Review* more generally.[17] Unfortunately, beyond socialists associated with IS, and its later reincarnation as the Socialist Workers' Party,[18] Thompson's was a relatively isolated voice at this juncture, such that, when a move occurred within Marxist circles to re-engage with ethical and normative theory in the 1970s and 1980s, in the ensuing discussions MacIntyre's name was conspicuous by its absence.

This dismissive stance was reinforced after the publication, in 1981, of the first edition of MacIntyre's magnum opus, *After Virtue*; which, despite its undoubted power, could be easily disregarded on the Left because of its concluding despair of the possibilities for building a moral community in the

[14] Blackburn 1970, p. 11.

[15] Ali 1972, p. 203, note 35.

[16] Anderson 1980, p. 108. cf. Anderson 1990, pp. 104–106.

[17] Thompson 1978, pp. 30, 33, 331, 349, 352, 358–66, 399–401.

[18] See the comments in Shaw 1974. Entries 1.6 ('Breaking the Chains of Reason'), 3.25 (*Marcuse*) and 16.5 (*Marxism and Christianity*); Harman 1983, p. 62; Callinicos 1983, pp. 5; 159, note 10; and Widgery 1976, pp. 14, 511, 519. Widgery reproduces MacIntyre's 'The Strange Death of Social Democratic England', in ibid., pp. 235–40. See Chapter 39, below.

modern world. Consequently, the Anglophone world's most sophisticated Marxist ethical theorist found his ideas doubly ignored on the Left: first, by the anti-moralists of the 1960s who were influenced by Althusserian Marxism, and then, once this sectarian attitude had faded, through his own break from Marxism just prior to the resurgence of forms of normative Marxism in the 1970s and 1980s. This was unfortunate, for, while some important contributions to a Marxist ethics were made in the 1970s and 1980s, these could all have benefited from an engagement with MacIntyre's surer sense of the historical contextualisation of ethical thought. Regrettably, the growing defeats suffered by the Left at the hands of resurgent neoliberalism in the 1980s militated against the appeal of MacIntyre's early gamble on the potential of the proletariat. And, as social-democratic régimes in the West and then Stalinism in the East collapsed in the face of the Thatcher/Reagan juggernaut, the assumption that Marxism too had been discredited informed a tendency on the part of MacIntyre's new found admirers to treat his early Marxism as either an aberration or a detour which had led to a dead end.

Another reason for the general ignorance of MacIntyre's early Marxism on the part of his interlocutors is the unavailability of many of the key texts published in this period. Important articles appeared in the relatively obscure journals of the Left: it is rare to find *The New Reasoner*, or *Labour Review* in a university library, and only slightly more common to find *International Socialism* (but not, usually, the very early editions to which MacIntyre contributed). In short, much of his work is unobtainable for practical purposes, while the groups that originally published the journals in which it appeared are either long since defunct or unwilling to republish. This would be less of a problem if MacIntyre himself had shown any interest in reproducing these early writings. However, until now, he has not; selecting for reprint in *Against the Self-Images of the Age* (1971) only those essays which appeared in what he described as 'professional philosophical journals' or 'journals of general intellectual culture'.[19] Similarly, in the most recently published selections of his essays, the earliest to be reprinted dates from 1972.[20]

In skirting over his more explicitly political writings, the essays brought together by MacIntyre in *Against the Self-Images of the Age* acted to distort

[19] MacIntyre 1971, p. vii.
[20] 'Hegel on Faces and Skulls' in MacIntyre 2006a.

the image of their author. One side of his persona in the 1950s and 1960s, the high-flying young academic, was allowed to eclipse another, the young revolutionary socialist. However, even in that limited selection, MacIntyre's ability to write clearly, on a spectacularly wide range of topics and for a general audience, differentiated his work from the bulk of his academic peers. In an apt comment on the young MacIntyre, Peter Sedgwick, writing in 1982, described his old comrade 'as an intellectual rather than solely as an academic'. This appreciation was related, partly, to the wide range of references deployed by MacIntyre, which encompassed areas far beyond his professional specialism. It was also partly related to 'his enviable capacity to take selected themes from the technical, professionalised debates among philosophers and social scientists and re-fashion them as material for the urgent attention of a non-specialised public, often using dramatic, poetic and prophetic devices in the casting of his arguments'.[21]

Sedgwick was right MacIntyre did and does have a remarkable talent for synthesis and clear exposition. However, in the 1950s and 1960s, he did more than this; he contributed to a series of important debates within the New and revolutionary Lefts, which we believe speak beyond the local concerns of the time. We particularly want to stress the contemporary relevance of MacIntyre's lasting contribution to Marxist theory. We suggest that his conceptualisation of a Marxist ethics through a historically mediated humanist interpretation of the concept of desire can fill an absence in contemporary radical thought; one that might outline a basis from which to draw a conceptual link between the real movement of workers and Marxist strategic demands. We believe that his early Marxism retains much of its power, and that it continues to offer insights through which contemporary theorists might relate the powerful strategic lessons of classical Marxism to the real desires of ordinary people in their struggles both in and against capitalism.

21 Sedgwick 1982, pp. 260, 261.

MacIntyre's Marxism

In an interview conducted in 1991, MacIntyre described the years between 1949, when he became a graduate student in philosophy at Manchester University, and 1971, immediately after his emigration to the United States, as forming a distinct period in his life and work.[22] We have broadly followed this periodisation in our selection of his essays. Thus, the opening essay is taken from his first published assessment of Marxism (1953), while the concluding pieces are three articles on Northern-Irish politics which appeared in close succession during 1974. His work during these years can be distinguished from his later comments on Marxism in that, to different extents, he was writing from within a Marxist theoretical framework. The chapters of this book trace the changes in MacIntyre's position, from his original attempt to synthesise Marxism and Christianity, to a wholly non-religious version of heterodox Trotskyism, to a final rejection of Marxism.

MacIntyre was born in Glasgow in 1929 of Irish descent. He took a degree in classics at the University of London during the late 1940s and subsequently a post-graduate degree in philosophy at Manchester University, where he stayed on as a lecturer between 1951 and 1957.[23] This was a period when the political bipolarity of Cold War international relations was refracted in Britain's organised labour politics through the Communist and Labour Parties. While the Labour Party, then as now, hegemonised the British Left, this position was not unchallenged; the Communist Party, most successfully in the trade unions, positioned itself as the left opposition to Labour. Unsurprisingly, the Communist Party had long since proved its willingness to perform any number of elaborate political contortions at the behest of its mentors in Moscow; while, more counter-intuitively, the Labour Party, though more pluralistic, had developed a parallel relationship to Washington. This situation was, of course, not conducive to the development of an independent left capable of articulating a political programme that went beyond the dualism of the Cold War.

The Asia-Africa Conference at Bandung in 1955 provided the first sign of an alternative to this bipolar world. At this conference, the grouping of states

[22] MacIntyre 1998b, pp. 267–9.
[23] *Who's Who* 2004, p. 1400.

which was later labelled the 'Third World' declared itself for the first time as a major independent player in international affairs. If this episode opened a crack in the world order, the events of 1956 – Khrushchev's secret speech, his suppression of revolution in Hungary, and the Anglo-French invasion of Egypt – together created a space for widespread criticism of the world order as a totality. In striking deep at the heart of the international system, these actions opened a space from which independent political forces could grow in Britain. In response to these events, a 'New Left' emerged which sought to map a third way between Eastern Communism and Western capitalism, and their left-wing political allies: Stalinism and social democracy.[24]

During his period in London, MacIntyre was both a member of the Communist Party of Great Britain (CPGB) and a communicant with the Church of England (C of E).[25] If Marxism appealed to him, in part, because of the power of the rich tapestry of historical-materialist analyses of the world as exemplified in the work, for instance, of George Thomson,[26] joining the CPGB did not necessarily involve, as one might suppose, a break with Christianity. For, from the onset of the Comintern's popular-front strategy in 1935 onwards, the CPGB had been involved in what it termed a 'dialogue' with various Christians: a process which climaxed when Hewlett Johnson, the 'Red Dean' of Canterbury Cathedral, joined the Editorial Board of the *Daily Worker* in 1943.

Whereas most contributions to this dialogue consisted of vague invocations of the supposedly shared humanist values of Communism and Christianity, MacIntyre's addition, *Marxism: An Interpretation* (1953), can be distinguished from the bulk of this literature by the seriousness of its attempt to discern intellectual links between Christian theology and Marxist theory.[27] Written from a radical Christian perspective and at the height of the Cold War, this book was remarkable in that it prefigured many of the themes that were to emerge a few years later with the birth of the New Left.[28] In particular,

---

[24] On the New Left, see Blackledge 2004b.

[25] His supervisor and later collaborator, Dorothy Emmet, claims that MacIntyre was on the verge of obtaining a candidature to become a minister in the Church of Scotland. See Emmet 1996, p. 86.

[26] MacIntyre 1998a, p. 256.

[27] See Chapter 1, 'Extracts from *Marxism: An Interpretation*'.

[28] McMylor 1994, p. 12.

MacIntyre began to explode the shared Stalinist and liberal myth of Marxism as a mechanical model of historical progress. We say began, because, in contrast to his essays published just a few years later, in 1953 he accepted the hegemonic critique of Marx's mature thought, while seeking to rescue what he perceived to be the revolutionary kernel of Marx's early writings. MacIntyre thus concluded *Marxism: An Interpretation* with the suggestion that the key text that should be read by Christians, alongside St Mark's Gospel, was Marx's *Economic and Philosophical Manuscripts* of 1844. For it was in this early text that Marx was at his prophetic, moral best; before succumbing to the allure of pseudo-scientific prediction that is evident in his work from *The German Ideology* onwards.

While this prefiguration of New-Left themes is important, MacIntyre's affiliation with the New Left did not simply emerge out of the congruence between his Marxism and their social practice. Rather, the experience of the New Left provided a practical source of inspiration for him, which helped raise his arguments from the level of theory to the level of practice. Indeed, the ideas embodied in *Marxism: An Interpretation* were deepened and transformed over the next few years as MacIntyre became more involved in political activity.

Adventures in the New Left, 1958–9

The New Left, as Peter Sedgwick pointed out in the wake of its collapse in the early 1960s, was less a coherent movement than a milieu within which many diverse political perspectives were aired.[29] It was formed of fragments from both the Labour and Communist Parties, alongside members of the revolutionary Left and student and other non-aligned elements radicalised by the events 1956. However, while the events of 1956 marked the point at which an independent Left first emerged in post-war Britain, it was a further eighteen months or so before a movement erupted that offered this milieu the opportunity to test its politics against those of the Labour and Communist Parties. The force that brought a new generation of activists onto the streets, and then into the New-Left meeting rooms, was CND; whose marches from early 1958 saw thousands of the dissatisfied youth come into

[29] Sedgwick 1964, pp. 15–18. On the New Left more generally see Blackledge 2006b.

conflict, not only with the government, but also with the leaderships of Labourism and Communism.[30] Indeed, it was through activity within CND that the New Left was able to break out of the political ghetto. However, the promise of radical change which nourished both the New Left and CND, was quickly stifled when the right wing of the Labour Party succeeded at the 1961 party conference in overturning the previous year's call for unilateral nuclear disarmament.[31] Subsequently, both the New Left and CND became casualties of shared overly optimistic hopes for the radicalisation of the Labour Party.[32]

MacIntyre seems not to have been actively involved in the New Left's formative debates. Nevertheless, by 1958 he contributed his first articles to the two main New-Left journals: *Universities and Left Review* and *The New Reasoner*. In the first of these essays, he argued that Marxism could learn from the best of bourgeois scholarship,[33] while, in the second, he insisted that, in discussions of the proletariat, the Left should not reify it as a revolutionary subject of history.[34] It was, though, in his third essay for a New-Left publication, written in the context of the New Left's debate on the nature of socialist humanism, that MacIntyre's early contribution to Marxism was most powerfully articulated.

Edward Thompson opened this debate in the first issue of *The New Reasoner*. His essay, 'Socialist Humanism: An Epistle to the Philistines' (1957), combined powerful criticisms of the inhumanity of Stalinism, with, on the one hand, a tacit acceptance of the consequentialist frame of reference through which the Stalinists had attempted to justify their actions, and, on the other, the suggestion that Stalin had forged his interpretation of Marxism from the more mechanical elements of historical materialism. Indeed, he commented that, although Stalin had employed brutal means, he had gone some way towards realising at least aspects of socialism in Russia. As was to be expected, Thompson's essay gave rise to a major debate within the New Left on the nature of socialism. For his part, Harry Hanson outlined a

---

[30] Both Labour and Communist parties initially opposed CND's demand for unilateral nuclear disarmament. See Thompson 1992, p. 116 and Thompson 1993, p. 64.

[31] Blackledge 2004b.

[32] Williams 1979, p. 365.

[33] See Chapter 3, 'On Not Misrepresenting Philosophy'.

[34] See Chapter 4, 'The Algebra of the Revolution'.

case for a more complete moral rejection of Stalinism as a strategy of forced industrialisation carried out through an assault on the basic human rights of the mass of Russians; while Charles Taylor suggested that if, as Thompson seemed to claim, Marxism had morphed into Stalinism then the New Left's critique of Stalinism implied a similar critique of Marxism.[35]

MacIntyre's contribution to this debate, 'Notes from the Moral Wilderness', aimed to outline a project capable of offering a powerful alternative to both Hanson's implied Kantianism and to Thompson's consequentialism by disentangling Marx's theory of history from Stalin's vulgarisation.[36] Moreover, in developing this perspective, he also instigated a process through which he outlined one of the most sophisticated defences of revolutionary-socialist politics of his day.

MacIntyre opened this essay with a critique of the implied Kantianism of Hanson's morality: 'The ex-Communist turned moral critic of Communism is often a figure of genuine pathos.... They repudiate Stalinist crimes in the name of moral principle; but the fragility of their appeal to moral principles lies in the apparently arbitrary nature of that appeal.' Despite the direction of this criticism, MacIntyre was even more critical of those apologists for Stalinism for whom socialism's moral core was lost amidst a mechanical theory of historical progress.

MacIntyre suggested that the Stalinists, through the medium of a teleological vision of historical progress, came to identify 'what is morally right with what is actually going to be the outcome of historical development', such that the '"ought" of principle is swallowed up in the "is" of history'. It was thus not enough to add something like Kant's ethics to this existing Stalinist theory of historical development if one wished to reassert moral principle into Marxism, for this theory of history negated moral choice. Conversely, neither was it adequate to reject, as immoral, any historical event from some supposed higher standpoint, for 'there is no set of common, public standards to which [one] can appeal'. Indeed, any such manoeuvre would tend to gravitate to an existing tradition of morality which, because these had generally evolved to serve some particular dominant class interests, would 'play into the hands

[35] Thompson 1957; Hanson 1957; Taylor 1957a; 1957b; For a more detailed discussion of this debate see Blackledge 2007c.

[36] See Chapter 5, 'Notes from the Moral Wilderness'.

of the defenders of the status quo'. Therefore, MacIntyre insisted, apologists for both the East and the West in the Cold War based their arguments upon inadequate theoretical frameworks. By contrast with these perspectives, MacIntyre argued that we should look for a 'theory which treats what emerges in history as providing us with a basis for our standards, without making the historical process morally sovereign or its progress automatic'. In his search for a basis from which to reconstruct a Marxist ethics, MacIntyre argued, contrary to 'the liberal belief in the autonomy of morality', that it was the purposive character of human action that could both distinguish human history from natural history, and which could provide a historical and materialist basis for moral judgements.

MacIntyre suggested that Marxists should follow Aristotle specifically, and the Greeks more generally, in insisting on a link between ethics and human desires: 'we make both individual deeds and social practices intelligible as human actions by showing how they connect with characteristically human desires, needs and the like'. He thus proposed to relate morality to desire in a way that was radically at odds with Kant; for where Kant's '"ought" of morality is utterly divorced from the "is" of desire', MacIntyre pointed out that to divorce ethics from activities which aim to satisfy needs and desires in this way 'is to make it unintelligible as a form of human action'. In contrast to the Kantian categorical imperative, MacIntyre therefore argued that we need a morality which relates to our desires. However, while human desires are related to human needs, MacIntyre refused to reify the concept of human nature. Instead, he followed Marx in radically historicising human nature, without losing sight of its biological basis. Indeed, part of Marx's greatness, or so MacIntyre argued, was that he succeeded in historicising Man: for Marx refused to follow either Hobbes's naturalisation of the war of all against all, or Diderot's utopian counter-position of the state of nature against contemporary social structures. By contrast, Marx comprehended the limited historical truth of Hobbes's insight, but counter-posed to it, not a utopia, but the real movement of workers in struggle through which they could become capable of realising that solidarity is a fundamental human desire.

Specifically, under advanced capitalism, in MacIntyre's reading of Marx, 'the growth of production makes it possible [for man] to reappropriate his own nature'. This is true in two ways: first, the increasing productivity of labour produces the potential for us all to lead much richer lives, both morally and materially; and, second, capitalism creates an agency – the proletariat – which embodies, through its struggles for freedom, a new collectivist spirit, through which individuals come to understand both that their needs and desires can best be satisfied through collective channels, and that they do in fact need and desire solidarity. Indeed, he claimed that the proletariat, in its struggles against capital, was beginning to create the conditions for the solution of the contemporary problems of morality: it embodies the practice which could overcome the 'rift between our conception of morality and our conception of desire'.

MacIntyre concluded that once the political Left had rid itself both of the myth of the inevitable triumph of socialism, and of the reification of socialism as some indefinite end which could be used to justify any action taken in its name, then socialists would truly comprehend the interpenetration of means and ends through the history of class struggle. Consequently, they would understand Marxist morality to be, 'as against the Stalinists', 'an assertion of moral absolutes', and, 'as against the liberal critic of Stalinism', 'an assertion of desire and history'.

A Year with the Leadership, 1959–60

The practical bent of MacIntyre's Marxism in this period lent itself to a re-engagement with Lenin's political thought at just that moment when the bulk of the New Left were theorising their break with the ideas of the leader of the Russian Revolution. This development is less paradoxical than it at first sight appears, for it is one of history's minor ironies that the New Left's break with Leninism, while explicitly conceived as a deepening of their break with Stalinism, was predicated upon the (Stalinist) assumption that the East-European régimes were, in a limited sense, socialist states. As one of us has argued elsewhere, the rejection of democratic centralism articulated by several contributors to *The Reasoner*[37] in 1956 – then still a magazine edited by critical members of the Communist Party – was predicated upon the assumption that 'socialist' states had been established 'peacefully' after the

[37] Three editions of *The Reasoner* were published in 1956 – the last in an act of explicit breach of party discipline. From 1957, *The New Reasoner*, was published outside the Party.

war without the leadership of Leninist parties. This 'fact' contradicted Lenin's claim that the necessarily revolutionary transition from capitalism to socialism required a centralised political leadership to counter the centralised power of the capitalist state. Thus assured of the possibility of a successful non-Leninist strategy for socialist advance, the dominant voices within the New Left felt able to distance themselves not only from Lenin's legacy, but also from any project of building an independent New-Left organisation.[38] In contrast with this perspective, MacIntyre's activist interpretation of Marx informed his reading of Lenin. Moreover, he read Lenin, not primarily from the vantage point of the Stalinist take-over of Eastern Europe after the War, but from the perspective of the limitations of mechanical Marxism: he came to view revolutionary organisations as necessary media through which proletarian unity might be won. This perspective sharply differentiated MacIntyre from many leading figures within the New Left, whilst simultaneously drawing him towards those whose break with Stalinism had brought them into the orbit of the Trotskyist Left.

There is an unfortunate tendency on the part of many students of the British New Left to dismiss the role of Trotskyism within it. This method belies an academic orientation on the part of many of these authors, which, as Dorothy Thompson has powerfully argued, acts to emphasise the theoretical and philosophical dimensions of New-Left activity at the expense of an analysis of its, primary, *political* nature.[39] Conversely, it is useful to remember that a number of key working-class activists, alongside some equally impressive journalists and intellectuals, upon leaving the Communist Party after 1956 found their way into the Trotskyist movement.[40]

Alongside a number of these activists, in June 1959 MacIntyre joined Britain's main Trotskyist organisation, the Socialist Labour League (SLL); which was then operating within the Labour Party. The following year MacIntyre aligned himself to a tendency within the organisation which favoured the creation

[38] Blackledge 2004b.

[39] Thompson 1996, pp. 94–5.

[40] Callaghan 1984, p. 72. These included Brian Behan who MacIntyre later described as 'the best man who was a revolutionary socialist in Britain in the last twenty five years'. MacIntyre 1965, p. 29.

of an open revolutionary party; and resigned from the organisation after the expulsion of the leadership of this grouping.[41]

The forerunner of the SLL – known simply as 'the Club' – had emerged as the British section of the tiny world Trotskyist movement in the late 1940s and early 1950s. The Club was the dominant local faction to emerge from the crisis of the international Trotskyist movement in the wake of the falsification of a number of Trotsky's key programmatic predictions after the end of the War. Led by Gerry Healy, the Club dealt with the debates within the organisation by expelling anyone who disagreed with an absurdly catastrophic set of perspectives drawn, dogmatically, from Trotsky's late political writings. In the British case, this meant expelling those, such as Tony Cliff and Ted Grant, later leading members of the Socialist Workers' Party and the Militant Tendency respectively, who challenged both these perspectives and Healy's authority.[42] By 1956, the details of what by this time seemed ancient struggles mattered less than the fact that the Club was the largest Trotskyist grouping in the country, and was therefore able to draw on Trotsky's undoubted moral authority as a critic of Stalinism to attract many of the best activists who had recently left the CPGB. If the undemocratic structure of the Club/SLL ensured that it continued to adhere to Healy's cataclysmic perspectives after 1956, this failing was not immediately apparent. Indeed, in the late 1950s, the Club/SLL seemed to offer the promise of the creation of a viable anti-Stalinist British Marxist party.[43]

A sense of the vibrancy of this new organisation is evident in a report of MacIntyre's contribution to the 'National Assembly of Labour', which gathered on 15 November 1959; drawing 700 delegates to St. Pancras Hall in London.[44] Described in a report in the SLL newspaper, the *Newsletter*, as a 'lecturer in philosophy at Leeds University and a delegate from the Leeds Branch of the Socialist Labour League', MacIntyre welcomed the fact that the conference included teachers and lecturers as well as traditional members of the working class. However, he warned his fellow intellectuals against acting as though

---

[41] Baker 1962, p. 65.

[42] Bornstein and Richardson 1986, p. 231.

[43] Hallas 1969.

[44] Contributors to the discussion included Jim Allen, the playwright, who was at this time still working as a miner, and Pat Arrowsmith of the Direct Action Committee.

they were 'sent from heaven or the Fabian Society in order to guide the labour movement from above with their theorising.'[45]

This democratic approach to political leadership is similarly evident in MacIntyre's critique of the sectarian attitude shown by some leading members of the SLL to the New Left. Thus, in 1959, he engaged Cliff Slaughter on the pages of *Labour Review*, the SLL's monthly theoretical magazine, over the issue of the SLL's relationship to the broader New Left milieu. Slaughter had argued that it was incumbent upon the SLL to 'state sharply were we differ on basic questions of theory and method' from the New Left. Consequently, he traced and criticised arguments regarding the nature of social class in the modern world as articulated by a number of important New-Left thinkers, principally, Dorothy Thompson, Charles Taylor and Stuart Hall.[46] In opposition to Slaughter's almost wholly negative indictment of New-Left theory, MacIntyre, in a reply published in the following issue of *Labour Review*, pointed out that the New Left was a more complex phenomenon than Slaughter's essay implied, and that many of Slaughter's own criticisms had been articulated within the New Left itself – most prominently by Edward Thompson. Therefore, while MacIntyre agreed with much of the substance of Slaughter's arguments, he felt that Slaughter's 'polemical and sectarian style' was mistaken, for it acted to create a barrier between the SLL and all that was positive within the New Left. 'The most important thing about the New Left', he argued, 'is that it exists'. Therefore, 'for a Marxist the question must be: What does the existence of this grouping point to in the changing character of our political life?'. On the basis of a generally positive answer to this question, MacIntyre concluded his internal critique of the SLL leadership with the argument that 'the relationship of Marxists to the New Left ought not to be one merely negative and critical but one which is continually looking for those points of growth in its theory that can lead on to common political action'. More generally, he argued in a way that reflected the influence on his ideas of the journal *Socialisme ou Barbarie* published by revolutionary ex-Trotskyists in France, that, as it was at the 'point of production' that people in 'our society... begin to act and think for themselves', then it was the duty of the SLL to argue, fraternally, within the New Left that that they should orientate

[45] *Newsletter*, v. 2, n. 127, 21 November 1959, p. 331.
[46] Slaughter 1959.

themselves towards the industrial struggles of the working class. Socialists, he wrote, 'can only carry through an effective educational effort as part of the industrial and political struggle'. Conversely, despite the good intentions of the New Left, its lack of focus on such struggles tended to 'dissipate socialist energy and lead nowhere'.[47]

While he was a member of the SLL, therefore, MacIntyre managed to combine a refusal of the sectarianism of the leadership of that organisation, with a defence of Leninist politics. To this end, he wrote a pamphlet for the SLL, *What Is Marxist Theory For?*, within which he articulated a humanist interpretation of Leninism. MacIntyre opened this pamphlet, which was in fact a collection of articles taken from the SLL's paper *The Newsletter*, with an outline of the Marxist theory of alienation, and the privileged position of the working class therein. In the second chapter, he deepened his defence of Marx's claim for the universal character of the working class, while, in the third chapter, he defended a nuanced Leninist model of the role of intellectuals within the labour movement. Finally, he concluded his argument with a call for theoretically informed revolutionary action both within and against the system.[48] He outlined the concrete contemporary shape of this practice in a second pamphlet, *From MacDonald to Gaitskell*, which concluded with a call to win the Labour Party to socialism.[49] MacIntyre further proselytised for the SLL on BBC radio, in a brief talk reproduced in *The Listener*, which provoked a debate with contributions from Edward Thompson, Harry Hanson and Peter Cadogan.[50] In addition to these popularisations, MacIntyre, in what was perhaps the most substantial of his writings for the SLL, attempted a sophisticated outline of the nature of revolutionary political organisation: 'Freedom and Revolution'.[51]

This essay was in large part an extension and deepening of his the humanist reinterpretation of Marxism set forth in 'Notes from the Moral Wilderness'. It opened with a defence of Hegel's conception of freedom as the essence of man, and Marx's deepening of this notion through his insistence on the

---

[47] See Chapter 9, 'The "New Left"'; cf. Castoriadis 1959.
[48] See Chapter 10, 'What is Marxist Theory For?'.
[49] See Chapter 11, 'From MacDonald to Gaitskell'.
[50] See Chapter 12, 'Communism and British Intellectuals'.
[51] See Chapter 13, 'Freedom and Revolution'.

inseparability of freedom and the achievement of a classless society. Alongside Hegel, MacIntyre refused to reify freedom as the endpoint of history, but rather historicised it as a series of moments moving towards this end. Thus, the free man 'in every age is that man who to the extent that it is possible makes his own life his own'. Within bourgeois society, MacIntyre located the freedom of the bohemian as an inauthentic model of freedom: 'a mere inversion of bourgeois values'. He counter-posed to this model the suggestion that as we exist as individuals through our relations with other people then the achievement of 'freedom is not a problem of individual against society but the problem of what sort of society we want and what sort of individual we want to be'. Indeed, given the validity of this claim, it was only logical for MacIntyre to conclude that 'to assert oneself at the expense of the organisation in order to be free is to miss the fact that only within *some* organisational form can human freedom be embodied'. Moreover, as capitalism emasculates freedom, then to be free means to involve oneself in some organisation that challenges capitalist relations of production: 'The topic of freedom is also the topic of revolution'. At this point, MacIntyre introduced a crucial mediating clause into his argument: while the working class through its struggles against capital might spontaneously generate emancipatory movements, it has proved incapable of spontaneously realising the potential of these struggles. However, if freedom cannot be handed to the working class from above, how then might it be realised from such unpromising material? MacIntyre answered that socialists must join revolutionary parties, whose goal is not freedom itself, but rather to act in such a way so as to aid the proletariat to achieve freedom:

> the path to freedom must be by means of an organisation which is dedicated not to building freedom but to moving the working class to build it. The necessity for this is the necessity for a vanguard party.

Moreover, MacIntyre suggested that socialists such as Thompson and the rest of the majority within the New Left who rejected the goal of building a socialist party, suffered from 'the illusion that one can as an isolated individual escape from the moulding and the subtle enslavement of the status quo'. By contrast, MacIntyre argued, 'the individual who tries most to live as an individual, to have a mind entirely of his own, will in fact make himself more and more likely to become in his thinking a passive reflection of the socially dominant ideas; while the individual who recognises his dependence on others has taken a path which can lead to an authentic independence of mind'. Given the efficiacy of the Bolsheviks, MacIntyre concluded his argument with the claim that 'the road to socialism and democratic centralism are... inseparable'.

With regard to his membership of the SLL, MacIntyre, in a response to critics of his defence of the SLL on the pages of *The Listener*, wrote that 'whether the SLL is or is not democratic or Marxist will be very clearly manifested as time goes on. I myself have faced no limitation on intellectual activity of any kind in the SLL'.[52] Ironically, within months of writing these lines, he resigned his membership of the organisation after the leading members of the tendency with which he was associated were expelled for the crime of contravening the 'correct procedure for forming a tendency'.[53] In a letter to Healy, MacIntyre observed that it was clearly impossible for a minority to exist within the organisation because of Healy's personal dominance – reinforced by the fact that he effectively owned the party as private property, since the assets were in his name. MacIntyre concluded, however, that these problems stemmed not simply from Healy's personal malevolence – real though that undoubtedly was – but because of the small size of the Trotskyist organisations which allowed individuals to play this role.[54] Consequently, despite his break with the SLL in 1960, MacIntyre saw no reason to break with Trotskyism *per se*.

In his next major essay for a New-Left publication, 'Breaking the Chains of Reason' (1960), MacIntyre conjured an image of two competing images of rival 'paths for the intellectual' in the modern world. On the one hand, Keynes, 'the intellectual guardian of the established order'; and on the other, Trotsky, the 'outcast as a revolutionary... providing throughout his life a defence of human activity, of the powers of conscious and rational human effort'. MacIntyre concluded this essay with an echo of Marx: 'the philosophers have continued to interpret the world differently; the point remains, to change it'.[55]

52 MacIntyre 1960, p. 500.

53 Callaghan 1984, pp. 77–8. While Callaghan claims that MacIntyre was expelled from the SLL, Baker suggests that he resigned following the expulsion of Brian Behan and others. Given the sectarian venom with which Baker criticises MacIntyre, it seems fair to assume that, had he been able to claim that the SLL had expelled MacIntyre, he would have done so. Baker 1962, p. 65.

54 Callaghan 1984, p. 78.

55 See Chapter 14, 'Breaking the Chains of Reason'.

International Socialist

MacIntyre's break with the SLL did not signal, therefore, the end of his affiliation with Trotskyism. Rather, it marked the point at which he joined the smaller, but more intellectually appealing and more democratic, International Socialism group. Knight pokes fun at MacIntyre's politics of this period, writing that after leaving the Communist Party, 'MacIntyre first joined a dogmatically Trotskyist group. Then... he joined another, less dogmatic one'. Fortunately, as Knight sees it, MacIntyre's resignation as an editor of the, 'less dogmatic', *International Socialism* in 1968 came 'just in time to avoid association with the posturing of the second and final wave of the New Left'.[56] The inadequacy of this critique of MacIntyre's political trajectory in this period is perhaps best illuminated through Edward Thompson's comment that *International Socialism* was 'the most constructive journal with a Trotskyist tendency in this country, most of the editorial board of which are active (and very welcome) members of the Left Club movement'.[57] Similarly, in his study of MacIntyre, McMylor described the International Socialism group as 'one of the more intellectually open and creative far left organisations'.[58]

Contra Knight, MacIntyre's shift in political allegiance in 1960 was significant. For, like MacIntyre, the Marxists around *International Socialism* were at this juncture involved in a project of rethinking the nature of revolutionary leadership. Moreover, like him, their goal was to build upon the ideas of Lenin, Trotsky and Luxemburg without collapsing into the caricatured ultra-Bolshevism of the SLL. Indeed, in a generally unsympathetic survey of the politics of IS in this period, Martin Shaw argued that it 'came to represent the polar opposite to the SLL: realistic in economic perspectives, able to explain the failures of labour bureaucrats as well as to condemn them, non-sectarian towards other socialists, the champion of thorough working-class democracy in all areas of practice'.[59] This perspective was, as Shaw suggests, informed by the break made with orthodox Trotskyism by IS's main theoretician, Tony Cliff. Trotsky had characterised the Soviet Union as a 'degenerate workers' state', and his 'orthodox' followers had generalised this model to account

[56] Knight 1998, p. 2; cf. Knight 2007, p. 119.
[57] Thompson 1960b, p. 22.
[58] McMylor 1994, p. 8.
[59] Shaw 1978, p. 104.

for the essentially similar régimes created in Eastern Europe and China after the War – 'deformed workers' states'. By contrast, Cliff insisted that it was nonsense to suggest that a workers' state could be realised without a workers' revolution. Moreover, as these states were locked into a process of military competition with the West, and as the producers within these states remained wage-labourers, the East European states could best be classified as bureaucratic state-capitalist social formations.[60]

According to Alex Callinicos, Cliff's theory of bureaucratic state capitalism afforded his Marxism a number of advantages over orthodox Trotskyism in the post-war period. First, in characterising the Soviet social formation's capitalism through its military competition with the West, Cliff was able to lay the basis for a powerful theory of the post-war boom: a theory of the 'permanent arms economy'. Second, this model of post-war capitalism in turn suggested a modification of the classical Marxist theory of imperialism, which immunised his followers from the worst excesses of 'Third Worldism'; the belief that the central locus of the struggle against capitalism had shifted from the point of production to the national-liberation movements in the South. Third, Cliff's model of the post-war boom informed his analysis of the changing locus of Western reformism: parliamentary parties of the Left were becoming increasingly irrelevant as the most visible improvements in workers' standards of living were won not through the ballot box but through their self-activity at the point of production: 'reformism from below' was undercutting reformism from above.[61]

The fundamental premise of the theory of bureaucratic state capitalism was that socialism could only be achieved through workers' self-emancipation. This assumption in turn informed both an orientation towards rank and file workers' struggles on the part of Cliff's group, and a critique of the SLL's model of leadership. Following Marx's democratic insistence in the third of his theses on Feuerbach that 'the educator must himself be educated', Cliff argued that the SLL's 'school-masterly' approach to the workers' movement had to be rejected. In its place, he insisted in two essays first published in

[60] Cliff 2003.

[61] Callinicos 1990, pp. 79–85. Cliff's analysis challenged the pessimism with which the bulk of the Left greeted the collapse of Stalinism between 1989–91. See Callinicos 1991.

1959 and 1960, that Marxists should act in their relations with other activists and workers as 'companions in struggle'.[62] This implied critique of the sectarianism of the SLL, paralleled MacIntyre's own assessment of the SLL's relationship to the New Left noted above. Read in this context, MacIntyre's shift from the SLL to the IS is best conceptualised as a moment in the process through which he deepened his understanding of the concrete implications of his radicalism: first, after his break with the CPGB he moved to the New Left, then towards a form of Trotskyism, and then towards a more vibrant interpretation of Marxism.

MacIntyre joined both IS and the editorial board of its newly launched eponymous journal in 1960.[63] His earliest contribution appeared in the third issue,[64] and he was first introduced to readers in Issue 6: 'Alasdair MacIntyre', the note revealed, 'teaches philosophy and has experience of the Communist Party, the Socialist Labour League, the New Left and the Labour Party; believes that if none of these can disillusion one with socialism, then nothing can'.[65] While this judgement proved to be somewhat premature, over the next few years MacIntyre did play a leading role within IS, within which, through his ability to combine political passion and classical learning with expert commentaries on a wide variety of contemporary issues, from Sartre's Marxism through the Common Market to Irish politics, he helped to inspire a new generation of its younger members.[66]

MacIntyre made explicit his heterodox interpretation of Trotskyism in a review, first published in 1963, of the third volume of Isaac Deutscher's biography of Trotsky. In this essay, he insisted that Trotskyism was a contested tradition, whose ossification in the hands of Deutscher, and by implication in the SLL, stood in stark contrast to its living force in the work of those such as

---

[62] Cliff 2001b, p. 129; 2001a, pp. 76–86.

[63] MacIntyre appeared as a member of the editorial board in Issue 2 and as co-editor alongside Mike Kidron from Issues 3–8 (1960–2). His name remained on the list of editors down to issue 32 in 1968.

[64] See Chapter 15; 'Is a Neutralist Foreign Policy Possible?'

[65] *International Socialism*, 6, Autumn 1961, p. 20. MacIntyre's membership of IS coincided with his break with Christianity (Chapter 18 below).

[66] On Sartre see Chapter 21, on the Common Market Chapter 26, and on Ireland Chapter 16. On Ireland see also MacIntyre, 1959, p. 239; 1962, pp. 2–3. For a discussion of MacIntyre as an intellectual in the 1960s, see Sedgwick 1982.

Alfred Rosmer, Trotsky's widow Natalya, and, again implicitly, within IS.[67] MacIntyre insisted that orthodox Trotskyism, through its reification of one moment of Trotsky's evolving attempt to achieve a scientific analysis of the Soviet Union, was built upon an indefensible and incoherent foundation. To cling, dogmatically, to the word of Trotsky's falsified prewar perspectives implied a necessary break with the critical and revolutionary spirit of his thought.

How did MacIntyre attempt to remain true to the spirit of Trotskyism in the early 1960s? Knight suggests that his position at this juncture involved him embracing dogma. Unsurprisingly, MacIntyre did not understand his allegiance to Marxism in such terms. Rather, as is readily apparent from his review of Lucien Goldmann's *The Hidden God*, his Marxism involved not a dogmatic faith in the working class, but, rather, a wager on its potential. The method of the wager, or so Goldmann argued, was at the heart of any approach to moral philosophy once the 'ideal of individual wisdom' had been replaced with an engagement with 'external reality'.[68] Goldmann, whose book is centrally concerned with the 'tragic vision' of Pascal and Racine, noted three periods when a form of the tragic vision became the dominant motif of the age: the moments of Sophocles, Shakespeare, and finally Pascal, Racine and Kant. He argued that the tragic vision itself expresses a particular social group's experience of 'a deep crisis in the relationship between [its vision of] man and his social and spiritual world'. Moreover, he noted that, after each of these historical moments, there occurred attempts by representatives of a new social group, to move beyond this crisis by showing that 'man is capable of achieving authentic values by his own thoughts and actions': Plato after Sophocles; 'European rationalism and empiricism' after Shakespeare; and Hegel and Marx after Pascal, Racine and Kant.[69] In each of these periods, once the move had been made from a faith in individual wisdom to an engagement with external reality, then 'man's life takes on the aspect of a wager on the success of his own action and, consequently, on the existence of a force which transcends the individual'.[70] In accordance with this model, Marxism involves

[67] Chapter 29; 'Trotsky in Exile'.
[68] Goldmann 1964, p. 301.
[69] Goldmann 1964, pp. 41–6.
[70] Goldmann 1964, p. 301.

a wager on the revolutionary potential of the proletariat. MacIntyre accepted this argument, and indeed deepened it when he wrote that 'one cannot first understand the world and only then act on it. How one understands the world will depend in part on the decision implicit in ones already taken actions. The wager of action is unavoidable'.[71] To label MacIntyre's wager dogmatic is thus to miss the point: one way or another, we all make the wager, and those who do not bet on the proletariat are compelled to retreat back to the tragic vision: if we reject Marx, then we are doomed, therefore, to fall back into one form or another of the incommensurable ethical perspectives dominant within bourgeois society. To fully comprehend MacIntyre's later break with Marxism we must consequently ask not what made him drop the dogma, but rather what made him change his bet?

In answering this question, we must first note that the mid-1960s were far from halcyon days for the British revolutionary Left. In fact, MacIntyre's stint as a member of IS more or less coincided with the period between the collapse of the first New Left, and the emergence, in 1968, of a second wave of radical political activism. This context posed a considerable problem for MacIntyre, for, just as the political dissent of 1956–62 had been the very lifeblood of his Marxism, the decline of the various elements of this radical milieu necessarily posed difficult questions of his revolutionary socialism. Nevertheless, MacIntyre's break with Marxism was no automatic response to the downturn in the level of political struggle; he actively interpreted the events of the 1960s and 1970s in an increasingly pessimistic way.

Interestingly, the response to the collapse of the first New Left chosen by the new cadre around *New Left Review* from 1962 onwards would have been unappealing to MacIntyre. The imagined role for *New Left Review* upon its formation through the unification of *The New Reasoner*, and *Universities and Left Review* in 1960 was, according to Edward Thompson, to facilitate the growth of a general socialist consciousness out of the multiplicity of radical struggles in contemporary Britain.[72] With the collapse of the first New Left, *New Left Review* fell into the hands of a small grouping around Perry Anderson who reorganised it as a journal of Marxist *theory* with little contact to socialist

---

71 Chapter 34; 'Pascal and Marx'.

72 Thompson 1960a, pp. 68–70.

practice.[73] Moreover, in so far as this new *New Left Review* team maintained a relationship with domestic politics, in the early mid-sixties it was as (not so) critical supporters of Harold Wilson's Labour Party.[74] In his 'Labour Policy and Capitalist Planning', MacIntyre strongly criticised those socialists who were moving to support Wilson for mistaking his neo-capitalist technocratic strategy as a progressive or even socialistic project. MacIntyre's rejection of the identification of socialism with statism in the West presupposed IS's critique of the socialist credentials of the Stalinist states in the East. While this perspective helped immunise him against the Wilsonite bug, he was equally wary of the abstractly theoretical practice of the new *New Left Review*. Indeed, the fact that MacIntyre's Marxism was rooted in a model of the actualised desires of workers in struggle meant that Anderson's project would have struck him as irredeemably formalist. However, in a context of political retreat for the Left, it was incumbent upon him to provide a viable alternative to *New Left Review*'s re-emergence as a medium for academic Marxism. The articulation of such a project necessitated at least two elements: first, a model of underlying tendencies which might generate future revolutionary-socialist upheavals and agencies; and, second, a model of socialist practice in the intervening period. Unfortunately, over the next few years, MacIntyre came to conclude that modern capitalism undermined fatally those tendencies which Marx had previously suggested would foster the creation of revolutionary-socialist agencies. First, he rejected Marx's theory of economic crisis; second, he argued that modern capitalism acted to fragment, rather than unite, workers' struggles; and, third, he rejected any concept of human nature as a standpoint from which to indict capitalism.

MacIntyre outlined his criticisms of Marx's theory of economic crisis in his essay 'Prediction and Politics', published in *IS* in 1963.[75] On the pages of *IS*, the post-war boom had been explained as a consequence of increasing international arms production. According to Michael Kidron, the co-editor with MacIntyre of *IS*, arms production forced a reciprocity between East and West in the Cold War, as each power was compelled to match the other's deadly potential through the medium of military competition. Moreover,

---

[73] Cf. Blackledge 2004a, p. 14.
[74] Blackledge 2004a, p. 39.
[75] Chapter 27.

spending on arms simultaneously acted to waste massive amounts of capital that would otherwise contribute to an increasing organic composition of capital and consequently to a decline in the rate of profit. Kidron went on to argue that, while post-war capitalism's tendencies to crisis were thus mediated, this process could not be relied upon indefinitely. For, on the one hand, the rise in the organic composition of capital had been slowed, but not stopped; while, on the other hand, the arms burden was shared disproportionately across the West, such that Germany and Japan, for example, could expand at the expense of Britain and the USA. According to this model, the contemporary economic boom could not be expected to continue uninterrupted, and therefore economic crisis was to be expected in the medium term.[76] Kidron's comments were aimed at Henry Collins's defence of a left-reformist political strategy on the pages of *IS*. Collins had argued that government planning had played the key role in the creation of post-war economic stability.[77] On this issue, MacIntyre seemed to take a middle way between Kidron and Collins; arguing that the role of the permanent arms economy was significant, but that this did not negate the importance of human agency in the transition from pre- to post-war capitalism. He suggested that post-war capitalism had been transformed by the 'conscious, intelligent innovation' of the bourgeoisie and its representatives: 'If capitalists had behaved in the forties and fifties as they did in the twenties the apparently mechanical laws of the economy would have issued in slump. But there are no longer slumps for the same reason that the pig-cycle is no longer with us: the changed self-consciousness of the participants'.

This proposition created an enormous tension at the heart of MacIntyre's Marxism; for he had previously insisted that workers' struggles against their alienation would tend towards socialism in the context of economic crises as explained by Marx in *Capital*. Thus, in 'Notes from the Moral Wilderness' (1959), he argued that

> Marx's explanation of capitalist crisis is not a matter of underconsumption, but of falling return on profit which leads the capitalist to lower his investment. And this explanation, like the explanation of proletarian

[76] Kidron 1962.
[77] Collins 1961.

> reactions to such crisis, rests on his view of what has happened to human nature under capitalism.

Similarly, in 'Rejoinder to Left-Reformism' (1961), he suggested that revolutionaries should develop a programme that sought 'to bring together three elements in our social life': 'the deep and incurable dissatisfaction with social life which capitalism breeds'; 'the recurrent state of objective crisis in capitalist social order'; and 'socialist theory'.

To remove Marx's analysis of the dynamics of capitalism from this model obviously weakened it as a theoretical basis for socialist practice. Moreover, elsewhere in 'Prediction and Politics', he argued that, far from tending to unite workers into a class for themselves, the division of labour associated with modern capitalism tended to fragment them.

> There is a sad case for saying that being in an economically strong position today against the employers in certain industries at least, means that the issues on which you are likely to fight and even possibly win are just the issues that are going to divide you from less skilled workers.

In such circumstances, the one remaining hope for socialism was to be found in the feeling, generated within the working class, that capitalism was constraining their potential for free human development. In the short term, this did not lead MacIntyre to break with his wager on the proletariat. Rather, he concluded 'Prediction and Politics' with the argument that as the condition for the fall of capitalism was the growth in socialist class consciousness within the proletariat, and that as this growth was neither inevitable nor impossible, the prospects for socialism 'depends upon us' to make that change in consciousness.

In 'Labour Policy and Capitalist Planning', he provided some meat to the bones of this suggestion, with the argument that socialists should aim to 'recreate a political trade unionism out of the existing links between the Labour Party and the unions'. Concretely, in a paper presented to an *International Socialism* day school in 1963, he argued that revolutionary leadership involved formulating a series of political demands which could be made upon the incoming Labour government, and which, whilst formally reformist, could, in practice only be realised through a revolutionary transformation of society. This argument drew on Trotsky's *Transitional Programme*, and shared a fundamental weakness with that document. For the effectiveness of Trotsky's model of transitional demands depended on the circumstances within which they were made, such that unfavourable circumstances would negate their revolutionary content. As Duncan Hallas argued, 'if at a given time "today's consciousness of wide layers" is decidedly non-revolutionary, then it will not be transformed by slogans'.[78] Unfortunately, the context within which MacIntyre wrote was characterised by decidedly non-revolutionary working-class consciousness, and no amount of transitional demands were going to change this. This criticism suggested a crucial flaw in MacIntyre's political theory. For his break with crude mechanical Marxism seems to have drawn him to a form of political substitutionism, according to which the will-power of revolutionaries played a disproportionately important role in the transition to socialism. Unfortunately, his model of that role appeared to be inadequate to the task of theorising a bridge between the existing consciousness of the working class and their potential revolutionary consciousness.

The pessimistic political implications that might follow the failure of this strategy was mediated in the short term by MacIntyre's deepening attraction to *Socialisme ou Barbarie*'s extreme spontaneist version of Marxism; an attraction that is evident in a report, carried in the journal *Solidarity*, of MacIntyre's 1965 debate with *Socialisme ou Barbarie's* leading intellectual, Cornelius Castoriadis (Paul Cardan). Billed as a debate between IS and Solidarity, MacIntyre provoked anger across the leadership of IS when he essentially accepted both the broad outline of Castoriadis's analysis of contemporary capitalism, and his critique of the project of building a socialist organisation.[79] The account of the meeting carried in *Solidarity* stated:

> The two main speakers, although approaching the problem from different angles, did not disagree on fundamentals. The similarity of many of their views led one comrade, who had come 'expecting a debate', to deplore the presence of 'two Cardans'.[80]

Concretely, MacIntyre's disagreement with other leading members of IS in the audience centred on his belief that a much more fundamental transformation in the nature of capitalism had occurred in the post-war years than they were

---

[78] Hallas 1979, p. 104; cf. Molyneux 1981, p. 182.
[79] *Solidarity* 1965, pp. 22–5.
[80] *Solidarity* 1965, p. 22. This criticism was made by Michael Kidron.

ready to admit. MacIntyre declared in his response to contributions from the floor that he detected 'a very bad tone in what Kidron and Cliff had said...because it was translated from the Russian, about the year 1905':

> The crucial difference between those who managed capitalism in the nineteenth century and those who managed it today was that the latter had achieved a degree of consciousness as to what they were doing.... Perhaps Cardan won't do either. But there is a problem posed here between the bureaucratic political forms and the economic transactions of our society which isn't in traditional Marxism and which Cardan's book poses very sharply.[81]

As we have intimated, MacIntyre had been drawn towards the ideas of *Socialisme ou Barbarie's* leading theoretician, Cornelius Castoriadis, from at least 1960 when, in 'Freedom and Revolution', he stressed the importance of politics at the 'point of production'. This essay was subject to important critiques on the pages of both *New Left Review*, and the SLL's *Labour Review*. Indeed, in *Labour Review*, Cliff Slaughter mounted a critique of MacIntyre through the proxy of an attack on both *Socialisme ou Barbarie's* 'spontaneist' deviation from (a caricatured interpretation of) Leninism, and its one-sided stress on politics at the point of production.[82] Similarly, on the pages of *New Left Review*, Edward Thompson argued that MacIntyre's thesis that the key antagonism in society lay at the point of production was 'the ABC of socialism with the B and C left out'. The B and C in this case were, Thompson insisted, the class struggle, which might take on any number of forms that are not reducible to industrial militancy.[83]

Thompson's was a powerful point; for MacIntyre's defence of the need to build a revolutionary party, organised along democratic-centralist lines that would act to lead the proletariat, while innocent of the ultra-vanguardist verbiage associated with the leadership of the SLL, suffered from an obverse problem; it only weakly addressed the problem of political practice within the working class. In fact, in MacIntyre's conception of its role, the party seemed limited to giving theoretical focus to the spontaneous movement

---

[81] *Solidarity* 1965, pp. 23–4.
[82] Slaughter 1960, pp. 105–9.
[83] Thompson 1960a, pp. 68–70.

of the working class.[84] This left a gaping hole at the centre of his political theory. For Lenin, and indeed Marx, had predicated their arguments for building revolutionary parties on the need to overcome the sectionalism of the spontaneous movement of workers; limitations that were a necessary correlate of the fragmentation of the working class through the technical, that is specifically capitalist, division of labour.[85] By contrast with these models, MacIntyre's one-sided stress on the spontaneous movement of the working class, while inadequate in any period of struggle, was doubly so in periods such as the 1960s, when workers' struggles remained sectional and did not to point in any obvious way towards socialism.

The tension created between the optimism of *Socialisme ou Barbarie*'s spontaneist-humanist interpretation of Marxism, and MacIntyre's pessimistic assessment of the concrete content of sectional struggles on the part of the working class, was eventually resolved when MacIntyre broke with Marxism. With regard to MacIntyre's relationship to IS, Ian Birchall has written that 'I don't think I ever saw MacIntyre again after [the Cardan debate]. I'm fairly certain he didn't contribute to the group press or attend any further meetings'.[86] This, therefore, appears to be the moment of break with IS; almost three years before MacIntyre posted his resignation letter to the editors in 1968.

Disengagement, 1964–8

MacIntyre's rejection of Marx's crisis theory, alongside his argument that the modern capitalist division of labour increased the fragmentation of the working class, implied that the workers' cries for freedom would remain atomised and therefore that the tasks facing socialists were much more daunting, indeed overwhelming, than more orthodox Marxists allowed. This is the conclusion implied in his works of the later 1960s, which, while written when he was still nominally an editor of *International Socialism*, universally suggested little or no hope for revolution. Thus, in his introduction to Marx's ideas for an academic audience, while he powerfully argued that 'the most

---

84 As he wrote in 'Breaking the Chains of Reason': 'Our deep need is... to provide all the growing points of human activity against the present social order with coherent theoretical expression, so that they may be rationally guided and effective'.

85 On this, see Blackledge 2005a and 2007a.

86 Birchall 2000.

crucial later activity of Marx', was not to write *Capital*, but was rather through his actions in 'helping to found and guiding the International Working Men's Association', he concluded that Marx 'still leaves the question of working-class political growth obscure'.[87] Whether or not this observation was correct of Marx, it certainly appeared to be true of MacIntyre, who was unable to conceptualise any contemporary conditions under which a mass movement might realise his vision of socialism. In fact, MacIntyre extended his political pessimism back into the nineteenth century. For instance, in a series of lectures originally given in 1964, but published some three years later as *Secularisation and Moral Change*, he argued that Engels had been mistaken in his overly optimistic perspective for the future secularisation of British society, and that this was a corollary of his overly optimistic perspectives for socialism. MacIntyre went on to suggest that 'the inability of men to discard Christianity is part of their inability to provide any post-Christian means of understanding their situation in the world'. Moreover, while he suggested that this failure was by no means 'ultimate', he noted no inherent tendencies with which socialists might engage that, belatedly, might help them prove Engels correct.[88]

Another reason why MacIntyre was drawn to such a pessimistic conclusion was that, by the mid–1960s, he moved to reject not only Marx's, but also all other competing theories of human nature which might act as a humanist basis for revolutionary politics. This position was made explicit in his classic *A Short History of Ethics* (1966), where, despite some tangential remarks as to the relationship between morality and desire, his own moral standpoint seemed disjoined from either any historical or materialist premises to which he had earlier been committed.[89] Consequently, he rejected the idea of human nature as a benchmark from which to adjudicate moral claims, and reduced individual morality to an existential choice.[90] While he chose Marxism in 1966, he refused any criteria by which this choice could rationally be defended. Therefore, without a theory of human nature with which to underpin it, his theory of revolution, at least as he had outlined it in 'Freedom and Revolution',

87 Chapter 31; 'Marx'.
88 MacIntyre 1967, p. 75.
89 MacIntyre 1966, pp. 210–14. Cf. Sedgwick 1982.
90 MacIntyre 1966, pp. 268–9.

remained baseless. MacIntyre's socialist morality, in this context, could boast no more compelling foundation than any competing moral claim. Indeed, by the late 1960s, it appeared that he had ceased to view Marxism as either a science or a guide to action, but rather as just one competing worldview amongst many others

One memoir of his performances at the time contains the following description:

> In 1965–6 MacIntyre delivered a lecture course at Oxford University entitled 'What was Morality?' to a packed room in the Examinations Schools. My image is of a short, jowelled figure in a corduroy suit, the latest in radical chic. The style was at once magisterial and provocative, deadpan but destructive.... Like Nietzsche and Sartre, MacIntyre saw 'the death of God' as a cataclysmic event in the history of moral systems which had, since the Enlightenment, become a series of failed attempts to attain the objectivity of theism without the embarrassment of theistic doctrines, an objective moral code without God as the author. In the heady 1960s MacIntyre was content to leave us with this deconstructed ruin of history. He viewed the situation with a cheerful irony and ended his lectures with a nod towards the Marxism then propounded by Sartre, which allowed us to seek the ephemeral community of the 'group in fusion', while keeping our distance from the supposed errors of historical materialism. If this was 'frivolous', said MacIntyre, perhaps that was not a vice. In any case, it was all that we could hope for.[91]

A couple of years later, *International Socialism* included a rather bemused note on a departure from the journal and its parent organisation

> Alasdair MacIntyre has resigned from the Editorial Board of *IS*. He offers no extended account of why he is resigning now, rather than earlier or later, nor has he accepted our invitations to lay out his criticisms of the journal in our columns. But resign he has.[92]

The closest MacIntyre came to a contemporary articulation of his differences with IS were aired in the new edition of *Marxism: An Interpretation*, republished

---

91 O'Hagan 1990, p. 19.
92 'Letter to Readers', *International Socialism*, First Series, 33, Summer 1968, p. 17.

in 1968 under the title of *Marxism and Christianity*. In this book, MacIntyre's interesting analysis of the lineages of Marx's ideas through Feuerbach and German idealism and into Christian theology remained. However, expunged from the text was any suggestion of the practical, Christian-socialist, purpose of the original. Moreover, MacIntyre ironically reduced Marx's theory of history to the caricature from which he had attempted its rescue in 'Notes from the Moral Wilderness'. Thus, he rejected historical materialism, in part, on the basis of a repetition of the common accusation that Marx's base-superstructure metaphor posited the existence of elements of the social totality which 'stand in external, contingent, causal relationship to each other', and suggested that the failure of Marxism as a theory of history informed its inability to provide a coherent ethical alternative to liberalism.[93] It was the retreat from socialist activity, even Christian-socialist activity, justified by this argument that led the reviewer for *International Socialism* to bemoan the re-write, proclaiming that the activist core of the first edition had made that much the better of the two books.[94] Interestingly, MacIntyre made a similar point in his 1995 introduction to this book,

> In the first version of this book there was a chapter on philosophy and practice that was omitted when I revised it in 1968. That chapter was originally included because it attempted to pose what I had rightly recognized as the fundamental problem. It was later omitted because I had by then learnt that I did not know how to pose that problem adequately, let alone how to resolve it. So in 1968 I mistakenly attempted to bypass it.[95]

In 1968, therefore, whereas MacIntyre had reached the negative conclusion that Marxists had not adequately theorised the problem of revolutionary practice, he failed to formulate a positive alternative. He concluded *Marxism and Christianity* with the suggestion that the desires of workers were irredeemably constrained by their fragmented practices, and that, in such a context, Lukács's defence of Lenin's politics amounted to a 'deification of the party' which was merely the flipside to Kautsky's earlier 'deification of history'.[96] A few years

[93] MacIntyre 1995, pp. 137; 122.
[94] Kuper 1970, p. 35.
[95] Epilogue; '1953, 1968, 1995: Three Perspectives'.
[96] MacIntyre 1995, p. 101.

later, he extended this argument to dismiss the membership of revolutionary organisations as pathetic caricatures of the experts of managerial capitalism.[97] When he repeated a similar claim in *After Virtue*, Peter Sedgwick tellingly suggested that it is 'only in a certain light, and at a certain halting-point in the argument' that such a comparison between capitalism's defenders and its revolutionary opponents could be rendered intelligible.[98] The 'light' through which MacIntyre made this assertion, included a dismissal of the potential of proletarian practice to underpin a realistic socialist movement, and the consequent belief that socialist activists, of whatever variety, were doomed to attempt, forlornly, to impose their ideas onto such unpromising material from the top down.

This in no sense meant that MacIntyre made his peace with capitalism. Thus, in the *New Statesman* in 1968, he argued that it was both a right and a duty to campaign against the war crimes being perpetrated by the Americans in Vietnam.

> when [George Kennan] condemns civil disobedience outright and when he supposes that what the student Left dislike about the Vietnam War is that they might be killed in it, he exhibits an ignorance of the contemporary student scene which is disgraceful in a member of a university.... What he does not begin to grasp – and what his dreadful paternalistic style must obscure from him – is that in Vietnam War crimes are being committed and that resistance to the Vietnam War by acts of civil disobedience is therefore not a right, but a duty.[99]

Nevertheless, despite the stridency with which MacIntyre defended this claim, within a couple of years he was to defend the authority of the university against student radicalism. In *Marcuse* (1970), he simultaneously emphasised his own continuing allegiance to the concepts of human liberation and freedom, whilst denouncing the contemporary student struggles as 'the first parent-financed revolts' which were 'more like a new version of the children's crusade than a revolutionary movement'.[100] This position involved MacIntyre

97 MacIntyre 1973, pp. 341–2.
98 Sedgwick 1982, pp. 264–5.
99 MacIntyre 1968, p. 714.
100 MacIntyre 1970, pp. 61 & 89.

in something of a performative contradiction, in so far as he rejected the argument that an ideal, pure Marxism can be deployed as an alternative to the reality of Marxism's history, while accepting an implicitly idealised vision of the struggle for liberation against which the student movement was found wanting. This was a far cry from the criticism he had made a decade earlier of the SLL's sectarian attitude towards the New Left. Indeed, just as Cliff Slaughter had maintained a formal allegiance to the emancipatory politics of the Left, whilst dismissing real struggles as they happened around him in 1960; in the late 1960s and early 1970s MacIntyre combined a formal radicalism with a much more conservative practice. Against the disruptive influence of 'Marcuse's students', MacIntyre extolled the virtues and 'authority' of the university of a seat of learning.[101] More generally, he explicitly rejected the applicability of Marx's categories to the modern world.

> [Marx] envisages the concentration of workers in large factory units and the limits set upon the growth of wages as necessary conditions for the growth of [political] consciousness; but he says nothing about how or why the workers will learn and assimilate the truths which Marxism seeks to bring to them.... Indeed, one might write the history of the age which Marxism illuminated so much more clearly than any other doctrine did, the period from 1848 to 1929, as one in which Marx's view of the progress of capitalism was substantially correct, but at the end of which the Marxist script for the world drama required the emergence of the European working-class as the agent of historical change, the working-class turned out to be quiescent and helpless.[102]

Consequently, MacIntyre argued that, in the modern world, 'to be faithful to Marxism we have to cease to be Marxists; and whoever now remains a Marxist has thereby discarded Marxism'.[103] This argument prefigures that expressed in his essay 'The *Theses on Feuerbach*: A Road Not Taken' (1994). Here, he suggests that while workers may have engaged in such social practices as facilitated the realisation of virtuous communities at certain

---

[101] MacIntyre 1970, p. 91.
[102] MacIntyre 1970, pp. 42, 43.
[103] Ibid., p. 61.

moments in history, by contrast with Marx's expectations the process of proletarianisation had simultaneously made resistance a necessary part of the lives of the working class, while robbing this resistance of its emancipatory content. Indeed, proletarianisation 'tends to deprive workers of those forms of practice through which they can discover conceptions of a good and of virtues adequate to the moral needs of resistance'.[104]

Conclusion

The power of MacIntyre's Marxism in the period of the first New Left was rooted in his ability to grasp that any moral claim, if it is to be universalised in the modern world, must be rooted both in a historically conceived theory of human nature and in a concrete understanding of human history. To this end, he did the Left a great service by retrieving the revolutionary kernel of Marx's theory of history from the deadening grip of Stalinism; and in thus releasing historical materialism from the cage of Stalinist determinism, he laid the basis for an ethical Marxism adequate to the tasks facing socialists in the modern world. In particular, he linked the concepts of class, revolution, and revolutionary party with those of need, want and desire such that his model of a workers' revolution answered a universal human desire for solidarity.

However, MacIntyre also asked a series of questions of the Left, regarding crisis theory, models of human nature, and models of proletarian social practice, that remain pertinent to this day. At one level, MacIntyre's recent reassessments of his earlier dismissals of the labour theory of value and essentialist models of human nature has narrowed the gap between his ideas and Marxism.[105] Nevertheless, he continues to believe that capitalism both creates the need for proletarian resistance while simultaneously subverting the radical content of that resistance. We would suggest that this argument does not correct, but rather inverts the errors committed by those mechanical Marxists who expected proletarian class consciousness to arise spontaneously as a response to the crisis of capitalism. Against both of these positions, we believe that MacIntyre's early wager on the proletariat retains its power to this day, so long as we recognise this wager as a call to action rather than

[104] MacIntyre 1998c, p. 232.
[105] MacIntyre 1995, p. xx; MacIntyre 1999. See Blackledge 2005b, p. 720.

as a mechanical prediction of future events. While it was a tragedy for the Left that MacIntyre did not develop his own insights into the sort of practice necessitated by such a wager, this does not negate the power of his early contribution to Marxism.

Ironically, MacIntyre broke with the Marxist Left just as, in the late 1960s and early 1970s, it entered its most exciting period of growth in conjunction with a series of working-class struggles whose very existence suggests the one-sidedness of MacIntyre's mature analysis of the proletariat.[106] Since then, while the Left has experienced many defeats, the contemporary anti-capitalist movement has once again placed the idea of the socialist transformation of society on the political agenda. This context has in turn re-opened, through the contribution of Hardt and Negri's *Empire*, the debate on the place of the desire for freedom within the socialist project. It is our belief that MacIntyre added much to our understanding of this relationship in the late 1950s and early 1960s, and contemporary radicals have much to learn from his writings of this period. For these essays, particularly 'Notes From the Moral Wilderness', 'Breaking the Chains of Reason', and 'Freedom and Revolution', provide the basis upon which Marxists might theorise the link between the struggles of ordinary people to meet their desires, with the goals of the anti-capitalist movement.

---

[106] On this period see especially Harman 1998.

A Note on the Selection and Annotation

Selection

The bibliography of Alasdair MacIntyre's writings between 1953 and 1974 which follows lists nearly 200 published pieces. These range from short poems in the *New Statesman* to substantial chapters in books as different as *Metaphysical Beliefs* and *Out of Apathy*. This collection reproduces less than a quarter of these items. How did we arrive at the final selection? The articles and essays had to meet one of two criteria.

The first is where they relate directly to Marxism itself – by which we mean not only theory and theoreticians, but the political movements which claimed (with varying degrees of accuracy) to be inspired by it. Most of the items which fall into this category are from the period during which MacIntyre considered himself to be a Marxist; some show him moving towards that position and some moving away from it, but all constitute part of the 'engagement' that the book seeks to document.

The second is where they are themselves Marxist analyses of the contemporary world. In most cases, these focus on British society and politics although, exceptionally, one deals with imperialist entanglements in Africa in the early 1960s (Chapter 20, 'Congo, Katanga and the UNO'). As we noted in the introduction, MacIntyre continued to employ Marxist analysis in specific ways, even after he had found it was inadequate as a general theory. His critique of Che Guevara in Chapter 41 ('Marxism of the Will'), for example, is essentially conducted from a classical-Marxist perspective.

We have not included everything that meets our criteria. The splendid series of one- or two-paragraph book reviews that MacIntyre wrote for *International Socialism* in the early 1960s are a model of concision, but would scarcely constitute individual chapters, and other potential contenders have been excluded for inclusion are simply occasional pieces, written to order and of little permanent value. However, we did not want to restrict our selection to the most obviously 'classic' essays which formed the basis of MacIntyre's early reputation, such as Chapter 5 ('Notes from the Moral Wilderness') and Chapter 14 ('Breaking the Chains of Reason'). In some ways, these major works can only be fully understood in the context of the broader, ongoing arguments which MacIntyre was developing in the shorter pieces included here. In any case, above a certain minimum length, brevity is not to be lightly dismissed. MacIntyre manages to say more about, for example, the early work of Raymond Williams (Chapter 17, 'Culture and Revolution') or the insularity of some British socialists (Chapter 26, 'Going into Europe') in a handful of pages than more inflated works have done in several chapters.

On the basis of our criteria it was relatively easy to exclude the majority of the religious writings from the 1950s. MacIntyre's technical philosophical writings, however, proved a more difficult and complex case. Throughout the years when he was politically active MacIntyre was employed as a lecturer by several university philosophy departments and regularly published in the academic journals of his profession. Former comrades in both the Socialist Labour League (SLL) and the International Socialists (IS) later expressed doubts as to whether his academic work was in any way informed by Marxism, but neither organisation seems to have formally raised the issue with him while he was a member.[1] In some cases, these writings do seem to exist in a parallel universe where Marxism is unknown – which, come to think of it, is a reasonably accurate description of the average British philosophy department during the 1950s and early 1960s. Others, however, employ the Marxist method in exemplary ways. For instance, his early (1959) remarks on the implications of the existence of class society for moral theory or his later (1971) discussion of the historical nature of the concept of 'ought' in *Against*

[1] In relation to the SLL, see Baker 1962, p. 67. In relation to the IS, Ian Birchall writes: '[Tony] Cliff…distrusted MacIntyre's academic philosophical work, which he believed had little to do with Marxism'. Personal communication, Birchall to Davidson, 24 August 2000. It should be added, of course, that MacIntyre was scarcely alone in producing professional work which did not reflect his Marxist beliefs. Indeed, even such cadres as the SLL's Cliff Slaughter produced fairly anodyne sociology during their day jobs. See, for example, Slaughter 1956.

the Self-Images of the Age.[2] In the end, we did not include essays of this type because they would have diluted the main focus of the book.

Our consideration of whether to include 'Ought' did however lead on to the more general question of our attitude to the minority of essays which are still in print. With one exception ('Notes from the Moral Wilderness' in *The MacIntyre Reader*) these are chapters in *Against the Self-Images of the Age*. In fact, this issue posed considerably less of a problem than the philosophical writings. We took the view that all the relevant essays should be included, as one of our main objectives was to contextualise them through reinsertion into the chronological trajectory of MacIntyre's work as a whole. An essay like 'Trotsky in Exile', for example, which first appeared in *Encounter*, can be seen as part of a far more consistently revolutionary argument alongside similar pieces from *International Socialism* than it does when read in comparative isolation in the pages of *Against the Self-Images of the Age*.

Annotation

One of the characteristics of MacIntyre's prose, at least in the material included here, is his employment of a classical essay style unencumbered by footnotes and references. In many cases this is because the pieces concerned originated as book reviews, where they are generally disallowed. Does it unnecessarily burden them by adding a formal scholarly apparatus? Reproducing these pieces as they first appeared would certainly have saved a great deal of editorial work, but that approach would have been inadequate, for two reasons. First, inserting references exposes the hitherto invisible skeleton, the theoretical underpinning supporting the argument as one reads down the page. Second, MacIntyre shared broadly the same cultural reference points as the members of his audience. He could therefore assume, with a reasonable degree of certainty, that it would be familiar with the theories of Popper or Wittgenstein, the novels of Koestler or Hemingway, or the editorial positions of *Tribune* or the *New Statesman*. That culture has long since passed into

---

2 A. MacIntyre, 'Hume on "Is" and "Ought"', in *Against the Self-Images of the Age: Essays on Ideology and Philosophy*, Duckworth, London 1971, p. 116; '"Ought"', in ibid., especially pp. 142–56.

history. References are therefore a necessary aid to the reader in mapping out the lost cultural world of the British New Left.

The vast majority of the footnotes in this collection have therefore been added by Neil Davidson. Where MacIntyre quotes from works which were only subsequently translated into English, such as Sartre's *L'Être et le néant* or Marx's *Grundrisse*, he has used the standard English translation. He has only made references to non-English editions either where the work concerned has not been translated or the translated version is now completely inaccessible.

MacIntyre tended to make reference to writings by other people in four different ways.

(i) *Complete references*. These were infrequent. Their rare appearances tended to occur in journal articles written towards the end of the period covered by these essays and to take the form of footnotes. These references have been left as originally written. In the very few cases where MacIntyre expresses an opinion in a reference – to commend a particular book or interpretation, for example – his comments have been enclosed in square brackets to indicate his authorship.

(ii) *Incomplete references*. These were more frequent and tended to appear in brackets within the text. In these cases, MacIntyre usually cites an author and refers to the journal in which their work appears without necessarily giving the title of the article or any other details, other than the date of the issue. These references have been transformed into footnotes with missing details added.

(iii) *Quotations without references*. These appeared with the greatest frequency. Typically, quotations were from novels or classical works of political theory without attribution other than author and title. In most cases, it has been impossible to trace the precise edition used by MacIntyre. In the case of novels, this was not an issue, since there are usually standard versions or translations of the text. Works of political theory posed greater difficulties. For Lenin, reference is made to the forty-five-volume *Collected Works* (1960–70) and these translations tend to be the same as those used by MacIntyre. In the case of Marx and Engels, there were greater problems. There are numerous translations and editions of their major works, some in which the text is rendered in significantly different ways. In order to introduce some consistency, reference is made, where possible, to the eight volumes of the Penguin Books/*New Left Review* Library (*Early Writings*, the three volumes of the *Political Writings*, the 3 volumes of *Capital*, and the *Grundrisse*). Any texts not included in these volumes have been referenced from the fifty-volume *Collected Works* (1975–2004). Where a quotation used by MacIntyre is significantly different from the version cited in the footnotes, the text of the latter version is also given.[3] The same procedure is followed in the case of a handful of other writers (Hegel, Lukács and – a name not usually found in this company – Bonhoeffer) and modern translations are referred to in the footnotes.

(iv) *Allusions*. MacIntyre frequently alludes to a remark by or idea associated with a particular thinker (often Hegel or Engels) without actually quoting them, let alone giving a reference. This can be particularly frustrating if, for example, you are anxious to find out where Herzen actually gave his much quoted description of Hegel's philosophy as 'the algebra of revolution' – a mystery which several generations of Marxist writers have apparently been unable to solve.[4] (It is, in fact, from his autobiography.) While full references are provided where the allusion has been identified, there has been no attempt to locate references for every single passing mention afforded to one writer or another.

Editorial comments have been kept to an absolute minimum, and are mainly concerned with clarification, such as alerting the reader to changes to the text of books which MacIntyre reviewed in their original edition, but which contemporary readers are only likely to encounter in subsequent revised editions (i.e. Raya Dunayevskaya's *Marxism and Freedom* or Eamonn McCann's *War and an Irish Town*). In one case (a reference to an article by Peter Townshend in Chapter 22, 'The Sleepwalking Society'), MacIntyre cites

---

[3] What counts as significant is a matter of judgement, of course. In Chapter 1, 'Extracts from *Marxism: an Interpretation*', MacIntyre quotes the famous passage from *Capital* which ends: 'The expropriators are expropriated.' The translation which he uses (from the Everyman edition) is essentially the same in all but minor details from the translation in the Penguin edition, so the latter is not reproduced. On the other hand, in Chapter 12, 'Breaking the Chains of Reason', MacIntyre cites Marx from the *Economic and Philosophical Manuscripts* as saying that Hegel's concepts are 'the money of the mind.' The Penguin edition renders this as 'Logic is the currency of the mind', which is rather different and worth highlighting.

[4] For examples of the 'as Herzen once remarked' strategy for avoiding looking up this reference, see S. Hook, *From Hegel to Marx: Studies in the Intellectual Development of Karl Marx*, Victor Gollancz, London 1936, p. 74, note 1 and J. Rees, *The Algebra of Revolution: the Dialectic and the Classical Marxist Tradition*, Routledge, London and New York 1998, p. 60, note 135.

the wrong article and this is noted and the correct details entered. In another, (a reference to a book by Clement Attlee in Chapter 30, 'Labour Policy and Capitalist Planning') he misidentifies *The Labour Party in Perspective* as *The Future of the Labour Party*. Other than these, the only comment offered in what follows is in relation to his interpretation of Engel's 1895 'Preface' to Marx's *The Class Struggles in France* from the same chapter. MacIntyre based himself on the edited version of this text – the only one available at the time – which seems to emphasise an electoralist strategy. The subsequent publication of the original text in the *Collected Works* has made the view that Engels had adopted a reformist perspective on the achievement of socialism at the very least more difficult to sustain. The comment which accompanies this reference simply draws the reader's attention to this fact. All other interpretative comments have been restricted to the *Introduction*.

Apart from presentational issues – corrections to spelling, changes to punctuation, insetting of quotations and breaking up the unbroken columns of prose favoured by the early New Left into more manageable paragraphs – these articles and essays are reproduced as they were written, with one exception. That exception is the one previously unpublished piece included here, Chapter 24, which we have titled 'The New Capitalism and the British Working Class'. The text is based on MacIntyre's hand-amended typescript for a talk given by to an IS day school during 1962. Unknown to all except, presumably, the few dozen members of the IS at the time, this was a valuable find, elaborating on many of the arguments which MacIntyre was making in more compressed form in articles of the time. We are grateful to John Charlton, who was present at the event, for supplying us with the document. However, it is written to be spoken, complete with asides, digressions, repetitions, and organisational in-jokes which would have made it either unreadable or incomprehensible in its pristine form. We have therefore cut the extraneous matter and compressed some passages, but have not, we trust, done violence to either the argument or to the informality of the presentation.

A Bibliography of Works by Alasdair MacIntyre, 1953–74

This bibliography attempts to give a comprehensive picture of Alasdair MacIntyre's work between 1953 and 1974, although I have no doubt that it is still incomplete. The main difference with existing bibliographies is that it includes the articles he wrote for the socialist organisations to which he belonged between 1959 and 1968. These tend to be ignored, through conscious attempts to suppress this aspect of MacIntyre's career, but mainly because his current admirers appear to be unaware of their existence, with a handful of exceptions. One particularly entertaining fact which emerges is that some of MacIntyre's most explicitly Marxist writings first appeared, not in the pages of *Labour Review* or *International Socialism*, but as radio broadcasts on the BBC Third Programme, subsequently published in *The Listener* – a situation difficult to imagine today.

Works are listed by date of first publication only. Within each year, books are listed first, then contributions to books, and finally contributions to journals and newspapers, which are shown by seasonal, monthly or weekly publication date. But, even in relation to these articles, absolute chronological accuracy is impossible, if only because order of composition and publication do not always coincide. In particular, the process of publication in academic publications, although quicker in these years than it is now, often means that articles appear months or even years after their original submission. Turnaround is usually quicker in the case of political journals, if only because they are more concerned with topicality.

The bibliography should nevertheless serve two purposes for readers. First, it situates the works we have chosen to include in this collection (highlighted with asterisks) within MacIntyre's output as a whole for the period. Second, it allows the reader to trace both how some subjects – notably religious themes – decreased in frequency with his increasing commitment to Marxism and how some others – mainly those relating to questions of morality – remained as common (hence the extremely unusual proximity of, for example, *International Socialism* and the *Proceedings of the Aristotelian Society* to each other within the entry for 1960).

1953

Marxism: An Interpretation, Student Christian Movement Press, London, 1953*.

'Review of G. Martin, *Immanuel Kant: Ontologie und Wissenshaftstheorie*', *Downside Review*, v. 71, n. 224, Spring 1953.

'Review of M. Pontifex and I. Trethowen, *The Meaning of Existence*', *Downside Review*, v. 71, n. 226, Autumn 1953.

1954

'Review of M. Pontifex and I. Trethowen, *The Meaning of Existence*', *Philosophical Quarterly*, v. 4, n. 16, July 1954.

'Review of K. Heim, *The Transformation of the Scientific World View* and *Christian Faith and Natural Science*', *Philosophy*, v. 29, n. 10, July 1954.

1955

'Visions', in A. Flew and A. MacIntyre (eds.), *New Essays in Philosophical Theology*, Student Christian Movement Press, London, 1955.

'Cause and Cure in Psychotherapy', *Proceedings of the Aristotelian Society*, supplementary volume 29, 1955.

'A Note on Immortality', *Mind*, v. 64, n. 255, July 1955.

'The Nature and Destiny of Man: Getting the Question Clear', *Modern Churchman*, v. 45, n. 3, September 1955.

1956

'Manchester: The Modern Universities and the English Tradition', *Twentieth Century* 159, February 1956.

'A Society without a Metaphysics', *The Listener*, 13 September 1956.

'Review of J. Brown, *Subject and Object in Modern Theology*', *Journal of Theological Studies*, v. 7, part 2, October 1956.

'Marxist Tracts' (review of G. Politzer, G. Besse and M. Caveing, *Principes fondamentaux de philosophie*; J. Lewis, *Introduction to Philosophy* and J. Lewis, *Marxism and the Irrationalists*), *Philosophical Quarterly*, v. 6, n. 25, October 1956*.

'Review of I. Trethowen, *An Essay on Christian Philosophy*', *Philosophical Quarterly*, v. 6, n. 25, October 1956.

'Review of T.B. Bottomore and M. Rubel (eds.), *Karl Marx: Selected Writings in Sociology and Social Philosophy and P. Laslett (ed.), Philosophy, Politics and Society*', *Sociological Review*, v. 4, n. 2, December 1956.

1957

'The Logical Status of Metaphysical Beliefs', in A. MacIntyre, S. Toulmin and R.W. Hepburn, *Metaphysical Beliefs*, Student Christian Movement Press, London, 1957.

'Determinism', *Mind*, New Series, v. 66, n. 261, January 1957.

'What Morality is Not', *Philosophy*, v. 32, n. 123, October 1957.

1958

The Unconscious: a Conceptual Analysis, Routledge and Kegan Paul and Humanities Press, London, 1958.

'Review of J.A. Hutchison, *Faith Reason and Existence*', *Mind*, v. 67, n. 266, April 1958.

'The Irrelevance of the Church of England", *The Listener*, 26 June 1958.

'On Not Misrepresenting Philosophy', *Universities and Left Review* 4, Summer 1958*.

'The Algebra of the Revolution' (review of R. Dunayevskaya, *Marxism and Freedom*), *Universities and Left Review* 5, Autumn 1958*.

'Notes from the Moral Wilderness 1', *The New Reasoner*, 7, Winter 1958–9*.

1959

Difficulties in Christian Belief, Student Christian Movement Press, London 1959.

'Review of L. Hodgson, *For Faith and Freedom*', *Philosophy*, v. 34, n. 128, January 1959.

'Review of B. Mitchell (ed.), *Faith and Logic*', *Philosophical Quarterly*, v. 9, n. 34, January 1959.

'Dr. Marx and Dr. Zhivago' (review of B. Pasternak, *Doctor Zhivago*), *The Listener*, 8 January 1959*.

'Symptoms of Disease' (review of W. Stark, *Social Theory and Christian Thought*), *New Statesman*, 7 February 1959.

'God and Conic Sections' (review of E. Mortimer, *Blaise Pascal: the Life and Work of a Realist*), *New Statesman*, 1 April 1959.

'Notes from the Moral Wilderness 2', *The New Reasoner*, 8, Spring 1959*.

'Telling Our Dreams' (review of N. Malcolm, *Dreaming*), *New Statesman*, 11 July 1959.

'The Claims of Philosophy' (review of S. Hampshire, *Thought and Action*), *New Statesman*, 18 July 1959.

'Marcuse, Marxism and the Monolith' (review of H. Marcuse, *Soviet Marxism*), *The New Reasoner*, 9, Summer 1959*.

'The Politics of the Belfast Airport Strike', *Newsletter*, v. 3, n. 115, 29 August 1959.
'Hume on "Is" and "Ought"', *Philosophical Review*, v. 68, n. 4, October 1959.
'The "New Left"', *Labour Review*, v. 4, n. 3, October–November 1959*.
'The Straw Man of the Age' (review of H. Thomas (ed.), *The Establishment*), *New Statesman*, 3 October 1959.
'What is Marxist Theory For? 1', *Newsletter*, v. 3, n. 121, 10 October 1959*.
'What is Marxist Theory For? 2', *Newsletter*, v. 3, n. 122, 17 October 1959*.
'What is Marxist Theory For? 3', *Newsletter*, v. 3, n. 123, 24 October 1959*.
'What is Marxist Theory For? 4', *Newsletter*, v. 3, n. 124, 31 October 1959*.
'The Hunt is Up' (review of E. Gellner, *Words and Things*), *New Statesman*, 31 October 1959.
'No Dilemma for the Archbishop' (review of C. Smyth, *Cyril Forster Garbet*), *New Statesman*, 5 December 1959.
'Resurrecting an Ancestor' (review of R. Wollheim, *F.H. Bradley*), *New Statesman*, 19 December 1959.

1960

From MacDonald to Gaitskell, Socialist Labour League Pamphlet, London, 1960*.
'Comment Upon "Commitment and Objectivity"' in Paul Halmos (ed.), *Moral Issues in the Training of Teachers and Social Workers*, *Sociological Review* Monograph 3, 1960.
'Purpose and Intelligent Action' (contribution to a symposium with the same title), *Proceedings of the Aristotelian Society*, supplementary volume 34, 1960.
'Deism', in J.O. Urmson (ed.), *The Concise Encyclopedia of Western Philosophy and Philosophers*, Hawthorn Books; New York, 1960.
'Pantheism', in J.O. Urmson (ed.), *The Concise Encyclopedia of Western Philosophy and Philosophers*, Hawthorn Books; New York, 1960.
'Theism', in J.O. Urmson (ed.), *The Concise Encyclopedia of Western Philosophy and Philosophers*, Hawthorn Books; New York, 1960.
'Breaking the Chains of Reason', in E.P. Thompson (ed.), *Out of Apathy*, Stevens and Sons, London, 1960*.
'Review of by R. Bultmann, *History and Eschatology*', *Philosophical Quarterly*, v. 10, n. 38, January 1960.
'Communism and British Intellectuals (review of N. Wood, *Communism and British Intellectuals*), *The Listener*, 7 January 1960*.
'Freedom and Revolution', *Labour Review*, v. 5, n. 1, February–March 1960*.
'Symptoms of Unease' (review of J. Fuller, W. Donaldson and R. McLaren (eds.), *Light Blue, Dark Blue* and D. Potter, *The Glittering Coffin*), *New Statesman*, 13 February 1960.
'On the Death of an Oxford Philosopher' (Poem), *New Statesman*, 12 March 1960.
'Positivism in Perspective' (review of A.J. Ayer, *Language, Truth and Logic*), *New Statesman*, 2 April 1960.
'Philosopher of Reaction' (review of A.R. Jones, *The Life and Opinions of T.E. Hulme*), *New Statesman*, 21 May 1960.
'Case History' (Poem), *New Statesman*, 8 October 1960.
'Huxley and Humanism' (review of A. Huxley, *Collected Essays*), *New Statesman*, 22 October 1960.
'The Barricades of Art' (review of J. Berger, *Permanent Red*), *New Statesman*, 29 October 1960.
'Is a Neutralist Foreign Policy Possible?', *International Socialism*, First Series, 3, Winter 1960–1*.

1961

'Beyond Max Weber' (review of R. Aron, *An Introduction to the Philosophy of History*), *New Statesman*, 3 February 1961.
'Irrational Book' (review of W. Barrett, *Irrational Man*), *New Statesman*, 17 February 1961.

'The Man who Answered the Irish Question' (review of C. Desmond Greaves, *The Life and Times of James Connolly*), *New Left Review* I/8, March-April 1961*.
'Iron Rationalism' (review of M. Ginsburg, *Evolution and Progress*), *New Statesman*, 7 April 1961.
'Culture and Revolution' (review of R. Williams, *Culture and Society, 1780–1950* and *The Long Revolution*), *International Socialism*, First Series, 5, Summer 1961*.
'Marxists and Christians', *Twentieth Century* 170, Autumn 1961*.
'Rejoinder to Left Reformism', *International Socialism*, First Series, 6, Autumn 1961.
Ehrenberg Explains' (review of I. Ehrenberg, *People and Life*, P. Black and M. Hayward (eds.), *Dissonant Voices in Soviet Literature* and A.S. Yessenin-Volpin, *A Leaf of Spring*), *New Statesman*, 15 September 1961.
'No to All Bombs', *Socialist Review*, First Series, October 1961.
'Welfare State Dismantled', *Socialist Review*, First Series, December 1961.

1962
'A Mistake About Causality in the Social Sciences', in P. Laslett and W.G. Runciman (eds.), *Philosophy, Politics and Society*, Second Series, Blackwell, Oxford, 1962.
'Statistics That Don't Lie' (as Stephen Hero), *Socialist Review*, First Series, January 1962.
'Congo, Katanga and the UNO', *Socialist Review*, First Series, January 1962*.
'Why Mergers?'(as Stephen Hero), *Socialist Review*, First Series, February 1962.
'Ireland Whose Own?', *Socialist Review*, First Series, February 1962.
'Wages: Lessons from Germany' (as Stephen Hero), *Socialist Review*, First Series, March 1962.
'Sartre as a Social Theorist', *The Listener*, 22 March 1962*.
'Cold Intensities' (review of O. Spengler, *The Decline of the West*), *New Statesman*, 23 March 1962.
'What's Left for Labour?', *Socialist Review*, First Series, April 1962.
'Stalin and History' (review of I. Deutscher, *Stalin*), *International Socialism*, First Series, 8, Spring 1962.
'Trotsky' (review of L.D. Trotsky, *Literature and Revolution*), *International Socialism*, First Series, 8, Spring 1962.
'Disengagement' (review of R. Coe, *Ionesco*), *International Socialism*, First Series, 8, Spring 1962.
'The Sleepwalking Society: Britain in the Sixties', *Socialist Review*, First Series, May 1962*.
'Open Letter to a Right-Wing Young Socialist', *Socialist Review*, First Series, June 1962*.
'Review of C.B. Martin, *Religious Belief*', *Philosophical Quarterly*, v. 12, n. 48, July 1962.
'C. Wright Mills', *International Socialism*, First Series, 9, Summer 1962*.
'The Factory' (review of G. Friedmann, *The Anatomy of Work*), *International Socialism*, First Series, 9, Summer 1962.

1963
'Going Into Europe' (contribution to 'Symposium III'), *Encounter*, v. 22, n. 2, February 1963*.
'Awful Warning' (review of D. Gabor, *Inventing the Future*), *New Statesman*, 22 March 1963.
'Review of I.T. Ramsey, *Freedom and Immortality*', *Philosophical Quarterly*, v. 13, n. 51, April 1963.
'Fromm's Dogma', *New Statesman*, 1963.
'Prediction and Politics', *International Socialism*, First Series, 13, Summer 1963*.
'God and the Theologians' (review of J. Robinson, *Honest to God*), *Encounter*, v. 21, n. 3, September 1963.
'Marx and Morals' (review of E. Kamenka, *The Ethical Foundations of Marxism*), *International Socialism*, First Series, 14, Autumn 1963.
'True Voice' (review of V. Serge, *Memoirs of a Revolutionary*), *New Statesman*, 30 August 1963*.

'Trotsky in Exile' (review of I. Deutscher, *The Prophet Outcast*), *Encounter*, v. 21, n. 6, December 1963*.
'Labour Policy and Capitalist Planning', *International Socialism*, First Series, 15, Winter 1963–4*.

1964
'Marx', in M. Cranston (ed.), *Western Political Philosophers: a Background Book*, Bodley Head, London, 1964*.
'Freudian and Christian Dogmas as Equally Unverifiable', in J. Hick (ed.), *Faith and the Philosophers*, St. Martin's Press, New York, 1964.
'Existentialism', in D.J. O'Connor (ed.), *A Critical History of Western Philosophy*, Free Press, New York, 1964.
'Against Utilitarianism', in T.H.B. Hollins (ed.), *Aims in Education: the Philosophic Approach*, Manchester University Press, Manchester, 1964.
'Freud as Moralist', (review of H. Meng and E.L. Freud (eds.), *The Letters of Sigmund Freud and Oskar Pfister*), *The New York Review of Books*, 20 February 1964.
'The Socialism of R.H. Tawney' (review of R.H. Tawney, *The Radical Tradition*), *The New York Review of Books*, 30 July 1964*.
'After Hegel', (review of K. Löwith, *From Hegel to Nietzsche*), *The New York Review of Books*, 24 September 1964.
'Pascal and Marx: on Lucien Goldmann's *Hidden God*' (review of L. Goldmann, *The Hidden God*), *Encounter*, v. 23, n. 4, October 1964*.
'Guide Through a Maze' (review of M. Black, *A Companion to Wittgenstein's 'Tractatus'*), *The Guardian*, 23 October 1964.
'Violence and All That Jazz' (review of L.D. Trotsky, *Terrorism and Communism* and A. Grossman, *Many Slippery Errors*), *International Socialism*, First Series, 19, Winter 1964–5.

1965
'Editor's Introduction', in A. MacIntyre (ed.), *Hume's Ethical Writings: Selections from David Hume*, University of Notre Dame Press, Notre Dame, 1965.
'Irrational Man' (review of C.G. Jung (ed.), *Man and His Symbols* and M. Phillipson, *Outline of a Jungian Aesthetics*), *The New York Review of Books*, 25 February 1965.
'Pleasure as a Reason for Action', *The Monist*, v. 49, n. 2, April 1965.
'Marxist Mask and Romantic Face: Lukács on Thomas Mann' (review of G. Lukács, *Essays on Thomas Mann*), *Encounter*, v. 24, n. 4, April 1965*.
'Modern Society: an End to Revolt?' (review of H. Marcuse, *One-Dimensional Man*), *Dissent*, v. 12, n. 2, Spring 1965.
'The Psycho-analysts: the Future of an Illusion?', *Encounter*, v. 24, n. 5, May 1965.
'Review of F. Ferré, *Language, Logic and God*', *Philosophical Quarterly*, v. 15, n. 60, July 1965.
'Weber at his Weakest' (review of M. Weber, *The Sociology of Religion*), *Encounter*, v. 25, n. 1, July 1965.
'Behan's Book' (review of B. Behan, *With Breast Expanded*), *International Socialism*, First Series, 21, Summer 1965.
'Liberal Marx' (review of I. Berlin, *Karl Marx*), *International Socialism*, First Series, 21, Summer 1965.
'Only Parts' (review of *The Essential Trotsky*), *International Socialism*, First Series, 21, Summer 1965.
'Imperatives, Reasons for Action, and Morals' (a contribution to 'Symposium: Ethics and Language'), *Journal of Philosophy*, v. 62, n. 17, 9 September 1965.

1966
A Short History of Ethics: a History of Moral Philosophy from the Homeric Age to the Twentieth Century, Routledge and Kegan Paul, London, 1967.
'The Antecedents of Action', in B. Williams and A. Montefiore (eds.), *British Analytic Philosophy*, Routledge and Kegan Paul, London, 1966.

'Recent Political Thought', in D. Thompson (ed.), *Political Ideas*, Penguin Books, Harmondsworth, 1966*.

'Modern Times', (review of G. Barraclough, *An Introduction to Contemporary History* and H. Rosinski, *Power and Human Destiny*), *The New York Review of Books*, 17 March 1966.

1967

Secularization and Moral Change: the Riddell Memorial Lectures, Oxford University Press, Oxford, 1967.

'Being', in P. Edwards (ed.), *Encyclopaedia of Philosophy*, v. 1, Macmillan, New York, 1967.

'Brunner, Emil', in P. Edwards (ed.), *Encyclopaedia of Philosophy*, v. 1, Macmillan, New York, 1967.

'Egoism and Altruism', in P. Edwards (ed.), *Encyclopaedia of Philosophy*, v. 2, Macmillan, New York, 1967.

'Essence and Existence', in P. Edwards (ed.), *Encyclopaedia of Philosophy*, v. 3, Macmillan, New York, 1967.

'Existentialism', in P. Edwards (ed.), *Encyclopaedia of Philosophy*, v. 3, Macmillan, New York, 1967.

'Freud, Sigmund', in P. Edwards (ed.), *Encyclopaedia of Philosophy*, v. 3, Macmillan, New York, 1967.

'Jung, Carl Gustav', in P. Edwards (ed.), *Encyclopaedia of Philosophy*, v. 4, Macmillan, New York, 1967.

'Kierkegaard, Søren Aabye', in P. Edwards (ed.), *Encyclopaedia of Philosophy*, v. 4, Macmillan, New York, 1967.

'Myth', in P. Edwards (ed.), *Encyclopaedia of Philosophy*, v. 6, Macmillan, New York, 1967.

'Ontology', in P. Edwards (ed.), *Encyclopaedia of Philosophy*, v. 6, Macmillan, New York, 1967.

'Pantheism', in P. Edwards (ed.), *Encyclopaedia of Philosophy*, v. 6, Macmillan, New York, 1967.

'Spinoza, Benedict (Baruch)', in P. Edwards (ed.), *Encyclopaedia of Philosophy*, v. 7, Macmillan, New York, 1967.

'The Idea of a Social Science', *Proceedings of the Aristotelian Society*, supplementary volume 41, 1967.

'*Review of* P.M. Blau, *Exchange and Power in Social Life*', *Sociology*, v. 1, n. 2, May 1967.

'Review of M. Gluckman (ed.), *Closed Systems and Open Minds*', *Philosophical Quarterly*, v. 17, n. 69, October 1967.

'Review of C. Levi-Strauss, *The Savage Mind*', *Philosophical Quarterly*, v. 17, n. 69, October 1967.

'Herbert Marcuse: from Marxism to Pessimism', *Survey* 62, January 1967*.

'The Well-Dressed Theologian' (review of V. Mehtal, *The New Theologians*), *Encounter*, v. 28, n. 3, March 1967.

'Sociology and the Novel' (in 'Crosscurrents – II'), *Times Literary Supplement*, 27 July 1967.

'Emasculating History: on Mazlish's *Riddle*' (review of B. Mazlish, *The Riddle of History*), *Encounter*, v. 29, n. 2, August 1967.

'Review of *Twenty Letters to a Friend* by Svetlana Alliluyeva', *Yale Law Journal* 77, 1967/1968*.

1968

Marxism and Christianity, Schocken Books, New York, 1968.

'The Reith Lectures are Discussed' (with P. Medwar and E. Leach), *The Listener*, 10 January 1968.

'Review of R. Rudner, *Philosophy of Social Sciences*', *British Journal for the Philosophy of Science*, v. 18, n. 4, February 1968.

'Secularisation', *The Listener*, 15 February 1968.

'How to Write About Lenin – and How Not To' (review of L. Schapiro and P. Reddaway, eds., *Lenin: The Man, The Theorist, The Leader*), *Encounter*, v. 30, n. 5, May 1968*.
'Son of Ideology' (review of G. Lichtheim, *The Concept of Ideology and Other Essays*), *The New York Review of Books*, 9 May 1968.
'Noam Chomsky's View of Language', *The Listener*, 30 May 1968.
'Death and the English', *The Listener*, 6 June 1968.
'Review of A. Schutz, *The Phenomenology of the Social World*', *Sociological Review*, v. 16, n. 2, December 1968.
'The Strange Death of Social Democratic England', *The Listener*, 4 July 1968*.
'Who Gets Killed – Alasdair MacIntyre Discusses the Death of Senator Kennedy', *The Listener*, 18 July 1968.
'Future Unpredictable?' (review of R. Aron, *Progress and Disillusion*), *New Statesman*, 16 August 1968.
'Doubts About Koestler', (review of A. Koestler, *Drinkers of Infinity*), *The Listener*, 12 September 1968.
'Living or Dead?' (review of J. Freund, *The Sociology of Weber* and H. Lefebvre, *The Sociology of Marx*), *New Statesman*, 27 September 1968.
'In Place of Harold Wilson?' (review of P. Foot, *The Politics of Harold Wilson* and T. Burgess (ed.), *Matters of Principle: Labour's Last Chance*), *The Listener*, 10 October 1968*.
'Le Rouge et le Noir' (review of D. Cohn-Bendit, *Obsolete Communism: the Left Wing Alternative* and G. Kennan, *Democracy and the Student Left*), *New Statesman*, 22 November 1968.
'Technocratic Smokescreen', (review of J. Meynaud, *Technocracy*), *The Listener*, 28 November 1968.
'Workers and Politics' (review of R. McKenzie and A Silver, *Angels in Marble* and J.H. Goldthorpe, D. Lockwood, F. Bechhofer and J. Platt, *The Affluent Worker: Industrial Attitudes and Behavior* and *The Affluent Worker: Political Attitudes and Behavior*) *New Statesman*, 27 December 1968.

1969

'Atheism and Morals', in A. MacIntyre and P. Ricoeur, *The Religious Significance of Atheism*, Columbia University Press, New York, 1969.
'Marxism of the Will' (a review of C. Guevara, *Venceremos! The Speeches and Writings of Che Guevara*; C. Guevara, *Reminiscences of the Cuban Revolutionary War*; C. Guevara, *The Complete Bolivian Diaries of Che Guevara and Other Captured Documents*; R. Rojo, *My Friend Che*; R. Debray, *Revolution in the Revolution? Armed Struggle and Political Struggle in Latin America*; J-P. Sartre, *The Communists and Peace*), *Partisan Review*, v. 36, n. 1, Winter 1969*.
'From Zutphen to Armageddon' (review of D. Eggenbegger, *A Dictionary of Battles*), *New Statesman*, 3 January 1969.
'Universities for the Rich?', *New Statesman*, 10 January 1969.
'Lumps of Thought' (review of T. Raison (ed.), *The Founding Fathers of Social Science*), *New Statesman*, 31 January 1969.
'Made in the USA', (review of D. Sills (ed.), *International Encyclopaedia of the Social Sciences*), *New York Review of Books*, 27 February 1969.
'The Self as a Work of Art' (review of E. Goffman, *The Presentation of Self in Everyday Life* and *Where the Action Is*), *New Statesman*, 28 March 1969.
'Philosophy and Sanity: Nietzsche's Titanism', (review of F. Nietzsche, *The Will to Power*), *Encounter*, v. 32, n. 4, April 1969.
'Review of J. Galtung, *Theory and Methods of Social Research*', *British Journal for the Philosophy of Science*, v. 20, n. 2, August 1969.
'Review of May Brodbeck (ed.), *Readings in the Philosophy of the Social Sciences*', *British Journal for the Philosophy of Science*, v. 20, n. 2, August 1969.
'On Marcuse', *New York Review of Books*, 23 October 1969.

1970

Marcuse: An Exposition and a Polemic, Fontana Modern Masters, London, 1970

'Is Understanding Religion Compatible with Believing?', in B.R. Wilson (ed.), *Rationality*, Harper and Row, New York, 1970.

'Gods and Sociologists', *Encounter*, v. 34, n. 3, March 1970.

1971

Against the Self-Images of the Age: Essays on Ideology and Philosophy, Schocken Books and Duckworth, New York and London, 1971.

'Conversations with Philosophers: Alasdair MacIntyre Talks to Bryan Magee about Political Philosophy and its Emergence from the Doldrums', *The Listener*, 25 February 1971.

'Mr Wilson's Pragmatism' (a review of H. Wilson, *The Labour Government, 1966–70: a Personal Record, The Listener*, 29 July 1971)*.

'Tell Me Where You Stand on Kronstadt' (review of P. Avrich, *Kronstadt 1921*), *New York Review of Books*, 12 August 1971*.

'A Perspective on Philosophy', *Social Research*, v. 38, n. 4, Winter 1971.

1972

'Hegel on Faces and Skulls', in A. MacIntyre (ed.), *Hegel: a Collection of Critical Essays*, Anchor Books, New York, 1972.

'Chairman's Opening Remarks', in W. Mays and S.C. Brown, eds., *Linguistic Analysis and Phenomenology*, Macmillan, London, 1972.

'Justice: a New Theory and Some Old Question' "Justice: A New Theory and Some Old Questions," (a review of J. Rawls, *A Theory of Justice*), *Boston University Law Review* 52, 1972.

'Praxis and Action' (review of R.J. Bernstein, *Praxis and Action*), *Review of Metaphysics*, v. 25, n. 2, June 1972.

'Rational Science', (review of K. Popper, *Objective Knowledge: an Evolutionary Approach*), *The Listener*, 14 December 1972.

1973

'Ideology, Social Science and Revolution', *Comparative Politics*, v. 5, n. 3, July 1973.

'Ancient Politics and Modern Issues', (review of D. Daube, *Civil Disobedience in Antiquity* and R. MacMullen, *Enemies of the Roman Order*), *Arion*, New Series, v. 1, n. 2, Summer 1973.

'The Essential Contestability of Some Social Concepts', *Ethics*, v. 84, n. 1, October 1973.

1974

'Durkheim's Call to Order' (review of S. Lukes, *Emile Durkheim: His Life and Work*), *New York Review of Books*, 7 March 1974.

'Irish Mythologies' (review of E. McCann, *War and an Irish Town*), *New Statesman*, 3 May 1974*.

'Sunningdale: a "Colonial" Solution', *Irish Press*, 5 June 1974*.

'Irish Conflicts and British Illusions', *New Statesman*, 19 July 1974*.

Chapter One

Extracts from *Marxism: An Interpretation*[1]

Marxism as theory and as practice

Our examination of Marx's intellectual development so far [in *Marxism: An Interpretation*] has been restricted to the period up to *The Communist Manifesto*. What I want to do in this chapter is to outline Marx's developed theory of exploitation in *Capital*, to show how the detail of his theory has been falsified by events, although many of his salient points stand, and then to examine how the attempt to make theory do the work of prophecy led to a refusal by Marxists to allow their theories to be measured by the facts: in other words how the religious background of Marxism has corrupted its would-be scientific attitude.

Marx's theory of exploitation rests on Marx's theory of value, and Marx's theory of value is inherited from Ricardo. Marx follows Ricardo in asserting that the value of a commodity is proportional to the socially necessary quantity of labour embodied in it. By the socially necessary quantity of labour Marx means the quantity of labour necessary to produce the commodity by means of the most efficient available

[1] Originally published as Chapters 8–10 of *Marxism: an Interpretation*, Student Christian Movement Press, London 1953, pp. 92–122. The original chapter headings have been used here as sub-headings.

methods. Labour is to be measured in hours of work. The labourer in capitalist society has for sale only his labour, that is, his potential working power. Since his labour is a commodity, its value can be calculated like that of any other commodity. The value of labour is calculated in terms of the number of hours that it takes to produce the necessary means for the physical existence of the labourer. Thus the wages he will receive will be such as will enable him to acquire these means and will be equal in value to the value of the working power that he has to sell. But the employer of the labourer must pay these wages in return not for the number of hours of labour necessary for the labourer's survival but in return for the number of hours of labour necessary to produce commodities – finished goods – which will sell for more than the cost of labour, the wages, since the employer must take his profit. Hence the worker receives the value of his labour-power, which embodied a certain number of hours of labour, but must work in return for a greater number of hours of labour than those for which he receives payment: thus the worker creates a surplus-value, which is appropriated by the capitalist. So labour creates surplus-value: so capital appropriates it. This means that the worker never receives more in wages than is necessary for bare subsistence, while the capitalist grows continually wealthier. As capitalism expands, as the economic system which depends on this exploitation becomes all-embracing, the lot of the working class necessarily becomes worse. The workers are condemned to increasing misery. The surplus-value which the capitalist appropriates is, in the competitive struggle of capitalism, ploughed back into enterprise in the form of capital development. In this competition victory is with the big capitalist as against the small. That is, there is a continual growth both of industrial plants and of the businesses controlling those plants. In the fight for profits the large-scale capitalist can always afford to undercut his small-scale rival – 'the battle of competition is fought by cheapening commodities'.[2] The growth of capital accumulation leads to an ever-increasing use of machinery. This in turn leads to unemployment and to still greater misery for the working class. Such is the capitalist process.

Be it noted that Marx broke with bourgeois economics not only in his particular analysis, but in his continual stress on the economic analysis of capitalism not simply as a state, but as a process. Marx's analysis is always

[2] See, for example, Marx 1977, pp. 222–3; 1976, pp. 434–5, 437.

an historical analysis. Secondly, we can recognise the basic themes of *National Economy and Philosophy* transmuted into economic science.[3] But since Marx is now concerned to give a scientific and historical analysis of the capitalist process he is forced to ask questions which are neither asked nor answered in the earlier writings. The most interesting of these are those which concern the beginning and the end of capitalism. For in order that the capitalist should be able to buy labour, he must initially possess capital. But capital, on Marx's theory, is the accumulation of surplus-value created by the labour which the capitalist has bought. Thus the capitalist apparently must possess capital in order to buy labour, but only labour can create capital for him. How then is there an original accumulation of capital which enables the capitalist process to begin at all? Marx's answer to this is quite simple: it is force which primarily creates the primitive accumulation of capital. The fruits of exploitation in feudal society provide the basis of exploitation in capitalist society. Marx dismisses as a story fit only for children the view that primitive accumulation is the fruit of thrift and energy on the part of certain enterprising individuals. So much for the beginning. The end of capitalism is the outcome of the simultaneous growth of large-scale industry and increase of working-class misery:

> Hand in hand with this centralisation, or this expropriation of many capitalists by few, develops... the entanglement of all nations in the net of the world market and with this, the international character of the capitalist régime. Along with the constantly diminishing number of the magnates of capital, who usurp and monopolise all advantages of this process of transformation, grows the mass of misery, oppression, slavery, degradation, exploitation; but with this too grows the revolt of the working class, a class always increasing in numbers, and disciplined, united, organised by the very mechanism of the process of capitalist production itself. The monopoly of capital becomes a fetter upon the mode of production, which has sprung up and flourished along with it, and under it. Centralisation of the means of production and socialisation of labour at last reach a point where they become incompatible

[3] These texts were originally published in German as *National Ökonomie und Philosophie* and it is to a German Democratic Republic edition of 1952 that MacIntyre refers. Since the first complete English translation appeared in 1959, they have been known as the *Economic and Philosophical Manuscripts*. For the edition referenced here and in subsequent chapters, see Marx 1975b.

> with the capitalist integument. The integument bursts. The knell of capitalist private property sounds. The expropriators are expropriated.[4]

This is magnificent, but it is not good economics.

To begin with, the labour theory of value does not work outside a state of perfect competition. It cannot be used to analyse problems of value without certain defects even in a state of perfect competition, for it does not apply unless it is assured that labour is the only means of production and that labour is all of one kind. The very phrase, 'socially necessary quantity of labour', begs some important questions. Thus the labour theory of value is not a theory of value as such which will tell you how economic value is determined: it is a theory of value for one special case, and even that one special case – perfect competition, labour the only means of production, labour all of one kind – can be dealt with in terms of the theory which replaced the labour theory of value, the theory of marginal utility. This has the advantage of applying to monopoly and imperfect competition as well as to perfect competition even if it also possesses substantial defects. On the other hand, while the theory of marginal utility has the great advantage of being generally applicable, if value is assessed in terms of it and the restrictions which are necessary to make the labour theory work are once more introduced, the marginal utility theory itself leads to an equation in which value is proportional to quantity of labour.

Secondly, Marx's account of primitive accumulation is only partly true. There is this much of truth in the account Marx rejected, that the 'factory' of the sixteenth and seventeenth centuries was often a one-man affair, which could be started on the basis of small savings, and which did depend for its success on the thrift and energy of the individual. But far more serious is the point that if Marx's analysis of the capitalist process were correct, his prediction of the increasing misery of the working class would have to be verified, and in fact the later history of capitalism has decisively falsified it. In the countries where capitalism is most highly developed – the United states, Germany and Great Britain – the standard of living of the workers has been raised within a capitalist economy. Furthermore, the quality of goods which the workers have been able to buy and have, in fact, bought has been the highest in the period of

[4] Marx 1976, p. 929.

capitalist development that has been controlled by large-scale industry. This is the exact opposite of what Marx's theory would lead one to expect. But, at the same time, Marx's prediction of the end of capitalism is being borne out. Nevertheless what is collapsing is not capitalist *economy*, but capitalist *civilisation*. Why has capitalist civilisation failed?

It has failed because it has offered freedom without security. Precapitalist society offered a certain measure of security, but the price of that security was the loss of freedom. What bound man to man in feudal society was the direct human intercourse of man with man in an economy that could never rise far above the subsistence level, an economy of which the essence is expressed in the stark phrase, 'from hand to mouth'. In such a society, economic relations are necessarily to some degree still personal relations. It is capitalism which creates a society where economic relations are necessarily impersonal in the main, and which offers instead a structure of political relationships. But the political rights that liberal capitalism confers can never make man at home in the world of capitalism. Capitalism breaks through the natural communities of an agricultural, subsistence economy, and replaces them with its own communities, the factory and the industrial city. This was recognised by Marx:

> The bourgeoisie, wherever it has got the upper hand, has put an end to all feudal, patriarchal, idyllic relations. It has pitilessly torn asunder the motley feudal ties that bound man to his 'natural superiors' and has left no other nexus between man and man than naked self-interest, than callous 'cash payment'.[5]

This process of capitalist development creates two proletariats: the workers and the intellectuals. They are proletariats because in capitalist society they do not belong. Their values are inevitably foreign to a world of competitive economic struggle. It is not a question primarily of having enough to eat. For the unemployed in capitalist times of crisis may well have sufficient to eat; there is no reason intrinsic to capitalism why they should not. What is demoralising is simply the lack of work in itself. And the indictment of a capitalist economy is that it works most efficiently when there is a pool of unemployed at its disposal. Similarly, the intellectual and, above all, the

[5] Marx and Engels 1973, p. 70.

artist are not at home in a capitalist civilisation. For capitalism, art is not only a commodity, it is the kind of commodity which must be classified as a luxury. And, as a luxury, art cannot survive. It is a necessity or nothing. Hence the essential failure of capitalism is not that the pursuit of profit is incompatible with the pursuit of social welfare: the essential failure is that the kind of society which capitalism creates is one that can never fully employ the skills of hand and brain and eye, the exercise of which is part of man's true being. Those whose skills capitalism rejects form the nuclei of the forces which are breaking down capitalism. On the one hand there is the proletarian organisation of trade unions: on the other the attacks upon capitalist culture by artists and intellectuals everywhere.

Marx's vision of capitalism's failure has then come true, but not in the way in which Marx predicted that failure. What, then, has happened to Marx's theory? When a theory leads to predictions which are falsified, one of three courses is possible. First, the theory can be frankly abandoned. This was the solution suggested in the case of Marxism by Eduard Bernstein and the revisionists. Bernstein in 1899 argued that Marxists should recognise that capitalism was not failing economically, and should work not for the overthrow of the system but for the achievement of reforms within the capitalist framework. But revisionism – which is the tacit ideology of the later Social-Democratic parties – is an impossible solution for Marxists, because it fails to recognise the religious dimension in Marx and treats Marxism as mere theory. Secondly, if one's theory is falsified by events, one can continue to hold one's theory and explain its failure by recourse to a series of auxiliary hypotheses. This is the course taken by most Marxists with regard to the theory of increasing working-class misery. The argument is that Marx was right in his prediction, except for the fact that he did not foresee two modifying factors which, although they do not change the course of events essentially, nevertheless disguise what is happening. The first of these factors is the rise of the trade unions and their protection of working-class interests by means of strikes and the threat of strikes. The second is the discovery by capitalism of new markets as a result of the colonial expansion of the late nineteenth century. This, so it is argued, allowed capitalism to expand until these markets too were saturated with goods: imperialism, the highest stage of capitalism, delays, but cannot stave off, capitalism's final ruin. Behind this line of argument there lies an attempt to interpret the slump of 1929 as being the first sign of the collapse that Marx predicted. Thus, on this view, the Marxist theory of capitalist crisis is based on a theory of the trade cycle, of the recurring periods of prosperity and of crisis which capitalism experiences. Furthermore, on this view, Marxism is committed to an explanation of such crises in terms of under-consumption. This explanation runs as follows, to quote from E. Varga, the leading Soviet economist:

> To put it more simply: prosperity continues so long as the process of real accumulation is in full swing, as long as new factories, harbours and railways are built, and old machines are replaced by new ones. But as soon as this process reaches a certain conclusion after a considerable number of new production plants have been completed, the demand for the commodities of Division I (means of production) diminishes, entailing a drop in the demand for consumer goods as well, since the workers in Division I are becoming unemployed. At the same time, the supply of commodities increases, since the new and reconstructed factories begin to pour goods into the market. Overproduction already exists, but the open outbreak of the crisis is delayed since the capitalists (who never believe that a prosperity phase will come to an end) are producing for inventory. But production exceeds consumption to an ever greater extent, until the crisis bursts into the open.[6]

We may note in passing that it is just not true that capitalists are blind to anything but the continuance of prosperity: a not completely implausible theory of the trade cycle has been put forward, which blames recurring crises on the capitalists' very fear of such crises. That is, the capitalist fearing a crisis restricts investment and so helps to cause the crisis which he feared. But whatever the merits or demerits of the underconsumption theory, one fact should be salient for Marxists: that Marx rejected it. To try and save Marx by explanations of this kind is, in fact, to cease to take Marx himself seriously as a theorist. For to take anyone seriously as a theorist is necessarily to see their work as a mixture of truth and error, and, in particular, as historically conditioned truth and error. This Marxists are willing to do with everyone except Marx. For they endow Marx's theory with the qualities which are rightly attributed to his prophetic vision. Hence the immense scholarship and analytical skill of the first volume of *Capital* and of *Theories of Surplus-Value* is

[6] Varga 1935, p. 24.

depreciated as much by Marxist exaggeration as it is by anti-Marxist carping. The sacredness of Marx's predictions is exemplified in the way in which no Marxist can allow for the possibility that Marx might have been wrong about the economic collapse of capitalism. Even so minor a deviation as Varga's opinion that the United states in the late 1940s was successfully staving off economic crisis and that both Britain and the US were, to some degree, solving the problems set by a capitalist economy was officially reproved in the Soviet Union and a recantation was exacted. Why is it that a religious term like 'recantation' can occur in a discussion of economic theory?

The answer to this is to be found in the fact that Marxism is not simply an economic doctrine: it is a doctrine about the universe, and such doctrines are held with religious rather than with scientific attitudes. Marx provided a view of history derived from Christianity through Hegel, and used that view as a framework for his economic analysis. Part of the work of Engels was to revive a Hegelian perspective and to make dialectical materialism a doctrine of nature as well as of history. Hence dialectical materialism became a doctrine which sought to explain everything; and failure at any one point must necessarily discredit to some degree the whole structure. In this growth of Marxist doctrine, the religious background to Marx's thought once more emerges. For it is a feature of religious thinking that it should inevitably make cosmological claims of some sort. But, more important in relation to the religious aspect, is the emergence of a conception of doctrinal orthodoxy within Marxism.

The existence of this concept is beyond question: the very notion of deviationism would be impossible without it. It is important to stress from the outset that the existence of canons of orthodoxy within Marxism inevitably destroys any pretensions that Marxism may have to the status of science. Scientific theories can be true or false; we can also speak in relation to established theory of their orthodoxy or otherwise. But their orthodoxy is irrelevant to their truth or falsity. It is a typical corruption of religion rather than of science to confuse truth with orthodoxy. In Christianity, the conception of orthodoxy has endangered even that of redemption. For Christianity begins by proclaiming the salvation of mankind. This proclamation is then summed up in a series of doctrinal propositions, which announce salvation and are therefore declared to be the way of salvation. So it comes about that to be saved is to assent to these propositions. Thus, from originally proclaiming the redemption of mankind, the Church time and again has fallen into the error of proclaiming the salvation of the orthodox, of those who assent to certain propositions of Christian doctrine. This conception of orthodoxy has two dangerous correlatives. First, redemption is so great an end that dissent from orthodoxy, the offer of a different salvation, becomes utterly damnable. The heretic is more dangerous than the unbeliever. Any means may be employed against him in the light of the overriding necessity of preserving the true faith. Secondly, if orthodoxy saves, then orthodoxy is the one important thing about a man and the orthodox must never be discredited. They must be protected against criticism. So pharisaism creeps in. This then is the pattern of that corruption of the human heart, religious orthodoxy. It is the tragedy of communism that its religious inheritance should have infected it with the conception of orthodoxy.

For communism inherits from Christianity the notion of a redemption, a reconciliation of all mankind. Then, just as Christianity turned salvation for man into salvation for Christians, so communism turned reconciliation for man into reconciliation for the proletarians. Engels, writing in 1892 of his own work of 1844, says of it:

> Thus great stress is laid on the dictum that Communism is not a mere party doctrine of the working-class, but a theory compassing the emancipation of society at large, including the capitalist class, from its present narrow conditions. This is true enough in the abstract, but absolutely useless, and sometimes worse, in practice.[7]

But what is not true for practice cannot in Marxist terms be true at all. So communism narrows the limits of its reconciliation. The second stage occurred in terms of a classical dispute between Plekhanov and Lenin after 1907. Plekhanov argued that 'history is made by the masses'. The revolutionary must wait until the masses spontaneously reach the point of revolution. There is warrant for this position in Marx's writings; but there is also warrant for Lenin's position, which emphasised the necessity of conscious leadership for the masses, to create the conditions of revolution. This conscious leadership is the role of the party, which in consequence must act as a small

---

[7] Engels 1990, p. 261.

highly-disciplined group bringing the truth to the masses. The issue between Plekhanov and Lenin took the form of a dispute about the nature of the party; but what was really at issue was whether it is the party or the working class which is to bring in the good society and in which the truth about society is found. Lenin's conception won the day and with it came the centralisation of power within the party. Trotsky in 1904 forecast a resulting development when 'the party is replaced by the organisation of the party, the organisation by the central committee, and finally the central committee by the dictator'.[8] This was to be the course of history: orthodoxy had mastered the party. The concomitant of orthodoxy is the persecution of heretics. This is the saddest record of modern times, and sadder still is the way in which orthodoxy has blinded otherwise honest party members. There is a place in communist ethics to justify any disloyalty provided loyalty to the party is served. So a Chinese Communist, Liu Shao-Chi, can write of the good party member:

> He should ensure that his personal interests accord with the Party's interests or even merge with them. Thus when his personal interests conflict with the Party's interests he will be able to submit to the Party's interests and sacrifice his personal interests without the slightest hesitation or reluctance.[9]

There is a standard communist defence against every charge. Orthodoxy has inhibited any possible repentance, and for actions like the handing over in 1940 at Brest-Litovsk of about one hundred Austrian, German and Hungarian Communists to the Gestapo, as part of the Russo-German rapprochement of 1939–40, repentance is the only adequate response.

This is not a history of communist good and evil; it is a study of the way in which fundamentally religious concepts entered into Marx's thought and afterwards into Marxism. The demonic element in Marxism is not unconnected with its religious background. But the religious significance of Marxism is brought out even more clearly if we consider the religious response which Marxism has evoked. For the patterns of guilt, repentance and conversion are largely meaningless in our day except for those with a pietist upbringing. It seems to be only Marxism that sufficiently illuminates man's relationship to

---

[8] Trotsky n.d., p. 77.
[9] Shao-Chi 1952, pp. 50–1.

the powers of this world to make men aware of the need for repentance. This is true in two quite distinct ways.

First, Marxism has proved capable of breaking through bourgeois self-satisfaction. Arthur Koestler is typical of the middle-class convert:

> At the age of nine, when our middle-class idyll collapsed, I had suddenly become conscious of the economic facts of life. As an only child, I continued to be pampered by my parents; but well aware of the family crisis, and torn by pity for my father, who was of a generous and somewhat childlike disposition, I suffered a pang of guilt whenever they bought me books or toys. This continued later on, when every suit I bought for myself meant so much less to send home. Simultaneously, I developed a strong dislike of the obviously rich; not because they could afford to buy things, but because they were able to do so without a guilty conscience.... Thus sensitised by a personal conflict, I was ripe for the shock of learning that wheat was burned, fruit artificially spoiled and pigs were drowned in the depression years to keep prices up and enable fat capitalists to chant to the sound of harps, while Europe trembled under the torn boots of hunger-marchers and my father hid his frayed cuffs under the table.... Every page of Marx, and even more of Engels, brought a new revelation, and an intellectual delight... the demonstration of the historical relativity of institutions and ideals – of family, class, patriotism, bourgeois morality, sexual taboos – had the intoxicating effect of a sudden liberation from the rusty chains with which a pre-1914 middle-class childhood had cluttered one's mind.[10]

So the conversion to Communism is a liberation today in the way in which early Christianity must have been a liberation: a liberation because both free one from the domination of the powers of this world. Both in their corruption into orthodoxy themselves can become dominating powers which experience has to break through. The illusions one loses when one joins the Communist party are real illusions: but so are those one loses when one leaves it. Koestler has described the experiences which broke through his Communism: they too are the more valuable for being typical. His views changed as the result of a spell in one of Franco's prisons in 1937:

[10] Koestler 1950, pp. 27, 28, 29.

> The experiences responsible for this change were fear, pity and a third one, more difficult to describe. Fear, not of death, but of torture and humiliation and the more unpleasant forms of dying – my companion of *patio* exercises, Garcia Atadell, was garrotted shortly after my liberation. Pity for the little Andalusian and Catalan peasants whom I heard crying for their *madres* when they were led out at night to face the firing squad; and finally, a condition of the mind...which would present itself at unexpected moments and induce a state of inner peace which I have known neither before nor since. The lesson taught by this kind of experience when put into words always appears under the dowdy guise of perennial commonplaces: that man is a reality, mankind an abstraction; that men cannot be treated as units of political arithmetic...[11]

But it is not simply the inhumanity of Marxism that has made the image of conversion real once more. The most important fact about conversion is that it is conversion into a community, and Communism has built up in the party a dedicated community of a kind rarely found outside the religious orders. Most modern religion has lost the dimension of commitment which is found in Communist parties: only the Communist to-day is committed both completely as regards himself and, more relevantly, as regards the contemporary world. Only the ex-Communist perhaps knows just what has to be given to the party, for the Communist himself is often blissfully unconscious of the degree of his commitment. Nor is it possible for us to take up a purely negative attitude towards Marxism. Far too many people in the West are using the experience of the ex-Communist, the Koestlers and the Silones, to reject a Communism which threatens their economic and moral complacency in a way in which the Christianity of the average parish will never do.

For Christianity is a stranger in the modern world. The Church has never come to terms with the world of science and Christian education has clung to classics and theology so that in their liberal humanism Christians have been at home with those who lived on the fringe of the modern world, the leisured classes of the eighteenth and nineteenth centuries. Methodism almost broke through, but the history of Methodism among the working classes bears

[11] Koestler 1950, pp. 75–6.

witness to the fact that religion inevitably breeds respectability, and that, whatever the pharisaisms of revolutionary politics, respectability is not among them.

Communism is in fact the form under which such strains in Christian thinking as were relevant had to enter the modern world: and because communism was religion it was open to the corruptions which always beset political religions. Nevertheless the motives that led and lead men to the Communist party are the motives which have led men into Christian faith. Equally, the motives that lead men out of the party are those which lead them out of the Church. In Ignazio Silone's novel, *Bread and Wine*, what emerges is that it is the same patterns of bread and wine, of harvest and vintage, which make up the fundamental patterns of human living, and which appear transformed in Christianity and Marxism. *Bread and Wine* is a story of Fascist Italy, of the returned Communist seeking as a fugitive to build a resistance movement. The Communist, Spina, says to another comrade of his dead teacher, the priest, Don Benedetto:

> It was his teaching that made me a Christian, but not a Christian in the appropriate manner. When I entered real life after leaving school, I developed in a direction quite opposite to that of religion, and I slowly substituted Marxism for Christianity.... During that time I never ceased trying to smother and repress my deepest impulses, solely because in my youth they had been bound up with religious symbols and practices. I tried, with an obstinacy and determination that sprang from my loathing of the Church, to substitute logic and intellectual ideas taken from the world of economics and politics for those deeper forces which I felt myself compelled to distrust.... Your coming to Pietrasecca and your confession finally broke down my last resistance. Don Benedetto's words penetrated to the depths of me. Within a few days all that remained alive and indestructible of Christianity in me was revived: a Christianity denuded of all mythology, of all theology, of all Church control; a Christianity that neither abdicates in the face of Mammon, nor proposes concordats with Pontius Pilate, nor offers easy careers to the ambitious, but rather leads to prison, seeing that crucifixion is no longer practical.[12]

[12] Silone 1936, pp. 278–9.

We began with a parable of Jesus. We have traced the pattern of the new humanity that is to be created from the poverty of man's estrangement from its origin in the gospel through its intellectualisation in Hegel and Feuerbach to the compassion of Marx. We have seen how the divorce of the Church from the modern world discredited prophetic vision and forced Marxism to seek a scientific mode for its prophecy. We have seen how the religious virtues and the religious vices alike found their home with the Marxists, and the lesson here is surely that it is only those who have seen these virtues and vices in their true contemporary, that is, Marxist form, who know the greatness that the gospel preaches, the degradation of the pharisee whom it denounces. The exchange of Roman Catholicism for Communism, the exchange that we have seen in the conversion of so many ex-Communists, bears witness to the likeness between those two systems. Roman Catholicism in its worst aspects is the corrupted religion of a subsistence economy; Communism, the corrupted religion of modern industrial society. But there is this great cleansing power in Communism – it never invokes the name of God to disguise its corruption. Hence Communism unlike the Church is preserved from the ultimate blasphemy. This is why the two most relevant books in the modern world are St. Mark's Gospel and Marx's *National Economy and Philosophy*; but they must be read together.

The consequences for philosophy

So ends our discussion of the relations of Christianity to Marxism. It is a discussion which has been conducted in unashamedly metaphysical terms. This whole discussion is however put in question by the contemporary analytical critique of ethics and of metaphysics. Here we can only indicate in barest outline how such a critique might be met. The core of such a critique is the way in which philosophical analysis can lay bare the logical confusions that underlie the metaphysical mode of speech and so suggest that in metaphysics we distort language to serve our emotional needs: in other words, this critique suggests that we disguise as factual assertion what is actually emotive and exclamatory. Let us begin by outlining the criticism of two essential Marxist positions by exponents of logical analysis.

Analytical philosophy has criticised Marxist materialism. The question put by materialism concerns the relation of our thinking to the external world. Ought we to attribute independent existence to the external world or is the external world a product of thought, of spirit? We have already noticed this question as one which divides Hegel from Feuerbach and Marx. An analytical philosopher would argue that any answer to this question is misleading because the question is logically improper. We cannot ask whether independent existence is an attribute of the world because independent existence is not an attribute. That is to say, the proposition 'The world has an independent existence' resembles grammatically the proposition 'Jones has independent means'. But existence is not a possession in the way in which money is. Nor is the independence of the world a quality in the way in which the independence of a man of property is. Since independent existence is not an attribute, it is equally improper to assert or to deny that it is an attribute of the external world. Thus the question put by materialism is meaningless.

Secondly, analytical philosophers have quarrelled with the question: What is the demiurge of history? For, they have argued, we can speak properly of this or that factor producing this or that train of events, but we cannot speak of any factor as *the* cause of the historical process. To pick out the material factor as the prime mover of history is merely to select, to draw attention to certain important features of history at the expense of others. The question: 'What is the prime mover of history?' is incompletely specified. For history as such cannot have a prime mover.

What separates this kind of philosophical analysis from both Marxism and Christianity is its divorce from practice and from all practical concerns. Marx asked the questions, what is the demiurge of history, is it thought or material conditions, because he wished to *change* history. This is his motive for trying to understand it. Thus Marx's questions are not theoretical, but practical. Or rather, his theory cannot be divorced from his practice. This separation of theory and practice is the key to analytical philosophy. It leads to a complete divorce of ethical theory from moral practice. It is indeed one of the contentions of the emotive theory of ethics that the analysis of moral judgments is itself a non-moral activity. So the emotive theory resolves itself into the following contentions: that 'This is right' means 'I approve of this: do so also'; that moral judgments therefore express feelings rather than assert facts; and that this analysis of moral judgments is a logical investigation which tells us what moral judgments mean, but does not pretend to tell us which moral judgments we should make in any situation. From the standpoint of our discussion of Christianity and Marxism the first contention is ambiguous, the second a dangerous half-truth, and the third false. I shall now proceed to justify these assertions.

First, let us begin by admitting the half-truth. 'It is wrong to exploit' is an emotive statement: but so is the multiplication table when an angry schoolmaster corrects a small boy who has formulated it incorrectly; so is any statement uttered with emotion. Hence the positivist division of statements into those of logic and mathematics which are formally true, those of the sciences which are empirically verifiable, and the emotive statements of poetry, ethics and metaphysics is a confusion of logical types. The distinction between emotive and non-emotive is a different one from that between formal truths such as $2 \times 2 = 4$, empirically verifiable statements and moral judgments. Any one of these latter three may be emotive, so that in asserting moral judgments to be emotive, we are no nearer to discovering what is the distinctive meaning and function of moral judgments.

Secondly, there is the analysis of moral judgments in terms of approval and disapproval. This assumes that we are clear as to the correct analysis of statements of the form, 'I approve of', whereas an analysis of such statements at once disposes of the view that moral judgments either report or express our feelings. For it may be quite true that Jones, who is a perfervid socialist, does have certain feelings whenever socialism is mentioned; just as Colonel Jones, his father, also has certain feelings – of anger and annoyance – whenever the topic occurs. But we would not say that Jones only approves or that his father only disapproves of socialism when they are actually experiencing certain feelings. When I say, 'Jones approves of socialism', I do not mean, 'At this moment Jones is experiencing certain feelings.' Jones may not be thinking about anything remotely connected with socialism, but it is still true that he approves of it. Hence approvals and disapprovals are not psychological symptoms or psychological reports: for they are neither exclamatory nor descriptive. They are semi-hypotheticals: that is when I say, 'Jones approves of socialism', I mean that Jones has in the past acted towards socialism in a way that has led us to expect similar behaviour in the future. If moral judgments have a reference, it is to behaviour.

This brings us to a third point: it is behaviour, it is practice that raises the question of morals at all. If we were never confronted with choices, if we never had to make decisions, there would be no point in making moral judgments. At the same time we often come to decisions of moral and political import without using specifically and explicitly moral language. Traditional moral philosophy has dwelt too much upon words like 'good' and 'right', disregarding the fact that a moral code which has only words of this kind at its disposal is committed from the outset to judge in terms of black and white a world where too often our choices are between different shades of grey. So both subjectivists and objectivists in traditional moral philosophy have concentrated upon questions like the meaning of 'good'. In so doing, they have misled us in two ways. For in looking for the meaning of statements such as 'This is good' they have too often asked for a referential meaning. Does 'this is good' refer to an objective quality of goodness just as 'this is yellow' refers to an objective quality of colour? Or does 'this is good' refer to a subjective emotional reaction, to a state of feeling, just as 'this is pleasant' refers to such a reaction? The dilemma posed by these questions is a false one. For it is not the function of statements like 'this is good' to *refer* at all, and therefore the question to what they refer can never be answered. Statements containing such words as 'right', 'good' and the subtler expressions of moral approbation and disapprobation are not answers to factual enquiries but to appeals for guidance. The function of moral judgments is brought out most clearly not when we are able to assert, 'this is right', but when we have to enquire: 'Which course of action is right?' For when we have answered the question as to how we settle our moral dilemmas, the problem of the nature of the moral judgment will have solved itself.

Moral judgments then announce our decisions. The problem is: what kind of argument do we use to solve problems of decision? The emotive theory suggests that it is all a question of feelings and that no rational pattern can be discerned in such an argument. But, if this were so, argument would be irrelevant anyway, since all reasons for acting in one way rather than another would be irrelevant except as emotional reinforcements, as slogans to influence our own feelings and those of others. The emotive theory assumes that language is either emotive or descriptive. A statement may be either a description of the facts or an evaluation of them: but it cannot be both. This is true at an elementary level: 'the garden is large' is factual; 'the garden is beautiful' is evaluative and emotive. But at any more complex level the description of the novelist or the dramatist is always itself the evaluation. Our language is such that we see the world as we value it: 'The world of the happy is quite another than that of the unhappy.'[13] It is not the case that we read Engels' description of England in 1844 and then draw the conclusion that this system ought to be condemned. Any such conclusion would be superfluous. The description itself is the condemnation.

How then do we settle problems of moral decision? Partly by appeal to general principles, partly by reference to the facts. But the facts are not, as it were, neutral. In most important moral disagreements the facts can be described in ways that support either side. Consider the argument in Koestler's *Darkness at Noon*:

> 'Wait a bit, Wait a bit', said Rubashov, walking up and down agitatedly. 'All this is just talk, but now we are getting nearer the point. As far as I remember, the problem is whether the student Raskolnikov has the right to kill the old woman? He is young and talented; he has as it were an unredeemed pledge on life in his pocket; she is old and utterly useless to the world. But the equation does not stand. In the first place, circumstances oblige him to murder a second person: that is the unforeseeable and illogical consequence of an apparently simple and logical action. Secondly, the equation collapses in any case, because Raskolnikov discovers that twice two are not four when the mathematical units are human beings...'
>
> 'Really', said Ivanov, 'If you want to hear my opinion, every copy of the book should be burnt. Consider a moment what this humanitarian fog-philosophy would lead to, if we were to take it literally: if we were to stick to the precept that the individual is sacrosanct, and that we must not treat human lives according to the rules of arithmetic. That would mean that a battalion commander may not sacrifice a patrolling party to save the regiment. That we may not sacrifice fools like Bogrov, and must risk our coastal towns being shot to pieces in a couple of years...' Rubashov shook his head: 'Your examples are all drawn from war – that is, from abnormal circumstances.' 'Since the invention of the steam engine', replied Ivanov, 'the world has been permanently in an abnormal state; the wars and revolutions are just the visible expressions of this state. Your Raskolnikov is, however, a fool and a criminal; not because he behaves logically in killing the old woman, but because he is doing it in his personal interest. The principle that

[13] Wittgenstein 1922, p. 185, remark 6.43.

> the end justifies the means is and remains the only rule of political ethics; anything else is just vague chatter and melts away between one's fingers.... If Raskolnikov had bumped off the old woman at the command of the Party for example, to increase strike funds or to install an illegal Press – then the equation would stand, and the novel with its misleading problems would never have been written, and so much the better for humanity!'[14]

This is a real moral argument and the point that I want to bring out is the way in which each side appeals to the facts, and although it is not like a physical scientist's appeals to the facts of observation and experiment, nevertheless in a quite crucial sense, there is such an appeal. The question is: 'Ought Raskolnikov to have killed the old woman?' Rubashov says, 'No, for while in certain abnormal circumstances such as wartime an action like this might be justified, normally the life of a human being ought not to be sacrificed for any end.' Ivanov fastens on Rubashov's concession. Whether or not an action is justified or not depends on what historical end it serves. Thus the question of what our actions accomplish in history is one of the crucial questions in this argument over Marxist ethics. This brings us to the point where we can begin to answer the criticisms of the materialist view of history. The question, 'What is the demiurge of history?' becomes intelligible when it is realised that it is asked from practical motives. If the answer, 'ideals are the prime mover in history' was correct, then those who would change the world would be those who propagated the right ideals. This was the answer of the young Hegelians, and their failure was the failure of that answer. Similarly, the whole question of materialism is not a speculative, but a practical one. Rubashov and Ivanov take a different stand on the moral problem, because there is a basic difference between them in their world-view. Thus world-views, however metaphorical, and apparently distorted uses of language, have practical consequences. But what are the criteria to be employed in distinguishing world-views? By talking of the consequences of a world-view are we not commending metaphysics on the grounds of its utility, rather than on the grounds of the truth of some one metaphysical system?

The question of metaphysics is bedevilled by talk which assumes that those who are commonly called metaphysicians were engaged on the same

[14] Koestler (ed.) 1947, pp. 126–7.

activity, and there can be no defence of metaphysics as such, simply because metaphysics is a rubric covering widely differing intellectual enterprises. Both Christianity and Marxism, however, claim truth as metaphysical systems rather than utility; and both vindicate that claim by laying themselves open to falsification on questions of fact. The Marxist asserts materialism in metaphysics because it is only the insights of materialism that will enable him to change the world effectively. Consequently the claims of Marxist materialism are vindicated, if, and only if, the predictions of Marxist social theory are verified. The achievements of communist revolution are the test of Marxist metaphysics. Christianity is, if anything, more intransigent than Marxism here. The Christian claims rest on the fact of the Resurrection of Jesus. Paul could put it quite bluntly: 'If Christ be not risen from the dead, then is our faith vain.'[15] Similarly, the Marxist can say: 'If the free society does not arise from the revolution, then Marxism is vain.' Both Christianity and Marxism assert patterns in history by pointing to vindicating events.

The Christian dilemma

The function of this last part of the argument is to bring out the way in which a discussion of the relations of Christianity to Marxism must, to be realistic at all, be relevant to practical decisions; and at the same time to show how ambiguous metaphysical doctrines are as instruments of decision. It has been argued that there is a prophetic element at the heart of Marxism which is both life-giving and corrupting. It would be easy to decide on the face of it that the corruption of Marxism should lead us to decide for the forces of anti-Communism. This would not allow however for the fact that anti-Communism as such is a mere negation of Communism, which shares its fundamental errors without its corresponding virtues. Communists and anti-Communists are agreed that there is a revolution in the modern world, a rising of the hitherto poorer peoples. They are agreed that the meaning of that revolution is the meaning that present-day Communism gives to it. They see the same significance in the revolt of the colonial peoples. The only difference is that the Communists support this revolution by every possible means, the

[15] I Corinthians 15: 17: 'And if Christ be not raised, your faith *is* vain: ye are yet in sin.'

anti-Communists oppose it. But what if one is not willing to concede that the ultimate truth about men is that they are divided into two opposing parties? Christians at least cannot concede this, for they are committed to the belief that men are at one in their common humanity which has been once and for all shown forth in the humanity of Jesus. The revolution of our time must receive in the light of Christian faith another interpretation. Such an interpretation we have already seen in the writings of the younger Marx, but when we set Marxism beside the Christian doctrine then the full extent of the Christian dilemma appears.

For Christianity speaks of a new age which God inaugurates in His Kingdom. The dilemma comes when we ask the question of the time of the coming of the Kingdom of God. On the one hand, there are those who would bring the Kingdom into history: but if the Kingdom is brought into history, then the cause of God must be identified with one historical cause as against others: If the Christian hope is to be realised in history, it must assume the form of a political hope; it must use the morally ambiguous means which are the only means to attain political ends. In other words, the religious content must be realised in political terms. But this is exactly what the young Marx did in his criticism of religion. Marxism is in essence a complete realisation of Christian eschatology. Contrasted with it is the kind of theology which seeks to place the Kingdom of God at the end of history, so that all historical causes are failures if they are measured against the hope of the Kingdom. This, course, delivers us from identifying the cause of God with the half-truths of political morality, but it does so surely at the cost of denying us any political guidance from Christian faith at all, and if Christian faith offers no political guidance, then it is fundamentally irrelevant to human life.

The solution adopted by the Church has been to distinguish between the full realisation of Christian hope at the end of history and a partial realisation of it now in the life of the Church. But this solution is discredited, at least for those outside the Church, by the way in which the Church has continually sanctified the political and social *status quo*. It must necessarily do so because it has accepted the existing property relations of society and so has become an institution with a vested interest in the continuance of these property relations. The financial difficulties of the Church of England consequent upon the nationalisation of the railways are a case in point. It is illuminating that the religious orders are, at least in origin, communities of poverty which are thus delivered from the domination of property relations. But the kind of disillusionment to which the Church's acceptance of property and privilege leads is strongly matched by the disillusionment of some with Communism. André Gide could write of his visit to Russia:

> There was in my Soviet adventure something tragic. I had arrived there a convinced and enthusiastic follower in order to admire a new world, and they offered me, to tempt me and win me, all the prerogatives and privileges which I abhorred in the old world.[16]

So that one is finally brought to the point where one must ask how the themes of the gospel and of Marx can be made relevant at all in the light of the corruption of the Church and of the Communist Party.

The task is to create a form of community which will exemplify the pattern of the gospel and which will be enabled to renew continually its repentance for its conformity to the patterns of human sin. After the histories of Church and party is there any hope for such a form of community? This essay should really end with that question, for its aim has been to formulate the religious dilemma before Marxism rather than to offer a solution of that dilemma. But the lines along which the dilemma might be solved can be indicated. First, it will have to be solved in the practice of Christian living, rather than in theory. Secondly, it must attempt to combine in its practice politics and compassion. Thirdly, there is only one hope in which this attempt is possible. In the last analysis, the difference between a Marxist world and a Christian lies in the fact that in a fully Marxist world prayer would be impossible. The true Christian community will be one of poverty and of prayer. In one sense it will not be specifically Christian, for it will be concerned above all with the truly human. Dietrich Bonhoeffer put this by saying:

> The Christian is not a *homo religiosus*, but simply a man as Jesus (in distinction from John the Baptist) was a man.... Not the flat and banal 'this-sidedness' of the Enlightened, of the Active, of the Comfortable and the Sluggard, but the deep 'this-sidedness' which is full of discipline and in which the knowledge of the Death and Resurrection is always present, this it is that

[16] Koestler (ed.) 1947, p. 176.

> I mean.... How can a man wax arrogant if in a this-sided life he shares the suffering of God?[17]

But in another sense this new community will be both human and Christian. For its prayer will be the classical prayer of Christendom. Paradoxically it is the contemporary study of Marxism which perhaps brings out most clearly what the classical methods of meditation have to say to us about the 'dark night of the soul'. It is a 'dark night', an *ascesis* of poverty and questioning which must renew our politics. A community committed alike to politics and to prayer would serve in the renewal of the whole Church, for it would give to us a new understanding of the central act of the Church's life which is in humble thanksgiving to eat the body of a Lord who hungered and thirsted and to drink the blood of a Lord whom the powers of Church and state combined to crucify outside the walls of the city.

[17] Bonhoeffer 2001, pp. 136–7.

Chapter Two
Marxist Tracts[1]

A Review of Georges Politzer, Guy Besse and Maurice Caveing, Principes fondamentaux de philosophie; *John Lewis,* Introduction to Philosophy and Marxism and the Irrationalists

Contemporary Marxism is a weird conglomerate of ideas, a few of them still with a hint of life, but most of them fossilised. This is partly a question of style. The mode of Russian polemic with which Plekhanov and Lenin infected Marxism is not a happy one. And partly it is a question of politically enforced conformity. What these two together can do to allegedly philosophical writing can be seen in the ignorant and dogmatic outbursts of the late A.A. Zhdanov or in the caricatures which pass for expositions of the thought of Bergson and Russell in the *Soviet Philosophical Dictionary*. Yet one might hope that in the writings of English and French Marxists, whose doctrine is certainly the fruit of intellectual conviction and whose opportunities to hear Marxism criticised are more than adequate, something better might be found. One's hopes are disappointed.

Take for instance three recently published books. The late M. Georges Politzer was a courageous militant, but his lectures on philosophy which have

[1] Originally published in *Philosophical Quarterly*, v. 6, n. 25, October 1956, pp. 366–70.

appeared posthumously remind one of nothing so much as those manuals *ad mentem Divi Thomae* which vex the lives of Catholic theological students. Here orthodoxy is proclaimed and its formulas are defended from a standpoint so certain and secure that we cannot but recall that passage in Hegel's *Logic* where the thoughts of the philosopher and the thoughts of God have become one and the same.[2] This reminiscence is not merely random. For the Marxist the history of pre-Marxist philosophy is a development of partial truth and partial error through a series of Hegelian conflicts into the full truth of Marxism. The history of post-Marxist philosophy is a history of the ideas of dying capitalism being confronted and overcome by the savants of Marxism. Dr. John Lewis has recently applied himself to these themes with some vigour, and he writes with an authority that permits us to take his views as typical of those current among Marxists. Let us examine just one of his assertions. Dr. Lewis says, for example, that we find in Aristotle 'a doctrine of "substance" and "attribute" and a rigidly formal logic which reflect and justify a static order of society'.[3] This statement is a specific application of the general Marxist doctrine of ideology and all the difficulties of that doctrine are apparent in Dr. Lewis's assertion. My first difficulty is with the expression 'rigidly formal logic'. I take it that Dr. Lewis intends to refer by this curious phrase to Aristotle's theory of the syllogism. If one says that the theory of the syllogism, as Aristotle expounds it, reflects and justifies the kind of Greek society with which Aristotle was familiar and of which he approved, one speaks unintelligibly. Consider for a moment the 'justifies'. Presumably Dr. Lewis does not hold that the theory of the syllogism does in fact justify a certain kind of Greek city-state. He must therefore mean that to Aristotle it seemed to constitute such a justification. This, as any reader of Aristotle's *Politics* knows, is false. The heart of the puzzle is to understand how anyone could ever think that the theory of the syllogism could have any political significance at all. Someone might reply to this by suggesting that what Dr. Lewis meant was that there is a

[2] See, for example, Hegel 1969, p. 50: 'Accordingly, logic is to be understood as the system of pure reason, as the realm of pure thought. This realm is truth as it is without veil and in its own absolute nature. It can therefore be said that this content is the exposition of God as he is in his eternal essence before the creation of nature and a finite mind.'

[3] Lewis 1954, p. 28.

psychological link between the kind of mind that is intrigued by the theory of the syllogism and the kind of mind that is politically conservative. But while this might turn out to be true, we should need the nature of the link defined more specifically before we could even begin to look for the evidence which would be appropriate in the testing of this hypothesis. Again, one might enquire, if Aristotle's doctrine of substance and attribute reflects a static order of society, what does his doctrine of change reflect? To press this point home we must consider the meaning of 'reflection'.

The relation of various works of intellect and imagination to the society in which they are produced is a legitimate and serious field for empirical study. But the metaphor of 'reflection' is a peculiarly infelicitous way of expressing this relation. A novel, of course, may in a quite obvious sense be said to reflect or to portray the contemporary social order and a Marxist critic like Georg Lukács may make of certain novels matter for penetrating comment in this respect. When we have given this example of the legitimate use of 'reflect' three points at once arise.

First, this reflection of the social order is a distinctive characteristic of the novel – and of similar genres – and just in so far as we allow 'reflection' a legitimate use in the context of a discussion of the novel we preclude its use elsewhere. To try and apply it to the relationship of other kinds of writing to the social order is to blur fatally the distinction between novels and other kinds of writing. It is to suggest that philosophical theses are aphoristic novels. They are not. It is worth noting that in this sense reflection is necessarily the explicit result of a conscious intention to reflect: it is not accidental or merely implicit. Philosophical doctrines do not spring from such an intention and thus could never be 'reflections' in this sense.

Secondly, in this legitimate sense of 'reflection', the more the novel reflects the less it justifies. Or rather, to reflect and to justify are two separate and distinct tasks and, in so far as the reality to be reflected is unpleasant, the more faithful the reflection the more difficult the task of justification. Reflection and justification are not necessarily compatible.

Thirdly, the Marxist theory of ideology usually suggests that some sort of causal relationship holds between the social order and the particular work of intellect or imagination. But in this legitimate sense of 'reflection' such a relation between the novel and the social order is precisely not causal. It is easy to see how the word 'reflection' misleads here with its mirror-image associations. Yet if a novel is not a mirror-image, far less so is any philosophical thesis.

I have begun from this point because crucial to the Marxist view of philosophy is the thesis that any given philosophical doctrine stands in a necessary relationship to some particular form of social order. The failure of Marxists to talk sense about this relationship vitiates most of the rest of their philosophical utterances. Because they conceive of philosophical controversy as a reflection of class war and because they see the contemporary class war as two-sided, so they have to force contemporary philosophy into the same pattern. Christian theology, existentialism and linguistic analysis are all to be comprehended under the label of 'idealism', their apparent differences dwarfed in the perspective of their disagreements with Marxism. It is obvious why Christian theology and existentialism should offend: the one asserts the sovereignty of God and the other the sovereignty of the individual human decision in a way that has seemed to beg questions about causal determination to many who are not Marxists. And part of what the Marxist means by 'idealism' is a failure to take causal explanation seriously. Yet if any school of philosophers has taken scientific modes of argument seriously, it has surely been those of a positivist or analytical stand-point. Whence then the charge of idealism? Contemporary Marxist writers frame this charge in two different ways. Sometimes they say, and a great many non-Marxists have said this too, that there is here a retreat from external reality into language and Dr. Lewis says explicitly that a preoccupation with problems of meaning has distracted philosophers from a suitable political awareness. Secondly, they see in the philosophy of science since Mach a refusal to treat scientific concepts as straightforwardly representative of material realities. The second is surely a special case of the first. The sin of modern philosophers in Marxist eyes is that they have rejected the view that language in general and scientific language in particular has the function of mirroring the facts. We are back at the metaphor of reflection. Lenin, whose terminology does not make for clarity, seems to have held both that the conceptual uses of language ('ideas') and perceptual experience itself ('sensations') were mirrors of reality and on this whole question had a classical disagreement with Plekhanov.[4] To see why

[4] Lenin 1968, pp. 41–2, 51–2, 151–3.

this Marxist view of language is mistaken is fundamental to understanding Marxism.

We are apt to suppose that there are only two possible alternative ways of viewing the relation between language and facts. Either language is external to facts and our problem is how to relate them or facts themselves are already incorporated in language somehow, so that we never get beyond the most primitive uses of language such as 'red now'. The first alternative perplexes us by raising the problem of how language applies to reality, the second baffles because we know that the facts are what they are independently of our saying so. The Marxist adopts the first alternative and says that language is related to reality after the manner of a picture or a mirror-image. Anyone who thinks that these are the only alternatives will oscillate desperately between them, thinking it intolerable to be imprisoned in language on the one hand, but conscious of the difficulties in any representative theory of language. The difficulties of any such theory have been so adequately dealt with elsewhere that here I shall restrict myself to suggesting that any theory which arises from the posing of this kind of alternative is bound to fall into error.[5] The basic misconception is to suppose that there is one activity which is apprehending reality and another which is using language and that there is a problem about relating these two activities. Certainly seeing is one thing and saying what you see is another; but the questions of whether and what you see have no answers until there is language enough to formulate them. To know anything is to know that a proposition is true, and knowing is not an activity, so that there is no problem of what it is that you know over and above the problem of saying what you know. Hence the investigation of the logic of our language, the analysis of its conceptual structure, can never be rightly conceived of as an activity totally distinct from and indeed to be contrasted with factual inquiry. Every factual enquiry, at the moment it embarks on the construction of theories – and even before this – has to become self-conscious about the type of concept employed. What can inhibit factual enquiry is a conceptual naïveté that assumes a certain kind of concept to be normative. Just as at one stage the formulas of the logical positivists concealed the complexity of our uses of language, so at an earlier stage the prestige of Newtonian mechanics provided

---

[5] [See, for example, E. Daitz, 'A Picture Theory of Meaning', *Mind*, New Series, v. 62, n. 246, April 1953.]

a conceptual scheme whose normative use is apparent in much nineteenth century materialism. Those whose lack of awareness over language leads them to hypostasise and to venerate certain ways of using language at the expense of others will inevitably think of their own conceptual schema as 'the facts'. This is what has happened to Marxists. Dr. Lewis, for example, wants to assimilate talk about electrons to talk about atoms, because he plainly thinks of the latter as the only kind of indubitably factual talk.

This linguistic rigidity of Marxist philosophers is the heart of the matter. Marx himself was one of those who see the world with such clarity that they conceive one of their principal tasks to be the furnishing of an explanation of why others do not see it in the same way. Hence his theory of ideology. Those ideas which seemed to blind men to the truth he termed 'mysteries', using this expression in ways that bear some resemblance to the positivistic use of 'nonsense' for example, in the eighth of the *Theses on Feuerbach* and in *Capital*, Volume 1.[6] His error was to locate nonsensical mystification in the adoption and use of certain concepts rather than of others, whereas the truth is that any concept can be used so as to mystify. The basic concepts of Marxism are a case in point. For such concepts as that of the economic explanation of political events or that of alienation are not without a legitimate use, without a point. It is the abuse of these and similar concepts by extending and applying them in a completely *a priori* way which creates a new set of mystifications.

That is why those Marxist writings which are formally devoted to philosophical questions are almost totally devoid of interest. Occasionally there is a hint of something better. When Lukács, for example, is discussing the portrayal of personality as a literary problem in his *Studies in European Realism*, he attacks the 'stream of consciousness' view of mind in ways that are reminiscent of Ryle and yet are stimulatingly different; and as a philosophical scholar writing on Hegel, Lukács has put us all in his debt.[7] But it is notable that even a thinker of the power of Lukács turns to the past for his problems. In the present there are no problems, there is only the refutation of error. So the books of English and French Marxists are either text-book expositions of Marxism, like M. Politzer's, or historical works or refutations of present errors, like Dr. Lewis's. It is both sad and significant that no Marxist undertakes

---

6 Marx 1975b, p. 423; Marx 1976, pp. 163–5.

7 Lukács 1972, pp. 7–10.

original philosophical work. For them there remains only the zeal of the evangelist. To read their books is to move in a dead world.

To report on the present state of Marxist philosophy is thus not a difficult task, but hardly a rewarding one. Yet if one goes behind Marxism to Marx himself, one becomes aware of a cluster of living problems which still leave their traces on Marxism. Marx was intimately concerned with two problems that necessarily arise for everyone who engages seriously in philosophy. He was concerned with the perspective of ultimate belief, with the problems which engage the philosophy of religion; and he was concerned with the question of how the philosopher should relate himself to his philosophy and the sense in which philosophy can or cannot affect one's ultimate views and commitments. The logical elucidation of these questions is urgent and important. If Marx's answers will not do, some of his questions are timely. To turn from the Marxists to Marx will at least suggest an explanation of why so many potentially able minds have been fatally attracted by and finally imprisoned within the jargon of Marxism.

Chapter Three

On Not Misrepresenting Philosophy[1]

A spectre is haunting the intelligentsia, the spectre of what they call 'linguistic philosophy'. Sunday newspaper reviewers and sociobiologists, theologians and dialectical materialists join in abhorring it. But as is the way with many who see spectres their reports are often incorrect and incoherent. Mr. Ernest Gellner who has joined the ranks of the philosophical ghost-seers in 'Logical Positivism and the Spurious Fox' is no exception.[2] Much of what he says is indeed not worth answering. The mixture of gossip and sociology, insinuation and condescension is likely to make the uninformed reader distrust Gellner just as much as he should. Yet the appearance of any discussion of contemporary British philosophy in a journal of the Left is itself an event of importance. The socialist intellectual tradition is at a moment of crisis when there are opening new possibilities of an approach to human culture that bears neither the frozen mask of Stalinism nor the glib smile of the cultural eclectic. At such a time it is peculiarly important that we should understand the impoverishment which Marxism has suffered as a result of its isolation from the best work in philosophy. (There is an interesting similarity

---

[1] First published in *Universities and Left Review*, 4, Summer 1958, pp. 72–3.

[2] Gellner 1958.

in philosophical style between Marxists and neo-Thomists, which springs from their sharing the same type of self-imposed isolation.) It would therefore be a misfortune if Gellner's misunderstanding and consequent misrepresentations were to gain currency. What is perhaps most misleading is his use of the label 'linguistic philosophy' to cover what are in fact very different philosophical attitudes and doctrines. All that I want to do in this article is to bring out with a single example how Gellner misdescribes the work of Wittgenstein; for he gives the impression at least of expounding doctrines connected with that work. If I have misunderstood his intentions, I may at any rate assist others in avoiding a misunderstanding which his obscure but abusive style of writing is likely to provoke. But at the outset it ought to be emphasised that Wittgenstein's work is complex and that its complexity is important. All that I can therefore hope to do, which is to indicate one theme of Wittgenstein's later thought and its possible importance, must be inadequate. But before I do even this two remarks may perhaps be in place. The first is that Wittgenstein's work stands in a far more complicated relationship to the history of philosophy than Mr. Gellner's article suggested. Plato, St. Augustine, Schopenhauer, William James, Moritz Schlick – these and more provided problems for Wittgenstein. And the truth that does lie in recent talk about a 'revolution in philosophy' ought not to blind us to the extent to which Wittgenstein provided new answers to old questions: 'What is knowledge?' 'What is perception?' 'What is understanding?' and so on. The second is that not only, as Gellner admits, did Wittgenstein not assert that the world is totally non-mysterious but also that those who have learnt most from Wittgenstein include a number of Christians who are presumably committed by their faith to something quite other than this. Wittgenstein's aphorism that 'Philosophy leaves everything as it is' says nothing of how things are.[3]

The theme from Wittgenstein's *Philosophical Investigations* on which I want to touch is that of the non-private character of language. What I shall try to do is three-fold. I shall seek to show why the conception of a private language is important and where the roots of this conception lie. Next is shall attempt to delineate part of Wittgenstein's attack on this notion. Finally I shall try to present one or two of Wittgenstein's key ideas (including one mentioned by Gellner) in the light of this discussion.

---

[3] Wittgenstein 1968, p. 49, remark 124.

The conception of a private language is rooted both in the history of philosophy and in our own conceptual inclinations. I know what the word 'red' means because I have seen red objects. I know what the word 'pain' means because I have felt pain. My understanding is totally limited by and totally dependent upon my experience: 'In short, all the materials of thinking are derived either from our outward or inward sentiment: the mixture and composition of these belongs alone to the mind and will.'[4] All our concepts are formed by abstraction from experience. This is the doctrine of a great philosophical tradition. That something has gone amiss with this tradition of empiricism very near its starting point is evident from the fact that it follows from its doctrines that language is primarily a private matter and only secondarily and as it were accidentally public. For since all my experience is mine and all your experience is yours, what I mean by 'red' and 'pain' is determined by one thing and what you mean by them is determined by another. My words take their meaning from my experience, yours from yours. How then is language public at all? Because we can point. It is not surprising that ostensive definition has a central role in much empiricist discussion. Our words have a common meaning because we can point at the objects to which they refer and which they describe. And for such a doctrine there will be necessary contrast between the outer world of material objects the outer world of material objects to which we can point and the inner world of thought and sensation to which we cannot point. The problem of how we can understand talk about the minds of others is necessarily crucial for empiricism.

That we can have a private language, at least, that there is something essentially private about language, at most, these are assertions to which adherence to this sort of tradition would commit us. So the assertion that there cannot be a private language, that language cannot be both language and private, puts this whole tradition in question. But what are the arguments which will back up this assertion? Wittgenstein has several of which I want to mention only one. Suppose someone has a private language. Every time that he feels a certain sensation he writes down or says 'E'. 'E' is the name of his sensation. But now is 'E' a private word? Can he himself understand 'E' without translating it into words which belong to our common public language? As Wittgenstein puts this:

[4] Hume 1999, p. 97.

> What reasons have we for calling 'E' the sign for a *sensation*? For 'sensation' is a word of our common language, not of one intelligible to me alone. So the use of this word stands in need of a justification which everybody understands – And it would not help either to say that it need not be a *sensation*; that when he writes 'E', he has *something* – and that is all that can be said. 'Has' and 'something' also belong to our common language.[5]

That is to distinguish the shape 'E' when he writes it or the thought when he utters it to himself he has to think of it as the *name* of a *sensation* (and not as just a capital 'E' or an abbreviation for 'Eric') and he cannot do this without such a word as 'sensation' which is learnt not simply by having sensations. Someone who tried to have a purely private language would in the end find himself merely uttering indiscriminable sounds (for to discriminate them he would have to fall back on public language) and these would not be language.

How do we learn to use words like 'sensation', 'pain' and so on? Not simply by having experiences, but by being introduced to ways of expressing what we feel in the context of what Wittgenstein calls 'language-games', that is a whole way of acting and behaving in which the language used has to be understood as part of the whole activity. A child cries and is asked: 'Where does it hurt?' The iodine is applied; the child is asked: 'Is the pain less now? Is the stinging over?' It is through this type of situation not only that the child does learn the meaning of words like 'pain', but that the child must learn them. The word in isolation attached to the sensation of pain in isolation: what would this be? We can only begin to understand the suggestion that the word might function thus because we ourselves do not understand the words 'pain' and 'sensation' in this way.

To make the same point differently, Mr P.F. Strawson has objected to Wittgenstein's thesis as follows:

> Wittgenstein gives himself considerable trouble over the question of how a man would *introduce* a name for a sensation into this private language. But we need imagine no special ceremony. He might simply be struck by the recurrence of a certain sensation and get into the habit of making a certain

---

[5] Wittgenstein 1968, p. 93, remark 261.

> mark in a different place every time it occurred. The making of the marks would help to impress the occurrence on his memory.[6]

What Strawson says might happen is of course almost exactly what Hobbes says does happen. Strawson's empiricist view of language may help to remind us how contemporary philosophy is far less homogenous than Gellner suggested. What is wrong with this view can be seen most easily if we begin by considering not a word like 'pain' or 'sensation' but a word like 'cow'. Suppose a man were to utter a certain sound every time that a cow appeared. Dr. Norman Malcolm, commenting on Strawson's argument has pointed out that:

> ...we need to ask, what makes the latter sound a *word*, and what makes it the word for *cow*? Is there no difficulty here? Is it sufficient that the sound is uttered when and only when a cow is present? Of course not. The sound might refer to anything or nothing.

That is, it need not be a word any more than, if I suffered from a nervous tick of the head every time I saw a cow, my movement of my head would be a word. Malcolm then says of the sounds in question,

> What is necessary is that it should play a part in various activities, in calling, fetching, counting cows, distinguishing cows from other things and pictures of cows from pictures of other things. If the word has no fixed place in activities ('language-games') of this sort, then it isn't a word for *cow*. To be sure, I can sit in my chair and talk about cows and not be engaged in any of those activities – but what makes my words *refer* to cows is the fact that I have already mastered those activities; they lie in the background.[7]

So too with a mark which a man made every time he felt a sensation. What would be needed to make that mark a word and a word specifically referring to the sensation would be a use for the word in expressing the sensation or calling attention to it or asking for its cause to be removed. In such a context of public uses the word would be more than simply a mark recalling the sensation; and it would have to be more than this even to be such a mark.

---

[6] Strawson 1954, p. 85.
[7] Malcolm 1954, p. 553.

This very compressed summary of one point, even though a central point, in Wittgenstein's philosophy is enough to dispose of some of Gellner's most misleading remarks. 'What it amounts to', says Gellner of what he calls the key image of linguistic philosophy, 'is *naturalism with regard to language,* seeing language as a natural process and activity and solving philosophical problems in the course of an investigation of this process.'[8] But nothing in this or, so far as I know, any other of Wittgenstein's arguments depends on such a naturalism. What Wittgenstein investigates are not the usages and idioms which people happen to employ, but the uses to which language is and can be put and especially the kind of use to which particular classes of expressions have to be put if they are to have sense. The way in which the notion of use appears in Wittgenstein's thought is clear from the above example. Neither 'cow' nor 'sensation' would be the words they are unless we knew how to relate them to the variety of uses to which they can be put. Language does not just happen: we do things with it, put it to certain uses. The notion of the uses of language is close to the notion of a language-game.

Moreover, for Wittgenstein this kind of investigation of language only has importance relative to its purpose of resolving philosophical perplexity. And although Wittgenstein had an important view of what philosophy was, his central contributions to philosophy consist in actual pieces of philosophising of which his remarks about philosophy are only one part. The impressiveness of his philosophy lies not, as Gellner seems to indicate, in any general thesis about how philosophical problems are to be solved, but in his own work on the problems. Indeed, his remarks about philosophy seem to me incomprehensible apart from that work.

I could of course have approached Wittgenstein's thought from a number of other points. All that I have indicated is one theme. I chose this theme for the following reason. Marx's actual philosophy was in part a dismissal of empiricism; but the philosophical tools available to Marx were such that his own positive philosophical statements are always liable to conceptual muddle. And Lenin falls back into the empiricist confusions about experience even in a work which purports to attack empiricism. But in his historical

---

[8] Gellner 1958, p. 69.

analyses of that culture of which empiricist philosophy was a part Marx helped to expose the myth of man as a private, isolated individual. Empiricist philosophy was a not undistinguished component of individualist culture, and a not unimportant background to that myth. So its exposure ought to matter to those who think Marx's insights on this point are of some importance. In a way the thesis that a private language is possible lies very near the heart of the dualism that has infected philosophy ever since the last scholastics and Descartes. What Wittgenstein has achieved in showing how our concepts of, for example, sensation are inseparably connected with our activities and behaviour is a possibility of overcoming that dualism. The connectedness of the inner life and the outer has been re-established. The importance of this cannot be underestimated. One has only to remember how psychology has been hampered by the apparent need to choose between the two unsatisfactory alternatives of introspectionism and behaviourism. Or one may recall Lukács's strictures on the way in which the introspectionism of Joyce and the behaviourism of Zola equally fail to portray human beings as human beings.[9]

I hope that no one will suppose that I have in this last paragraph *established* a connection between Wittgenstein's work and such large issues. All I have done is to indicate one small point where the importance of what Wittgenstein did can begin to be grasped. There is, however, another and a more elementary issue raised by Gellner's article. Of all the ideas that minister to the sickness of our age none is more influential in the university than the conception that there are only two alternatives – the kind of objectivity that dwells in the ivory tower or the kind of partisanship that does not care about truth. The triviality of the academic who wants his work to raise no large issues and the falsification of the Stalinist who wants everything to be secured to one immediate issue reinforce each other. Those propagandists against contemporary academic philosophy, from Joad to Gellner, who promote the view that it is an essentially trivial pursuit, unwittingly strengthen the bands of those who seek to present us with this alternative.

---

[9] On Joyce, see Lukács 1962, pp. 17–18. On Zola, see Lukács 1972.

One last point: of course, there is plenty of bad philosophy about today. If this was all Gellner wanted to say, no one would have disagreed. And the bad philosophy of an age is always a parody of the good. But any attempt to present Wittgenstein's work and influence in the way that Gellner does is bound to fail. To present Kant as essentially holding two propositions, or Marx, would be to make oneself ridiculous. So it is too with Wittgenstein.[10]

[10] For a response to this article see Gellner 1958b.

Chapter Four
The Algebra of the Revolution[1]

A Review of Raya Dunayevskaya, Marxism and Freedom

'Hegel's logic is the algebra of the revolution'.[2] Herzen's aphorism is often quoted, but rarely taken seriously. That Herzen had a real insight here is suggested by the fact that key periods in the thought of both Marx and Lenin followed hard upon a close reading of Hegel. The first classic statement of Marxism in *The German Ideology* was an outcome of Marx's struggle with the *Phenomenology of Mind* in 1844. The re-evaluation of Marx by Lenin after 1914 follows on his reading of the *Science of Logic*:

> It is impossible fully to grasp Marx's *Capital,* and especially its first chapter, if you have not studied through and understood the whole of Hegel's *Logic.* Consequently none of the Marxists for the past half century have understood Marx!![3]

What gives this crucial role to Hegel's philosophy? Hegel's picture of human activity as rational activity, and of rational activity as activity that has freedom as its goal. Certainly for Hegel this

[1] Originally published in *Universities and Left Review* 5, Autumn 1958, pp. 79–80.

[2] Herzen 1974, p. 237: 'The philosophy of Hegel is the algebra of revolution: it emancipates a man in an unusual way and leaves not one stone upon another of the Christian World, of the world of tradition that has outlived itself.'

[3] Lenin 1960–70d, p. 180.

picture is ambiguous, hovering between assertions about the real human condition and statements of the ideal, not yet realised, form of human life. Certainly Marx had to transform Hegel. But the ferment of the concepts of freedom, reason and consciousness in Marx's philosophy is the Marxist debt to Hegel. Hegel without Marx is unrealistic, and in the end obscurantist. Marx without Hegel would have been rigid, mechanical, inhuman. And when later Marxisms display these characteristics it is often a sign of a neglect of the Hegelian stimulus in Marx. 'The question of Hegel was settled long ago', said A.A. Zhdanov in 1947: 'There is no reason whatever to pose it anew.'[4] When would-be Marxists talk like this, it is usually a sign that the freeing of human nature is no longer the central goal of their socialism.

This is perhaps the most important theme of Raya Dunayevskaya's *Marxism and Freedom*. Miss Dunayevskaya was at one time Trotsky's secretary. When Trotsky declared in the last war that Russia was genuinely a workers' state which ought to be defended, she broke with him, and since then has played her own very individual part in the American labour movement.[5] She only wrote the final draft of her book after earlier drafts had been discussed and criticised by groups of miners, steelworkers, auto-workers and students.[6] A book that is the product of an interest in Hegel on the one hand and participation in a miner's strike in West Virginia on the other promises to have unusual qualities. And this book is unusual. It has three great merits.

The first is that she has tried to write a history of Marxist theory in which the development of the theory is linked at every point to the corresponding developments both in society and in the political experience of socialists.

The second is that she has utilised some of the source material of Marxism more fully than any previous commentator. I have spoken already of her Hegelian concern. In this connection she has included in appendices translations of a major part of Marx's *Economic and Philosophical Manuscripts* of 1844 and of those portions of Lenin's *Philosophical Notebooks* which deal with Hegel.[7] But she has also been in a position to make use of the stenographic

---

[4] Zhdanov 1950, p. 102.

[5] For Trotsky's final substantive statement of his position on Stalinist Russia (dated 18 October 1939), see 'Again and Once More Again on the Nature of the USSR', in Trotsky 1971.

[6] Dunayevskaya 1971, p. 24.

[7] The appendices to which MacIntyre refers were the first publication of these texts in English. Dunayevskaya excluded them from the second (1964) and subsequent

reports of the early congresses of the Russian party and especially of those of the Ninth party congress of 1921 when the crucial debates on the role of the trade unions in a socialist society took place.[8]

The third merit of this book, and it arises out of the other two, is that it provides a framework for a revaluation of Lenin in which a change can be noted from an emphasis on the party as the revolutionary manipulator of a passive working class to emphasis on the potential revolutionary spontaneity of the working class. And this change goes along with what we may call Lenin's Hegelian conversion.

It will be already clear that this book is an important contribution to socialist thought. What has to be said in addition is that it is a book in which important insights and scholarly research is often sacrificed to a new framework of dogma. For Miss Dunayevskaya this is the age of state capitalism, a form of economy common to both USA and USSR. This leads her into a fantastic under-valuation of socialist achievement in the Soviet Union. She writes of the Soviet state as though the Moscow trials, Vorkuta, and Hungary were its supreme and authentic expressions. And because of this standpoint she tends to treat as Soviet crimes and heresies what are in fact at least attempts to face the problems of a socialist society. Miss Dunayevskaya criticises Soviet industrialisation; she says nothing of how industrialisation ought to proceed in a socialist society. She attacks Soviet collectivisation of agriculture; she says nothing of what socialist agriculture should be. And the result is that this portion of her book is negative and sterile. She sees no more hope in Yugoslavia than in Russia. Her only hope is the world-wide working class. And the suspicion grows as one reads that she has an entirely idealised view of that class.

What has happened to her book seems to be something like this. She has been repelled by the arid, seminary text-book Marxism of the Stalinists and the Trotskyists (who share all the dogmatism of the Stalinists without any of their achievements). She has gone back to the sources and reread her Marx and Lenin. But what she has in the end extracted from this is a new dogmatism, a new fixed scheme. And in doing this she misses seeing in Marxism a

---

editions of *Marxism and Freedom* as they had by then been translated into English in their entirety. See ibid., pp. 17–18. For the texts themselves, see 1975b.

[8] Dunayevskaya 1971, pp. 196–201.

perspective on human affairs which her return to Hegel might have brought home to her. We are so used to having Marxism interpreted for us as the science which lays bare the laws of society that we tend to take it for granted that Marxism presents us with a picture of man as a being whose behaviour is essentially predictable. But in fact it is truer to say that Marxism shows us how in class-divided society human possibility is never fully revealed. There is always more potentiality in human beings than we are accustomed to allow for. And because of this, human development often takes place in quite unpredictable leaps. We never perhaps know how near we are to the next step forward.

It is when Marxists lose faith in the possibilities of human life in our age that they begin to look for some substitute faith. In Stalinism it is belief in the party and above all in the party bureaucracy. For Miss Dunayevskaya it is her largely idealised version of the working class. And of course those who have to idealise the workers are precisely those who have lost their faith in the real flesh-and-blood working class.

Many socialists want to look out on society and be able to read off the signs of hope with some sort of theoretical barometer. Out of Marxism they have tried to fashion such an instrument. But if we look back at Marx and Lenin, perhaps the most impressive thing about their lives is the way in which they were prepared to live without signs of hope. I think of Lenin reorganising among despairing Russian socialists after 1905 or isolated after the betrayals of 1914. It is from Lenin's stance of hope in a situation which to the ordinary eye would be one of hopelessness that we have to learn. And if we learn what Marx and Lenin have to teach here, and what Miss Dunayevskaya can help us learn from them, one outcome will perhaps be that we shall no longer want to write books like hers.

Chapter Five

Notes from the Moral Wilderness[1]

A position which we are all tempted into is that of moral critic of Stalinism. One point to begin thinking about socialism from is that of dissatisfaction with this figure. This dissatisfaction may force us into a rereading of the Marxism which such a critic rejects. What I want to ask is whether our dissatisfaction with the moral critic and a contemporary rereading of Marxism may not together suggest a new approach to moral issues. It is worth mentioning that this is what I want to do, because this is so much a question to which I still lack an answer that even as a question what follows may seem too tortuous and indefinite. Moreover I cannot even say with certainty from what standpoint I ask this question. And this, I suspect, is not merely a matter of my own private confusions: the various characters who walk through these pages, the Stalinist, the moral critic, the revisionist and so on, if they succeed in being more than lay figures do so not just because they are present in the real world, but also because they represent moments in the consciousness of all of us, masks that we each wear or have worn at some time or other. The need to overcome and transcend their

[1] Originally published in *The New Reasoner*, 7, Winter 1958–9, pp. 90–100 and *The New Reasoner*, 8, Spring 1959, pp. 89–98. Reprinted in Knight (ed.) 1998, pp. 31–49.

limitations and mistakes, their 'false consciousness' in moral matters, is the need to find a way out of our own wilderness.

I

> Don Quixote long ago paid the penalty for wrongly imagining that knight errantry was compatible with all economic forms of society. (Karl Marx)[2]

The ex-Communist turned moral critic of Communism is often a figure of genuine pathos. He confronts the Stalinist with attitudes that in many ways deserve our respect – and yet there is something acutely disquieting about him. I am not speaking now, of course, of those who exchange the doctrines of Stalinism for those of the Labour Party leadership, the Congress for Cultural Freedom or the *Catholic Herald*. They have their reward. I mean those whose self-written epitaph runs shortly, 'I could remain no longer in the Party without forfeiting my moral and intellectual self-respect; so I got out.'[3] They repudiate Stalinist crimes in the name of moral principle; but the fragility of their appeal to moral principle lies in the apparently arbitrary nature of that appeal. Whence come these standards by which Stalinism is judged and found wanting, and why should they have authority over us? What disturbs me in the character of these moral critics of Stalinism is not just their inability to answer this question. It is that this inability seems to me to arise from a picture of their own situation, a picture profoundly influential among ex-Communists, which is at the root of much contemporary self-deception.

What is this picture? It is a picture of independence regained, of a newly won power to speak with a voice of one's own, instead of being merely a gramophone for the Stalinist bureaucracy. What this picture conceals from those whose minds and imaginations it informs is the extent to which they have merely exchanged a conscious dependence for an unconscious. The form of their appeal to moral principle is largely the outcome of the pressures upon them both of Stalinism and of the moral liberalism of the West, pressures which produce a surprisingly similar effect. So far as Stalinism is concerned, it provides a pattern which the moral critic simply inverts. The Stalinist identifies what is morally right with what is actually going to be the outcome

[2] Marx 1976, p. 176, note 35.
[3] Hanson 1957, p. 79.

of historical development. History is for him a sphere in which objective laws operate, laws of such a kind that the role of the individual human being is predetermined for him by his historical situation. The individual can accept his part and play it out more or less willingly; but he cannot rewrite the play. One is nothing in history but an actor and even one's moral judgments on historical events are only part of the action. The 'ought' of principle is swallowed up in the 'is' of history. By contrast the moral critic puts himself outside history as a spectator. He invokes his principles as valid independently of the course of historical events. Every issue is to be judged on its moral merits. The 'ought' of principle is completely external to the 'is' of history. For the Stalinist the actual course of history is the horizon of morality; that what belongs to the future is progressive is made into a necessary truth. For the moral critic the question of the course of history, of what is actually happening and the question of what ought to happen are totally independent questions.

So far I have represented the moral critic's standpoint as a kind of photographic negative of Stalinism. And this would not in any case be surprising since the typical critic of this kind is an ex-Stalinist. But the hold of this pattern on the mind is enormously strengthened by the fact that it is the pattern of the liberal morality which prevails in our society. For it is of the essence of the liberal tradition that morality is taken to be autonomous. What this means can be made clear by considering it first at a fairly sophisticated level. In the philosophical text-books it is the doctrine that moral principles can have no non-moral basis. Our judgements on specific moral issues may be supported by the invocation of more general principles. But in the end our most general and ultimate principles, because they are that in terms of which all else is justified, stand beyond any rational justification. In particular, they cannot be justified by any appeal to facts, historical or otherwise. This isolation of the moral from the factual is presented as a necessary and ineluctable truth of logic. The argument here is that all valid argument is argument in which the premises entail the conclusion; and the concept of entailment can be sufficiently explained for our present purpose by saying that one set of propositions entails another proposition or set of propositions, if and only if nothing is asserted in the latter which was not already implicitly or explicitly asserted in the former. And since clearly in going from factual to moral assertions one is clearly not merely repeating oneself, factual assertions cannot entail moral assertions. But, as entailment is accepted as the only form of valid argument, it follows that moral assertions cannot be backed up rationally at all by factual or any other non-moral assertions. And this has as its central consequences the view that on ultimate questions of morality we cannot argue, we can only choose. And our choice is necessarily arbitrary in the sense that we cannot give reasons for choosing one way rather than another; for to do this we should have to have a criterion in moral matters more ultimate than our ultimate criterion. And this is nonsensical. About this doctrine we may note two things.

First, it is remarkable how much it has in common with Sartrean existentialism. Those philosophical journalists who lament the lack of relationship between British analytical philosophers and Continental metaphysicians might take heart from seeing how the moral philosophy of both can breed the notion of unconditional and arbitrary choice as a, if not the, crucial feature of the individual's moral life. In both there is a picture of the individual standing before the historical events of his time, able to pass judgement on them exactly as he pleases. His values are for him to choose; the facts in no way constrain him. And we can see at once how this dovetails with and reinforces the negation of Stalinism.

Secondly, leaving aside the question of whether this view of morality is correct or not, we can see how strikingly it corresponds to the actual moral condition of many people in our society. For them their moral principles are completely isolated from the facts of their existence and they simply accept one set of principles rather than another in arbitrary fashion. They affirm this or that 'ought'; but their morality has no basis. I am not speaking here of the morality of intellectuals which might be thought (albeit wrongly) to reflect the philosophical currents; I am speaking of the largely inarticulate whose moral discourse nevertheless provides the standard and normal usage in our society.

There are then some grounds for a suspicion that the moral critics of Stalinism may have done no more than exchange one dominant pattern of thought for another; but the new pattern gives them the illusion of moral independence. Yet the very nature of their new morality must make their answer to the question which I originally posed seem extraordinarily thin and unconvincing even to them. Why do the moral standards by which Stalinism is found wanting have authority over us? Simply because we choose that they should. The individual confronting the facts with his values condemns. But he can only condemn in the name of his own choice. The isolation which his mode of moral thinking imposes on the critic can tempt him in two directions. There is the pressure, usually much exaggerated by those who write about it, to exchange the participation in a Stalinist party for some other equally intense form of group membership. But there is also the pressure, far less often noticed, to accept the role of the isolated moral hero, who utters in the name of no one but himself. Ex-Stalinists who pride themselves on having become hard-headed realists seem to be peculiarly prone to this form of romanticism. They are the moral Quixotes of the age.

The value of their Quixotry varies of course with the circumstances in which they proclaim it. The reassertion of moral standards by the individual voice has been one of the ferments of Eastern European revisionism. But, because of the way in which it is done, this reassertion too often leaves the gulf between morality and history, between value and fact as wide as ever. Kolakowski and others like him stress the amorality of the historical process on the one hand and the moral responsibility of the individual in history on the other. And this leaves us with the moral critic as a spectator, the categorical imperatives which he proclaims having no genuine relationship to his view of history.[4] One cannot revive the moral content within Marxism by simply taking a Stalinist view of historical development and adding liberal morality to it. But however one may disagree with Kolakowski's theoretical position, the kind of integrity involved in reasserting moral principles in the Polish situation is entirely admirable. To speak against the stream in this way means that, even if the morality in question seems somehow irrational and arbitrary, in the protest which sustains it can find its justification. But to assert this position in the West is to flow with the stream. It is merely to conform.

The pressures towards conformism, moral and otherwise, do not need re-emphasising. And it ought to be said for the moral critic of Stalinism that he is usually also the moral critic of Suez, Cyprus, and the H-Bomb. At least he delivers his censures impartially. Yet even here I want to put a question mark against his attitudes. For the Western social pattern has a role all ready for the radical moral critic to play. It is accepted that there should be minorities of protest on particular issues. And it is even a reinforcement for the dominant picture of morality that the moral critic should exhibit himself choosing his

[4] See, for example, Kolakowski 1971, pp. 207–27.

values of protest. For they remain *his* values, his private values. There is no set of common, public standards to which he can appeal, no shared moral image for his society by means of which he can make his case. And if he chooses his values in the spirit of *Hier steh' ich, ich kann nicht anders* [Here I stand, I can do no other], is it not equally open to his opponents to do the same? It is this that seems to be the cause of the deep suspicion of and muddle over moral arguments among the leaders of the Campaign for Nuclear Disarmament. Thus the isolation of the moral from the factual, the emphasis on choice, the arbitrariness introduced into moral matters, all these play into the hands of the defenders of the established order. The moral critic, especially the ex-Stalinist moral critic, pays the penalties of both self-deception and ineffectiveness for imagining that moral knight errantry is compatible with being morally effective in our form of society.

The argument as I have presented it so far is highly schematic. It could be reinforced at many points. And in concluding this stage of the argument it is perhaps worth noticing one of them very briefly. Just as the ex-Stalinist critic of Communism reflects both the negation of Stalinism and the dominant temper of Western liberalism in his moral attitudes, so also with his approach to matters of fact. The Stalinist approaches the historical developments of our time with a tightly organised general theory; the ex-Stalinist repudiates theory. But what he means by 'theory' he tends to take over from the Stalinist. And in his repudiation of general theories he falls in with the prevailing empiricism of our society. I want to follow through this pattern, not for its own sake, but for the further light it may throw on contemporary thinking about morality.

What the Stalinist thinks that he possesses, what the empiricist critic thinks to be logically impossible, is a blueprint of the social clockwork. For Stalinist theory the laws which govern social development are treated as if they have a character closely similar to that of the laws which govern the behaviour of a mechanical system. In Sartre's novel *La Mort dans L'Âme*, a member of the French C.P. in 1940 is made to say:

> ... it is *conceivable* that the Politburo might founder in the depths of stupidity: by the same token, it is *conceivable* that the roof of this hut might fall on your head, but that doesn't mean you spend your time keeping a wary eye on the ceiling. You may say, of course, if you feel like it, that your hopes are founded on God, or that you have confidence in the architect – but any reply of that kind would be mere words. You know perfectly well that there are certain

> natural laws, and that it is the way of buildings to stay standing when they have been built in conformity with those laws. Why, then, should I spend my time wondering about the policy of the USSR, and why should you raise the question of my confidence in Stalin? I have complete confidence in him, *and* in Molotov, *and* in Zhdanov – as much confidence as you have in the solidity of these walls. In other words, I know that history has its laws, and that, in virtue of those laws, an identity of interest binds the country of the workers and the European proletariat.[5]

When Popper attacks historicism, it is essentially this doctrine that historical development is governed by laws and that its future course is therefore predictable which he is concerned to undermine. Equally this is what Stalin defends. But in the definition of what is at issue Stalin and Popper shake hands. The Marxism that Stalin presents is recognisably the Marxism that Popper also presents. And it is this same conception of theory which is evident throughout the contemporary anti-theoretical empiricism that is fashionable in the West both in academic and in political circles. Its relevance to the present topic is solely that it provides the straitjacket within which it is possible to confine and misrepresent the Marxist alternative to liberal morality. If it were the case that Marxism was a system in which the clockwork of society was laid bare, then it would be true that 'the *essence* of the Marxist ethic... is its futurism'.[6] For it would be true that the only effective way of remedying the evils of class society would be to manipulate into existence the classless society; the blue-print of a mechanical system will tell us which levers we must pull to transform the system. And we pull the levers to contrive some new state of the system. The counterpart to a mechanical theory of society is a means-ends morality. But so too the counterpart to a rejection of a mechanical theory may be a very similar sort of morality. How can this be so?

'We have no general theory; we approach each issue on its merits. We can remedy this or that detail of the social set-up; it would be Utopian to hope for more. History eludes theory; it just happens. And the theorists and even the legislators merely trot along in its wake, writing up and codifying what has already happened.' So run the slogans of the contemporary mood. We can see how the rejection of Stalinism leads easily into this frame of mind. It is

[5] Sartre 1963, p. 311.
[6] Hanson 1957, pp. 80–1.

less obvious perhaps how much the moral attitude of the political empiricist has in common with that of the Stalinist. First of all, for both, human agency is essentially ineffective. History occurs, whether theory can grasp it or not, independently of human will and desire. For both, a favourite charge is utopianism, the accusation of trying to extend the sphere of human initiative in ways beyond those which history will allow for. And both too often have an enormous faith in the 'levers' of social engineering: the empiricist in an *ad hoc* way, the Stalinist systematically. One result of this is that the rejection of Stalinism by the empiricist is for the most part based only on the charge that Stalinist means do not as a matter of fact produce the requisite ends; the means-ends model of morality survives unscathed.

What I am contending in this final part of the first stage of my argument is that the moral helplessness of the ex-Stalinist critic of Communism is deepened by his lack of any general theory; that this lack of theory reflects an identification of theory with Stalinism; and that once again his new attitudes have far too much in common with his old. And the only point of the analysis so far is to enable us to formulate with more precision the question of whether there can be an alternative to the barren opposition of moral individualism and amoral Stalinism.

2

> The idea of the translation of the ideal into the real is profound: very important for history... (V.I. Lenin).[7]

The moral critic of Stalinism, as I have tried to depict him, largely is what he is because he sees no other possibility. He envisages only two moral alternatives, Stalinism on the one hand and his own new position on the other. It is therefore only a first step to argue that his new position is a frail one. What has to be done positively is to show that there is a third moral position. And any attempt to do this will have to satisfy a number of different requirements. If it is to avoid the defects of a purely empirical approach, it will have to provide us with the insights of a general theory without falling into the dogmatic ossifications of Stalinism. If it is to avoid the arbitrariness of liberal morality, it is going to have to provide us with some conception

[7] Lenin 1960–70d, p. 114.

of a basis for our moral standards. If it is going to perform either of the preceding tasks successfully it is going to have to produce arguments, not just assertions; and it is very important to remember that although in the first section of this essay I may have shown, or tried to show, that the position of the ex-Stalinist moral critic of Communism is more fragile, more ineffective and more liable to self-deception than is often supposed, I have not provided the arguments which would be necessary to exhibit it as mistaken. In order to do this I want in the next stages of the argument to work backwards through the themes touched on in the first section.

This makes my first task vindication of the possibility of a general theory of society. And this is nothing other than the task of replacing a misconceived but prevalent view of what Marxism is by a more correct view. The misconceived view is the one contained in the quotation from Sartre, and what I want to fasten on in it is its conception of the present age, the age of the transition to socialism. It is notorious that Marx himself says very little about the details of the transition. The Stalinist interpretation of the transition is however quite clear. For the Stalinist Marxism is in essence the thesis that a given level of technology and form of production as a basis produces a given form of social life and consciousness. What Stalin did in Russia was to provide the necessary basis on which superstructure of socialism must arise. The transition from capitalism to socialism must therefore take the form of a manipulation of the economic and industrial arrangements of society and this will have as its effect the creation of a socialist consciousness among the mass of mankind. Because this transition is an exemplification of the general laws governing social development its form and nature are essentially predictable and inevitable. Side by side with this doctrine of the transition is a doctrine as to the predictable and inevitable collapse of capitalism. And it is noteworthy that when Hanson, for example, asserts that the ethic of Marxism is essentially futurist he does so on the grounds that this is the age of 'immiseration' and that all we can do, if we are Marxists, is contrive the shortest path out of it. About all this I want to make a number of separate, but connected points.

(1) Stalinism is, as it were, a meta-Marxism. That is, it not only asserts certain Marxist doctrines, but it is itself a doctrine as to what sort of doctrines these are. And under Stalinism the title 'scientific socialism' is accorded to Marxism on the basis of a view which takes physics to be the paradigm case of a science, or worse still elementary mechanics. Engels in a famous remark compared

Marx's achievement to that of Darwin. And the theory of evolution seems to me to provide a far more illuminating parallel to historical materialism than does Newtonian mechanics. Here two points can be stressed. One is that the evolution of species was established as a general truth long before it was possible to say anything of the genetic mechanisms which play such a key role in evolutionary explanation. And the thesis of historical materialism can equally be established in a way that leaves open all sorts of questions about how at a particular epoch basis and superstructure were in fact related. A second point is that the fact that the past history of species not only can but must be viewed in terms of evolution does not entail that the future history of species is predictable. For we do not necessarily know how to extrapolate from past to future. Someone may ask how if we are not concerned with predictability here the theory can ever be verified. The answer is to be found by reading *The Origin of Species*. Darwin states his own thesis with remarkable brevity. He then takes hard case after hard case and shows how in fact all can be fitted into the evolutionary picture. How many hard cases does he need to dispose of before his case is established? Clearly there is no simple answer; but at a certain point conviction becomes overwhelming. Equally historical materialism is established by showing the amount of history that is made intelligible by it; and once again there is no hard and fast rule as to the point at which such a view becomes plausible. Moreover there is the same distinction to be drawn between our ability to see the laws of development in the past and our inability to extrapolate into the future. Inability to extrapolate? Isn't Marxism most importantly a matter of prediction, a matter of what comes next in history? To answer this we must pass on to a new point.

(2) The predictability which Stalinism offered rested on its conception of a mechanical relation between basis and superstructure. But as Marx depicts it the relation between basis and superstructure is fundamentally not only not mechanical, it is not even casual. What may be misleading here is Marx's Hegelian vocabulary. Marx certainly talks of the basis 'determining' the superstructure and of a 'correspondence' between them.[8] But the reader of Hegel's *Logic* will realise that what Marx envisages is something to

[8] Marx 1975d, p. 425: 'The totality of these relations of production constitutes the economic structure society, the real foundation, on which arises a legal and political superstructure and to which correspond definite forms of social consciousness.'

be understood in terms of the way in which the nature of the concept of a given class, for example, may determine the concept of membership of that class. What the economic basis, the mode of production, does is to provide a framework within which superstructure arises, a set of relations around which the human relations can entwine themselves, a kernel of human relationship from which all else grows. The economic basis of a society is not its tools, but the people co-operating using these particular tools in the manner necessary to their use, and the superstructure consists of the social consciousness moulded by and the shape of this co-operation. To understand this is to repudiate the end-means morality; for there is no question of creating the economic base as a means to the socialist superstructure. Creating the basis, you create the superstructure. There are not two activities but one. Moreover it is no use treating the doctrine that the basis determines the superstructure as a general formula in the way Stalinism has done. For the difference between one form of society and another is not just a difference in basis, and a corresponding basis in superstructure, but a difference also in the way basis is related to superstructure. And the crucial character of the transition to socialism is not that it is a change in the economic base but that it is a revolutionary change in the relation of superstructure to base. That liberation which Marx describes as the ending of prehistory and the beginning of history is a freeing of our relationships from the kind of determination and constraint hitherto exercised upon them. It is therefore absolutely necessary to grasp the nature of this determination correctly. What may have misled here is the fact that particular features of the basis of any given society are always causally related to what may be counted as features of the superstructure. But this is not to say that the basis as such is causally related to the superstructure as such.

(3) The question of predictability often takes the form it does for the Stalinist, because Marxist economic theses are detached from Marx's general view. And predictions about the transition to socialism are tied to predictions about immiseration, under consumption and the business cycle which seem to stand or fall as verifications of immutable laws governing our economic development. Here I want to say only that our stock picture of Marx's economics needs a lot of revision. I have mentioned the role of 'immiseration' in Hanson's argument. It is worth remembering that Marx did not think capitalist crisis an automatic outcome of under consumption; and those like Hanson who see 'immiseration' as summarising a Marxist view

need to be reminded that in Volume 2 of *Capital* Marx wrote that 'crises are precisely always preceded by a period in which wages rise generally and the working class actually get a larger share of the annual product intended for consumption'.[9] So far as I can see, Marx's explanation of capitalist crisis is not a matter of under-consumption, but of a falling return on profit which leads the capitalist to lower his investment. And this explanation, like the explanation of proletarian reaction to such crisis rests on his view of what has happened to human nature under capitalism. That is Marx's economics make sense only if related to his general view of human nature. Marx's view of human nature is not a pious addendum to his economic analysis.

(4) Socialism cannot be impersonally manipulated into existence, or imposed on those whose consciousness resists, precisely because socialism is the victory of consciousness over its previous enslavement by economic and political activity. All other forms of society have been suffered by men; socialism is to be lived by them. And this is where the threads in the previous points come together. Marx inherits from Hegel a conception of the 'human essence'. Human life at any given moment is not a realisation of this essence because human life is always limited in ways characteristic of the basis of a given form of society. In particular human freedom is always so limited. But in our age we have reached the point where this can change, where human possibility can be realised in a quite new way. But we cannot see the realisation of this possibility as the predictable outcome of laws governing human development independently of human wills and aspirations. For the next stage is to be characterised precisely as the age in which human wills and aspirations take charge and are no longer subservient to economic necessity and to the law-bound inevitability of the past. But Marxists surely say, not that this might happen, but that it will? If they say this, they are no longer predicting. They are re-affirming Marx's belief that human potentiality is such that men will take this new step, and this affirmation is of a different order from predicting. For the Marxist view of history can be written up in the end as the story of how the human ideal was after many vicissitudes translated into the human reality. And at this point we can perhaps begin to establish

[9] Marx 1978, pp. 486–7: 'we need only note that crises are always prepared by a period in which wages generally rise, and the working class actually does receive a greater share in the part of the annual product destined for consumption'.

the connection of all this with the previous argument about the moral critic of Communism.

The moral critic rejected Stalinism because it represented the historical process as automatic and as morally sovereign. And for moral values encapsulated wholly in history he substituted moral values wholly detached from history. To this he added a thorough distaste for general theorising. But if we bring out as central to Marxism the kind of points which I have suggested, may not this suggest a third alternative to the moral critic, a theory which treats what emerges in history as providing us with a basis for our standards, without making the historical process morally sovereign or its progress automatic? In order to ask this question properly we ought to re-examine some of the traditional questions about human nature and morality. What is the relation between what I am, what I can be, what I want to be and what I ought to be? These are the topics to which we must next turn, so that we shall be able to see the questions to which Marx's conception of human nature sought to be an answer.

3

'Men make their own history, but', this phrase echoes through the Marxist classics.[10] The political aim of Marxists is to liquidate that 'but'. Their theoretical aim is to understand it. In order to understand it we must first be clear what it is for men to make their own history, for men to act and not just to suffer. So the concept of human action is central to our enquiry. What is it to understand any given piece of behaviour as a human action? Consider the following example. If my head nods, it may be a sign of assent to a question or it may be a nervous tick. To explain the nod as a way of saying 'Yes' to a question is to give it a role in the context of human action. To explain the nod as a nervous tick is to assert that the nod was not an action but something that happened to me. To understand the nod as a nervous tick we turn to the neurophysiologist for a causal explanation. To understand it as a sign of assent is to move in a different direction. It is to ask for a statement of the purpose

---

[10] Marx 1973a, p. 146: 'Men make their own history, but not of their own free will; not under circumstances they themselves have chosen but under the given and inherited circumstances with which they are directly confronted.'

that my saying 'Yes' served; it is to ask for reasons, not for causes and it is to ask for reasons which point to a recognisable want or need served by my action. This reference to purpose is important. When social anthropologists come across some unintelligible mode of behaviour, obedience to a primitive taboo, for example, they look for some as yet unnoticed purpose, some want or need to which such obedience ministers; and if they find none they look for some past want or need which the practice once served, even though now it is nothing but a useless survival. That is to say, we make both individual deeds and social practices intelligible as human actions by showing how they connect with characteristically human desires, needs and the like. Where we cannot do this, we treat the unintelligible piece of behaviour as a symptom, a survival or superstition.

One of the root mistakes of the liberal belief in the autonomy of morality now stands out. The believer in the autonomy of morality attempts to treat his fundamental moral principles as without any basis. They are his because he has chosen them. They can have no further vindication. And that is to say among other things that neither moral utterance nor moral action can be vindicated by reference to desires or needs. The 'ought' of morality is utterly divorced from the 'is' of desire. This divorce is most strikingly presented in the position taken by Kant that it is a defining characteristic of moral actions that they shall not be performed 'from inclination'. It is repeated in contemporary terms by those writers who deny that one moral judgment can be based on anything except another more fundamental moral judgment, on the grounds that no 'is' can entail an 'ought' and that entailment is the only logically respectable relationship between statements. And this position does not need to be attacked any further for my present purposes, for it is obvious that to represent morality in this light is to make it unintelligible as a form of human action. It is to make our moral judgments appear like primitive taboos, imperatives which we just happen to utter. It is to turn 'ought' into a kind of nervous cough with which we accompany what we hope will be the more impressive of our injunctions.

At this point it is worth recalling one way of reconnecting morality and desire, namely that produced by the shock effect on eighteenth century moralists of travellers tales from Polynesia. A rationalist like Diderot is able to contrast powerfully the simple moral code of the Polynesians, which expresses and satisfies desire, with the complex moral code of Europe, which represses and distorts it.[11] But this contrast may be used to support a simple hedonism, belief in which is as destructive of moral understanding as is belief in moral autonomy. It is no use saying simply 'Do as you want', for at first sight we want many and conflicting things. We need a morality which orders our desires and yet expresses them. The myth of the natural man who spontaneously obeys desire is only comprehensible as the myth of a society where desire appears utterly cut off from morality. How did this divorce occur?

The short and obvious answer would perhaps run like this. Morality expresses the more permanent and long-run of human desires. But for most human history, such desires rarely achieve fulfilment. And so the objects of desire disappear from consciousness. And the rules survive, as a primitive taboo survives. Only the rules still have point, but men have forgotten what their point is. And then as the possibility of the abolition of class society and the possibility of new forms of human community appear, the objects of desire come back into the moral picture. Men recall to consciousness the lost purpose of their moral rules. And if at this point they insist on treating the rules as purposeless and autonomous they contribute only to the frustration of morality. Thus the history of morality is the history of men ceasing to see moral rules as the repression of desire and as something that men have made and accepted for themselves and coming to see them instead either as an alien, eternal, disembodied yet objective law, which constrains and represses, or as an entirely arbitrary subjective choice.

Hegel in his early anti-theological writings thinks of the Jewish law written on stone tablets as the archetype of the objectification of morality, and such objectification is for him symptomatic of human alienation. We can see why. Men objectify moral rules, have to objectify them, when the desires which they repress are too painful or too dangerous for men to know them as their own. (The resemblance between what Hegel says about society and what Freud says about the individual hardly needs remarking on). They appear instead as the voice of the other, the non-human, the divine; or they just appear. Belief in the autonomy of morality expresses this alienation at the level of philosophy.

One way of writing the history of morality would be this: to see it as the coming together of three strands which have been held apart in class society. The first of these is the history of moral codes, meaning by this not so much

[11] See, for example, Diderot 1992a, pp. 66–75.

the history of which rules commend themselves in each society as the history of how different societies have conceived of the nature of moral rules. If I suggest in outline the type of thing that I mean it will obviously be no more than a caricature. But even caricatures have their uses.

For the Greeks the connection between the moral life and the pursuit of what men want is always preserved, even if sometimes very tenuously. The desires which the moral life is alleged to satisfy are sometimes a little curious, as for example Aristotle's conception of doing philosophy as the supreme fulfilment of human aspiration. But desire is always kept in the picture. So it is too in the Bible. What God offers is something that will satisfy all our desires. (The commandment that we love our neighbours as ourselves both presupposes and sanctions a high degree of self-love.) And desire remains at the heart of morality in the Middle Ages. It is true that now morality becomes a matter of divine commandments, but the God who commands is the God who created our human nature and His commandments are in consequence desired to be such as will fulfil his purpose of blessedness for that nature. So that in Thomist ethics an Aristotelian view of desire and a Christian view of the moral law are synthesised, even if somewhat unsatisfactorily. But the Protestant reformation changes this. First, because human beings are totally corrupt their nature cannot be a function of true morality. And next because as totally depraved beings, indeed even perhaps as simple finite beings, we cannot judge God. So we obey God's commandments not because they and He are good, but simply because they are his. The moral law becomes a connection of divine fiats, so far as we are concerned totally arbitrary, for they are unconnected with anything we may want or desire. At this stage two other considerations suggest themselves. The first is that if the moral rules have force, they surely do so whether God commands them or not. The second is that perhaps there is no God. 'Do this, because it will bring you happiness': 'Do this because God enjoins it as the way to happiness'; 'Do this because God enjoins it'; 'Do this'. These are the four stages in the development of autonomous morality. At each stage our moral concepts are silently redefined so that it soon appears self-evident that they must be used in the way that they are used.

The second threat in the history of morality is the history of human attitudes to human desire. For as morality becomes thought of as objective and eternal, so desire becomes something anarchic and amoral. Diderot and his friends could appeal to the 'natural man', his wants uncontaminated by the evils of society, and suppose that desire could be recalled to its central place in the moral life by such an appeal. But in class society desire itself is remoulded, not merely suppressed. Seeking to find an outlet it legitimates itself by becoming respectable. Men try to want what the ruling ethos says that they want. They never succeed, because desire is spontaneous or it is not desire. 'A man's self is a law unto itself', wrote D.H. Lawrence, 'not unto *himself*, mind you'. And again, 'The only thing man has to trust to in coming to himself is his desire and his impulse. But both desire and impulse tend to fall into mechanical automatism: to fall from spontaneous reality into dead or material reality'.[12] But when social life takes on dead, acceptable, mechanical forms, desire reappears as the negative, as the outlaw. The counterpart of Diderot's myth of the happy Polynesia is the reality of 'Rameau's Nephew', a work which stimulated both Hegel and Marx. This is a dialogue between Diderot himself, the voice of the man who accepts the forms and norms of society, and Rameau, who represents the suppressed desires, the hidden anarchic consciousness.[13] Freud saw in this dialogue an anticipation of his own contrast between conscious and unconscious mental life.[14] But in the dialogue Diderot goes far beyond any individual psychology: here the voice of desire is not the voice of happy Polynesian society, but something become purely individual, the voice that can live only by hypocrisy and an extreme care for self-interest. One remembers Engels's comment on a remark by Hegel:

> 'One believes one is saying something great', Hegel remarks, 'if one says that "man is naturally good". But one forgets that one says something far greater when one says 'man is naturally evil'. With Hegel evil is the form in which the motive force of historical development presents itself. This contains the two-fold meaning that, on the one hand, each new advance necessarily appears as a sacrilege against things hallowed, as a rebellion against conditions, though old and moribund, yet sanctified by custom; and that, on the other hand, it is precisely the wicked passions of men – greed

---

[12] Lawrence 1950, pp. 89, 91.

[13] Diderot 1897, p. 152: 'Were the little savage to be left to himself, were he to keep all his imbecility and unite to the want of reason of the infant in the cradle the violence of the man of thirty, he would wring his father's neck and dishonour his mother.'

[14] Freud quotes the passage from Diderot in the preceding note in Freud 1922, pp. 283–4.

> and lust for power – which, since the emergence of class antagonisms, serve as levers of historical development...[15]

Desire becomes recognisable only as something individualist, which tends, as in Hobbes, to the war of all against all, and morality, when it is related to desire, becomes at best an uneasy truce or peace between warring desires, embodied in a social contract. So that even desire conceived as selfish is never conceived of as more than partly satisfied. And desire as a driving force is stripped of all these qualities which unite men. Nietzsche's superman is pure dehumanised desire despising the values of those who accept the autonomy of morality and 'transvaluing' them. Figures such as Nietzsche's are the reflection in a romanticising consciousness of an entirely non-fictional capitalist type. E.M. Forster in *Howard's End* makes Helen Schlegel say:

> 'Perhaps the little thing that says "I" is missing out of the middle of their heads, and then it's a waste of time to blame them. There's a nightmare of a theory that says a special race is being born which will rule the rest of us in the future just because it lacks the little thing that says "I". There are two kinds of people – our kind, who live straight from the middle of their heads, and the other kind who can't because their heads have no middle. They can't say "I". They *aren't* in fact... Pierpont Morgan has never said "I" in his life. No superman can say "I want" because "I want" must lead to the question "Who am I?" and so to Pity and to Justice. He only says "want" – "Want Europe", if he's Napoleon; "want wives" if he's Bluebeard; "want Botticelli", if he's Pierpont Morgan. Never "I" and if you could pierce through him, you'd find panic and emptiness in the middle.'[16]

---

[15] Engels 1975–2004b, p. 378. The 'quote' from Hegel is actually what the editors of the *Collected Works* describe as a 'summary' of his ideas by Engels. Ibid., p. 378, note e. The passage in Hegel which is closest in meaning occurs in Hegel 1985, vol. 3, p. 298. Here Hegel contrasts the statements 'humanity is by nature good' and 'humanity is by nature evil': 'From the formal point of view, since the human being has volition and will, it is not an animal any more; but the content and purposes of its volition are still natural. It is from this standpoint – obviously the higher standpoint – that humanity is evil by nature; and it is evil just because it is a natural thing. What we vacuously represent to ourselves, in taking the original condition of the human being to have been the state of innocence, is the state of nature, the animal state. Humanity ought not to be innocent [in this sense], it ought to be brutish.... Rather it is its responsibility [*Schuld*], its will, to be good – it ought to be *imputable*.'

[16] Forster 1910, pp. 231–2.

The peculiar contribution of the Marxist critic here is the understanding that the 'I' can only be put back into 'I want' if the 'we' is put back into 'we want'. What Forster calls the non-existence of those who say 'want', what Lawrence calls their 'mechanical automatism', these are the outcome of a type of society in which paradoxically it is both true that individuals are isolated from each other and that their individuality is lost to them as the system demands an increasing identification of them with itself. How to regain the 'I' by asserting 'we'?

The fundamental answer to this is the whole Marxist theory of class struggle. To have set the problem properly I ought to have set those changes in the moral consciousness about which I have written in their real, material context. The rift between our conception of morality and our conception of desire will never be overcome until the rift between morality and desire is overcome in action. But since we are already on the margin of the transition that will heal that breach, we can see in outline at any rate how the two may come together in consciousness. At this point the crucial concept for Marxists is their concept of human nature, a concept which has to be at the centre of any discussion of moral theory. For it is in terms of this concept alone that morality and desire can come together once more. How this is so can be seen if beside the sketchy histories of morality and desire I have given, I place an equally sketchy account of the emergence of this concept.

One can begin with the Bible. In the Bible the dealings of individual men with God are all parts of the dealings of Man with God. Man appears like a character in a morality play, passing from his first nature as Adam (the Hebrew word for 'man') to his second nature as Christ (the 'last Adam', as St. Paul calls him).[17] But the unity of human nature is something perceived only at rare moments and in symbolic form; original sin has broken it. So there is no necessary drive within Christianity to incarnate human unity. (This is not to say that some Christians have not looked for such an incarnation. The difficulty is that all the formulations of the Christian religion are politically double-edged. 'All men are equal before God and God wills them to be at one' can either be interpreted to mean that inequality and disunity are a scandal that Christians ought to strive to abolish, or they can be interpreted to mean

[17] 'And so it is written. The first man Adam was made a living soul; the last Adam *was made* a quickening spirit.' I Corinthians 15: 45.

that it is only before God that men are equal, and only God that can make them at one, so that a merely human equality and unity are neither desirable nor possible.[18] I do not doubt that the original Gospel commands imply the former interpretation; but any Christian who wants to can always rely on the second. As most do.)

In the eighteenth century God becomes a deistic ghost in progressive thought. But the conception of Man remains as central. Only whereas the religious conception of Man was ideal in the sense of being a representation of what was believed to be ultimate human destiny, the eighteenth-century conception is ideal in the sense of being concerned with what is human only in an abstract and formal way. Human rights are inalienable and eternal; only it is compatible with their possession that men should suffer poverty and exploitation. Man in the Bible has a cosmic history; Man in the eighteenth century has a rational nature whose history is the slow emergence of Reason into Enlightenment or as often a history in which Reason passes again into darkness (Gibbon); it is only with Hegel that Man begins to possess and with Marx that Man achieves a real history. The point of the word 'real' here is that in Hegel and Marx the history of Man becomes one with the history of men; with empiricist historiography the history of men becomes all the history that there is and the final outcome is Sidney Webb's view that there can only be the history of this or that particular institution, but that there can be no such thing as history as such. This is to say that in Hegel and Marx the history of man is seen as the history of men discovering and making a common shared humanity. For Hegel the subject of this history is Spirit. And individual human lives appear only as finite fragments of the Absolute. For Marx the emergence of human nature is something to be comprehended only in terms of the history of class struggle. Each age reveals a development of human potentiality which is specific to that form of social life and which is specifically limited by the class structure of that society. This development of possibility reaches a crisis under capitalism. For men have up to that age lived at their best in a way that allowed them glimpses of their own nature as something far richer than what they themselves lived out. Under capitalism the growth of production makes it possible for man to re-appropriate his own nature, for actual human beings to realise the richness of human possibility

[18] See, for example, I Corinthians 12–27 or Galatians 3: 28.

But not only the growth of production is necessary. The experience of human equality and unity that is bred in industrial working-class life is equally a precondition of overcoming men's alienation from this and from themselves. And only from the standpoint of that life and its possibilities can we see each previous stage of history as a particular form of approximation to a climax which it is now possible to approach directly.

How does this conception of human nature close the gap between morality and desire? I have given a one-sided and partial view of Marx's approach to history; I now have to give an equally one-sided and partial account of how this view of history bears upon morality. Capitalism provides a form of life in which men rediscover desire in a number of ways. They discover above all that what they want most is what they want in common with others; and more than this that a sharing of human life is not just a means to the accomplishment of what they desire, but that certain ways of sharing human life are indeed what they most desire.

> When Communist workers meet, they have as first aim theory, propaganda and so on. But they take for their own at the same time and by this token a new need, the need for society, and what seems a means has become an end.[19]

So Marx. One meets the anarchic individualist desires which a competitive society breeds in us, by a rediscovery of the deeper desire to share what is common in humanity, to be divided neither from them nor from oneself, to be a man. And in this discovery moral rules reappear as having point. For their content can now be seen as important in correcting our short term selfishness, and thus helping to release desire. Moral rules and what we fundamentally want no longer stand in a sharp contrast.

To discover what we share with others, to rediscover common desire, is to acquire a new moral standpoint. One cannot, of course, make this discovery by introspection whether systematic or random. Whether one makes it at all will depend on whether capitalism places men in a position in which so deep dissatisfaction is born that only a realistic answer to the question 'What do I really want?' can be given. The history of all false consciousness is a history of evasions of this question. And this question can only be answered by a

---

[19] Marx 1975b, p. 365.

discovery that 'I want' and 'we want' coincide; I discover both what I want and how to achieve it, as I discover with whom I share my wants, as I discover, that is, the class to whom I am bound. In a class-divided society, my desires draw me to this or that class. And because the rediscovery of moral rules as having their point in the fulfilment of desire is this sort of discovery, one sees how Marx's contention that all morality is class morality has to be taken. But what content has *our* morality?

The viewpoint we have to meet is the view shared by both the Stalinist and the moral critic of Stalinism, that the only Marxist criterion in moral action is the test of how far the proposed action will take us along the road to socialism. But we have already seen that for a Marxist who realises that the progress to socialism is not automatic, that the transition is a transition to freedom and not one that can be calculated, there can be in this sense no predetermined 'road to socialism'. Means and ends interpenetrate not just in some moral ideal, but in history itself. Yet this is still only to say what a Marxist morality is not. What is it?

4

As against the Stalinist it is an assertion of moral absolutes; as against the liberal critic of Stalinism it is an assertion of desire and of history. To begin with the contrast with the liberal. The liberal sees himself as choosing his values. The Marxist sees himself as discovering them. He discovers them as he rediscovers fundamental human desire; this is a discovery he can only make in company with others. The ideal of human solidarity, expressed in the working-class movement, only has point because of the fact of human solidarity which comes to light in the discovery of what we want. So the Marxist never speaks morally just for himself. He speaks in the name of whole historical development, in the name of a human nature which is violated by exploitation and its accompanying evils. The man who cuts himself off from other people (and this has no content unless we realise that the vast mass of other people is the working class) says at first 'I want' and then just 'want'. His 'I ought' is the most tremulous of moral utterances. For it represents nothing but his own choice. So the liberal moral critic of Stalinism isolates himself, makes his utterance unintelligible and has no defence against the patterns of conformism which his society seeks at every point to enforce upon him.

To speak for human possibility as it emerges, to speak for our shared desires, this is to speak for an absolute. There are things you can do which deny your common humanity with others so that they isolate you as effectively as if you were a liberal. It is for this reason that the Marxist condemns the H-Bomb. Anyone who would use this has contracted out of common humanity. So with the denial of racial equality, so with the rigged trial. The condemnation of Imre Nagy was an act which cut off its authors from humanity. Because in denying the rights and desires of others you deny that they and you share desires and rights in exactly the same way. You only possess either in so far as you have them in common with others. And thus Communist morality is by no means futurist. I think of Dzerzhinsky in gaol, volunteering for the most servile tasks in order to show that labour dishonours no man no matter of what degree culture. I think of all those Communists who died; what made the moral stuff of their actions was not that it contributed to some future state of society. They may not have contributed at all. What was at the heart of what they did was an embodiment of a human nature of which Communism will be the great release.

The argument at this point, as indeed perhaps throughout this paper, has been so compressed that I may be in some danger of replacing precision by rhetoric. What is it in fact, it may be asked, that leads us as socialists to view with equal contempt those who failed to protest at Nagy's murder and those who jump to protest at the late Cuban trials? The answer to this could only begin from a detailed account of what Nagy did and what happened in Cuba. But to give such an account would be to see, for example, that Nagy abided by and his executioners fought against certain principles and values. The values in question may be only partly expressed in human nature to date, but the attempt to give them full embodiment in human life is that which alone can give meaning to the history of morality. That we take up this point of view is not, as I have already argued, simply the fruit of our own choice. We discover rather than choose where we stand as men with particular aspirations at a particular point in history. What the Stalinist fails to see is that although choice is not the sole basis of socialist affirmation, nevertheless as socialists we confront issues which cannot be understood in terms of the so-called 'objective' laws. It is not that Stalinists take a different view of the moral issues which I have raised in this article. It is that within their framework of thought such issues cannot even arise.

The concept of human nature is therefore what binds together the Marxist view of history and Communist morality. What it teaches is in part that the liberal moral critic is the one person who has no right to criticise Stalinism. The separation of morality from history, from desire discovered through the discovery of that common human nature which history shows as emerging, leaves morality without any basis. But this is not a logical necessity for morality, as the liberal would have it. For we can depict a moral alternative which is not without any basis. The liberal critic may speak against Stalinism; but he speaks for no-one but himself and his choices. We saw the fragility of his position at the outset; we can now see why it is fragile. Furthermore we can now see more clearly what the liberal critic and the Stalinist have in common.

The liberal critic accepts the autonomy of ethics; the Stalinist looks to a crude utilitarianism. The liberal accepts the divorce of morality and desire, but chooses morality; the Stalinist accepts the divorce and chooses desire, renaming it morality. But this desire that he chooses is not the desire to be fundamentally at one with mankind. It is desire as it is, random and anarchic, seeking power and immediate pleasure only too often. So one finds under Stalinism the moral belief in an ultimate justifying end, combined with immediate power-seeking. The two do not go as ill together as they seem to at first sight. Both the autonomy of ethics and utilitarianism are aspects of the consciousness of capitalism; both are forms of alienation rather than moral guides. And to see how even the Stalinist perpetuates a class consciousness is to become aware of how liable one may oneself be to be putting forward merely a set of self-justifying attitudes.

For at the end of these notes I am aware only of how little has been achieved in them. Of one thing I am sure: that they are an attempt to find expression at a theoretical level for a moral vision that is being reborn to-day among socialists, most of whom are not theoreticians. Even if my analysis is wholly mistaken, the historical power of that vision is untouched. That, and not any amount of analysis, is what will lead us out of the moral wilderness.[20]

20 For two responses to this article see Hanson 1959 and Jones 1959.

Chapter Six
Doctor Marx and Doctor Zhivago[1]

A Review of Boris Pasternak, Doctor Zhivago

Tragedy has been defined as the conflict of good with good. In this sense the conflict between Boris Pasternak and his Russian critics has been a tragic one. No one who has read the letter which the editors of the Russian literary journal *Novy Mir* sent to Pasternak when they rejected *Doctor Zhivago* can doubt that they are intelligent, humane, and sensitive men within their limitations.[2] But these limitations have tilted them from seeing a crucial point, that the Marxist insights which they value so highly are central to Pasternak's novel. 'Marxist insights in Pasternak!' it will be exclaimed: 'Surely Pasternak's novel has been denounced as precisely anti-Marxist.' But is just this thesis that I want to deny most vehemently. Pasternak is in many ways a Marxist author. And anyone who has read the writings of the young Hegelian Marx, the young Doctor Marx of whom his contemporaries spoke so enthusiastically, will find reminiscence after reminiscence in *Doctor Zhivago.*

---

1 Originally broadcast on the BBC Third Programme and published in *The Listener,* 8 January 1959, pp. 61–2.

2 'Letter to Boris Pasternak from the Editorial Board of *Novy Mir*', reproduced in Crankshaw 1959, pp. 151–71.

Argument between East and West

But I ought to begin from what the critics have said. The most striking feature of the controversy over *Doctor Zhivago* has been the agreement between most Eastern and Western critics. All the clamour over the prize-giving has certainly created an impression of violent dissension, but when the slogans and the shouting are set aside, to what does this disagreement amount? On the one hand, Communist critics such as the editors of *Novy Mir* say that Pasternak has written a pessimistic novel in which the hero selfishly asserts his own personality and thus cuts himself of from the community, and that Pasternak libellously depicts the Bolshevik revolution and state as essentially productive of terror and suffering. Whereas the Western critics tend to say that Pasternak has produced a tragic novel in which the worth of the lonely individual is courageously affirmed over against the community, and that he bravely depicts the Bolshevik revolution in suffering. The tone of voice differs, but on both sides of the Iron Curtain Pasternak's novel has been given the same interpretation, an interpretation that seems to me to spring from a critical vision that is still suffering from Cold War distortions.

I want at this stage to try to place *Doctor Zhivago* as a work of art. It is a poet's book rather than a novelist's book. The comparisons that have been drawn with Tolstoy appear to me grotesque. The technique of building the narrative through a long succession of short scenes in which small incidents bear the weight of large transitions in a time and a place, sometimes reminds one of the technique of the film, and sometimes, as Mr. Stuart Hampshire has acutely pointed out, of Shakespeare.[3] And this dramatic approach of Pasternak's precludes one from identifying the author directly with any of his characters, certainly from identifying his standpoint with that of Zhivago. For although Zhivago is in the obvious sense the central character, there is a far more significant character than Zhivago, namely the Revolution itself. The Revolution is a character before which all the characters tend to insignificance, have to clutch desperately at their own significance but always on the verge of becoming nothing but leaves in the wind. And this is the fate of his characters because they belong to a class, the pre–1914 Russian intelligentsia, who in spite of their sensitivity and human generosity, and perhaps in part because

---

[3] Hampshire 1958.

of them, is alienated from the Revolution. It is something external to them, something that happens to them.

Human substance of the Revolution

Pasternak gives us a sense of the human substance of the Revolution. Institutions and ways of life may be such that they no longer express the life that people used to live. They appear as alien and oppressive shams, and when human life breaks in on them they fall to pieces. Such was the way of life of pre-revolutionary Russia as it crumbled before the Revolution. And Zhivago and his friends hang uneasily between what they see as the barren emptiness of the old and what they see as the brutal substance of the new. One can bring out the ambiguity of Zhivago's position by looking at the charge which the editors of *Novy Mir* bring against Pasternak that there is a distorted Christian commitment in his depicting of Zhivago.

The use of Christian symbolism is particularly explicit in Zhivago's poems printed at the end of the book. The clue to how this symbolism is to be taken is found in Zhivago's own meditations on Christianity and in those of his uncle. Here what Christ did was to introduce in his own person a new conception of humanity, and the truths of Christianity are not dogmas concerning the supernatural but statements about the essence of human nature. Christianity is turned into an ideal for human nature, an ideal that finds its most natural expressions in lyric poetry, especially the poetry of Blok, the ideal of a humanity at once tender and fragile. This ideal fails Zhivago and his friends. Just as the human Christ they pictured was crushed by Judea and Rome, so Zhivago as a Christ-figure is crushed, but crashed not so much by the Revolution as by his own inadequacy and the inadequacy of his ideal.

Unsuspected connexions

At this point, one begins to see unsuspected connexions. I have referred to Zhivago as alienated from the humanity of the Revolution; I have also referred to his attempt to translate the essence of Christianity into a human ideal. But the question of alienation and that of the essence of Christianity have been brought together before: in Hegel, in Feuerbach, in Marx. Hegel and Feuerbach both made it the task of philosophy to secularise the image of man in Christianity; Marx made it the aim of his thought to show how this essential human nature emerged in the reality of history from the distortions and enslavement of class-divided society. And in this work the concept of alienation has a key role.

Men are divided from each other and from themselves by the forms of class society. One result of this is that the whole institutionalised way of life in modern bourgeois society is at once hollow, alien, and oppressive. Humanity, and the one true bearer of the human essence in our time, the industrial proletariat, has to break through and make new forms. So alienated man remakes and regains himself. This is the picture which the young Marx elaborated, the picture out of which mature Marxist theory grew. In this picture there is a place for those members of bourgeois society who, humane and sensitive as they are, cling to the ideals and culture that they know and therefore cannot make the transition to the new society.

Such, surely, is Zhivago. He can think of 'his loyalty to the Revolution and his admiration of it, the Revolution in the sense in which it was accepted by the middle classes and in which it had been understood by the student followers of Blok, in 1905', and contrast this with the real effective blood-stained Bolshevik Revolution.[4] He can envisage the Christ-like figure of humanity transcending its alienation as an ideal, but he cannot face the results of that alienation being overcome in actuality. Surely the diagnosis of Doctor Zhivago's predicament has to be made in terms of the young Doctor Marx's concept of human nature and its alienation.

But on this I shall be fiercely attacked from both East and West. The Western critic will say that I am talking as if the Bolshevik Revolution were a real redemption of humanity, whereas it was a series of horrors, horrors which Pasternak makes frighteningly real. The Eastern critic will say that Pasternak gives scarcely a hint of the heroism, self-sacrifice, and revolutionary generosity that was incarnated in the men who made the Soviet Union. As to the accusation from the West, I ought to point out that the freedom of the spirit which is Zhivago's ideal is at the end of Pasternak's book a thing which Zhivago's friends can sense as something almost tangible in the streets of Moscow; and what brought it there was not Zhivago but the whole revolutionary history

---

[4] Pasternak 1958, p. 148.

of the Soviet Union. Zhivago's own inability to be at one with the Revolution leads in the end to his moral disintegration. To the accusation from the East it should be said that of course this is only part of the historical truth about the Revolution. It is the experience of the Revolution as the bourgeois intelligentsia felt it, as a series of inexplicable blows. Both the evil and good that Zhivago encounters from Communists fall on him as though by turns of chance. It is not just that the good revolutionary is outside his comprehension. The limits of Zhivago's vision make both good and bad revolutionaries alike an uncomprehended force that is simply there. It is just because Pasternak is able to portray the limitations of Zhivago so strikingly that I find it impossible to accept the view that Zhivago's standpoint is Pasternak's own.

The critics' mistake in approach

But there is something much more fundamental at stake here. Both Eastern and Western critics have read Pasternak as a pessimist on the subject of the Russian Revolution because he narrates not the victory of the Revolution but one man's tragedy during the Revolution. Both seem to assent to the thesis that an optimism about human nature in general and the Bolshevik Revolution in particular is incompatible with stressing the fact that the course of human history, and especially of revolutionary history, generates countless tragedies. This is to make a fatal mistake in approach to Pasternak. For the essence of the tragic is that it provides a measure of what man is and can hope for. Only the depth of the tragic suggests the potential height of the man who suffers it. And Pasternak's narrative of the events which encompass the tragedy of Zhivago's destruction suggests the inarticulate weight of human resource behind those events, a resource which can outgrow the patent absurdity of so many of the revolutionary trappings. So, in one of the prophetic meditations with which the narrative is interspersed, one character passes from a comparison of the Old and the New Testaments to say:

> In everything to do with the care of the workers, the protection of the mother, the struggle against the power of money, our revolutionary era is a wonderful era of new, lasting, permanent Achievements. But as to its interpretation of life and the philosophy of happiness which it preaches – it is simply impossible to believe that it is meant to be taken seriously, it is such a comical remnant

> of the past. If all this rhetoric about leaders and peoples had the power to reverse history, it would set us back thousands of years to the biblical times of shepherd tribes and patriarchs. But fortunately it cannot do this.[5]

This union of the hopeful and tragic creates the dilemma which destroys Pasternak's central characters. What is important is that Pasternak for the most part, although not always, succeeds in holding on to both sides of the dilemma. Lara, Zhivago's love, always looks back to her early happiness with her husband, Antipov. And he at the end explains to Zhivago how he was torn between his private and his political loyalty. He describes his own struggle both for his wife and for the Revolution. And he hymns the whole history of Marxism, culminating in a vision of the 'immeasurably vast figure of Russia, bursting into flames like a light of redemption for all the sorrows and misfortunes of mankind'.[6] Then he turns back to the subject of his wife and Zhivago reveals to him how much she loved him. And at once he has to know precisely how she told Zhivago this, and to imagine the way in which she was shaking the carpet as she said it. The small, tragic personal incident reveals the whole pathos of Antipov's revolutionary life.

Over-rated book?

I hope I have made clear how impressive Pasternak's book seems to me. For it is only if I have succeeded in doing this that I ought to say that I think it has been a good deal overrated by some Western critics. The true achievement is the whole body of Pasternak's poetry with which *Doctor Zhivago* finds its place. But *Doctor Zhivago* has a central flaw and it would be a false and dishonouring respect to Pasternak not to remark on it. For there is an ambiguity in Pasternak's attitude which I can perhaps locate like this. Pasternak treats his characters like the cast of a play, or rather like the dancers in a formal masque. He brings them together and separates them again and again, and their coincidental re-encounters are a necessary part of his technique. But he continually suggests and occasionally makes explicit claim that these meetings and partings have a mysterious pattern of an almost supernatural character.

---

[5] Pasternak 1958, p. 371.
[6] Pasternak 1958, pp. 408–14 (quote p. 413).

In this suggestion, which I find unconvincing, I sense a hesitation. Pasternak after all did not disintegrate like Zhivago, did not commit suicide like Essenin or Mayakovsky. He lived through and with both the Revolution and Stalinism. He saw the pre-1914 intelligentsia from the outside and judged their limitations. But he still hangs on to the half-hearted supernaturalism of that age, to the humanised Christianity of Zhivago. Oddly enough, one feels that it is Christianity and not Marxism with which Pasternak has failed to make an adequate reckoning, and the editors of *Novy Mir* are right to stress Pasternak's dubiously Christian attitude.[7] So you have, in the novel, rather contrived and shamefaced suggestions of a more than this-worldly agency in which Pasternak seems to share Zhivago's weaknesses and which tempts one towards the view that Pasternak identifies himself with Zhivago.

In one sense, I am taking the side of the Soviet critics over Pasternak, although not in a way that they would welcome. For I certainly agree with them that the question of Pasternak's aesthetic achievement is essentially linked to that of his attitude to the political events which he recounts. But, unlike the Soviet critics, I feel that, whatever his own intention, he has brought home the human reality of the Revolution with a rare force, the more tellingly because he has been at such pains to put the evils and tragedy in the foreground. The paradox of *Doctor Zhivago's* reception is the way that it underlines the truth of some of the things that Pasternak seems to be trying to say. For in the West the misreading of *Doctor Zhivago* leads to a welcoming of the book because the Western critic finds it so easy to identify himself with the main character. He too is characteristically an intellectual whose culture and ideals are divorced from the political movements of the age, who even prides himself on this divorce. This leads him to note Pasternak's sympathy for Zhivago, but to ignore what Pasternak shows of the limitations of Zhivago's vision and morality. In the East the misreading of *Doctor Zhivago* leads to a condemnation because the ruling class in Russia cannot bear to look at the tragic side of the growth of revolutionary history.

---

7 'Letter to Boris Pasternak from the Editorial Board of *Novy Mir*', pp. 167–8.

'Genuine power'

Part of the genuine power of Pasternak's book is manifest by the way in which the reactions of both East and West to it reveal how each is in its own way a victim of those alienations to which Pasternak points. The paradox is deepened by the fact that in Russia *Doctor Zhivago* would be an important corrective to current views of the Bolshevik Revolution, but there they are not permitted to read it. Whereas a far more plausible case might be made out for preventing people from reading it in the West, where thousands of readers will not recognise the one-sidedness of Pasternak's history, and where the chances of those readers turning to a full account of the Bolshevik Revolution are very small indeed. It is in Russia that *Doctor Zhivago* needs to be read.

I do not suppose that the view of Pasternak which I have suggested will do other than arouse hostility on all sides. But if I have done anything to break up the dusty stereotypes of both communism and anti-communism, which have been brought out by the editors of *Novy Mir* and by Pasternak's would-be defenders in the West, I shall be satisfied. I think, and it is a terribly impertinent thing to say after having talked my own fill about Pasternak, that perhaps we are all talking about it far too much. In so doing we may have lost the sense of the vast and inescapable order of time and nature which pervades Pasternak's lyricism and which provides a back-cloth for the time-bound incidents at the front of his stage. With all those faults which it would be absurd to deny, it remains true of him that he has let the years of the Revolution live through him. As he says in one of Zhivago's poems:

In me are people without names.
Children, Stay-at-homes, trees.
I am conquered by them all
And this is my only victory.[8]

---

[8] Pasternak 1958, p. 496. For responses to this article see the letters from P. Einsyning and J. Lindsay in *The Listener* 15 January 1959.

Chapter Seven

Marcuse, Marxism and the Monolith[1]

A Review of Herbert Marcuse, Soviet Marxism

'Why, they're people just like us!' This is the cry with which the popular press warns their readers not to believe everything else they have told them about the Russians. One of the few occasions on which this naïve and usually dishonest slogan needs to be brought out again is on reading Doctor Herbert Marcuse's tough book about Soviet Marxism. The toughness comes partly from Marcuse's stiff, academic style. But it comes also from the sheer difficulty of what he is trying to do – to present Soviet Marxism as an ideology, a mask worn by Soviet society. The rulers can use it to present their policies and to justify them; at the same time it does really express a good deal of what is going on in Soviet society.

So, for instance, the priority assigned to the growth of heavy industry is justified in terms of the shortening of the working day and other such advances and is, at the same time, an expression of the structure and interests of the established bureaucracy. The interests of the workers and the interests of the bureaucracy are made to seem to coincide by a liberal use of redefinitions of traditional Marxist vocabulary. So far, the most striking, perhaps, of these – it is too

[1] Originally published in *The New Reasoner*, 9, Summer 1959, pp. 139–40.

recent for Marcuse to notice it – is Khrushchev's assertion that the economic competition between East and West is a contemporary form of the class struggle. Anyone who has wondered how in a country where Marx's writings circulate freely so vulgar an error could be published will learn a lot from Marcuse.

Marcuse relies on Soviet official sources almost entirely both on matters of doctrine and on matters of fact. He sees Soviet society as built on 'repressive production relations', which perpetuate ways of thinking and living which are in themselves liable to reproduce regimentation and oppression. Soviet ideology mirrors the determinism of Soviet society in its neglect of the dialectic and of the creative role of consciousness. He quotes for example from an article in *Voprosy Filosofii* for 1955 the assertion that 'under socialism, too, the laws of the social development are objective ones, operating independently of the consciousness and will of human beings'.[2]

I do not doubt that everything Marcuse says is true. But in an odd way he is trapped by his own method and it is at this point we need to be reminded that Russian socialism is human beings, not just theory and power stations. For Marcuse, by retelling the official tale, connives at the denigration by Soviet officialdom of the USSR. The evidence here comes from a mass of personal reports, from novels such as Dudintsev's *Not by Bread Alone* (not because it is oppositional – for it is not; but for the sense of the texture of everyday life which it gives) and films like *The Cranes Are Flying*.[3] What these make clear is the way life itself does break through. And one gets no sense of this in Marcuse. He reproduces without any sense of irony the voice of the Monolith desperately asserting that it is a monolith. Whereas the multifarious voices of living Russian socialist consciousness and will suggest that the objective laws are in for a pretty thin time.

What Marcuse really provides is a source book for Soviet theory and this is valuable enough. He may help us to avoid taking the path of too many non-Stalinist Marxists and looking for some too easy formula to explain what happened in Russia. 'state capitalism' is one much over-worked candidate. What we have to do is to trace in detail the role of the Stalinist bureaucracy

[2] M.T. Iovchuk, 'Rol' sotsialisticheskoi ideologii v bor'be s perezhithami kapitalizma' ['The Role of Socialist Ideology in the Struggle with Survivals of Capitalism'], in *Voprosy Filosofi* [*Problems of Philosophy*] 1955, n. 1, p. 4, quoted in Marcuse 1968a, p. 125.

[3] Dudinstev 1957.

interposing itself between the socialist foundations in the original revolutionary drive, and the new life of the Soviet people. In doing this we have to avoid Marcuse's error of taking too seriously the self-appraisal of the bureaucrats. But Marcuse helps all the time by suggesting approaches which he doesn't follow through.

Chapter Eight

The Straw Man of the Age[1]

A Review of Hugh Thomas (ed.), The Establishment

One of the ways in which societies avoid the reality of dissidence and revolt is by encouraging imitations of rebellion. The licensed rebel is encouraged to huff and puff a great deal, both satisfying himself and annoying the less discerning defenders of the status quo. But the more intelligent conservatives know very well that the provision of straw men to be attacked is a useful device to divert attention from the more important social targets. The latest straw man in our society is the concept of 'the Establishment'. 'The Establishment' has had a curious history; it first appeared on as the malign force that tried to protect Mrs Maclean from the press. Since then it has proliferated until now Hugh Thomas has edited a collection of essays in which the connections of the Establishment with the public schools, the Army, the Civil Service, Parliament, the City and the BBC are discussed.[2] The quality of the essays varies enormously, from the engaging brilliance of Simon Raven on the officer caste, where the form of autobiography is used to convey a serious piece of social analysis, to the turgid mutterings of Henry

1 Originally published in *New Statesman*, 3 October 1959, pp. 433–4.
2 Thomas (ed.) 1962.

Fairlie about the BBC, where the form of social analysis is used to convey a bad-tempered piece of one-sided polemic.[3] It was Mr Fairlie, of course, who first popularised the phrase in print. He complains bitterly that its original meaning has now been lost to sight. By doing so, he helps to bring out the very different ways in which 'the Establishment' has been used and in which it is used by the contributors to this book. At least three meanings have been distinguished and every one of them is politically unhelpful.

First of all, it may simply refer to 'the powers that be'; as such it could serve no special purpose, for it would tell us nothing about who exercises power in our society and how they do it.

Secondly, there is the meaning which Mr Fairlie originally intended to give it: 'The idea of the establishment is concerned less with the actual exercise of power than with the established bodies of prevailing opinion which powerfully, and not always openly, influence its exercise.' The members of the Establishment do not represent established interests or power blocs; or, if they do, this is irrelevant to their membership of the Establishment. It 'has roots in no class and no interest'.[4] Who are the members of this mysterious rootless group? Vice-Chancellors, Lady Violet Bonham-Carter, the Archbishop of Canterbury, the Governors of the BBC, the Warden of All Souls – these appear in Mr Fairlie's Honours List. At once it is clear that, in Mr Fairlie's sense, the Establishment is a mythological creature. It just is not there. For the members of this group can be divided into those who certainly have their roots in class and interest and those who equally certainly have no strong influence upon the exercise of power. The Governors of the BBC are among the former and the Warden of All Souls is among the latter. Mr Fairlie helps to undermine his own contention by pointing out how sensitive throughout its career the BBC has been to the demands of established authority.

The third sense which can be attached to 'the Establishment' is that which Mr Thomas editorially sanctions. 'The word "Establishment" simply indicates the assumption of the attributes of a state church by certain powerful institutions and people; in general these may be supposed to be effectively beyond democratic control.'[5] Mr Thomas's own development of this sense is so

---

[3] Raven 1962.
[4] Fairlie 1962, p. 186.
[5] Thomas 1962, p. 18.

incoherent as to be almost silly. On one page he can write: 'An Establishment point of view in painting undoubtedly, to an unbelievable extent, reflects mid-nineteenth century canons of judgement; there are still circles in England for whom an appreciation of the Impressionists is an esoteric taste and for whom El Greco is still "insane"', and on the next he can cite as a pillar of the Establishment, as one of its 'saints', Sir Kenneth Clark.[6] But if Mr Thomas makes nothing out of his own definition, something can still be made out of it, and something important at that. For the notion of a state church carries with it notions of ritual and of prestige which are important. It is not just that power is exercised in our society; there are certain trappings of power, certain ritual performances and sacred offices associated with its exercise. Thus the concept of the Establishment is connected not with power or authority themselves, but with the masks which they wear.

If the first meaning that can be attached to the phrase was unhelpful because vague, and the second was unhelpful because based on misconceptions, this third meaning is a positive menace to clear political thought. For, by associating the expression with the mask of power rather than with power itself, it distracts attention from the reality and provides a convenient substitute object for attack. As the cohorts is licensed rebellion surge into battle against the Royal Academy and the Warden of All souls, one can hear in the distance faint cheers coming from the Banks, the treasury, and the Boardroom of AEI. Once again the real centres of political and industrial power are safe.

In three essays in this book the real issues are touched on. Victor Sandelson provides an introductory guide to the workings of the City; Thomas Balogh pierces through the myth that the Civil Service is a neutral and impartial instrument waiting to implement whatever economic policy the statesman may decide upon; and Christopher Hollis vigorously lays bare the impotence of Parliament.[7] But none of them begins to raise adequately – and one can see how the concept of Establishment gets in the way of raising adequately – the question of how the masks of power are related to the faces behind the masks. For the simple fact is that established opinion and the established rituals of authority can only be understood once we understand where power actually lies, and what class and what interest hold power. It may be said that this

[6] Thomas 1962, pp. 16–17.
[7] Sandelson 1962; Balogh 1962; Hollis 1962.

is a matter which lies outside the scope of the present essays; this is indeed so, and it is the concept of the Establishment which makes it so, and which assists towards the fiction that all the panoply of power and authority can be considered apart from considering power and authority in themselves. Yet if we look at the points raised in this connection by these essayists three clear political morals emerge.

The first is the interlocking character of all the institutions of established power. Why does the question of the ownership of industry haunt this book? Because the City is unintelligible, the issues debated in Parliament are trivial, the failures of economic policy-making by Civil Servants have no substance, and the financing of the public schools is a mystery until this question is raised. But to raise it is to bring out the fact, which this book does not bring out, that the masks of power wear two faces. On the one hand, there is the face presented by the BBC, by *The Times* and by all that Mr Fairlie equates with the Establishment; on the other hand there is the face presented by the popular press and ITV. There is the face of Mr Macmillan and the face of Mr Charles Hill. They belong together. For in a society radically decided by private ownership of the means of industrial production there is going to be a sharp division between the face presented to the executives of the established order and those who aspire to be such (Top People and Those on the Way Up), and the face presented to those who provide merely their labour at one end and their consumer power at the other end of the economic system. The one mouth cries that it knows and wishes to propagate only what is really best, that it knows what is good for you better than you do yourself; the other mouth says that it gives you what you want, that it is the obedient servant of the demands of the public. Mr Fairlie identifies the Establishment with the former and consequently identifies opposition to commercial television with opposition to democracy and to creating a 'population with independent tastes'.[8] By doing so he plays his part in accepting the alternatives as being either that of doing good to people self-consciously, or else that of surrendering them to the pressures of the mass media, while thinking this is giving them what they want. What we have to do is to refuse to accept the choice as lying between these two alternatives. But so long as we have our kind of class-divided society these are just the alternatives we shall continually be presented with.

[8] Fairlie 1962, p. 192.

The second moral relates closely to the tasks of the next Labour Government, Doctor Balogh with great skill exposes the failure of previous Labour Governments to create an Establishment of their own. They failed to give us socialism partly because they tried to use institutions and people who were profoundly anti-socialist.[9] But while the substance of Dr Balogh's argument seems to me to be unassailable, the crucial fact about socialism is that it will be a society in which power and decision making are more widely diffused, not a society in which one oligarchy has replaced another. The problem of how to avoid falling prey to the bureaucracy is a permanent problem for socialists.

Finally, there is a general moral which I should like to draw. This book helps to demonstrate the way in which political thinking that starts from the concept of the establishment is likely to lead nowhere. For, because it leaves the true centres of power unnoticed and unexamined, it can offer no general picture of the possibilities of our society, of the changes that are necessary, of the way in which the substance of human life could be transformed and enriched through political action. And this lack of any assessment of potential alternatives to our present system means that the attacks on the Establishment are not only aimed in the wrong direction, but even in that direction they are too negative. To many this book will seem like a piece of mere querulousness. It is far more than that. But it remains a book in which the contributors are trapped by the concept of the Establishment so that they appear among the latest and most distinguished victims of the straw man of the age.

---

[9] Balogh 1962, pp. 101–8.

Chapter Nine

The 'New Left'[1]

The most important fact about the New Left is that it exists. When Cliff Slaughter opened up discussion on "The 'New Left' and the Working Class" he made important criticisms of the theories about our society which some writers in the *New Reasoner* and *Universities and Left Review* have advanced.[2] But while I agree with almost everything that he wrote, I feel that he chose the wrong starting-point for discussion. For a Marxist, the question must be: what does the existence of this grouping point to in the changing character of our political life? Slaughter too easily talks of 'the petty-bourgeois intellectual' and by so doing slides the New Left into a category which gives us no illumination as to the *specific* characteristics of this movement. And when one begins to look at the New Left carefully it is clear that the views with which Slaughter disagrees have also been challenged from within the New Left. John Saville has disagreed with Dorothy Thompson, and both Ralph Samuel and Edward Thompson have criticised Stuart Hall fairly trenchantly. What characterises the New Left is not the holding of an agreed set of doctrines, but

---

[1] Originally published in *Labour Review*, v. 4, n. 3, October–November 1959, pp. 98–100.

[2] Slaughter 1959.

something more difficult to characterise, a frame of mind. Indeed it has more than once been argued on the New Left that it is among its merits that it is so open a movement, that it is not endangering itself by becoming constricted within some new orthodoxy. What it has created are two journals, both with far larger circulations than would have been thought possible a few years ago. *Universities and Left Review* for example has a circulation of between six and seven thousand. It has brought hundreds, and perhaps thousands, of young people into contact with socialist discussion. And it has provided, as Slaughter does not fail to recognise, important contributions to those discussions. How has all this been achieved? The answer comes, I think, from the meeting of two different groups. There are on the one hand the ex-Communists of 1956 and some like-minded people who abandoned Stalinism and have tried to rethink their socialism from the ground up. When they rebelled against the bureaucracy of the Stalinist party machines and the mechanical determinism of Stalinist ideology they did so in the name of a conception of human nature which was authentically Marxist. And the tone of voice in which they spoke caught the ears of a whole generation of young people who had not as yet been caught and moulded into political shape by the orthodoxies of our own society. The New Left finds its audience in the generation that marched to and from Aldermaston. What it has done is to provide leadership for and articulate expression of the feelings of an age-group that no one else has succeeded in influencing so strongly.

Who are these young people and what is their mood? Certainly most of them are middle-class, students and ex-students, teachers, office-workers, journalists and so on. But they are people who could make an impressive contribution to the fight for socialism. And they are in many ways the group who are most nakedly exposed to the pressures of conformism in our society. They do not normally meet working-class people very often. They are fed from all sides with the reports of what is happening to the workers brought back by the middle-class sociological explorers from the proletarian jungle. What they do respond to sharply are the threats which meet them in their own experience: the impact of the mass media, the debasement of values under capitalism, the appalling official cynicism in face of the H-bomb. Their vitality is a sign of the inability of the official set-up to impose its orthodoxies, of the continual revolt of people against the patterns that the bureaucrats try to impose upon them.

These young people are not impressed by the Labour Party or the Communist Party. What happened in Spain, in the Moscow Trials, in 1848 or 1905, these are things of which they have usually only the most fragmentary knowledge. They are generous and are attracted above all by the seriousness and integrity that mark so many on the New Left. But their thinking is imprisoned by two contradictions which prevent growth in socialist thought beyond a certain point. The first of these concerns the relation between a capitalist economy and the variety of social institutions within such an economy. The second concerns the problem of socialist organisation. So far as the first is concerned the contradiction arises from the fact that the New Left wants to stress *both* the all-pervasive corrupting influence of capitalism *and* the possibility of transforming institutions within capitalism. Thus there is no hesitancy on the part of writers on the New Left in rejecting classical reformism. Their analyses of advertising, of architecture, of films, of television and all our other cultural forms press towards the insight that it is the whole way of life which capitalism imposes which tends to the corruption of these things. If you are going to be effective, you are going to have to oppose not this or that feature of the system but the system itself. Yet there is also the strong emphasis, which Slaughter has criticised, on the possibility of building in the 'here and now'. But anything built in the 'here and now' will be subject to all the pressures of the system. The trouble with this demand for building in the 'here and now' is its ambiguity. If this is offered as an alternative to building a working-class movement then it is doomed to frustration and failure. If on the other hand it is, as it could be, a way into the class struggle then it is important and full of possibility. For clearly, trying to create forms of community or culture which are opposed to the values of capitalism will at once bring one into social conflict. And the danger is that one will fight a series of guerrilla engagements on cultural questions which will dissipate socialist energy and lead nowhere. What one hopes is that opening up these questions will lead one to see the basic antagonism in our society *at the point of production*.

There is a good deal of talk on the New Left about releasing the energies of people from the bonds of the system. There is a good deal of talk about the need for people to do things for themselves and not have them done for them. But the key point in our society at which people begin to act and think for themselves is the point at which they react in their work. The spontaneity of rank-and-file movements in the unions – what has the New Left said or done about this? One suspects strongly that many of the readers of *Universities and Left Review* draw their picture of present-day working-class life almost entirely from Richard Hoggart.[3] Hoggart's analysis is open to criticism on many points. But the most crucial fact about it is that it pictures the worker entirely at leisure and not at all at work. And this is to miss both the point at which people are formed in their social activities most effectively, the only point at which one can begin to understand the relation of the capitalist system to people who live within it.

So we in fact arrive at a situation in the thought of the New Left where two alternative roads open up. Without the insight that working-class action against capitalism is basic to the whole struggle (and 'basic' is not a strong enough word) the assertions that capitalism tends to corrupt our whole cultural and social life and that it is possible to build community under capitalism remain a bare contradiction liable to sterilise socialist thought. With that insight new ways into the class struggle are opened up. The danger that faces the New Left is a clear one. It is characteristic of our political system that it has built into it a place for a licensed radicalism. Provided the system is not itself menaced, opposition on this or that point is encouraged as a safety-valve and the critics are praised and patronised into place. Who are to be the licensed radicals of the 1960s? Classical reformism is no longer radical enough to need a licence. Building socialism in the 'here and now' could menace capitalism as little as reformism ever did. It can be clothed in the left vocabulary which reformism has abandoned. And it could be used to separate off the young radicals of the New Left from the working-class struggle.

This danger is the more urgent because of present tendencies in the labour movement. Whatever the outcome of the General Election a swing towards 'Bevanism without Bevan' is becoming increasingly probable. This will find an immediate point of contact with the New Left in, for example, opposition to NATO. The Communist Party leaders are working towards a new period of 'Popular Frontism'. Those of vaguely left tendencies will feel themselves on the crest of a wave. The chief danger in all this will be that it will suggest false hopes of victory through parliament, through capturing the 'machine'; it will distract attention from the rank and file

[3] Hoggart 1958.

industrial struggle. It will foster illusions of every kind about the 'here and now'.

Nonetheless the possibilities are quite as great as the dangers. For the New Left has so far shown a determined resistance to being incorporated as the radical wing of the Establishment. And the core of this resistance has been the extremely useful work done on where power lies in Britain today. The *Universities and Left Review* pamphlet *The Insiders* and Michael Barratt-Brown's essay on 'The Controllers' are only the two most outstanding examples of information which the New Left has disseminated in such a way that a background has been provided which explains to those who feel alienated from the powers which make and threaten their lives why this is so.[4] This makes it all the more urgent that Marxists should be prepared to make their contribution within the New Left. The very openness of the discussion makes it possible for Marxists to enter into a dialogue in which they will learn as well as teach. And if Marxists do not enter into this discussion the one necessary insight, that into the role of the working class, will remain lacking. But if one is to do this effectively one must begin where people are. One cannot bring in the theory of working-class action from outside the discussion as a kind of magical cure-all; one has to begin with the problems that engage people on the New Left and show in detail how their solution is impossible without an understanding of the centrality of that action. This is to say that if Marxists are to participate effectively in the New Left, they must really participate. This is not everybody's job; but there is no inconsistency for some of us in being both members of the Socialist Labour League and within the New Left.

One additional fruit of this might be that it would assist in dissipating the personal misunderstandings that still too often interfere with political work. These have two sources. The struggles of the past twenty-five years bred into many people a polemical and sectarian style of approach and with all of us this is easier to see in others than in ourselves. But more than this Stalinism with its bureaucracy bred an intense suspicion of personal motives. And this has been carried over into a far too great openness to gossip and suspicion. I think that people on the New Left and in the League have only to meet properly and argue properly for this to be avoided. If Marxists will take such initiative as is open to them (and I am well aware what efforts many Marxists

---

[4] Hall et al. 1957–8; Barratt-Brown 1958; 1959a; 1959b.

have already made in this direction) they could break through this particular mist.

So far I have only dealt with the first of the two contradictions which I mentioned. The second arises because the New Left wishes both to assist in building socialism effectively and yet to remain outside the form of any type of organisation which might lead to the actual capture of power. The roots of this lie in the repudiation and criticism of the bureaucracies both of social democracy and of communism. But this is extended to a suspicion of any organised political work which could provide a revolutionary leadership. The attempt to work inside the Labour Party and the trade unions is apt to be dismissed as 'factionalism' and for work outside them the loosest and most informal forms of organisation are thought appropriate. How then is it expected to achieve socialism? The answer seems to be that the building up of a socialist consciousness through educational and other work will lead to a permeation of society so that finally the capitalist integument bursts asunder. But in fact there is here a failure to measure up to the forces of the bureaucracies inside and outside the labour movement. The most brilliant criticisms of the mass media are likely to reach the attention only of those already least susceptible to those media so long as the control of the media remains in the hands of those faithful to capitalism. How do your reach the rank and file of the labour movement? By playing your part in it and above all at the point of industrial struggle where the rank and file is itself responding to the pressures of capitalism. In other words you can only carry through any effective educational effort as part of the political and industrial struggle.

There is also a confusion abroad about freedom of discussion. British Marxists today are likely to be under no illusions about the importance of completely open discussion; but at the same time they find in Marxism a hard core of theory which can guide them into common action, while they still disagree on a wide variety of topics. The danger of loose and informal methods of organisation is that they cannot impinge upon the class struggle in any effective way. The Left Book Club is a misleading model here: it was only able to do the work it did – whatever we think of that work – because of all the other organisations which were also at work, and especially because of the Communist Party. Likewise the New Left can only hope to be effective if its discussions assist people in a kind of political activity which the New Left itself is unwilling to foster. Here again the role of Marxists is clear. Whether the discussions on the New Left serve action or not depends partly on whether we are willing to take part in them or not. Once again this is only a task for some comrades. But we could help to meet the need for a marriage between working-class spontaneity and adequate theory, on which the League has rightly laid so much stress, by utilising the discussions on the New Left.

The most paradoxical fact about the New Left is the way in which sometimes in New Left discussions the fight on cultural questions and the fight for political power are treated as if they were two quite separate matters. This is not the place to develop the thesis that the only way to overcome the corruption of our culture is through the achievement of working-class power. But it is this thesis which Marxists must consistently develop in discussions on the New Left. And it is at this point that all the arguments which Slaughter develops become relevant and important. What I have tried to do is give a context to those arguments which would make it clear that the relationship of Marxists to the New Left ought not to be one merely negative and critical but one which is continually looking for those points of growth in its theory that can lead on to common political action.[5]

[5] For a response to this article see Thompson 1960.

Chapter Ten

What Is Marxist Theory For?[1]

1. Theory and activity

A Marxist movement is apt to be attacked from two sides. Intellectuals see the militant participation in strikes and lock-outs and cannot connect this with anything in their own experience. So we get the charge of 'mindless militancy'! Militant workers are equally puzzled by our stress on discussion, on argument, on theory. 'What good is theory to us?' they ask: 'We want action.'

At the centre of Marxism is the belief that theory which does not issue in action is mere talk; and that action which is not guided by theory is in the end always condemned to failure. But how does Marxist theory guide Marxist action? This is the question which I want to ask in these articles.

We can begin from the feeling of helplessness which many workers have. They feel that their lives are shaped and dominated by powers and forces far beyond their control. The operations of society appear as a set of impersonal happenings which impinge on men and dictate to them, whereas in fact

[1] Originally published in *Newsletter*, v. 3, n. 121, 10 October 1959, p. 289; *Newsletter*, v. 3, n. 122, 17 October 1959, pp. 293–4; *Newsletter*, v. 3, n. 123, 24 October 1959, pp. 299–300; and *Newsletter*, v. 3, n. 124, 31 October 1959, p. 309. Reprinted as a *Newsletter* pamphlet, London 1960.

what happens in society is always the outcome of human intentions, decisions and actions.

The young Karl Marx learnt from the philosopher Hegel that it is human activity, the power of setting oneself purposes and carrying them out rationally, which makes men different from all other beings in the universe. But of course, what men set out to achieve and what they want, are often very different from what they actually achieve and what they get.

So they come to see society and human institutions, such as the state, not as the products of human agency, but as powers with an independent existence. Man appears to himself the plaything of non-human forces, part of a system whose laws operate independently of what he thinks and wills. This is what Hegel called 'alienation'. But Hegel thought that all this came about because of the inadequacies of human thinking. Men are enslaved by these alien powers because they have not progressed far enough intellectually. Marx argued that this alienation is created by the working of the economic and social system. 'Alienation' is not a word which described men's mistakes about their relation to society; it is a word which describes their real situation in capitalist society.

Under capitalism the vast majority of men, the industrial working class, do not and cannot have lives that are genuinely their own. They have to sell their labour-power to an employer in order to live. The employer expends their lives in making such goods as he hopes will satisfy the demand. The lives of working people are turned into somebody else's property and become something 'alien' to them, first in the form of their working day which is given to another, and then in the form of the goods which they make, which belong to the employer and are sold as he wills and as he can, and finally in the form of the social system which exists only by virtue of their work, but whose chief effect so far as the working class themselves are concerned is the loss of their own lives. It is worth remarking that this essential loss of control over one's own life occurs under capitalism (and under earlier systems of exploitation) even when capitalism appears temporarily to be alleviating its ordinary ills of poverty, unemployment and war. Even under boom conditions, the workers' life is dictated to him by others.

Capitalism then is a system in which men's lives are dominated by a power which takes shape as the power of money, the power of ownership of the means of production. Men appear to themselves as helpless, because they are in the grip of a system which makes their labour-power into a commodity, which needs their labour to produce as the system demands and their consumer power to buy as the system demands. The satisfaction of real human need disappears as a purpose. In one sense all men are equally victims of the system. What happens to the capitalist depends upon its workings as much as what happens to the worker. But the important difference is in what happens. 'The possessing class and the class of the proletariat represent the same human self-estrangement' wrote the young Marx:

> But the former is comfortable in this self-estrangement and finds therein its own confirmation, knows that this self-estrangement is its own power, and possesses in it the semblance of a human existence. The latter feels itself annihilated in this self-estrangement, sees in it its impotence and the reality of an inhuman existence.[2]

Because of this, the working class is the only class that has the will and the need to abolish capitalism. The only solution to its problems is the abolition of the system, in order to create a society in which human activity is not deformed into a commodity, and in which men begin to shape their own lives. This is the starting point of Marxism, but it is a starting point which already rules out any attempt to solve working-class problems by finding some way out within the system. The question that is raised is how human activity can become an effective means of ending the system altogether.

2. Class and history

One of the things that bewilder workers who have no theory to guide them is the difficulty of finding some order in the variety of forces which seem to operate in society. What Marx did was to show how one could only make sense of these if one looked at the way in which a particular society produces its livelihood at a particular time. As the mode of production changes, different classes become dominant in the community. So at one time it is the land-owning class which governs, at another time the factory-owning

---

[2] Marx and Engels 1975–2004a, p. 36: 'But the former class feels at ease and strengthened in this self-estrangement, it recognises estrangement as *its own power* and has in it the *semblance* of a human existence.'

class. What survives through all these changes is the basic division between those who own and control the means of production and those who perform the labour of human society. For these last create the wealth which is taken away from them and which provides the basis for the leisure, the luxury and the culture of the owning classes.

There are, therefore, two senses in which all previous history is the history of class struggle. In the first sense, there is the history of the struggle between different ruling classes. The rising capitalist class, based on trade and manufacture, gradually build up their power inside the existing social framework and finally take over the institutions of government. In the second sense, the landowners and capitalists struggle in turn against the working class, trying to extract the maximum possible wealth from their labour. Both these reach their historic climax at the point at which the working class can for the first time take the initiative and move to achieve power and to end exploitation. But we may see this and still fall victims to misunderstanding.

For those who look at the rise and fall of the ruling classes of the past and present may be tempted to see the rise of the working class to power as just the rise to power of one more class within the framework of the existing order. But the working class cannot enjoy power within that framework; they can rule only by abolishing the old form of society. It is not required to take over the institutions of class-divided society; it is required to replace them by institutions which are not designed for purposes of exploitation. This fact, that the working class has only the alternative of continuing capitalism or of ending class society for good, is one that marks off the struggle of the working class from all previous class struggle.

A second difference concerns the greatness of what is at stake. On the one hand, industrial capitalism has revolutionised the means of production and created such vast wealth that an end to exploitation is possible. On the other hand, it is capitalism whose social forms maintain exploitation, competition and conflict and their outcome in poverty, unemployment and war. All human values hang on the victory of the working class over the forces that keep these forms in being. Survival itself hangs on this.

Thirdly, and crucially, the working class can only hope to triumph if they are conscious of their task. Earlier classes came to power through the operation of forces which they could not understand. The working class can only come to power if it has become conscious of its own existence as a class. It is important that the upholders of the existing order spend so much effort in trying to obliterate class consciousness, in trying to make workers think of themselves as anything but members of a class.

Thus one central use of Marxist theory is in helping us to understand the need for theory to create a working-class conscious both of its past history and its future possibilities.

3. Intellectuals and workers

I have argued that Marxist theory shows us the need for a politically self-conscious working class, which is aware of the possibility and the necessity of a break with the whole existing order of class society. In this article, I want to discuss the respective roles of intellectuals and workers in bringing this about. Lenin saw the unity of intellectuals and workers in a Marxist party as a precondition of a proper unity of theory and practice. We can see what he meant by looking at what happens when each group tries to act alone.

A working-class movement without intellectuals is apt to despise theory. Because it despises theory, it has no perspective, no sense of a way forward beyond immediate needs and demands. It fights upon this or that particular issue and is defeated more often than it need be because it lacks any larger strategy. And because of the narrowness of its aims its working-class members are themselves hindered from developing intellectually. The whole British labour movement has been infected by this narrowness. One reason why it is not surprising that this narrowness has prevailed is that the two alternatives which have been most obvious seem equally unattractive. The first of these alternatives is the recruitment of intellectuals to be mere technicians and propagandists for the labour movement. Since 1926, the Labour Party has increasingly had its shop-window full of bright young men, who are able to offer academic justifications for the policies of the trade-union leadership. The alliance of such intellectuals with the party and trade-union bureaucrats is one of the factors that lead to a suspicion of all intellectuals among honest militants. At the same time, the Communist Party has equally perverted the role of the intellectuals. It has had a theory, but a rigid, mechanical and prefabricated theory which has inhibited those intellectuals who have joined it. In a genuine Marxist party, the theory is neither something simply brought from outside by the intellectuals to the party nor something already complete which the intellectuals have simply to accept. The theory is at once something to which the Marxist intellectual contributes and something through which he grows. Faced with the alternatives of either acting as backroom boys for the social-democratic bureaucrats or as office-boys for the Stalinists, many intellectuals have retreated into a socialism which lacks roots in the working class altogether.

If workers without intellectuals tend to become narrow and lose sight of ultimate aims, intellectuals without workers become pipe-dreamers who see the ultimate aims clearly but can envisage no immediate steps which might lead towards them. (This happens among the 'New Left'.) When such intellectuals realise their predicament, the danger is that they try to remedy this lack of working-class connexions by jumping straight into the existing, bureaucratised labour movement and accepting this as if it were the authentic working class.

Another tendency which is sometimes an effect of this is that which separates 'politics' and 'culture'. 'Politics' becomes restricted to the immediate objectives, 'culture' becomes a matter only of ultimate ends. The only way of fighting this is to start out from envisaging the relation between intellectuals and workers in a quite different way. When theorists like Marx, Lenin and Trotsky (and no Marxist theorist can ever be only a theorist) came into the working-class movement they achieved two different things. They both helped workers to generalise their experience and they helped them to use that experience as a guide to future action. Without the working-class experience they would have had nothing to generalise from. Without the working-class revolt against exploitation they would have had no signposts into the future. Moreover it was Marx's experience of the class conflicts of the present which was an essential part of his equipment in understanding the class conflicts of the past. Then by understanding the past he was able to throw still more light on the present and the future. A lot hangs here on the way in which intellectuals and workers come together. If Marx had approached the working-class movement from the outside as a middle-class sociologist, he would never have had working-class experience made available to him in the way in which it was. Mere speculative curiosity leads nowhere. The only intellectual who can hope to aid the working class by theoretical work is the one who is willing to live in the working-class movement and learn from it, revising his concepts all the time in the light of his and its experience. Finally, a more fundamental point.

The distinction between intellectuals and workers itself reflects the divisions of class society, rooted in the most basic division of labour and in the facts of exploitation.

One of the experiences which people have who work in the Marxist movement is that already in our political work this distinction begins to disappear. As workers become increasingly guided by theory, as intellectuals become increasingly close to the workers' struggle, so the two groups become one. This is our continual experience in the Socialist Labour League as it was in the experience of the Russian Bolsheviks.

4. Good and bad theory

The whole aim of Marxist theory is to bring the working class to a point of consciousness where successful political action becomes possible. Marxism, therefore, clashes with all those forms of political theory which argue that men cannot understand and guide social change. The doctrine that men must remain victims of circumstance and environment and cannot hope to master them is essentially a conservative one. The conservative pictures society as growing like a tree and just as twigs and leaves cannot affect the growth of the main trunk, so individuals cannot affect changes in society. This conservative theory reappears in various forms in the labour movement. It appears, for example, in the appeals so often made by right-wing Labour Party leaders to be 'realistic'. What 'realism' means for them is usually an acceptance of the limitations imposed by existing circumstances. Behind such an acceptance there lies a conviction, which is often never made explicit, that circumstances cannot be changed, or at best very, very slowly. This belief in the domination of man by environment is also reproduced in Stalinism. Revolutionary failure and collaboration with class enemies are always excused on the grounds that the so-called objective conditions have not yet ripened, that we must wait until circumstances become favourable. This inner link between social democracy and Stalinism is illustrated by their attitudes to the future development of British capitalism. The Stalinists believe that the inner mechanism of capitalism is such that in the long run it must automatically break down. The social democrats believe that the devices used by modern capitalists ensure that the machine will keep going. Both speak from the standpoint of passive observers outside the system who ask: 'Will it keep going or not?' The

Marxist standpoint starts from the view that this question is not a question about a system outside us, but about a system of which we are a part. What happens to it is not a matter of natural growth or mechanical change which we cannot affect. We do not have to sit and wait for the right objective conditions for revolutionary action. Unless we act now such conditions will never arise. For one of the aims of contemporary capitalism is to have its crises by instalments, with a dislocation in this industry or in that, which will avoid any total breakdown.

Whether this policy succeeds or not depends partly, and perhaps largely, on how the workers whose conditions of life are under attack in a particular industry respond to that attack. If they accept their isolation from other workers, the employers' offensive will almost certainly succeed and any general crisis for capitalism will be still further delayed. If, however, the workers begin to co-operate with workers in other industries in planning and implementing a strategy of counter-offensive, then capitalism will be forced back towards crisis. But whether workers will be able to do this depends upon whether they believe in the possibility of effective social action. Only Marxist theory can provide and support such a belief.

Finally, there are three general points about the place of theory in politics which we ought always to keep in mind.

The first is that even the view that theory cannot help us or is unnecessary is itself a theory. It implies a whole view of society as something whose progress is beyond our control. And this theory is the more powerful for so often being accepted and propagated by people who believe themselves entirely free from theory.

Next, it is worth emphasising how much a grasp of theory can help the individual worker to play his part in the class struggle, not just because it helps him to understand and to act, but also because it can give him confidence in what he is doing. It is no small thing for a man to consciously take part in class battles. It is easy when times are hard or discouraging for a man to have doubts about the possibilities of advance towards socialism. It is in these circumstances that people are tempted to rely not on themselves, nor on the working class, but on some large, apparently strong organisation which can solve their doubts by exhortation and command and which can protect them against the worst of the storm. This is one of the temptations that leads people into and keeps them in Stalinist organisations. It is a temptation against which the best safeguard is a sure grasp of Marxist theory.

Finally, it is only by means of reference to theory that we can remind ourselves, as we ought to, of how great the possibilities in front of us are. The whole point of revolutionary struggle is lost if we think, for example, simply in terms of a series of defensive actions against employers' attacks. Every event in the struggle is a stage towards a society in which we will have destroyed class antagonism and removed all the waste and frustration in human life which is caused by capitalism. Socialists before Marx saw how urgent and desirable this was; Marxist theory teaches us how to bring it about. And a first step is to grasp once and for all that just as theory without action is dead, so action without theory is blind.[3]

[3] The original series of articles/pamphlet ended with the following advice from MacIntyre: 'Further reading: The work in which readers who want to ask questions about what has been said in these articles ought to look for answers is *The Communist Manifesto*. After they have read this, they should pass on to *Socialism: Utopian and Scientific* by Engels and *What Is to Be Done?* by Lenin.'

Chapter Eleven

From MacDonald to Gaitskell[1]

He who fights and runs away
Lives to fight another day. (Nursery Rhyme)

It looks as if Mr. Gaitskell has had second thoughts. Clause 4 is not to be omitted from the Constitution; it is merely to be added to.[2] But only those who are taken in by Mr. Gaitskell's tactical changes of emphasis will rejoice. For what Mr. Gaitskell has been doing ever since Mr. Jay's famous article is seeing how far he can go and in what direction.[3]

There are various ways in which socialism can be evicted from the Labour Party, and if Clause 4 is not omitted it can always be reinterpreted. The interpretation which is contained in Mr. Gaitskell's proposals to the National Executive Committee, and which in the main has been accepted, is essentially a rewriting of Clause 4 and a restriction of public ownership to little more than its present extent.

Thus, Mr. Gaitskell's change is not a retreat. But he has managed to give the appearance of one who

---

[1] Originally published as a Socialist Labour League Pamphlet, London 1960.

[2] Prior to 29 April 1995, Clause 4 of the Labour Party Constitution stated that one of the 'Party Objects' was: 'To secure for the producers by hand and brain the full fruits of their industry, and the most equitable distribution thereof that may be possible, upon the basis of the common ownership of the means of production and the best obtainable system of popular administration and control of each industry or service.'

[3] Jay 1959. The article in question occupied the front and back pages of the paper under the headline: 'Are We Downhearted? Yes! But We'll Win Back'.

has retreated. This could assist him in two ways. It is liable to disarm the Left and delude them into thinking that they have won a victory when they have in fact been defeated. And it could help to build up an image of Mr. Gaitskell as a reasonable man who is willing to compromise, unlike those rabid fellows on the Left.

The origin of Clause 4

Why is it so easy for Clause 4 to be reinterpreted? Because ever since it was included in the Labour Party constitution, it has been continually understood in different ways. The phrase 'common ownership' has been assigned no unambiguous meaning and the phrases 'the most equitable... that may be possible' and 'the best obtainable' leave everything open. This is no accident. The clause was included in the constitution in 1918 (and amended in 1929). The original draft was by Sidney Webb and Arthur Henderson and, then as now, the aim was to produce a formula wide enough to embrace radically different tendencies. The Labour Party had been formally constituted in 1906; but it was only in 1918 that it adopted what is substantially its present constitution. In 1918 three main steps were taken.

First, the foundation of constituency Labour Parties, with individual members, began the effective destruction of the power of the ILP inside the Labour Party. Till then one could only join the Labour Party by joining an affiliated organisation, and the ILP provided the only counterweight to the power of the trade unions. Since the ILP provided the essential *political* organisation within the Party, its views and members had to be respected. When the Labour Party built its own political organisation in the form of the constituency parties, this was no longer necessary.

Secondly, the trade-union representation at both local and national levels was weighted so as to secure trade-union control of the NEC.

Thirdly, the Labour leadership, divided into pacifist and pro-war factions during the War, reunited. It was not until 1922 that James Ramsay MacDonald was re-elected to Parliament and became leader of the Party again. But MacDonald's position in the Party was assured from 1918 onwards. Because of the Tory attacks on him he won the partial support of the 'Left'; for his policies he had the support of the Right.

In the Labour Party as it existed in 1918 and after, we can discern three separate interpretations of Clause 4, so far as 'common ownership' is concerned. There is first of all the most leftward of these views, that of some of the members of the ILP who were to a limited extent influenced by Marx as well as by Keir Hardie. On this view it is industry as a whole that is to be taken over by the state. Production for use is to replace production for profit. The enemy is the capitalist *system*. The agency of change is to be Parliament. What the forms of common ownership are to be remains vague.

Ramsay MacDonald and Clause 4

The most rightward of the three views had been expressed in MacDonald's book, *Socialism and Government*, published in 1909.[4] On MacDonald's view in 1909 it might be the case that the Labour Party would be rendered unnecessary, since either the Liberals or the Tories (and probably the Liberals) might take its aims for their own. Thus for MacDonald common ownership was an idea with no particular class affiliation. Central to MacDonald's thought is the conception of a national interest, which is more important than class or party interest. Common ownership is commended only insofar as it can be defended in terms of such a national interest. The national interest is, of course, the interest of capitalists as well as of workers and so, in effect, MacDonald was prepared to commend common ownership only if it could be made acceptable to the capitalist class.

What divided MacDonald from the ILP 'Lefts' and what united them? What divided them was that the ILP 'Lefts' did see political issues as *class* issues, whereas MacDonald did not. The ILP 'Lefts' saw common ownership as a taking away of industry from the capitalists and giving it to the people as a whole. But the agency which would do this was the bourgeois state and, in particular, Parliament. In their acceptance of the British state the ILP 'Lefts' were at one with MacDonald. It is quite wrong to call MacDonald a Fabian. The class struggle, even although misunderstood, is still central to 'Fabian Essays'. Where the ILP 'Lefts', MacDonald and the Fabians were at one was

---

[4] MacDonald 1908.

in their supposing that bourgeois democracy, plus the enlightened activity of the more rational members of the upper class and the middle class could secure common ownership. The state will bring in common ownership *for* the workers, to whom the parliamentary Labour Party is to stand much as the Victorian philanthropists stood to 'the poor'.

A source of confusion

One source of confusion here was the fact that very often such municipally-owned enterprises as gas and water were taken to be small-scale models of socialist common ownership. Since such enterprises had often been taken over from private enterprise by Tory or Liberal local authorities, it looked as though the capitalist class could be convinced by rational argument. These enterprises priced their products only at the cost of production, and were in this sense non-profit-making, so they appeared both to be cases of production that was no longer for profit and to be cheaper and more efficient than comparable private enterprises. (It was at this point in the argument that *cheapness* as a principal argument for nationalisation came into the picture.)

The error here is seen as soon as we ask: *for whom* did the local authorities provide these cheap and efficient services? The answer is that they were provided largely for private industry and that their cheapness was thus essentially a source of profit for such industry. The workers in municipal enterprises do not cease to be exploited; it is merely that the surplus-value which is extracted from them appears not on the balance sheets of the municipality but on those of the capitalist enterprises which get subsidised gas or water or whatever it is. Thus there is no difficulty in understanding why Tories accept such enterprises. Far from being a victory against capital, they are its cheap handmaidens.

This erroneous worship of the dustbin as the symbol of socialism was shared by the third view which existed in the Labour Party alongside that of MacDonald and that of the ILP 'Lefts'. This was the view that although common ownership in the interests of the 'workers by hand and brain' was the eventual goal, it was to be approached gradually by the nationalisation of particular enterprises. The profit from these enterprises would be taken away from the capitalist class and they would be further impoverished by taxation upon unearned income and heavy death duties. This taxation would gradually wear down the economic power of the capitalist class.

The public enterprises would be cheaper and more efficient and would thus discredit private ownership in the eyes of all rational men. They would be state monopolies with government-appointed Boards of Directors. Once again, Parliament would be the means whereby they were brought into being and the capitalist state was accepted as the framework inside which they could exist. They would be 'oases of socialism'. This was Herbert Morrison's view in 1934; it is advanced by some members of the 'New (!) Left' in 1960. It dominated the Labour Party in the 1930s, and it largely underlay the Labour programme of 1945, 'Let Us Face the Future'.

Syndicalism and Clause 4

We cannot however pass on to 1945 without noticing another important influence on Labour's view of common ownership. In the period when MacDonald formulated and worked out his views the gulf between the parliamentary Labour Party and the trade-union militants was as wide as it has ever been. Many militants were influenced by the syndicalist movement, then at its peak. For the syndicalists, ownership meant ownership by the workers in each particular industry with the state power pushed on one side. Ownership would be *taken* by the workers, not given to them. Syndicalism worked itself out in the industrial struggles immediately after 1918 and the defeat of the General Strike marked the handing over of the trade-union movement to a leadership which drew the sharpest of lines between political and industrial action.

Thus the trade-union representatives on the NEC have always been the element most anxious to see public ownership as a series of limited measures enacted by Parliament and to condemn any action by the workers against the employers which sought to change the ownership of industry. The rise to power on the political side of the Labour Party of the protagonists of a right-wing interpretation of 'common ownership' has usually been the outcome of the pressure of the trade union leaders. Hugh Gaitskell, for example, is Arthur Deakin's legacy to the Labour movement. Without Deakin, Gaitskell would be merely a testimonial to what an education at Winchester can do for you.

Already in the 1930s, public ownership had been argued for on other grounds. Some industries, severely hit by the depression, could only recover with extended government subsidy. Public ownership, it was argued, would allow the government to subsidise these industries more efficiently and would provide a means for making them more efficient. For it would rescue them from the dangers of competition. The industries for which such proposals were made included some which the Labour Party afterwards nationalised, and some which it did not, such as cotton.

By 1945, two deep inconsistencies were embedded in the Labour Party's doctrines about common ownership. For the Labour Party proposed to take over profitable enterprises and use the profit for the community, to provide social services, for example. But it also proposed that such public enterprises should produce cheaply in the way in which municipal enterprises do, and we have seen that municipal enterprises are cheap because they do not make a profit for themselves. Thus, if such enterprises were both to produce a sufficient profit and to be models of cheapness in their pricing policies, they were going to have to be profitable on a really enormous scale. But here the second inconsistency appears: the principal industries which it was proposed to nationalise, coal-mining and railways, were scarcely profitable at all. The mines and the railways were both in desperate need of re-equipment and so of investment. On the other hand, gas and electricity had operated and were to continue to operate typical municipal enterprise pricing policies, so that there was no surplus produced from them.

The nationalisation policy of the 1945 Labour government

About the nationalisation of the Labour government of 1945 three main points need to be made.

1. *What* was nationalised? Was the vast capital wealth of the industrialists handed over? The answer is, No. The compensation payments meant that the capital was largely turned into money and handed over to the private owners in the case of the mines. The mines then had to be refinanced, as did the railways. The money came partly from budget surpluses, but more and more has had to be borrowed on the open market. The development of the electricity and gas undertakings has been similarly financed. The repayment of loans raised in this way has been a first charge on the industries in question,

so that the profits in the form of interest payments have been handed over, whether the industries made a surplus or not. Where you have had successful development, as in gas and electricity, the increases in efficiency have been used to keep down prices, and so have helped to subsidise private industry. Artificially low pricing for industry, both in coal and on the railways, has produced an even more unjustified subsidy for private capitalism. What has effectively happened is that the labour force in the nationalised industries has been made available to the employing class in forms in which the maximum of profit could be extracted from their labour. This is not to say that there have not been important improvements in wages and welfare for both miners and dockers since 1945 (although these are now seriously threatened); but if there had not been such improvements it is doubtful whether capitalism could have maintained an adequate labour force in these industries under boom conditions. Had these industries been left in private hands, the labour force would have been very unprofitable for capitalism. So that a Hull docker went to the heart of the matter when he said recently, 'What was nationalised was the labour force'.

2. The expansion and contraction of the nationalised industries is governed by the needs of private capitalism, and the policy-decisions in the nationalised industries are taken by the agents of private capitalism. The key positions in nationalised industries are almost entirely held by men who have close links to private capitalism and the Tory government has added numbers of part-time directors to the boards, who retain their posts as directors of private companies as well.

3. The nationalised industries therefore make sense only on the assumption that they perform a function inside a capitalist economy. They mark a use of the British state by the capitalist class for its own economic purposes; they mark also the ability of that class to utilise Labour Party politicians for its purposes. They are a sign of the strength, not of the weakness, of the British capitalists.

It was therefore not a fundamental break with the past when 'Industry and Society' proposed state share-buying in private industry. The utilisation of profit for social services was part of Morrison's concept of public ownership. The investment in private capitalism goes well with the Labour Party's actual measures of nationalisation. Gaitskell represents a strain out of the Labour Party's past, just as much as Barbara Castle does.

The socialist attitude towards Clause 4

The political task at the moment therefore, is not just that of defending the place of Clause 4 in the constitution. We have also to give it socialist content. There are at least three tasks here.

First, we have to make it clear that any transitional programme of nationalisation should be designed to hit the capitalist system where it hurts – at the point of profit. We want not investment in profitable private capitalist industry, but the *ownership* of such industry. Moreover, any programme for the ownership of specific industries must have in mind the aim of securing as quickly as possible the ownership of all industry. Unless every gain is utilised immediately for further inroads on the capitalist system, we shall face the strongest economic counter-attack and not be able to meet it. We have to own the industrial system as a whole, to plan it not for profit, but for use.

Secondly, common ownership cannot be divorced from workers' control. This has implications both for our future objectives and for our immediate programme. We must press now for the workers to refuse to be passive objects of administrative command in the nationalised industries. The Coal Board must open its books to the miners, and the miners must demand a share in the making of key decisions, for example.

Thirdly, Clause 4 must be defended in such a way that the issues are clearly defined. Gaitskell will, if he cannot eliminate socialism from the constitution, seek to keep it out of the programme. The struggle over Clause 4 could make this much more difficult for him in future, for it would make Labour Party members and trade unionists much more conscious of the issues. What they need above all to be conscious of is that the British state is not a politically neutral administrative machine which can be used to change ownership. The British state, with all its parliamentary institutions, is the political expression of private ownership. Achieving common ownership means smashing the state power and creating a new kind of state. Failure to see this has hitherto been the common element in Fabianism, MacDonaldism and the views of the old 'Lefts'.

The time has come when the Labour Party must be made to face this issue. It may mean that Gaitskell will follow MacDonald out of the party. If he does, we must certainly see that as few as possible follow him. But we must equally not allow it to happen, as it happened in 1931, that a man is counted a socialist just for not leaving the party. Morrison, Attlee and others got a quite spurious credit for this. And one result was that Morrison's thinking on nationalisation was able to bridge the gap between MacDonald's betrayal in the '20s and Gaitskell's in the '50s.

Chapter Twelve

Communism and British Intellectuals[1]

A Review of Neal Wood, Communism and British Intellectuals

Disillusionment with revolutionary politics has been a theme among British intellectuals ever since Wordsworth. Since 1917 autobiographical accounts of disenchantment with Marxism have multiplied until we have all come to believe that the history of British intellectuals between 1929 and 1956 was a kind of rake's political progress; generous young minds moved by prewar unemployment and fascism were drawn into the nefarious revolutionary clutches of the Communist Party and imprisoned there until some particularly repulsive deed of Bolshevism brought them back to the clear light of liberalism. In the thirties, British intellectuals were concerned which class owned the means of production; in the fifties what mattered to them was which class put the tea in before the milk and vice-versa.

Like all good mythology, this piece of folk-lore contains a large element of truth. But it contains some error and distortion too. Fortunately a number of studies of the history of the British Communist Party have recently been published which makes it possible to sift out the truth and the error. One is Doctor

---

[1] Originally broadcast on the BBC Third Programme and published in *The Listener*, 7 January 1960, pp. 21, 23.

Neal Wood's *Communism and the British Intellectuals*.[2] From this one can draw some striking conclusions about the role of the Communist Party in British political life. The most important of these is that, for the last thirty years, the Communist Party has been an essentially conservative force.

Ritualised pseudo-conflict

Anthropologists have familiarised us with the idea that what looks like conflict in a society may not really be so. Where there are possibilities of destructive struggle, the risk of destroying the established order may be avoided by providing outlets in the form of ritualised pseudo-conflicts. The motions of conflict are gone through and by doing this the tensions are relieved and the real conflict is avoided. This happens in some African tribal societies and it has sometimes been thought to be the function of British parliamentary life. But the imitation of conflict can be effective only if the imitation is plausible and if it secures the belief of the actors who have to carry it through. The life of Parliament obviously fails to meet this criterion. Yet, if the larger political parties have ceased to head off and tame down the young disruptive radicals, they have hardly had cause for anxiety. The Communist Party has done the job for them. Radical militancy has swept into the Party and by it been diverted, dissipated, and finally disillusioned.

This contention will be so new to most people that it will inevitably meet with strong resistance; not just from present supporters of the Communist Party, but from all those defenders of Western civilisation for whom the Communist Party has been the chief target, not to mention all the memoir writers who cherish a secret nostalgia for what they like to think of as their red revolutionary days. So the tale must be carefully told. And the first thing to be said is that it was not always so. The founders of the Communist Party were authentic Marxists and revolutionaries, almost all of then industrial workers, held back by the sectarian traditions of the small socialist groupings from which they came, but immensely serious in going about their political tasks. It was their misfortune to be overwhelmed by two catastrophes, the rise of Stalinism in the Soviet Union and the events that culminated in the defeat

---

2 Wood 1958.

of the British working class in the General Strike. Among the stages in the Stalinisation of the British party, two stand out. There is the fatal break with subjective truth in the acceptance of the Stalinist slanders about Trotsky; and there is the fatal break with democratic control of the Party which ended with the Moscow-dictated reorganisation of the Party in 1929. This placed Harry Pollitt and Palme Dutt in power. And it transformed the party's Marxism into a prefabricated strait-jacket. Into this party came the intellectuals of the thirties.

University reds of the thirties

Doctor Wood's study describes social climate from which most of the Communist intellectuals of the thirties came. They came like their more conformist fellows, from upper-middle-class homes and public-school backgrounds. They were almost all products of Oxford and Cambridge, especially Cambridge. Some of the best of them, died in Spain: David Guest, a young Oxbridge mathematician who spent a year at Göttingen in 1930 and saw what national socialism really was; John Cornford, son of a poet and a classical scholar, himself a poet and a historian; and the best of them all: Christopher Caudwell, not upper-middle-class, but a journalist, an engineer, and a genuinely original thinker. Cauldwell stands out from the British Communist intellectuals of the thirties as one for whom the Marxist classics were an incentive to, not a substitute for, thought. And the existence of Cauldwell's work illuminates by contrast the passivity of most other Communist intellectuals in the thirties. 'Passivity!' those who remember the period will exclaim with horror. And they will recall the endless meetings, the *Daily Worker* selling, the posters and the circulars, the endless round of meetings, the ceaseless round of activity. But what they could not recall – despite much authentic anti-fascist heroism – is a specifically intellectual contribution. Nor could they find an instance where the work of intellectuals would have built policy or transformed theory. There could be no contribution to the making of policy and theory by intellectuals; policy and theory were handed down to them.

What then did they contribute? Part of the answer is prestige. 'In the heart of bourgeois England', boasted Karl Radek in 1934, 'in Oxford, where the sons of the bourgeoisie receive their final polish, we observe the crystallization of a group which sees salvation only together with the proletariat'.[3] Later, during the Spanish war, Communist intellectuals formed the link between middle-class liberalism on the one hand and the forces of the Comintern at the other. This was the age when fellow-travelling on a large scale was born, and itself begot countless journals and organisations. The usual picture of a fellow-traveller is of a milder, slightly less committed supporter of Communist Party policies than is the card-carrying member. What Dr. Wood suggests is that party members in the thirties were merely slightly extremer versions of fellow-travellers. It is the fellow-travelling ethos that predominates. Indeed, it had to be. Stalin had put revolution into cold storage. The wickedness of the Trotskyists in Stalinist eyes was essentially that they still attempted, in Spain for example, to carry through a revolutionary programme. Communists revealed themselves as champions of bourgeois democracy. Communist intellectuals purveyed a curious blend of moderate reformist socialism on the one hand and dishonest apologies for the Moscow trials on the other.

A party no longer Marxist

However, the charge that British Communists were only a kind of fellow-traveller has more to it than the abandoning of revolutionary politics. Trotskyist dissenters from the British Party had already challenged the leadership on this point and appealed to Marxism. Why was this appeal to Marxism not listened to? Partly because of the bureaucratic control of the Party and the ceaseless blackening of all critics, especially Trotskyist critics; and partly because the British Party was no longer Marxist. A Marxist vocabulary was still employed, but what it was used to express was quite different from Marxism.

In the third of the 'Theses on Feuerbach', Marx wrote:

> The materialist doctrine that men are products of circumstances and upbringing, and that, therefore, changed men are products of other circumstances and changed upbringing forgets that it is men that change circumstances and that the educator must himself be educated. Hence this

[3] *International Press Correspondence*, v. 14, 14 September 1934, p. 1270, quoted in ibid., p. 51.

> doctrine necessarily arrives at dividing society into two parts, of which one is superior to society.[4]

Marx attacks here one of the doctrines dominant in Europe since the eighteenth century. According to this doctrine, there are objective causal laws both of nature and of history, knowledge of which enables men to control their own destiny. So far as social life is concerned, the manipulation of society is possible to those who possess the secret of these laws. As Marx saw it, this doctrine implies the sharpest of divisions in society between those who know and those who do not, the manipulators and the manipulated. Classical Marxism stands in stark contrast to this: it wants to transform the vast mass of mankind from victims and puppets into agents who are masters of their own lives. But Stalinism treated Marxist theory as the discovery of the objective and unchangeable laws of history, and glorified the party bureaucrats as the men who possessed the knowledge which enabled and entitled them to manipulate the rest of mankind.

Society controlled by scientists

In this, Stalinism coincided with an entirely different version of doctrine which flourished in Britain. This was the doctrine the rational society would be run by scientists. All that was needed was the discovery by scientists of the laws governing development; and then these scientists should be given power so that they might apply their discoveries. H.G. Wells, Sir Richard Gregory, Sir Julian Huxley and countless others all expressed themselves in this sense. Sir Julian could speak in 1937 of the need for 'some sort of scientific control of society'. H.G. as early as 1906 for the management of society élite of scientists whom he named 'the Samurai'.[5]

The cultural ancestry of this view was, in Britain at least, entirely non-Marxist, but its propagation in scientific and other circles just what was needed to bridge the ideological gap between liberals and Stalinists. Russia's achievements were primarily those of scientific control and manipulation rather of revolutionary participation. The rise of the bureaucracy in the USSR, from the standpoint of Marxist critics such as the Trotskyists, represented what

[4] Marx 1975c, p. 422.

[5] Wells 1905, Chapter 9, 'The Samurai'.

had gone chiefly wrong in Russia; this was now represented as the dominance of Wellsian élite, although H.G. Wells himself was never taken in.

Wells had tried and failed to transform the Fabian Society into a school for his Samurai. But Fabianism was a theory of social manipulation similar to that which Wells advocated and to what Stalinism was. What mattered to the Fabians was the conversion of those in power so that the masses might be rationally and benevolently controlled. To see this kinship between Fabianism and Stalinism is to understand that the visits to the Soviet Union of the Webbs and their conversion to Stalinism are not eccentricities of aged liberals cunningly duped by the guile of the Stalin Constitution. They are an authentic expression of the ideology of left intellectuals of the thirties. If I am right, this ideology exercised such dominion that Communist intellectuals cut their Marxism to fit its cloth rather than *vice versa*. This is what I meant when I said they were really no more than an extreme type of fellow-traveller, producing a left-wing version of H.G. Wells and projecting this on to the Soviet Union. The Webbs made the passage from Fabianism to Stalinism; Mr. John Strachey made the journey in the opposite direction. The British Communist Party was therefore able to live in a climate which allowed its intellectuals both to act as office-boys for the Soviet bureaucrats and to share the essential outlook of their liberal colleagues.

I have already mentioned the uncreative role of the intellectuals inside the party. This is of course entirely different from what Marx had intended. 'Philosophy', wrote Marx in 1844, 'cannot be realised without the abolition of the proletariat, the proletariat cannot abolish itself without the abolition of philosophy'.[6] The liberation of the intellectuals and the liberation of the workers had to go hand in hand. Lenin saw the intellectual as having an absolutely essential role in a Marxist party; without Marxist intellectuals a workers' party can never attain more than a trade-union consciousness, can never pass to a revolutionary consciousness. To do this, the intellectuals must be prepared to accept the discipline of such a party and to learn from the workers who will form the vast majority of its members; but they must make their own specifically intellectual contribution or they might as well not be there. An intellectual work cannot be chained down

6 Marx 1975a, p. 257: 'Philosophy cannot realise itself without the transcendence [*Aufhebung*] of the proletariat, and the proletariat cannot transcend itself without the realisation [*Verwirklichung*] of philosophy.'

by non-intellectual considerations. Trotsky was not unfaithful to Lenin's views when he wrote that 'art, like science, not only does not seek orders but by its very essence cannot tolerate them'.[7] Compare with this Edward Thompson's description, from experience, of the British Communist intellectual 'in the toils of a bureaucracy which demands everything from them, from stamp-licking to *Daily Worker* selling, except honest intellectual work'.[8]

Three types of intellectual career

This situation has led to three types of intellectual career in the British Communist Party.

There have been first of all those in whom idealism has been transformed into straightforward time-serving. Consider for instance the career of such utterly devoted party members as Palme Dutt or James Klugman. Klugman was an apologist of Tito's until the expulsion of Yugoslavia from the Cominform; its chief denouncer in an appalling book, *From Trotsky to Tito*, where the old slanders against Trotsky are allowed to father Moscow's new lies about Tito; and finally an obedient member of the party hierarchy when Tito was restored to favour and Klugman's own book was withdrawn.[9] Twists and turns like this do not merely spell the death of the intellect. They spell the political immobilisation of the intellectual in anything more than the shortest run.

The second type of career is what the mythology I referred to has taught us to regard as the standard one. This is the man who goes so far along the road and then returns to liberalism. But, if I am right, his stay inside the Party was not really as far removed from a liberal position as he may now believe. And he was not a dangerous revolutionary; the party provided the safety-valve of a revolutionary vocabulary and little more. When one hears ex-Communists

---

7 Trotsky 1970, p. 114.

8 Thompson 1957, quoted in Wood 1958, p. [155]. As Thompson pointed out in a letter responding to this article, the full quotation conveys a slightly more complex picture: 'Second, in a period of such significance for socialist theory as this [i.e. 1957], they can no longer waste time and energy in the toils of a bureaucracy which demands everything from them, from stamp licking to *Daily Worker* selling, *except* honest intellectual work; which hedges ideas around with dogmatic anathemas, and inhibits their expression with disciplinary measures.' See the letter from Thompson in *The Listener*, 4 February 1960, p. 224.

9 Klugman 1951, especially pp. 81–7, 123–5 for comparisons between Trotsky and Tito.

who have rejoined the ranks of parliamentary democracy speak about their party days, one is reminded of John Bunyan's extremes of self-denunciation for such things as playing tip-cat on the village green on a Sunday.

Where the mythology really lets us down is in ignoring the third type of career – an entirely different type. In this career, one leaves the Party because one realises that in joining it one was stultifying all one's revolutionary impulses and beliefs. That is, there is not only the much publicised exodus to the right; there is the as important – or more important – exodus to the left. Most of those who left the Communist Party over the Soviet aggression in Hungary left in this direction. They did so after a series of internal party revolts, the publishing of an internal opposition paper and an appeal to moral principle which one member of the Party's executive described as 'an immodest parading of conscience'. Almost all of them remain on the Left in British politics; many of those who remained Marxists joined with their predecessors the British Trotskyists in founding a new Marxist revolutionary organisation, the Socialist Labour League.

Future encounter?

Dr. Wood's book is limited because he does not consider this alternative with sufficient seriousness. He considers the possibility of the intellectuals being corrupted because of inherent defects in Marxism; he does not consider the possibility that the intellectuals were corrupted because of the Party's desertion and distortion of Marxism. Intellectuals who have left the Party have testified in both directions. Both need to be examined. Historians who take the first alternative for granted are apt to see the relations of British intellectuals to Marxism as an episode now beyond recall. But, if I am right in my argument, then to indict the British Communist intellectuals of the thirties is to indict the Marxism of Stalin, not the Marxism of Marx. Any encounter between British intellectuals as a group and authentic Marxism is a matter not of the past but of the future.[10]

[10] For responses to this article, see the letters from A.H. Hanson and MacIntyre in *The Listener*, 21 January; R.E. Dowse in ibid., 3 March 1960; P. Cadogan in ibid. 10 March 1960; and R.E. Dowse and MacIntyre in ibid., 17 March 1960.

Chapter Thirteen

Freedom and Revolution[1]

The danger to the non-Marxist Left is that lack of theory leaves its discussions blind and formless; the danger to the Marxist Left is that it tends to treat theory as something finished and final, and so the inherited formulae can become a substitute for thought. To guard against this, we ought every so often to re-open old discussions in new ways. The particular old discussion which I want to take up is that about freedom. No word has been more cheapened by misuse. No word has experienced more of the tortuous redefinitions of politicians. So it may be of use to go back to the bare essentials of the Marxist concept of freedom and in so doing lay one or two ghosts. What ghosts do I particularly hope to exorcise?

First and most immediately the view that socialism and democracy can be separated – if by democracy we mean something more and other than the forms of parliamentary democracy. In left Labour Party circles, one sometimes hears it argued that 'the West' has democracy, but not socialism, while 'the East' has socialism, but not democracy and what we need is a (blessed word!) synthesis. Secondly, I want to expose the view that the problem of

---

[1] Originally published in *Labour Review*, v. 5, n. 1, February–March 1960, pp. 19–24.

freedom can be stated in terms of 'the individual' and 'the collective'. This, so I shall argue, is not a pure mistake, like the first view, but it contains the germ of dangerous confusion. Thirdly, we need to guard against the view that the threat to freedom arises out of certain specific forms of organisation and in particular from democratic-centralist forms. These views have haunted the labour movement for many years now. One reason for their prevalence is the habit of separating the discussion of freedom in relation to the nature of society from the discussions of freedom in relation to the forms or organisation appropriate to a Marxist party.

Freedom and humanity

Hegel spoke of freedom as 'the essence of man'.[2] What did he mean? It is a distinctive feature of human as against merely animal or natural life that men act upon their environment and do not just react to it. Every other species has fared well or ill as the environment allowed; men have transformed the natural and social environment. This specifically human initiative cannot be understood except in terms of the concepts which belong to what Marx called 'practical consciousness', such concepts as those of desire, intention and choice.[3] To say that men are free is to say that they are able to make their desires, intentions and choices effective. But this by itself is far too abstract.

It is too abstract in two different ways. For, on the one hand, this initial definition might suggest that the free man is the man who gets what he wants, and this is obviously wrong. For one can be free and dissatisfied; indeed, in our society, the more the ferment of freedom is at work in a man the more dissatisfied he will be. And one can be satisfied and unfree. At least, one can be satisfied in the short run and be unfree. The drug addict gets what he wants; but he is a slave to his short-term craving. So we have to distinguish between two senses of 'getting what one wants'. There is the sense in which to get what one wants is to follow and satisfy one's immediate and short-term impulses; but there is also the sense in which to get what one wants is to attain what will in the long run and at every level in fact satisfy. Often, to get what

[2] See, for example, Hegel 1956, p. 18.
[3] Marx and Engels 1975–2004b, p. 44.

one wants in the first sense can stand in the way of getting what one wants in the second sense. Moreover, to know what will really satisfy one, one has to rely on the decisions that other men have made throughout history. And the discovery of the kind of life that will satisfy is the discovery of the kind of life in which fundamental desires, intentions and choices are made most effective, in which man is most agent and least victim. Hence the relevance of all this to the topic of freedom.

What kind of life would this be? To answer the question properly would be to write from one point of view the history of class society. Every new class that comes to power brings to light new possibilities for human nature; each new form of exploitation that accompanies such a rise to power brings new frustrations of human possibility. Progress, as Marx and Engels always saw, bears two faces: it remains progress. But, in our society, the development of capitalist economy has brought us to the threshold of something new. The rise of the working class to power will not be the sign of a new class society and consequently a new form of exploitation; it will be the sign of an end to class society and an end to exploitation. Human possibility will no longer be frustrated in the ways in which it has been throughout all previous history.

I have, in the last three paragraphs, presented an argument that could do with three books. But I have done so in order to draw an outline, parts of which can now be filled in more detail. Before doing this, however, two central points can be made. The first is that, if this argument can be vindicated, the achievement of freedom and the achievement of the classless society are inseparably united. The second is that, in our era, to free oneself from the pressures and limitations on one's actions is to move towards that society, and only he who begins to move towards it with some degree of consciousness can begin to feel that his life is his own, what he has made it and not what society has made it. This second point is important because it brings out the relevance to freedom of both the final goal and of the movement towards it. Whether a man himself moves into the classless society is not within the individual's power to decide; whether a man moves towards it is within his power. Hence the great tragic moments of our history are those in which the individual fails in one way or another, even though indissolubly united to the working-class movement. One can think here of the death of Trotsky at the hand of another, or of the death of Joffe by his own hand.

The free man, then, in every age is the man who to the extent that it is possible makes his life his own. What happens to him, whether good or evil, wisdom or stupidity, happens to him as far as possible by his own choice and is not the outcome of the blind workings of nature or of the will of others. And this use of the term 'free' appears in some measure in all the various versions of the concept which different phases of class society have bred. In all of them, too, there remains something of the notion which Hegel makes so prominent, that unless you are free you are not an authentic specimen of humanity, not really a man. This emerges clearly in slave society; in the early Greek society pictured by Homer, to be a slave is for one's life to be wholly another's and not at all one's own. Consequently one is not really a person, but a thing and a chattel at that.

Capitalism and history

The paradox of bourgeois society is that it at one and the same time contains both the promise of greatly enlarged freedom and the denial of that freedom. In two directions, capitalism enlarges freedom by destroying bonds and limitations. In transforms nature and ensures an effective human domination of nature. More than that, it makes men assume that they are not bound down by nature. In precapitalist societies, one finds a sense of inevitability and fatality about natural catastrophes such as floods and famine. In capitalist societies, men learn that there is no inevitability here. Where they come to feel inevitability and fatality is not in nature, but in society. Yet even here there is a first promise of freedom. The 'Marseillaise' and 'John Brown's Body' are bourgeois hymns. The feudal ties of the serf and the ownership of the slave are destroyed by capitalism and in their place there stands the free labourer, free to sell his labour, if there is a buyer, or starve.

It is important to pick out the different ways in which freedom is specifically denied by capitalism. All class society involves the rule of some class at the expense of others; that is to say, the making of the desires, intentions and choices of a minority effective at the expense of those of the majority. But the ways in which this happens differs from society to society. Under capitalism, we can distinguish three different ways in which freedom is denied. The most obvious of these is perhaps the direct oppression of the worker in time of unemployment, the coercion by poverty or by force of colonial workers all the time, of all some of the time. But this coercion and oppression, it will be said, is surely absent in times of prosperity.

Those who believe that welfare capitalism has brought permanent prosperity will argue that economic oppression has been abolished, because they identify it with this first form of unfreedom. But, even if we were to concede (which I do not), their claims about prosperity, there remains even for the prosperous worker a second form of unfreedom. For even the prosperous worker is prosperous by reason of the decisions of others; his life is as much made for him and imposed on him as is that of the unemployed worker. The capitalist decides upon investment; the capitalist sites his factory here or there; the capitalist looks for markets in this or that direction. In this sense the capitalist determines what jobs are open to the worker, what wages can be offered to him and so on. The capitalist disposes of his own life and of the life of others in a way in which the worker never can. By accumulating surplus-value he wields the power of capital, the power of what Marx called 'dead labour', over living labour. He does this equally whether the worker prospers or suffers.

Surely, someone might argue (the ghost of Arthur Deakin perhaps), this ignores the role of trade unions. Surely through them the worker can negotiate (some have even said dictate) his own terms with the employer and so make his life his own, something he has helped to determine for himself. The short answer to this is, of course, that the official trade-union structure in our society very often presents itself to the individual worker as part of the alien power that dominates and shapes his life. The officials are as much 'they' as the employers. They move within the limits of capitalism as the employers do. And, over many of them (for whatever reason), the rank and file exercises no effective control at all.

The limits set by capitalism mark the third type of unfreedom. For there is an important sense in which both capitalists and workers are victims of capitalism. The laws of the system bind both; both are carried along by semi-automatic processes, at best half understood and half controlled. Economic laws appear as laws of nature, the power of the market appears as an inscrutable chance, and every feature of life assumes the aspect of a commodity. Here, money reigns and triumphs over capitalist and worker alike. The capitalist is both better and worse off than the worker. Better in the obvious and crucial sense that he escapes poverty and insecurity. Worse in the sense that he has no reason to become dissatisfied and frame the questions which might reveal to him the less-than-human quality of his life.

Individual versus the collective?

It is typical of class society that social life appears as something given outside our control, in which we can only play a pre-arranged part. This makes conformity to the established order appear as, not just a virtue, but almost a necessity. Life in a period of relative stability becomes therefore heavily coloured by conformism and many who do not feel the weight of economic tyranny directly as proletarians feel it indirectly through the pressure of social convention. The revolt against this under capitalism takes a variety of forms. We ought to remember that the contemptuous ring which the word 'bourgeois' has in our mouths was given to it by Flaubert as well as by Marx. It is significant that we have to mention a novelist here. For a number of reasons the type of the free individual in a bourgeois culture, who is free just because he rejects the social conventions, is the artist. In a bourgeois society, the artist has the choice of being either a solid fellow who sells poems by the line or canvas by the yard as a grocer sells tea by the pound, or else an eccentric in a garret for whom art exists solely for its own sake.

This sense of 'free' in which to be free is to reject the conventions has left its mark upon phrases as various as 'free love' and 'free verse'. But this freedom is too negative and destructive to be much worth praising. It is the freedom of the bohemian and the beatnik. As such, it is too much like a mere inversion of bourgeois values. Instead of the cog playing its part in the machine, the cog runs free or grinds destructively against other cogs. Instead of contracting in, contracting out. Instead of the public world of the stock exchange and the labour exchange, the private world of fantasy. In this world, too, one is a victim and a product of a system not understood.

It is this conception of freedom in a somewhat more sophisticated version which underlies the posing of the problem in terms of a tension between 'the individual' and 'the collective'. This type of thinking is often found in Liberal Party publications. We can use these terms without danger in some contexts; but, in general, they suggest the antithesis of two false abstractions. For we have to remember *both* that the individual has no effective human existence outside the sum total of his social relations *and* that the collective has no existence apart from the concrete individuals which compose it. Moreover, the terms 'individual' and 'collective' are so general and abstract and can be used to cover such a wide variety of historical situations, that their use in this connection makes the problem of freedom appear as a timeless problem needing to be solved in all sorts of organisations, rather than as a problem whose resolution depends on the emergence in history in the future of certain specific social forms. Used by a careful writer in a careful way (as Trotsky for example uses them in discussing the nature of tragedy) these terms can aid thought.[4] As they are normally used they are the kind of rhetoric which only clouds our thinking. Because the individual exists in his social relations and because the collective is a society of individuals, the problem of freedom is not the problem of the individual against society but the problem of what sort of society we want and what sort of individuals we want to be. Then unfreedom consists in everything which stands in the way of this.

To see the mistake here, to see that 'the individual' and 'the collective' are false abstractions, is not something that will keep us from this error once and for all. All of us will pass through phases in which both rightly and wrongly we sharpen the line between ourselves and others. This self-imposed isolation is a feature of every normal adolescence. It is also a normal experience in political organisations in which the first experience of membership and friendship may give way dialectically to a consciousness of distance between oneself and others. Some conclude at this point that there is something wrong with them (and, of some individuals, this is in fact the truth). Others conclude that there is something wrong with the organisation (and, of some political organisations, this is in fact the truth). But to objectify this as a struggle between 'the individual' and 'the collective' is to treat an experience which is a part of normal political growth in a highly misleading way. To assert oneself at the expense of the organisation in order to be free is to miss the fact that only within *some* organisational form can human freedom be embodied.

[4] See Trotsky 1991, pp. 268–74.

Freedom is revolution

The individual then cannot win his freedom by asserting himself against society; and he cannot win it through capitalist society. To be free is only possible in some new form of society which makes a radical break with the various oppressions of capitalism. Thus the topic of freedom is also the topic of revolution. But we still need to be clearer than we are as to what we have to revolt against if we are to be free. I have already described some features of capitalist society in general. It is perhaps worthwhile to fasten on some features of Britain in 1960 which exemplify capitalist unfreedom. I can bring out what I mean here by describing our society as one of grooves, ladders and espresso bars.

Grooves – because so much of life is preordained. To be born in a particular family in a particular place means for most people a particular type of home, schooling and job. Choice is hideously limited, often in fact non-existent. Where there ought to be choice, there can only be more or less grudging acceptance. To marry, to build a home takes place under the same constricting conditions. Hence the dream of a win on the pools is not just the dream of material advantage, it is, in very inadequate form no doubt, also a dream of escape from limitation, a dream of freedom. But where there is money, high wages or good luck, there is still the groove. Capitalist production pushes you along the groove of work; capitalist consumption holds you in the advertisers' groove. The stick of work and the carrot of television, these mark out how so-called consumer capitalism has additional techniques for limiting and holding the worker down. Old age puts you back in the final groove of pensioned need.

So much for grooves. Ladders – because the only escapes from the grooves that are offered are competitive ones. The prizes are all financial and there are a few – very few – large ones. You compete at eleven plus for the grammar stream. On that ladder you compete for higher rewards. In the commercial world you compete in offering your skill or your savings in the service of capitalist enterprise. At least in the grooves you were *with* your fellows, on the ladders you are against them. So we go from working-class grooves on to middle-class ladders, from middle-class grooves on to still other ladders and so on.

Grooves, ladders *and* espresso bars. There are those not yet captured for grooves and ladders, adolescents clutching Modern Jazz Quartet L.P.'s, coffee bar bohemians who sense the phoney everywhere (and rightly) except in themselves (wrongly).

These three represent the types of capitalist unfreedom which I described earlier. The grooves along which working-class people are hurried by bourgeois decision-makers, the ladders up which the system hurries and harries the decision-makers themselves, the suffocatingly negative response of those who merely contract out. And over them all the shadow of the Bomb, symbol of man's power over nature more than a symbol of how that power has become the instrument of a status quo that will destroy us if we do not destroy it.

What all this makes clear is that the liberation of ourselves from this society can only be by a revolution of a certain kind. We cannot hope for a liberation by means of the formal democracy of representative institutions. For, first of all, in fact all representative institutions are biased in favour of the status quo. No decision of importance is even discussed before the electors: where and when were our electors asked about the 'mixed' economy or NATO or oppression in Africa? They were offered Tweedledum who was for them and Tweedledee who was for them, too. No choice was here, so no question of a free choice, let alone of a choice leading to freedom, could arise. But this has been often said. What has been less often discussed is that in a society ridden with grooves and ladders what representative institutions will represent will be the world of grooves and ladders. The road to freedom is the road out of what we are; so to represent what we are will not help us. The rise to parliamentary fame is made up one particular social ladder; the controllers of the parties who monopolise electoral discussion move along the same grooves. To break with this society, and to realise their potentialities men will have to break with parliament, too.

Freedom and revolutionary discipline

But how? We cannot achieve freedom by merely wishing it. And to see what is wrong with capitalism and what is right with socialism is still not to see how to pass from one to the other. About this I want to make simply two last points. The first is that because our society is unfree in specific ways, the working class will not and cannot find the road to freedom spontaneously. And, since the participation of every worker in the decision-making which governs his life is a condition of freedom as I have discussed it, it follows that, until the working class finds this way, no one else can find it for them. So the free society cannot be a goal for the politically conscious individual, except by way of moving with the working class into conscious political action. Thus the path to freedom must be by means of some organisation which is dedicated not to building freedom but to moving the working class to build it. The necessity for this is the necessity for a vanguard party. Moreover, such a party will have to find some form of existence which will enable its members to withstand all the pressures of other classes and to act effectively against the ruling class. To escape these pressures two things will be necessary.

First, it will have to keep alive in its members a continual awareness of the kind of society in which they live and of the need to change it and of the way to change it. It will have to be a party of continuous education. And, in being this, it will have to vindicate freedom in yet another way. Bourgeois democrats and Stalinists have often argued as to whether art and science ought to be controlled by state authority or not. The point which this discussion misses is that such control is impossible, logically impossible. You can stop people creating works of art, or elaborating and testing scientific theories; you can force them instead to do propaganda for the state. But you cannot make them do art as you bid them or science as you bid them; for art and science move by their own laws of development. They cannot be themselves and be unfree. To rescue and maintain genuinely free enquiry is in a class society itself a partisan activity. But a revolutionary party has nothing to lose by the truth, everything to gain from intellectual freedom.

Secondly, one can only preserve oneself from alien class pressures in a vanguard party by maintaining discipline. Those who do not act closely together, who have no overall strategy for changing society, will have neither need for nor understanding of discipline. Party discipline is essentially not something negative, but something positive. It frees party members for activity by ensuring that they have specific tasks, duties and rights. This is why all the constitutional apparatus is necessary. Nonetheless there are many socialists who feel that any form of party discipline is an alien and constraining force which they ought to resist in the name of freedom. The error here arises from the illusion that one can as an isolated individual escape from the moulding and the subtle enslavements of the status quo. Behind this there lies the illusion that one can be an isolated individual. Whether we like it or not every one of us inescapably plays a social role, and a social role which is determined for us by the workings of bourgeois society. Or rather this is inescapable so long as we remain unaware of what is happening to us. As our awareness and understanding increase we become able to change the part we play. But here yet another trap awaits us. The saying that freedom is the knowledge of necessity does not mean that a merely passive and theoretical knowledge can liberate us. The knowledge which liberates is that which enables us to change our social relations. And this knowledge, knowledge which Marxism puts at our disposal, is not a private possession, something which the individual can get out of books and then keep for himself; it is rather a continually growing consciousness, which can only be the work of a group bound together by a common political and educational discipline. So the individual who tries most to live as an individual, to have a mind entirely of his own, will in fact make himself more and more likely to become in his thinking a passive reflection of the socially dominant ideas; while the individual who recognises his dependence on others has taken a path which can lead to an authentic independence of mind. (In neither direction is there anything automatic or inevitable about the process.)

Someone will object here that what I have posed as the two necessities for a party of revolutionary freedom are incompatible. How can intellectual freedom and party discipline be combined? The answer to this is not just the obvious one that a certain stock of shared intellectual conviction is necessary for a man to be in a Marxist party at all. But more than this that where there is sharp disagreement it is necessary that discipline provides for this by allowing minority views to have their say *inside* the party on all appropriate occasions. If this is provided for, then disagreements can remain on the level of intellectual principle without on the one hand hindering action or on the other hand degenerating into mock battles between 'the individual' and 'the collective'.

After all this, I hope that some ghosts no longer walk. The thread of the arguments leads on to the conclusion that, not only are socialism and substantial democracy inseparable, but that the road to socialism and democratic centralism are equally inseparable. Those among socialists who have written most about freedom have tended most often to reject democratic centralism. But, if I am right on the main points of this argument, this rejection must necessarily injure our understanding of freedom itself.[5]

[5] There was no direct response to this article in *Labour Review*, although a subsequent article made some rather oblique criticisms of MacIntyre's conception of the party, perhaps because it was not yet clear that he intended to leave the Socialist Labour League. See Slaughter, p. 109: 'Some Marxists seem to conceive of the party as simply a contractual discipline to stop individuals from going off the class rails as they react to class pressure. But it is more than that: it must become the vanguard of revolutionary action, the representative of the general interest of the working class.' More explicit criticism followed his departure from the organisation. See Baker 1962, p. 70.

Chapter Fourteen

Breaking the Chains of Reason[1]

I

> I am contending for the right of the *living*, and against their being willed away...by the manuscript-assumed authority of the dead. (Tom Paine)[2]

There is not much enthusiasm abroad among intellectuals in our time for the day when the last king will be strangled with the entrails of the last priest.[3] It is not just that the liberation of mankind has come to seem an impossibly utopian enterprise. To most present-day British intellectuals, the very concept of commitment to such a cause has become suspect. They are, on the whole, content with what they have; if they want anything else, it is more of the same sort of thing that they have already. An American sociologist has written of them that 'never has an intellectual class found its society and its

---

[1] Originally published in E.P. Thompson (ed.), *Out of Apathy*, Stevens and Sons, London 1960, pp. 195–240.

[2] Paine 1970, p. 64.

[3] The original phrase is: 'All the great ones of the earth and all nobles should be hanged, and strangled with entrails of the priests.' Often ascribed to Voltaire, these words were actually written by Jean Meslier (1664–1729), the parish priest of Etrepigny in the Champagne district of France. They appear in a testament found after he had starved himself to death during a dispute with the feudal superior and which reveal him to have held atheist and, indeed, virtually communist views. Parts of the manuscript were published by Voltaire in 1762 as *Extrait des sentiments de Jean Meslier* and it is from this publication that the association with him derives. The testament has not been translated into English.

culture so much to its satisfaction', and has pictured our university teachers in a state of complacent delight, drinking port and reading Jane Austen.[4] Remember the Spitalfields silk-weavers of the 1840s spending their Sunday leisure drinking porter and reading Tom Paine and you have a clue to how far and in what direction our society has travelled. The great-great-grandsons of the Spitalfields weavers are competing for scholarships to sit at the feet of the port-drinkers; their great great-granddaughters are keen readers of those women's magazines in which the blue-eyed, fair-haired, six-foot-tall hero is increasingly likely to turn out to be an academic of some sort.

The sweet smell of the academic's social success helps to explain his unease when presented with images of radical change. He does not seek to be in any sense a prophet of hope; indeed, the very notion seems to him pretentious and vulgar. Those prophets of hope, the great Marxist intellectuals, are treated as the authors of antique texts for commentary and refutation; the idea of 'left intellectuals' is such that, when that glittering reflection of the contemporary intellectual scene, Mr. Anthony Crosland, wants to speak of them he has to guard himself by the qualification 'if one may use the awful phrase'. Small wonder that, when the contemporary intellectual's preoccupations are translated into terms of imaginative vision, he appears as one without hope. The repeated assurance of Mr. Butler that we can double our standard of living in the next twenty-five years if we only refrain from rocking the boat sounds very thin and unconvincing compared to the threats of what may happen to us if we don't. The increase in human powers which once seemed the very root of hope is now far more often a source of dread. The fantasies of Orwell, who was obsessed by the danger of the techniques of power getting into the hands of men of bad will, have only been outdone by the fantasies of Huxley, who sees just as dire consequences in the possibility of them getting into the hands of men of good will.

Yet fantasy here as always reflects life. If the intellectual has nightmares of a conformist future, he has only to wake up to find himself in a conformist present with the intellectuals conforming as hard as anyone else. The writers elevate Western values in *Encounter*. The scientists play their part at Hartwell, Aldermaston and Porton. The teachers and the journalists purvey second-

---

[4] Shils 1972, p. 137.

hand versions of the dominant ideas. It is in this conformist culture that power has become a means not to possibility but to a destruction of all possibility. That comparatively primitive technology which took us from gas-light to gas-chambers has been replaced by the achievement which took us from the disintegration of the atomic nucleus to the disintegration of Hiroshima and Nagasaki. Intellectual achievement hovers between the imagination and the reality of destruction.

It was not always so. We inherit from other times and places a series of images of the intellectual as rebel and critic: Condorcet, hiding from his executioners so that he may finish his *Sketch of the Progress of the Human Race*; Marx in the Reading Room at the British Museum, surviving on a pittance; Sartre playing his part in the Resistance. On the threshold of our society, the intellectual appeared as liberator and revolutionary. But, both before and after that eighteenth- and nineteenth-century stimulus to reason, the intellectual has too often been a victim of the bureaucracies of the mind. Before, there were those corporations of learning, the universities, providing a vital link between the powers of church and state. Since there have been the growing administrative tasks of industry and the civil service on the one hand, with the diffusion of ideas on the other through the press, television and schools, the universities once more providing an important link. Between the collapse of the older order and the rise of the new, the intellectual achieved a short-lived independence during which he appeared as a voice of hope, speaking to men who might hear.

It is a mark of the conformism of contemporary intellectuals that not only do they not see themselves as able to speak in this way, but they are no longer able to conceive of there being an audience which might hear and respond. One component of the apathy of the intellectuals is a deep-seated belief in the apathy and conformism of the working class. Yet an addiction to ITV is perhaps no more likely to reduce one to being an impotent spectator of life than is a habitual reading of *The Times* or the *Guardian*. The grooves of conformism are different for different social groups. What unites all those who live within them is that their lives are shaped and driven forwards by events and decisions which are not of their own making. A lack of will to change this situation and an inability even to recognise it fully infect all classes in our society.

Where intellectuals are specifically concerned, an explanation may be looked for in terms of the specialisation of thought. The formal logician, the prehistorian, the neurologist and the poet all count as intellectuals: why should they have anything to say of outstanding social significance? Should this not be the province of yet another specialist, the sociologist or the political theorist? Part of the answer to this ought to start from the way in which what the sociologists and political theorists have to say today often seems as devoid of immediate political significance as the study of butterflies or Buddhism. But the core of the answer lies in the change in the characteristics of the intellectual. Among our intellectual ancestors, the thinkers of the eighteenth-century Enlightenment and their immediate heirs, it was taken for granted that to participate in intellectual life at all was to be committed to the ideas of reason and freedom and to the politics that could make these effective. What we have to ask about the intellectuals is not just what social pressures have driven them into their present unhappy state; but what has happened to emasculate their ideas and what in our culture has robbed the intellect of its social power. To ask this is not, of course, to ask a question that is only relevant to intellectuals; it is to ask what hinders intellectuals from contributing to a general break-through from apathy.

2

The inheritors of the Enlightenment are, in their different ways, Hegel and Marx. In their writings, there is a ferment of concepts whose life derives from their close interrelationship, the concepts of reason, of freedom, of human nature and of history. 'When individuals and nations have once got in their heads the abstract concept of full-blown liberty, there is nothing like it in its uncontrollable strength, just because it is the very essence of mind'.[5] So Hegel. His belief in the strength of this concept is not surprising in one who wrote in the shadow of the American and French Revolutions, above all in the shadow of the Tree of Liberty planted in his student days at Tübingen. Unlike all his successors in disillusionment with revolutionary politics from Wordsworth to Malraux, Hegel never came to think his youthful belief in

[5] Hegel 1894, p. 401, para. 482.

freedom mistaken. Even when, in old age, he combined detestable political attitudes with bad logic in order to prove that the Prussian monarchy was an authentic embodiment of freedom, he would on every anniversary of the taking of the Bastille drink toasts with his students in commemoration of that great liberation. What survived every twist and turn in Hegel's career was the conviction that freedom is the core of human nature.

It is so because human action can only be understood in terms of such concepts as purpose and intention. To know what someone is doing is to know what ends he is pursuing, what possibilities he is realising. Human history is a series of developing purposes, in which, through the exercise of reason in the overcoming of conflicts, freedom is attained. To understand a particular episode is to place it within the context of that history. Men are understood not in terms of that which they have been but in terms of the intersection of what they have been and what they can be. Because possibility grows through conflicts of principle and purpose history is a dialectic of contradictions, intelligible not as natural events are or as a machine is but rather as a conversation or an argument are.

At every stage in human history, the growth in reason and the growth in freedom are inseparable. Only in so far as reason guides action are men free to discern alternative possibilities and to frame purposes. Only in so far as the realm of freedom extends does reason have force against the non-rational. Without freedom, reason operates only within limits, and so its constructions, however intricate, remain beyond those limits uncriticised, and, in so far as uncriticised, irrational. Without reason, freedom becomes merely a lack of constraint which leaves the individual the plaything of all the forces which impinge upon and influence him, but of which he remains unconscious.

Post-Hegelian discussions of freedom have not often preserved this vital link between freedom and reason. The discussion has usually been carried on in terms of the contrast between negative freedom, belief in which is cherished by utilitarians, and positive freedom, belief in which was cherished by Victorian and post-Victorian idealists. Negative freedom is what I enjoy when I escape criticism by other people; positive freedom is what I enjoy when I am in that state which reason advises to be best calculated for my self-realisation. Both are ghosts of dead political philosophies which still haunt contemporary thinking. Both need to be exorcised. In the name of positive freedom, men have been called free so long as they are being tyrannised over for their own good. In the name of negative freedom, men have been called free when enclosed by ignorance and their natural situation, provided only that nobody was actively coercing them. Certainly, belief in negative freedom is less obviously vicious than belief in positive freedom, but so long as the choice is between these two, one can understand both why belief in freedom is not an active inspiration in much of our social life and why intellectuals have not felt that their vocation committed them to a devotion to freedom. For, in both these concepts, the interconnection between reason and freedom which is essential to the Hegelian concept is lost sight of.

Two other features of the Hegelian concept are also important. The first is the way in which the concept of freedom is firmly located in Hegel's overall historical scheme. Freedom is not something which at any given moment men either do or do not possess; it is always an achievement and always a task. The concrete content of freedom changes and enlarges from age to age: in the dialectical growth of human nature, what was the freedom of the past may be the slavery of the present. Moreover, the tasks of freedom in any age are defined partly by the goal to be reached, partly by the obstacles to be overcome. It is this necessity of referring to what has to be overcome which makes 'the negative' so important a notion to Hegel. The particular form of the negative which matters in this discussion is the alienation of man from himself which leads men to envisage as objective, impersonal and enslaving forces which are in fact creations of human consciousness and reason. God, the state, the Moral Law; these are but false objectifications by which we deceive and enslave ourselves. So at least the younger Hegel. The human task is to tear away the masks, to recognise our own faces behind them and so free ourselves from the domination of the mask.

To take the argument to this point is to feel the mounting irritation in most readers at this apparently abstract concern with expounding fragments of Hegel. Why, for the Absolute's sake, Hegel? The answer is that, in Hegel's elucidation of the essential connections between the concept of human action and the concept of freedom and reason, something is restored which is lost in the contemporary academic mind. The view that human activity can be reduced to patterns of response to the stimuli of conditioning is continually fed to us. And perhaps it is not accident that so many who want to eliminate from our concept of the human those features of it which are distinctively human have had no good words for Hegel. The anti-metaphysical positivism of the American exponents of 'rat psychology' joins hands with the Pavlovian determinism of the Stalinists. 'The question of Hegel was settled long ago', snapped Zhdanov in 1947: 'There is no reason whatever to pose it anew.'[6]

Not that there is not a peculiarly Hegelian way of betraying freedom and reason. Hegel's critics have pointed out that while Hegel was right to point to freedom and reason as essential possibilities of human nature, the translation of the possible into the actual is not to be achieved by making conceptual connections, but only by a transformation of human life. (This is a central point of Marx's criticism of Hegel.) But the mature Hegel retreats from the inadequacies of actual human life into the twin sophistries of the Absolute Idea and the Prussian monarchy. And Hegel's followers have too often fled into abstraction, so that they have seen the misleading character of our concepts, but failed to see that the distortion of our concepts cannot be corrected apart from correcting the distortion of our lives. When Marx wrote of the role of concepts in Hegel's *Logic* he spoke of them as 'the money of the mind'.[7] What he had in view was the way in which we can be deluded into supposing that monetary transactions can occur independently of an actual transfer of goods. So we may wrongly suppose also that we can change our basic concepts, but not our lives. Because we are reasoning animals (even if we do not always reason well) the shape of our concepts shows in the outline of the shape of our lives.

Part of our reaction against Hegel and one effect of the reign of positivism has been that specialisation of the intellect which has been mentioned already. Not that the very growth of knowledge and especially of scientific knowledge would not have rendered specialisation necessary anyway. But it is not clear that specialisation had inevitably to be accompanied by a complete fragmentation of our culture. If there were only unity in our concept of human nature, for example, we should have at least a clue to the relations between the most diverse elements in our thinking. In past times, some unity was given to our education by means of classical literature, history and ideals. The ancient world provided a backcloth for the modern. To learn the inner history of the modern academic is in part to write of the decline and fall of the ideals of a classical education.

---

[6] Zhdanov 1950, p. 102.

[7] Marx 1975b, p. 383. '*Logic* is the *currency* of the mind'.

3

'Absorbed in money making and in the peaceful warfare of competition, it [bourgeois society, that is] forgot that the shades of ancient Rome had sat besides it cradle.'[8] So Marx. But how did the bourgeoisie come to forget? For nascent bourgeois society, the Greco-Roman world provided the mantle which human values wear, and this not only on the battlefields and amid the terror which brought that society into being, but also in its academic syllabuses. The prototype of all arts disciplines, as they exist in our universities today, is the Greats school at Oxford; and the Greats school in its inception was a study of a whole society, of the language, literature, history and philosophy of Greco-Roman culture. The small-scale in physical size of that culture, its relatively self-contained character, made it a suitable object for study. It was far enough away to be viewed dispassionately, near enough to provide a model for social behaviour. Lord Milner's young men building the modern empire, the Asquithian liberals – these in their own way echo Thucydides and Cicero.

But, from very early on, the school tends towards becoming a group of separate disciplines; the vision of a whole society – inaccurate as it may have been – is lost. The language and literature, history and philosophy, it becomes a model for the fragmented disciplines of modern civic universities. Sometimes, when schools of English are founded in modern universities, Anglo-Saxon is deliberately introduced to parallel the linguistic demands of classical studies. And what happens in these fragmented disciplines in both older and newer universities is that a great many specimens of human culture are inspected without any connections being established which would bring out what it is anyway to be part of human culture or society.

There is lacking any conception of the human as such, in terms of which relations between history and literature and philosophy might be established. So, to do a course in one of these subjects is usually like going round a museum; exhibits are there neatly labelled and you the spectator stand outside the case. But you can think of any connection between them and you only by imagining yourself dead and stuffed under the glass. For the alternative of seeing the exhibits as living, living as you are living, has never been opened to you by

---

[8] Marx 1973a, p. 148.

the demonstration of any vital connection between yourself and them. Such a connection could only be established by the concept of a common human nature. And to serve its purpose, such a concept would have to be historical, have to be a means of showing the past growing into the present. Marxism possesses such a concept; why it has not been fruitfully in British academic life we shall have to ask presently. But, for the moment, this is to rush ahead of the argument. What does matter is simply the divorce of arts subjects from the study of human society as such.

This lack of unity in arts subjects makes them all the more open to victimisation by administrative pressure. And administrative pressure in the university today exhibits that curious blend of the planned and the unplanned so characteristic of welfare capitalism.

On the one hand, there is the pressure to produce more scientists and technologists and the consequent building programmes. On the other hand there is a general expansion in size of universities with very little, if any, thought as to what the purpose of arts faculties may be. The universities design their courses either to produce the kind of trained scientist that industry and the government demand or to produce the kind of arts graduate (I think here of the vast mass of those of middling ability, not of the few more distinguished) that nobody demands at all. The content of science courses is almost entirely non-problematic; how to get enough of the required subject-matter into three years teaching is the limit of the problem. The content of arts courses is almost entirely problematic; our only *firm* criterion is what has been done in the past.

In this situation, the examination system and the tasks which it imposes become the limits of academic vision for many. About the ends of what one is doing no questions are asked, in the sciences because decisions about the ends have been taken by powers outside the universities, in the arts because there are no accepted and effective standards by which such decisions could be made. Thus, all discussion is about means; the university teacher is turned into an administrator who has to accept a framework imposed from elsewhere – from industry and government in the sciences, from the past in the arts. And administrators are notoriously conservative; their criteria are, have to be, those of efficiency in producing *given* results. Theirs is not to reason why, but only how.

So the universities have few answers to offer to their students when they ask why they should do what they do. They have to fall back on two extremes: either disciplined study is worth while just because of the sheer value of the experience-in-itself or it is a professional training which has as its end the getting of a certain sort of job or it combines these. The first answer which sounds idealistic is in fact cynical because everyone knows, although few will admit, how few worthwhile intellectual experiences the mass of students encounter in a university career. (The best students are different here: but they would mostly achieve what they achieve anyway. One is sometimes tempted to think that the only students with whom the university teacher does not largely fail are those for whom he is really superfluous.) The second answer, which sounds cynical, is in fact idealistic, at least for arts students, because they are not in fact being trained to do anything except to teach others subjects which will land them in the same predicament. Unless, that is, they too, like the scientists, become the servants of the great corporations. The editor of *The Times Educational Supplement* has said recently that

> ...it can still be maintained that the classics, for pure educational value, are outstanding amongst all other subjects. 'Greats' at Oxford, which is the crown of a classical education, still produces men and women with minds ideally prepared for work in the world. 'Why do you recruit firsts in Greats?', a former chairman of a great oil company was asked. 'Because they sell more oil', he replied.

What I have tried to depict in this section is an academic scene in which the breakdown of the admittedly inadequate norms of a classical education had left the academic world without any inner strength to resist the moulding pressures of industry and the state. The university assumes the shape of the social *status quo*. So does the university teacher. A product of the system which he now helps to administer, he can hardly avoid sharing the mood which I described in the first section of this essay. Himself without initiative or much room to manoeuvre, he becomes an admirable representative of conforming society. As the supporter of the dominant ideas in our culture he is gradually transformed into a trustworthy guardian of our society's ideology. The concepts of reason and freedom are not even a temptation to him.

To use the word ideology here may seem to give the discussion a quaint Continental flavour. European intellectuals have ideologies, Croceans,

Marxists, existentialists or whatever it is. We British, so the refrain runs, are less pretentious, less hospitable to these inflamed general theories. And this immediate reaction if of course one to be characterised not just in terms of our various professed doctrines and theories, but in terms of the absence of general theories and unifying ideas. In particular, as I am going to repeat to the point of weariness, we lack any unifying concept of human possibility.

This is, of course, to say that the key point in our intellectual failure is in the human sciences. It is to what has happened to psychology, sociology and history that we need to turn. And now we need to pass beyond the patterns of administrative pressure. Certainly, the human sciences too have been fragmented, becoming on the one hand abstract academic disciplines, or on the other hand being turned into training schools for personnel managers and almoners. But the depth of our dilemma lies not in the way that they have been presented, but in what there has been to present. To approach this topic is to reach the heart of the matter.

4

The dream which still haunts and informs the human sciences is the dream of mechanical explanation. Engels has narrated vividly how, after 1848, with the death-knell of Hegelianism there was a revival of the mechanistic materialism of the eighteenth century.[9] To do for society what Newton had done for nature was the revived hope. It looked back to the thought that Diderot had expressed when he spoke of 'the complicated machine called society'.[10] It looked forward to the physiological laboratories of Germany and America where the anatomising of nerve-endings and the experimental study reflexes was envisaged as a preliminary to the grand task of explaining human behaviour. What the psychologist looked for in the individual, the social scientist was to search for in the group. His task was to discover laws as simple as Newton's laws of motion, from which observed regularities in human conduct might be deduced and which would at one and the same time provide causal explanations of particular human actions and a basis for

[9] Engels 1975–2004a, p. 26; 1975–2004b, p. 364.

[10] In fact, Diderot refers to the state rather than society. Diderot 1992b, p. 209: 'The state is a very complicated machine, which one can neither assemble nor set in motion without knowing all the pieces.'

general and unifying theories. To explain, to predict, to control; to be able to see human behaviour as the outcome of physiological or environmental determinants; and to unify this understanding in a scheme as simple as Newton's: these have been the goals.

The assumption is, of course, that there is nothing distinctive in human behaviour which might render it unamenable to modes of explanation appropriate for understanding the behaviour of molecules of mainsprings or muscles or maggots. And, with this assumption, goes another, that the mode of understanding human beings resembles the mode of understanding natural objects in that to understanding is to control, or at least is to take the first steps towards controlling. For to understand is to give causal explanations; to explain an event causally is to state under what given conditions the event occurs and under what conditions it does not occur; and to state this is to tell us what we have to contrive if we wish to produce this type of event. So to understand is to be in a position to manipulate. To carry through this programme would be to acquire possession of that power the exercise of which is depicted in *Brave New World* and *1984*.

The central paradox of this mechanistic view of human life is well brought out by the third of Marx's *Theses on Feuerbach*:

> The materialist doctrine that men are products of circumstances and upbringing, and that, therefore, changed men are products of other circumstances and changed upbringing, forgets that it is men that change circumstances and that the educator must himself be educated. Hence, this doctrine necessarily arrives at dividing society into two parts, of which one is superior to society....[11]

That is, if we think of society as a machine and recognise that we are part of society, then to discover the mechanics of social change is to discover those laws of which we are the victims as much as anyone else. If on the other hand we think of knowledge of the mechanics of society as affording us levels of change, we at once have to think of ourselves as outside the machine, operating it, as a part 'superior to society'. In other words, to conceive of ourselves as acting to change society is at once to recognise the inapplicability of the machine model to ourselves; the machine model will do to explain how

[11] Marx 1975c, p. 422.

we come to be modelled and acted upon, but not how we act. And we can only apply the mechanistic type of explanation to this by making an arbitrary distinction between them and ourselves.

That the mechanistic type of explanation must therefore break down we can see. That it did break down in practice was revealed simply by its failure to yield results except in limited small-scale contexts. But the project of an overall mechanical explanation of human life continued to dominate the human sciences. For such alternative approaches to human nature as are considered receive their definition in terms of the breakdown of that project. So much is this so that those features of human life which render it unamenable to mechanistic explanation still fail to receive their due. Such features, which I have already connected with the notion of activity, are twofold. First, human activity is never to be equated with physical movements. Physical movements are certainly susceptible of mechanistic explanations. And every human action involves physical movement. But to understand the physical movement is not to approach understanding the human action. The same physical movements involved in signing my name may be the bearers of quite different actions. The same physical movements may be involved in indorsing a cheque, signing a peace treaty or putting my name to a proposal of marriage. What differentiates these are the socially recognised conventions, the rules, in virtue of which the movement is taken as signifying this or that. So that I cannot explain the action except with reference to established rules and meanings. A society constituted by such an ability to communicate presupposes, but cannot be explained in terms of, physical movement.

More than this, as Engels pointed out, mechanical explanations are unhistorical.[12] A machine runs or breaks down; it has no historical development. To explain a particular human action is to place it in relation to the circumstances out of which it arose and the goal which the agent sought. Stages in a mechanical operation can be explained in terms of preceding and following sequences of events. But they have no goals and they do not respond to circumstances by means of understanding. They simply follow out predetermined paths.

The insight that human activity is intelligible and explicable only in a social and only in a historical context is lost sight of, not only in the dream

12 Engels 1975–2004b, p. 370.

of a general mechanistic theory of human behaviour, but also in the various intellectual adaptations to the breakdown of that dream. The first and most striking of these adaptations is social and psychological science as it actually exists amongst us. The assumption behind it is that what went wrong with the dream was not its mechanistic character, but the *a priori* character of its generality. What we need is to amass particular studies of particular cases. From these we shall derive low-level generalisations and correlations; the study remains causal, mechanistic and manipulative, but it is accepted that as yet we cannot ascend to the simplicity of an overall theory. This entails that our studies are essentially statistical and out of social and historical context. The study of man in nature gives way to the study of delinquents in a Chicago suburb. 'Twenty-five years ago and earlier', wrote Bernard Berelson, an American social psychologist, in 1956,

> ...prominent writers as part of their general concern with the nature and functioning of society, learnedly studied public opinion not 'for itself' but in broad historical, theoretical and philosophical terms and wrote treatises. Today, teams of technicians do research projects on specific subjects and report findings. Twenty years ago the study of public opinion was part of scholarship. Today it is part of science.[13]

The equation of science with the study of social phenomena out of social context is what is striking. This equation leads on to two other fallacies.

The first is that significant generalisations can arise out of material collected without any general principles of significance. I think here of a recent volume of statistical information about contemporary British social life from which you can learn how many people in our society spend their holidays in caravans, but not how many own shares.

The second fallacy is that the use of formal, mathematical devices might make other than trivial at the level of generalisation what is trivial at the level of the particular case. The human sciences are haunted in any case by the view that what is less complex is necessarily more comprehensible than what is more complex; that understanding technologically primitive societies is therefore a step towards understanding technologically complex ones, and that understanding the nervous system is a task prior to understanding

[13] Berelson 1956, pp. 304–5.

thought. This misses the point that you may not be able to comprehend the goals for which men in the primitive society strive unless you look beyond it to the more advanced; and you certainly cannot hope to even embark upon the project of explaining thought in terms of the nervous system until you understand thought sufficiently to know what it is you are hoping to explain by your own neurophysiology. The point which I am making was made by Marx against some of Darwin's disciples. Marx first agreed with them in rejecting that one-sided teleology which wants to explain an earlier stage only as a preliminary to a later one; but he then rejected their mechanistic assumption that the earlier can be made sense of without the later, but not the later without the earlier (and for 'earlier' and 'later' one could also read here 'simple' and 'complex') in the bold statement that 'the anatomy of man is a key to the anatomy of the ape'.[14]

To ignore this is necessarily to condemn the human sciences to become a collection of particular observations and cases without any overall unity or significance. Dignified by the name of empiricism it can then become the received doctrine that this is how the human sciences should be. Academic standards of objectivity and impartiality are invoked to show how admirable our lack of standards of importance is. But, even among those who take up this attitude, there are divisions of standpoint. There are those who hold that the limited and particularising nature of the human sciences at the moment merely reflects a temporary phase in their development. To such sociologists as Lundberg or Lazarsfeld, the only misleading feature of the attempt to assimilate the human sciences to physics is that expectations were pitched too high too soon. The human sciences still await their Newton. We continue to collect data and to hope. There is, however, another possible response, and one as much in vogue in British circles as that which I have just indicated is in American. This is the doctrine that the limited and particularising nature of the human sciences, as we have them, is due not to the slowness of our progress nor to the fact that we searched for the wrong sort of general theory, but to the fact that the concept of any general theory or overall understanding of society is nonsensical. For any general theory of society will be an overall theory of the historical development of society. To advance such a theory is to

[14] Marx 1975–2004b, p. 42.

fall into what Professor Karl Popper has called 'historicism' and castigated as the original sin of the modern intellect.

I have, in this essay, criticised the contemporary human sciences as non-historical, atomistic, content with limited, contextless, low-level generalisations, and unable to discern or construct theories of overall social structure. These are, for Professor Popper, precisely the features which any well-constructed human science would have to have. He thus provides a splendid rationalisation for the contemporary sociologist. The most interesting feature of the arguments of Popper's social philosophy is that they systematically persuade when they do persuade (and the incense which so many acolytes burn at his shrine is evidence of how often that is) by presenting us with pairs of what are alleged to be exclusive and exhaustive alternatives. One alternative is then exhibited as fallacious in its logic and destructive in its moral consequences. This involves us in a vindication of the other. If these false alternatives were merely Popper's, they would not be so important to discuss; but, as I have already remarked, Popper's thought in many ways systematises and represents the assumptions of the age.

The most obvious of these dichotomies is that which allows us only to be *either* historicists or without any overall view of history. Popper defines historicism as the belief in unconditional trends in history. He ascribes such a belief to the error of supposing that an historical process can be explained solely in terms of a law or laws without adding a statement of the initiating conditions from which the process commenced.[15] Clearly, if anyone supposed this, he would both be committed to a belief in 'absolute trends' and be in gross error. But who has ever believed this? Certainly neither Hegel nor Marx. To bring Marx into the picture is to make clear at once how Popper is involved both in historical and logical error. For Marx both believed in the possibility of overall theorising about history and did not believe in 'absolute trends'. Knowledge of the trends that are dominant is, for Marx, an instrument for changing them. So his belief that he has uncovered 'the economic law of motion of capitalist society' is not a belief in an absolute trend, but a trend whose continuance is contingent on a variety of factors including our activity. It is interesting here that the error of which Popper believes Marx to be guilty, namely that of treating historical processes as if they were explicable in the same way as

[15] Popper 1957, especially pp. 35–54.

physical events were, is one which Marx himself indicated. But Marx goes on to explain human history in a different way, beginning with the family of concepts which belong to what he called 'practical consciousness': the concepts of intention, deliberation and desire, those concepts which are essential to understanding men as agents and not a mere passive reflexes of non-human forces.[16] Then Marx asks what the limiting factors upon human agency are in every age and finds these in the basic economic relationships which are built into particular modes of production. Human history is the successive liberation of possibility as economic limitation of this kind is removed. In each age, the economic relationships mean that the rules in accordance with which social and economic life are carried on are different and differ with the mode of production. In each age, the character of the rules is determined by the relationships between men which are involved in that particular mode of production, and these relationships are not between individuals but between groupings of men, who are united by their common economic and social role, and divided from other groupings by the antagonisms of economic and social interest. So, 'all history is the history of class struggle'.[17] This is not a generalisation built up from instances, so much as a framework without which we should not be able to identify our instances; yet also a framework which could not be elaborated without detailed empirical study. We see its growth not just in Marx, but also in historians like Michelet and Taine. The relevant feature of Marxism for the present argument is the way in which the economic basis appears as a limiting and conditioning of human actions, but not as an exhaustive explanation of it dynamic. This enables us to see how Marxism cannot be labelled 'historicist' in Popper's sense. And this is important to my whole argument, both because of my Marxist approach, and because is exposes the misleading character of the choice which Popper's alternatives offer us.

The second false dichotomy in Popper's thought is that expounded in terms of what Popper calls 'methodological individualism'. This is the doctrine that groups are to be understood as collections of individuals and that individuals are concrete while societies are abstract.[18] 'The army' is an abstract concept;

---

[16] Marx and Engels 1975–2004b, pp. 43–5.

[17] Marx and Engels 1973, p. 67. 'The history of all hitherto existing society is the history of class struggle.'

[18] Popper 1957, pp. 82, 130–43, 147–8, 157.

'the soldier' is a concrete one. An army is a collection of soldiers. The vice to which 'methodological individualism' is opposed is 'holism', the view that social groups can and ought to be viewed as more than, or other than, just a collection of their members. This is supposed to involve us in a belief in the reality of fictions and abstractions. *Either* we take Popper's nominalist view *or* we fly to super-empirical entities. Once again the choice posed is utterly misleading. What is important is that no individual can be characterised except in terms applicable to other individuals. To characterise a given individual by any predicate at all is to exhibit that individual as a member of a class. (This is, of course, to use the word 'class' in the logicians', not the sociologists', sense of the word. Many logicians have made the point, including Hegel.) Moreover, of classes many things may be said which cannot be said of individuals; one consequence of this is that no class can be characterised by referring only to the individuals who compose it. You cannot characterise an army by referring to the soldiers who belong to it. For, to do that, you have to identify them as soldiers; and, to do that, is already to bring in the concept of an army. For a soldier just is an individual who belongs to an army. Thus we see that the characterisation of individuals and of classes has to go together. Essentially, these are not two separate tasks. What Popper no doubt fears, and fears rightly, is a belief in social groups and historical trends as states existing apart from individuals, of which individuals are but the playthings. Popper is right to stress that there is no history and no society which is not the history or the society of concrete individuals; but, equally, there are no individuals who exist apart from their history or apart from their society. So that to insist on the latter truth also is to realise that we do not have to choose between 'methodological individualism' and a vicious, supra-empirical 'holism'.

The third false dichotomy is presented by the alternatives that *either* we must be illegitimately partisan in the social sciences *or*, and this is Popper's view, we can be concerned only with means and not with ends. The fallacies in this thesis are twofold. It assumes a possible total separation of means and ends in social life. This only needs to be stated for dubiety to become evident. What is more immediately important is that Popper's thesis is self-refuting. For, to assert that our concern can only be with the means and to add that the result of that concern can only be limited and particular statements of social correlation is already to be partisan. An example of what Popper takes to be a genuine discovery of the social sciences is that 'You cannot have full employment without inflation' (the rider 'in our type of economy' is not added).[19] If such limited discoveries are all that we can hope for from the social sciences, it follows that we cannot hope to transform society as such; all that we can hope to change are particular features of social life. To adopt this view of the means available for social change is to commit oneself to the view that the only feasible ends of social policy are limited reformist ones, and that revolutionary ends are never feasible. To be committed to this is to be partisan in the most radical way. Popper again presents us with a false choice, and one that depends of course on the other false alternatives which he presents. In all of them, he mirrors so aptly the actual condition of the social sciences that we can understand the almost religious consolation which his views offer social scientists. What might have otherwise appeared to them as lamentable incoherence and impotence appears now as necessary and unavoidable. More than this, it appears praiseworthy, for Popper is apt to insist that historicism is the doctrine of totalitarianism. So that not to share his condemnation of it is not merely to be mistaken, but also to be wicked. Thus, the practitioner of the social sciences who cannot transcend their present condition finds his state not only a necessary but even a virtuous one.

This is perhaps a point at which to recover the general thread of the argument. I have argued that the human sciences have been dominated by the conceptual ideal of laying bare the clockwork of human nature. For this ideal has shaped the thought both of those who have accepted it and of those who have rejected it. Those who have rejected it have accepted it as only the form in which the ideal of a general understanding of society might be formed; and so in rejecting it they have rejected the concept of any such general understanding. Or else they have accepted the mechanistic ideal as the paradigm of rational explanation; and in rejecting it they have fallen back upon treating human life as irrational and inexplicable. We can merely record and amass our records; or we have to point to irrational and incomprehensible forces. The dilemma thus presented arises from a failure to see that the point of Hegel and Marx; and this failure is endemic not just in the minds of our sociologists but in the life of our society.

---

[19] Popper 1957, p. 62.

Surely, however, it will be replied, I have not allowed for the variety of positions taken up in non-Marxist sociology. Within the scope of this essay, I am necessarily concerned to indicate and outline a position rather than to argue for it exhaustively. But it may help to underline the point I am trying to make to append to this section something on the work of two very different sociologists who are in their own way submerged by the situation which I am trying to describe. Both are contemporaries.

The first contemporary at whom I want to look is Talcott Parsons, because in Parsons's massive work on *The Social System* some of the most basic patterns of non-Marxist sociology are revealed. I almost in this last sentence said 'bourgeois sociology' and if I have done so I would have not only been classifying the social order to which Parson's work belongs. For Parsons begins by recalling that early bourgeois thinker, Hobbes, and he explicitly states his problem in terms reminiscent of Hobbes.[20] We begin with individuals and their desires at one pole and we ask how social order is created at the other. Parsons is about three hundred years more sophisticated than Hobbes in his psychology; the elaborate devices of the theory of 'socialisation' replace the simple Hobbesian psychology of the fear of death and the desire to dominate. But, as with Hobbes, society and the individual are counterposed and the task is to explain how the individuals are brought into a state where social equilibrium is maintained. With Parsons, we are back in a mechanistic theory designed to explain order and stability. It is no wonder that Parsons finds it difficult to provide plausible speculations for social disorder. He can explain stability; but how does change arise? Parsons's work is therefore profoundly non-historical and this is perhaps also a consequence of his attempt to discuss the life of social groups in a general, comparative, timeless way. More than this, his starting point in the motivation of the individual and the reasons why the individual has come to share the values of his society pushes into the background all questions about the hierarchy of power-relations and the political and social institutions which embody them. Both history and politics become marginal to society in Parsons's social theory; and when Parsons does write, as he has done, directly on political and historical questions, he notoriously abandons his own concepts and has even been accused of Marxist ideas.

---

20 Parsons 1952, pp. 36, 43, 71, 118–19, 121, 123.

The contemporary sociologist whom I want to compare with Parsons is that fierce critic of Parsons and hero of radicalism, C. Wright Mills. Wright Mills might be thought to be close to my own position on a superficial reading. 'Freedom' and 'reason' are for him key words and he has criticised these tendencies in sociology which are criticised in this essay. But Wright Mills's position seems to start far away from Parsons's and end close to him. Where, for Parsons, the institutions of power were marginal, for Wright Mills they are central. Whether it is the internal development of American society that is in question or the approach of another world war, Wright Mills is concerned to locate the effective decision-makers and why they are who they are and where they are. Yet Wright Mills still has to stress the autonomous character of contemporary social processes.

> Great and rational organisations – in brief, bureaucracies – have indeed increased, but the substantive reason of the individual has not. Caught in the limited milieu of their everyday lives, ordinary men often cannot reason about the great structures – rational and irrational – of which their milieu are subordinate parts. Accordingly they often carry out a series of apparently rational actions without any ideas of the ends they serve, and there is the increasing suspicion that those at the top as well – like Tolstoy's generals – only pretend they know.[21]

When social scientists, such as Wright Mills himself, discern what is happening, what are they to do? Wright Mills's only answer is that they must speak both to those at the top and to 'ordinary men', but, on Wright Mills's own showing, those at the top are unlikely to want to hear and ordinary men are unlikely to be able to hear. If Parsons showed us a social equilibrium in which individuals are wholly absorbed, Wright Mills shows us a machine in which individuals are trapped.

There is not picture in Wright Mills of the resistances that men can and do offer to such pressures, no conception of the Hegelian 'negative' with all of what Hegel called its 'patience, labour and suffering'. The only independent power in human life that Wright Mills can see is the independent reason of social scientists of integrity. This kind of misconception rests not just on factual error; it rests above all on the image of human nature with which the

[21] Wright Mills, 2000, p. 168.

social scientist approaches the evidence. That Parsons from the political Right and Wright Mills from the political Left should both be submerged by the determinist image of man in testimony to its continuing strength; that Wright Mills should be so conscious of this in Parsons and so unconscious of this in himself is even more impressive testimony on the same point.

We are now in a position to frame the fundamental dilemma with which the human sciences confront us. Psychologists, sociologists and the rest, they offer us two possibilities so far as large-scale human change is concerned, so far as man's control of his own life is concerned. Either men can discern the laws which govern social development or they cannot. If they can, then they must avow that their own behaviour is subject to those laws and consequently they must admit that they have discovered themselves to be not agents, but victims, part of a social process which occurs independently of human mind, feeling and will. If they cannot discern such laws, then they are necessarily helpless, for they have no instruments of change in their hands. So that in any case human agency is bound to be ineffective. Of course, so far as small-scale adaptive changes are concerned, it may be otherwise. All sociologists leave room for reformist manoeuvre.

The important characteristic of this dilemma is that it separates understanding and action. Understanding and the lack of it are both a condition of inaction. At the heart of the concept of explanation there is the insight that we should not ever be in a position to assert that one event is the cause of another, unless we could produce the second event by means of the first and avert the second event by averting the first. Unless our activity was effective in bringing about changes we could not give causal explanations; how odd then that the concept of causal explanations should underpin a thesis which culminates in the conclusion that our activity must necessarily be impotent.

Those who swallow the oddness of this and indeed live so inside the dilemma that they cannot hope to see it as a dilemma must therefore see men either as rational subjects in an irrational world (they can frame concepts of social explanation, but cannot find application for them) or as objects in an irrational world (they can find explanations, but discover that they too are among the explained). It is scarcely surprising then that the human sciences reflect and reinforce the prevailing apathy and conformism of the intellectuals. In the first section of this essay, I pointed to the fact of this conformity; in the second it was contrasted with the intellectual and moral hope offered by the intellectuals of the Enlightenment and by Hegel and Marx. In the third section, I argued that the traditional educational norms of our culture now offered no source of strength to withstand the prevailing mood and I argued that we lacked any proper concept of human nature. Now we have seen why. In one sense, at this point in the essay, the ideology of the age has already been unveiled. At the heart of the theorising of those self-appointed therapists of our culture, the social scientists, we find precisely those ideas necessary to define and to buttress our intellectual malaise. As Herzen remarked of some of their predecessors, they see themselves as the doctors of a sick society, whereas they are in fact symptoms of its disorder.

5

Diseases know no frontiers. This is as true of intellectual as of physical disorders. If it were not so we might treat the human sciences as an infected area which could be quarantined off, rather as anxious but misinformed middle-class parents in 1930s hoped to shelter their children from Marxism by forbidding them to go to the LSE. In fact, however, there is no discipline which is not touched by our present condition. Yet the vast quantity of detailed, specialised, hard-working study by means of which academics disciplines endure is apt to conceal this. For the numerous tasks to hand distract from attention to that total picture, without the possibility of which the individual tasks would no longer have any point. And, where any sort of total picture does begin to emerge from the individual pieces of research, it seems to be just a consequence of the research, something whose acceptance is as inevitable as is the result of a chemical analysis or the dating of a document.

What picture in fact emerges? One in which the absence of a central concept of human nature and the non-historical features of the social sciences continually invade other disciplines. It might be thought paradoxical that this should be above all true of history. After all, contemporary history is strikingly different from liberal history. The descent from the Whig view of English history as freedom broadening down from precedent to precedent to H.A.L. Fisher's boast of being unable to discern any purpose or pattern in historical sequence is a tale of the past.[22] Whatever the disciples of Namier have brought into historical studies, they have brought a realism about power and a cynicism about ideals which is a change from the Whigs. All that one wonders is whether having caught the Whigs bathing they are not now merely wearing their clothes turned inside out. For history has now become the history of the arrangements of power. The Namierite attention to the day-to-day events of the rise and fall of politicians in the reign of George III, for example, works on the assumption that it is almost a work of nature that there are positions which are positions of power and influence and positions which are not. Given the ladders up and down which our rulers ascend and descend, their climbing can easily enough be described. But is it adequately described if we never ask how the ladders come to be there?

This attention to the individual cases of power-holding, power-gaining and power-losing may appear superficially to underline the activity of individuals. But because it does not raise questions of context it in fact presents the individual as hemmed in by social circumstances, always responding to external pressure and never a fully autonomous and responsible individual. Consider, for example, a recent account of the Peterloo Massacre. The government had to keep public order and rely on local information. They never willed it. The local magistrates faced what they understandably – in the context of time and place – took to be a seditious uprising. The troops were under orders from the magistrates. No individual is responsible; and since the story contains nothing but the doings of individuals there is no responsibility to be ascribed.[23] The system in which such things happen is accepted as a framework to the story in such a way that it never appears inside the narrative as a culprit. There are no culprits. When the readers of such histories report to us that ideals and aspirations have no historical leverage and that what matters is power, the reply should be that the powerlessness of ideals is written into the methodology of this sort of history from the outset.

This is the other side of the sociological coin. We have seen how Popper's rejection of the equation of social science with history reflects in sociology. Now we see what it reflects in history. With history and sociology in this state

---

[22] Fisher 1935, v. 2, p. vii.

[23] Presumably, MacIntyre is referring to Read 1958, especially Chapter 8 and pp. 207–8.

it would be strange if political theory were not similarly placed. What should we deduce that the state of political theory would have in these circumstances to be? If it reckoned with the actual state of the human sciences and history, it would have to see social development as a self-making process or tradition since men cannot consciously or rationally move it. The role of reason in this development would at best be that of understanding or recording after the event. What reason could not hope to do would be to prescribe before the event. Since it would be an illusion to suppose that reason might do this, political rationalists would be not just intellectually mistaken but politically and morally dangerous. Since political activity cannot be rationally guided, how shall it take form? The only possible answer is that it should be adaptive, a matter of knowing how to secure the safe passage of the institutions we inherit into changing circumstances with the least possible derangement and disturbance. If we were to ask for a political theory to be tailor-made to fit the state of the social sciences and history, this would have to be its content. But a tailor has anticipated our needle and already done the job and the cloths are being worn. For this is none other than the political theory of Michael Oakeshott, a theory which has certainly the merit of being self-confirming, since it is so splendidly adapted to the prevailing climate.[24] It is almost superfluous to point to the profoundly conservative and anti-revolutionary nature of this theory.

If creative, rational human activity has disappeared from the intellectual scene so thoroughly, why has it done so? The answer which I am approaching is that our social life and our intellectual vision reinforce each other. Our social life is one in which human activity is rendered uncreative and sterile. We live in a society of grooves and ladders, a society created out of human activity and which human activity could abolish. Yet it cannot be simply reasoned out of existence; reasoning can give direction to human activity, can make it effective. But there must be human activity to be informed and directed. Where is it? It is there wherever those whose lives are most made and imposed upon them, the working people in the industrial and in the colonial centres, revolt against the conditions of their life. Cut off from those revolts, and over-impressed by the reports which sociological explorers have brought back from the proletarian jungle, the intellectuals see the working class as being the most

[24] See, for example, Oakeshott 1962, especially pp. 30–6.

helpless, inactive group of all. They come from a mechanically moulded and conditioned way of life and they describe what they see in mechanised and deterministic terms. Then their own concepts blind them and those to whom they speak to there being any alternative possibilities. The vices of our lives and the errors of our concepts combine to keep both in being.

How great the intellectual pressures are may perhaps best be grasped by looking at the typical distortions to which genuinely independent thought in our culture is subjected. Probably the two greatest thinkers of our age were Freud and Wittgenstein, both of them conscious inhabitants of a fallen world who had lived through the collapse of the Austro-Hungarian Empire. Both of them thought against the intellectual climate of their time. What is interesting is the way in which each has been domesticated and rendered harmless by the spreading abroad of versions of their theorising from which all the bite has been removed.

Freud was in revolt against the mechanistic climate of the age. That he was so has been concealed by most of his expositors, not least by himself. He abandoned neuro-physiology and the search for causes of neurotic and psychotic disorders in order to connect them with motives and desires. He invented a technique whereby one could become conscious of unconscious motives and thereby free oneself from their compulsive hold. He saw in the rational comprehension of desire the path to freedom. We can free ourselves from the infantile demands which oppress, and remake ourselves. We can pass from super-ego morality to the morality of the ego-ideal. As to the content of this ideal Freud stops short; honesty, reasonableness, a care for people – having prescribed a practice of life dominated by these he does not ask how such a life could be realised against the weight of our social institutions. This, then, becomes the vulnerable point at which his interpreters are able to rewrite him back into an adaptive and deterministic setting. At the level of therapy the ideal, especially among American neo-Freudians, becomes one of 'adjustment', of fitting the individual into a social niche. At the level of theory the explanation of unconscious motivation becomes not a prelude to freedom but a prelude to explaining away social dissatisfaction as neurotic. We tread the path here from the important to the trivial, from Freud to Kingsley Amis.

When the Nazis burnt Freud's books they testified to the essential anti-fascism of his stress on rationality and freedom. The next stage is that of Koestler's novel *Arrival and Departure* where the hero discovers the roots of his anti-fascist activity in repressed guilt at a forgotten injury which he had done to his brother in childhood.[25] But at least Koestler's hero goes on as an anti-fascist. With Amis, in his Fabian Society pamphlet on *Socialism and the Intellectuals,* the watering down and misunderstanding of Freud reaches its climax. Politics is a matter of temperament; love of the established pulls you to the Right and hate of it to the Left. 'And behind that again lies perhaps your relations with your parents.'[26] No hint is here that those whose adult politics are merely patterned after their relationship with their parents need to be freed and can be freed. No hint is here that one might free oneself through social action.

Or take the case of Wittgenstein. Wittgenstein is a philosopher about whom it is hard to write without distortion. His own thoroughness, patience and integrity mean that he never elaborated views easy enough to be fitted into neat summaries. If I pick out from his though just one theme it will indicate again the type of intellectual pressure that is in question. A variety of tangles in philosophy have arisen around the view that we are able to talk about our experiences because words are names for specific experiences with which they have become associated. I know what 'red' or 'pain' means because I have seen red lights or felt pain and the words and the experiences have come to be marks which remind me of these experiences. Against this view, Wittgenstein argued that what matters is the *use* to which an experience can be put in the context of human activity, its role, point, or purpose. Consider a word like 'cow'. Norman Malcolm, expounding Wittgenstein, has commented on an imagined case where a man utters a certain sound every time that a cow appears, and said that

> ...we need to ask, what makes the latter sound a word, and what makes it the word for *cow*? Is there no difficulty here? Is it sufficient that the sound uttered when and only when cow is present? Of course not. The sound might refer to anything or nothing.

That is, it need not be a word any more than if I suffered from a nervous tick of the head every time that I saw a cow, my movement of my head would be a word. Malcolm then says of the sound in question,

---

25 Koestler 1943, pp. 116–24.
26 Amis 1957, p. 4.

> What is necessary is that it should be playing a part in various activities, in calling, fetching, counting cows, distinguishing cows from other things and pictures of cows from pictures of other things. If the word has no place in activities ('language-games') of this sort, then it isn't a word for *cow*. To be sure I can sit in my chair and talk about cows and not be engaged in any of these activities – but what makes my words *refer* to cows is in fact that I have already mastered these activities: they lie in the background.[27]

This supposition makes it clear how, for Wittgenstein, language is essentially social, essentially a matter of human activity and not at all to be understood mechanistically. It recalls Marx's assertion that 'language is practical consciousness'.[28]

Yet, in many accounts of Wittgenstein from both hostile and sympathetic viewpoints, everything has been turned upside down, Wittgenstein set out to elucidate 'ordinary language'; he is represented as having tried to argue from it. Instead of the purposive concept of 'use' we get the naturalistic concept of 'usage'. The philosopher's task is not that of understanding the standards for success in language-using: it is the bleakly conservative one of recording and classifying how we all talk anyway. Language is not something that men do and make, it becomes merely a part of the given and made environment. This sort of reinterpretation fences round Wittgenstein's thought just at the point at which it might help us to break through the prevailing miasma.

Thus in every field there has come into its own an intellectual conservatism protected against change by the alleged impossibility of change. The villain of the piece, it ought to be clear by now, is not that scapegoat so often invoked, positivism. Positivism, with its narrowed view of rationality, its acceptance of physics as the paradigm of intellectual activity, its nominalism, its atomism, its lack of hospitality to all general views of the world – positivism with all these merely recorded after the event what the intellectual landscape of our culture had become. Those who could not bear to hear what it reported fled often not from an alien force but from the mirror-image of their own minds.

---

[27] Malcolm 1954, p. 553.
[28] Marx and Engels 1975–2004b, p. 44.

6

This, then, is the ideology of apathy and conformism. It provides the ideal climate in which to disarm the intellectual and transform him into an educational technician who can safely be charged with training the social administrators of the established order. How are we to break it hold upon us? Many of the fallacies in it have been exhibited in the course of the argument, and the Hegelian and Marxist alternative has appeared to point the context from time to time. But how are we to live out that alternative in both our thinking and our action? Not by manipulation of people so that they will move in some direction that we desire, but by helping them to move where they desire. The goal is not happiness, or satisfaction, but freedom. And freedom has to be both means and end. The mechanistic separation of means and ends is suitable enough for human manipulation, not for human liberation.

This entails a decisive break with utilitarianism. Marxists have in the past crippled themselves intellectually by adapting even their Marxism to a determinist, mechanistic mould. I think here of the career of George Lukács. Lukács faced the dilemmas of bourgeois sociology as they are classically presented in the work of Max Weber and found a solution in the work of Hegel and Marx. He participated in the Hungarian Soviets of 1919 and was Minister of Education in Bela Kun's government. Then when he expounded Marxism in 1923 he came up against the mechanistic attitude of the right-wing Soviet Marxists. He recanted and allowed that he had underestimated the objective weight of historical determination and overestimated human possibility. Weighed down by the specious arguments of determinism he lived through the era of objective necessity. We must do the lesser evil for the greater good; we must use the means for that end; we must pull the levers at the trials of Bukharin, Radek and the rest to move on the machine of Soviet society. Then in 1956 when Nagy broke through the smoke-screen if the Stalinist ways of thinking, Lukács again became Minister of Education. He vindicated his philosophical work in his life.

In the social-democratic tradition too, utilitarianism has dominated and with it mechanistic modes of thought. And social democracy has been quite self-conscious in its Benthamite approach. What Benthamite utilitarianism lacked, as J.S. Mill saw at once, and what liberalism by becoming utilitarian came to lack, was any critique of satisfaction. The ultimate criterion is 'happiness' and 'happiness' is simply that state in which people are getting what they avowedly want. There is no scope within the terms of utilitarianism for criticising their preferences. So that one seems condemned if one remains within the terms of Benthamism to say that people are satisfied if they get what they think they want. And if one attempts to emerge from those confines and says that one knows what people really want (that is, in the long run, if they only had the relevant experiences) better than they do themselves, one seems bound to adopt policies which will necessarily compel and coerce people. The second course is a violation of negative freedom, the first an abdication to all the unconscious pressures which mould popular taste, and to those who are able to contrive and control such pressures. And it is the first course that classical utilitarianism adopts as its own.

It is thus the case that utilitarianism can become an instrument for removing immediate dissatisfactions rather than a doctrine of genuine reform and that it easily becomes and instrument for contriving people's good rather than for activating people themselves. J.S. Mill's characteristic doctrines on happiness and liberty point to what is absent in Benthamism rather than succeed in repairing the gaps. What matters is that the utilitarian spirit accords exactly with the changing purposes of capitalism. Dickens has remarked through the characters of Gradgrind and Bounderby how early capitalism found application for utilitarian themes; it has less often been remarked how easily the utilitarian spirit wears a Fabian dress and appears as the maximiser of common interests in the promotion of pleasure and the diminution of pain.[29] At two points the utilitarianism informs Fabianism: by setting in front of all men the common goal of the greatest happiness of the greatest number (in itself a harmless and humane slogan) it encourages the belief that there is a common interest in society. So that what is needed is an adjustment of interests. Whereas Marxists differ from Fabians in asserting that in class-divided society there is a fundamental conflict of interests; and that there can be no reconciliation of these interests. Again, utilitarianism offers to Fabianism the idea that it is

[29] Dickens 1969, pp. 48, 58: 'Thomas Gradgrind, sir. A man of realities. A man of fact and calculations. A man who proceeds upon the principle that two and two are four, and nothing over, and who is not to talked into allowing for anything over.... With a rule and a pair of scales, and the multiplication table always in his pocket, sir, ready to weigh and measure any parcel of human nature, and tell you exactly what it comes to.... Mr Bounderby was as near to being Mr Gradgrind's bosom friend, as a man perfectly devoid of sentiment can approach that spiritual relationship towards another man perfectly devoid of sentiment.'

the group of intelligent and benevolent administrators (whose native wit and training have provided them with the relevant knowledge which the masses lack) who will contrive this adjustment of interests for society.

This is precisely in the spirit of welfare capitalism. Profoundly as the interests of different under capitalism are divided, it remains the case that there is a need for this clash to be concealed, for the mask of common interest to be worn. Thus demands for social insurance, health services, and educational opportunity up to a certain limited point can express militant dissatisfaction with capitalism and yet be skilfully tamed by the capitalist administrative machine. Bismarck was a pioneer here and the Fabian tradition is uncomfortably close to Bismarck.

The breakthrough comes from awakening what Marx called self-activity. The dissatisfaction with the established order, which is that awakening, appears spontaneously at many points in our society. But it is too often allowed to die or is discouraged; or – if sufficiently militant a specimen of working-class activity – receives direct hostility. Our deep need is instead to provide all the growing points of human activity against the present social order with coherent theoretical expression, so that they may be rationally guided and effective. What is necessary for the intellectual is to accept his responsibilities for this, both in the working-class movement and to those for whom he is profoundly responsible.

Anyone who has taught in a university since the war has seen three phases of student life. There was the ex-service generation, for whom many of the causes and motives of the thirties remained alive. Their maturity and experience have been remarked on often enough. What gave to that maturity its edge was a sense of the enormous possibilities that the war had opened up, possibilities which were gradually to disappear in the Cold-War climate. The next generation were essentially the children of the war and Cold War, their younger days surrounded by consciousness of shortage and uncertainty, their adolescence presented with the newly made careerism of welfare capitalism. They were the non-political, the non-anything, the universities' gift to Lord Hailsham. For they were conservatives in the profound sense that they accepted the environment as *given*: all that they had to do was to find a suitably sheltered niche. But this started to change as the fifties wore on and it ended in 1956 not with a whimper but a bang. The twin crimes of Suez and Hungary, the premeditated crime of nuclear warfare, and moreover the apparent deadness and dull cynicism of official politicians in the face of these things – these launched students along with other adolescents into the world of political questions.

Of political questions, not of political answers. All that tremendous adolescent energy, which the very rawness of the emotion makes so impressive, is still looking for intellectual satisfaction at the political level. If no coherent answers are found, then as the student generations pass on they will become all the more frustrated and disillusioned for having been so hopeful in the past. And this is what the reactionaries hope for. 'I was a socialist when I was young, too.' The unspoken completion of this – 'How good to grow middle-aged, conservative and self-satisfied like me' – points to the danger: the silting up of the poetry of adolescence into the prose of bourgeois middle age. All the pressures are there: the need to get a job, to succeed in it, to bring up a family, to pay for a house. Not to succumb to these the feeling and the questioning must find a theory and a way of life which will transmute the poetry of adolescence into continuous life-long activity.

Two images have been with me throughout the writing of this essay. Between them they seem to show the alternative paths for the intellectual. The one is of J.M. Keynes, the other of Leon Trotsky. Both were obviously men of attractive personality and great natural gifts. The one the intellectual guardian of the established order, providing new policies and theories of manipulation to keep society in what he took to be economic trim, and making a personal fortune in the process. The other, outcast as a revolutionary from Russia both under the Tsar and under Stalin, providing throughout his life a defence of human activity, of the powers of conscious and rational human effort. I think of them at the end, Keynes with his peerage, Trotsky with an icepick in his skull. These are the twin lives between which intellectual choice in our society lies.

7

The philosophers have continued to interpret the world differently; the point remains, to change it.[30]

---

[30] Marx 1975c, p. 423: 'The philosophers have only *interpreted* the world, in various ways; the point is to *change* it.'

Chapter Fifteen

Is a Neutralist Foreign Policy Possible?[1]

What weighs most heavily against unilateralism with those willing to consider its claims seriously is that it appears to be a demand without a context, a demand isolated from other questions of policy. The jockeying in the Labour Party which has followed upon the Scarborough decision has revealed the danger of this very clearly. Even those willing to accept Conference demands seem determined to interpret unilateralism in such a way that if it were implemented the arrangements of international power should be as little disturbed as possible. It so happens that technical developments in the field of nuclear weapons make this an easy task. The existence of Polaris missiles already makes Britain a less important aircraft-carrier than she was. In two years, Britain will be an obsolete component in the American defence system. Britain's contribution to NATO will then be compatible with the renunciation not only of the independent deterrent but also of any British-based American missiles. Moreover, the same developments will change the function of all America's satellites. They will become a conveniently placed set of buffer states that will no longer be required for possible offensive purposes.

[1] Originally published in *International Socialism*, First Series, 3, Winter 1960–1, p. 26.

Thus a Britain which demanded that the defensive aspects of NATO should be emphasised rather than the aggressive would fit easily into a necessary and prudent realignment of American policy.

The danger is then that unilateralism is reinterpreted by such Labour leaders as Harold Wilson until it becomes compatible with what CND has already declared to be incompatible, the NATO alliance. Socialists therefore have a responsibility to elaborate a foreign policy which will express an authentic break with present policy. There are, of course, unilateralists who have already done this but on whose policies we need scarcely waste printing ink. The Communist Party wants to create at best a passive satellite, at worst a non-combatant opponent for the Soviet Union. Other socialists content themselves with insisting that the abolition of the bomb is part of the abolition of capitalism, a truism that enables them to avoid the difficult and specific questions of foreign policy. The most serious restatement of such policy has in fact been made on the New Left by E.P. Thompson, John Rex and others.[2] It is about some features of the kind of policy which writers such as those have elaborated that questions ought to be raised.

There are generally three elements in such a policy. The first is the notion of Britain as strengthening and partly leading a Third Force of the uncommitted nations, especially the Afro-Asian powers. The second is the notion of the United Nations as a viable instrument for such a Third Force not merely to express and advocate but actually to enact its policies. The third is the notion of such action as relaxing tension and bringing about controlled multilateral disarmament of the two major world blocks. What this policy shares both with Mr Cousins and with Mr Gaitskell is the view that international politics is a matter of the conflict of nations rather that of the conflict of classes. It is in the light of this shared assumption that the questions about 'positive neutralism' of this kind must be framed.

To the view of Britain as leading a Third Force the objection must be raised that the colonial revolution divides Britain from those states which on this view she should aspire to lead. To this it can be said that positive neutralism demands a Britain committed to support for the African revolution. But this is not a homogeneous affair. And, in any case, such a commitment would make

[2] See, for example, Thompson 1958, pp. 50–1.

a radical break with all Labour Party colonial policy. Britain's trading patterns would have to change to at least some extent and this requires a more radical internal change of economic policy. Perhaps this chain reaction could occur. But we need, as a first task, to become more precise about this possibility.

Secondly, the experience of the Congo certainly does not speak unambiguously for the possible independence of United Nations action. It is very sad that Mr Khrushchev's inadequate tactical sense should have helped to conceal how true the Soviet Union's accusations against Mr Hammarsköld were. The original resolution on which the UN force entered the Congo was simply defied. The action of the African states with their extremely opportunist swinging to and fro raises parallel doubts about the United Nations and the third force.

Thirdly, where we have had apparently independent political action it has been because the US and the USSR have been in a tense position where neither dared to move forward. In such positions, UN action has left American and Russian policy untouched. Such policy appears more responsive to internal pressures than to world events.

Fourthly, the absence of China from the United Nations has to an unknown extent made the United Nations a scene of negotiations when it might have been one of much more continuous bitter acrimony. The conflicts of East and West have simply not been exposed to the full in the UN because the Chinese have not been there to expose them.

These are questions which it may be possible to answer. But until they have been answered at length or an alternative policy has been proposed the statement of the unilateralist case is greatly weakened.

Chapter Sixteen

The Man Who Answered the Irish Question[1]

A Review of C. Desmond Greaves, The Life and Times of James Connolly

Mr Greaves has given us one of the books which was waiting to be written about James Connolly and has made a fine, scholarly job of it. Those who have a picture of Communist scholarship as partisan, falsifying, careless of fact could not do better than read Mr. Greaves. Here is enormous and scrupulous care over every detail of fact. We need no longer to puzzle over the dates or the places of Connolly's different activities. All the evidence has now been set out for us, all the conclusions are fairly drawn. Except the political ones. The field for a political biography of Connolly remains open and the need is urgent. For Mr. Greaves's book is a monument of bourgeois objectivism. On the one side there are the facts; on the other there are the political judgements. And this separation of factual material from political judgement means that, in these pages, Connolly is a dead man. The organic development of his thought is obliterated. His life is a mere chronicle of activity.

If Mr. Greaves's book had only brought Connolly to life it would have shown up all those who prefer him dead. The politicians of Fianna Fail, Fine Gael and

[1] Originally published in *New Left Review*, I, 8, March–April 1961, pp. 66–7.

the Labour Party in the Irish Republic, for example. They would like to forget what they dare not teach their own school-children, that the greatest founder of the Republic was a Marxist. But the majority of present-day Marxists are not that fond of Connolly either, for he was a syndicalist and a democrat. There has never been a revolutionary further away from elitism. To try to judge Connolly by the standards of Leninism, as Mr. Greaves does, is to miss the point, both by being unhistorical, and thus wronging Lenin as well as Connolly, and also by not seeing that Connolly's teaching provides some of the material for a critique of Leninism.

Who was Connolly?

'Who *was* Connolly anyway?' the English readers of *New Left Review* will be crying by now and although I hate to have to tell them, the circulation of *NLR* in Dublin and Donegal is probably not high enough to justify leaving this bit out. Connolly, like many other Irish nationalists (such as Parnell and Patrick Pearse) had strong non-Irish connections. He was born in Edinburgh in 1868. It was around 1890 that he learnt his socialism from the small group of SSF (Scottish Socialist Federation) and ILP members in Edinburgh. Invited to Dublin as a socialist organiser, he set himself the task of giving a socialist content to the Irish national movement:

> If you remove the English army tomorrow and hoist the green flag over Dublin Castle, unless you set about the organisation of the socialist republic, your efforts would be in vain. England would still rule you. She would rule you through her capitalists, through her landlords, through her financiers.[2]

When Connolly went to the United states, he joined Daniel De Leon's Socialist Party and was a founder of the International Workers of the World, the 'one big union' of the songs. The arguments with De Leon and others led him to formulate slowly a Marxism with which he later analysed Irish history and politics. Connolly, like Marx himself, has no conception of the vanguard party. He would have agreed with Marx in seeing the essential *political* movement being that of the class as a whole and the party as merely an expression of the class. The transition is from the trade-union movement concerned with

[2] Quoted in Greaves 1976, p. 85. See also Connolly 1987, v. 1, p. 307.

purely isolated economic issues to the trade-union movement concerned with the political issue of class power. This transition did not take place for Connolly merely in thought. What he thought as a syndicalist in the USA he did as a socialist trade union organiser in Ireland. The political action of the Easter Rising in 1916 would not have occurred without the Citizen Army. And the Citizen Army was in part members of the Irish Transport Workers Union with guns in their hands. They learnt to take up arms as a result of their experience with the police in the great lock-out of 1913. So from trade unionism of a militant order political action was born.

Just as Connolly never knew the vanguard party, so he would never have recognised the idea that the middle-class intellectual is a necessary element in the vanguard. Connolly was that rare thing, a working-class intellectual. As such he knew the potentialities of workers. The working class (pace Kautsky, Lenin, Wright Mills and some readers of *NLR*) goes out under its own leaders. The middle-class intellectual has no privileges in the movement.

What of the Easter Rising? Lenin wrote that: 'The misfortune of the Irish was that they rose prematurely when the European revolt of the proletariat had not yet matured.'[3] If the Irish had waited for that – they would still be waiting. When Connolly was going out to the Rising, he said: 'We are going out to be slaughtered.'[4] Was it then just romanticism? No, it was action to change consciousness. It showed that just over 800 men could shake British rule. It produced a new sense of possibility in Ireland that bore fruit for the Republican Army in 1918 and afterwards. The Easter Rising reminds us how people have to be delivered not just from their oppressors, but from their own inability to believe in the possibility of liberation.

But the Republic failed? One looks at the mean-spirited men who rule over Ireland's poverty today and thinks:

> Was it for this the wild geese spread
> The grey wing upon every tide,
> For this that all that blood was shed...?[5]

---

[3] Lenin 1960–70f, p. 358.
[4] Greaves 1976, p. 410.
[5] Yeats 1986, p. 335. Yeats continues: 'For this Edward Fitzgerald died/And Robert Emmet and Wolfe Tone/All that delirium of the brave?/Romantic Ireland's dead and gone/It's with O'Leary in the grave.'

Yet, the National Progressive Democrats, Ireland's new socialist party, has two deputies in the Dail (and under fifty members in the country) and even out in the countryside they are beginning to talk about socialism. The students, especially in Trinity, are moving. Connolly could never have forgiven a piece about him that did not look to the present and the future. When Ireland rises again it will speak with Connolly's voice.

Chapter Seventeen

Culture and Revolution[1]

A Review of Raymond Williams, Culture and Society, 1780–1950 and The Long Revolution

Hegel said that the function of philosophy was to make man at home in the world.[2] The effect of a good deal of socialist theorising is almost the opposite. The categories of thought are often so alien to the detail of everyday experience that theory becomes not a kind of insight, but a kind of blindness, and a blindness almost deliberate and willed. On the one hand, there is the fabric of life at work and in the family, the worries about children and schooling, the pub and the trade-union branch, housing and money and holidays. On the other hand, there is some imposed abstract political scheme, a mechanical rendering of Marx's view of history or, worse still, of Lenin

---

[1] Originally published in *International Socialism*, First Series, 5, Summer 1961, p. 28.

[2] Hegel nowhere states this directly, but it is implied in several passages. See Hegel 1952, pp. 6, 7. 'To recognise reason as the rose in the cross of the present and therefore to enjoy the present, this is the rational insight, which reconciles us to the actual, the reconciliation which philosophy affords to those in whom there has at once arisen an inner voice bidding them to comprehend, not only to dwell in what substantive while still retaining subjective freedom, but also to posses subjective freedom while standing not in anything particular and accidental but in what exists absolutely.... Just as reason is not content with an approximation which, as something "neither hot nor cold" it will "spew out of its mouth", so it is just as little content with the cold despair which submits the view that in this earthly life things are truly bad or at best only tolerable, though here they cannot be improved and that this is the only reflection which can keep us at peace with the world. There is less chill in the peace with the world which knowledge supplies.'

or the Fabians. These, coexisting in a single mind, produce in turn theoretical sterility and frustration, a violent refusal to face the complexity of thought and temporary relief in the substitution of easy slogans and formulas for well-founded conclusions.

Raymond Williams has done more than any other writer to liberate us from this. His novel, *Border Country*, makes it plain why he was so well equipped for the task. For those who have traversed in their own lives the journey between working-class and university life, or between Wales and England, the felt experience is a movement towards and not away from theorising.[3] To travel in class and in place is also to travel in time through the social strata laid down at different periods in the past hundred years. One can be forced to ask for a view of history because one discovers that one is oneself what the past has made one. All of Raymond Williams's work is touched with an entirely admirable and unobtrusive self-consciousness of this kind.

This personal quality is linked to a method of approach which in one respect at least promises well. Williams approaches social change through thought about social change. In *Culture and Society* he discusses the variety of descriptions which people have offered in theories, in novels, in polemical tracts and literary criticism, of social changes since the industrial revolution. This, as *The Long Revolution* makes clear, is not a substitute for describing such change itself. But the changes did not happen, did not exist, except as an incarnation of human purposes and projects, and we do not know what men were doing who contrived these changes unless we know how they envisaged them. The cultural images which men throw up are a first attempt at a history of human action in their time; but even before that they themselves are also part, and the articulate, conscious part, of the change which such history aspires to describe. We cannot describe a period first in our terms and then ask how good contemporaries were at describing it; for we do not know what they were doing unless we know how they described it. It is in the incoherences of such descriptions that we discover the key to the difference between the true story and the story as told. So Marx began not by going straight to capitalism and measuring up his own description of capitalism against that of classical political economy. He began with the classical economists, whom he treated

---

[3] Williams 1960.

as the voice of capitalist society, and only later pierced through the veil of half-understanding with which capitalism protects itself.

The danger of such an approach is that by accepting the terms in which a culture makes itself articulate we become imprisoned within those terms and unable to transcend them. This danger is particularly acute when the culture we study is that of our own age or the recent past. For then we cannot get outside ourselves unless we *already* possess a theoretical background of the kind which Marxism aspires to provide. I do not mean, of course, that Marxism enables us to leave our skins: but it suggests that we can find a standpoint to judge what we are by what we can be. Marxism brings contemporary possibility on to the stage in order to pass judgment upon contemporary actuality.

Although Williams is not a Marxist, he escapes imprisonment by the present in *Culture and Society* because he brings together such a host of conflicting witnesses that no one conceptual scheme dominates us. Cobbett, Mill, Disraeli, Gissing, Lawrence, Tawney and many others all contribute to a growing, if contradictory, consciousness of the possibility of a common culture. But, in *The Long Revolution*, where the question is asked how far that possibility has in fact been realised, the situation is much worse. Put briefly, Williams accepts as authentic the unity of our society and his long revolution is a revolution against nothing except the inertia of the past. The false consciousness of gradualism is allowed to be judged in its own terms.

This comes out clearly in Williams's essay on the individual and society, where the beginnings of a good discussion never come to fruition because Williams does not allow for the fact that particular framings of the antithesis always took place in a context of specific institutions. To place what Williams says about Freud in the context of the situation of the intelligentsia in the decline of the Austro-Hungarian Empire or Williams's metaphors of vagrancy and exile in relation to actual vagrancy and actual exiles would be to transform his discussion.[4] The result of Williams's abstraction is a loss of tension. We escape the fact that every individual exists at a point where life is a conflict between his unrealised potentialities and the barriers which confront their realisation. We are defined both by what we can be and by what we have to struggle against. Every form of class society up to our own has been at once a release of and an inhibition of human possibility. In our society class is wholly

4 Williams 1965, pp. 95–7, 107–10.

inhibiting. Or so at least the Marxist argues, Williams never confronts this thesis. Instead of the splendid, tentative discussion of Marxism and literature in *Culture and Society* we get in *The Long Revolution* a presentation of Marxism as the ghost of a theory in which most of human life is omitted.[5]

What Williams himself omits is three-fold: work, class, power. This is not to say that in occasional paragraphs their importance is not recognised. But these lonely banners of traditional socialism are never integrated into the book. Instead of class consciousness, we get as the subject of this book far too often an unidentified 'we'. Instead of work and its organisation we get 'the concept of the market'.[6] Instead of power we get public opinion. And the whole argument is weakened by its insularity. Capitalism never appears on the scene properly because no world movement appears there as such. British development is treated as though autonomous.

There have been since the Industrial Revolution in Britain two main critiques of our form of life. One was the romantic protest against capitalist ugliness whose culmination is in Lawrence and Leavis. The other was the socialist protest. William Morris held them together in his own day: it is a prime victory of bourgeois ideology to have kept them apart ever since. Raymond Williams has done more than anyone else to bring them together again. But, so far, at the key points in his writings the argument always breaks down. I have not begun to do justice to the richness of the books: but it is clear from *The Long Revolution* that unless Williams can learn from Marx what Morris learnt he will continue to disappoint as well as to teach.

---

[5] Williams 1961, Part 3, Chapter 5, 'Marxism and Culture'.
[6] Williams 1965, pp. 124–5.

Chapter Eighteen

Marxists and Christians[1]

It is an interesting paradox that large statements of doctrine are more usually aimed at heresies amongst one's own adherents than at those who hold other doctrines. This is true not only of Christians. The recent papal encyclical on politics was aimed at casing and accommodating Christian socialists rather than at setting out a polemic against Marxists. Similarly the recent Soviet encyclical on communism addressed itself only to those who already accepted the basic premises of Soviet orthodoxy. More than this, the tendency to official peaceful co-existence is present in both documents. The papal document affirms its own positions rather than denies those of what the English translation of an earlier encyclical called 'Atheistic Communism'. And there have been Marxists who would have stressed in their

---

1 Originally published in *Twentieth Century* 170, Autumn 1961, pp. 28–37. The original article contained the following introductory passage by the editors: 'Outside Britain in the 1960s, a huge section of the world has been changed and is still changing under the impact of Marxism, while Christianity is (relatively speaking) in retreat. Inside Britain, as Alasdair MacIntyre says, Christianity has become "more respectable than ever" and Marxism "more disreputable". Is it possible to be both a Christian and a Marxist? Here the question is discussed by a leading young philosopher, who – after teaching philosophy at Manchester and Leeds – goes to Nuffield College, Oxford this autumn as Research Fellow. Alasdair MacIntyre sums up his own standpoint for us: "Was a Christian. Am not. It is less misleading when asked if I am a Marxist to say 'yes' rather than 'no'. But other Marxists have been known to say 'no'."

description of the coming state of communism the withering away of religion. The Soviet document notably does not.

Yet if the discussion appears lifeless at the level of official exchanges between the not always Christian bureaucracy of the Vatican and the much more dubiously Marxist bureaucracy of the Kremlin, it is even more difficult to arouse interest in this debate at what one may call local level. What makes it difficult to discuss Christianity and Marxism in the British 1960s is that the one has become more respectable than ever, the other more disreputable. To be a Marxist in our society is to be a member of a tiny isolated minority; to be a Christian is to be part of the at present rising wave of bourgeois piety. Where, in the 1930s and 1940s, Christian students in British universities would have been pushed by circumstance into confrontation with Marxism, today pietism and ecclesiasticism absorb them more and more. The Communist Party exerts an attraction on few people of any kind and where Christians encounter it today it is likely to be in the guise of a public relations firm in the service of Khrushchev Enterprises Inc. Other Marxist groupings are usually numerically insignificant. When Marx is discussed in universities or schools it is normally a subject for academic refutation. The Christianity of the 1960s has a quality of complacent self-sufficiency that does not seem to destine it for painful encounters and the Marxism of the 1960s is unlikely to make an immediate impact on anybody, at least in Britain.

This framework of deep pessimism about the whole enterprise is a necessary starting-point. Otherwise anything more positive that I have to say will appear out of proportion. What I want to do is first to characterise the kind of dialogue that might go on between Christians and Marxists in the 1960s at occasional moments in odd places. I then want to look at the problems for Christianity that *might* be created by this dialogue. But I have to say *might*. And, in so far as this discussion is important, it is not just for people who wear the official labels, who think of themselves as Christians or Marxists. The Christianity of Pasternak (so different from that of the bishops) and the Marxism of Brecht (so different from that of his bishops) infect the consciousness of many people who will think themselves quite alien to this dialogue. But it will cast its shadows in their minds.

Can one be both Christian and Marxist? The first cynical, but historically vindicated answer, is that one can be Christian and anything. In the Cold War, as in almost all hot wars, Christians were on both sides. So rephrase the question. Can one be both consistently Christian and consistently Marxist? Here the answer that I want to suggest is that Marxism and Christianity are most obviously incompatible when Christianity is given an explicit political interpretation and most notably akin in areas that are at one remove from political action.

The first fact that Marxists have to face about Christianity is that it is politically ambiguous. Ever since in England the sufferings of King Charles I were likened to those of Christ the King at the same time as the Levellers were preparing to institute Christ's kingdom understood in a very different sense, it has been clear that Christianity admitted both of radical and of conservative interpretations. Marxism is at odds with both. The radical utopian strain in Christian politics is suspect for Marxists just because it is utopian. By utopian Christians I mean those who believe that the Kingdom of Heaven can be domesticated upon the earth forthwith. For such Christians, politics is a matter of an immediate and radical break with the existing order. Individuals or communities attempt to sell all they have and live without material possessions; they refuse military service and espouse non-violence. With varying degrees of eccentricity, they establish new forms of community, or new political movements. The essence of this type of politics is the belief that Christianity can be incarnated in a programme which can be applied forthwith to the solution of political problems.

Marxists may often sympathise with such movements, especially when they belong to the past. And Marxists do not usually fail to applaud genuine radical charity of a kind which does not attempt to be a substitute for political change. Consider the very high regard in which Danilo Dolci's work is held by them (as it certainly ought to be).[2] What they castigate in Christian utopianism is what this has in common with other forms of utopianism, its escapism and its lack of insight into the means of social change. Utopianism is escapist because, in societies where large-scale transformation is in fact impossible, it contents itself with creating small pockets of change, which cannot in any case hope to survive. Because it concentrates on this, it fails to accept responsibility for the slow, patient tasks of large-scale transformation.

---

[2] See, for example, Dolci 1965.

This is not why most Christians reject Christian utopianism. They have done so because they have seen Christianity as scarcely politics at all. The powers that be are ordained of God; one must make one's peace with them except when they persecute the church or force it into obviously un-Christian acts.) Otherwise the Christian is indistinguishable from the good citizen. This is the starting-point for a much more influential doctrine than Christian utopianism, Christian conservatism. On the conservative view, the Kingdom of God belongs not to belief in God or disbelief in God as a mere intellectual mistake. For Marxists, belief in God is a characteristic 'mystification' functioning to conceal the realities of nature and society. Just as Christians do not see belief in God as a belief in just one more being additional to other beings, so Marxists see belief in God as a distortion of our total vision. In having an overall view of the world, both Marxists and Christians find themselves at odds with liberal empiricists. Again, for liberal empiricism, fact is one thing and value is another. Discovering what sort of place the world is and deciding how to act in it are two quite distinct and separate tasks. Here again there is an insistence on the unity of theory and practice by Christians and Marxists (even if in different senses of those much abused terms) which does violence to the most fundamental categories of the liberal mind. More than this, both Christianity and Marxism insist upon trying to make people aware of their cosmic and social situation, on trying to make people transcend the horizons of private life. Adolescents are always more open than others to this insistence; the adult life of our society is built on the premise that most people cannot hope to understand, far less to change, the social universe.

I have suggested that the trouble for Christianity in the 1960s (from a Marxist point of view) is likely to derive from the fact that Christians inherit from their past values which cannot be realised within the structure of capitalism. Some of these values are ascetic ones which are purely religious and are also alien to Marxism. Others are akin to values of Socialism. 'The history of early Christianity', wrote Engels:

> ...has many characteristic points of contact with the present labour movement. Like the latter, Christianity was at first a movement of the oppressed; it began as a religion of the slaves and the freed, the poor and outlawed, of the peoples defeated and crushed by the force of Rome. Both

> Christianity and Proletarian Socialism preach the coming deliverance from slavery and poverty...[3]

Engels saw the key difference in the other-worldliness of Christianity. But Kautsky, rightly or wrongly, saw Christianity as itself originally concerned with an earthly deliverance:

> The liberation from poverty which Christianity declared was at first thought of quite realistically. It was to take place in the world and not in Heaven.[4]

Only later was Christianity perverted by other-worldliness. This strain of political radicalism is usually evoked to some degree by unjust social orders and is likely to be evoked in the 1960s. But the strain for Christians, especially younger Christians, will arise when they find Christianity once again blessing the established social forms. Although the affluent society can afford other and more expensive opiates, it will contrive to find Christianity indispensable.

One reason for this is that our social structure will generate in individuals deep anxiety about status. Another more important one is that to celebrate the great movements of birth and death and marriage there are no rituals but those of religion. Only religion seems to give meaning to those occasions which are felt to be important. In Christianity there are cases of symbolism imperfectly comprehended in which the undernourished imagination can find refreshment. Moreover, Christianity provides some release from the sense of helplessness which is so widespread. Every few months, the world seems liable to nuclear destruction; the social units are so large as to be clearly out of control; all the conquests of space by science often deepen the individual's sense of insignificance. The very simple need to believe in a loving father outside whose care not a sparrow, not a fundamental particle, perishes is unlikely to die. But because the rift between the symbolism of Christianity

---

[3] Engels, London 1975–2004e, p. 445: 'The history of early Christianity has notable points of resemblance with the modern working-class movement. Like the latter, Christianity was originally a movement of oppressed people: it first appeared as the religion of slaves and emancipated slaves, of poor people deprived of all rights, of peoples subjugated or dispersed by Rome. Both Christianity and the workers' socialism preach forthcoming salvation from bondage and misery'.

[4] Kautsky, n.d., p. 463: 'On the other hand, the liberation from misery proclaimed by Christianity was at first quite material, to be realised on this earth, not in Heaven.'

and the social structure is now so great the individual's helplessness will in fact be increased. His resort to religion will console him at the cost of leaving him understanding still less. For so long as he believes he is helpless, he grasps something important about himself, a small first step towards ending his helplessness. Whereas a religious belief that he is helpless only in an earthly sense deprives him of the stimulus to look further.

At the same time, the assimilation of the church to the social order means that churchmen for the most part passively reflect the dominant values. Where one does find social protest, it is always neatly balanced by the presence in the church of defenders of the *status quo*. The vast mass of church members are unradical middle-class people. Thus the church milieu in which the Christian lives and the motives which lead people to the church will be socially conservative. This will intensify the strain upon those Christians whose values do lead them into conflict with the existing order, especially young Christians. What sort of question will confront them?

From time to time issues arise such as that of apartheid or those raised by the Campaign for Nuclear Disarmament. Christians find themselves working side by side with Marxists and other non-Christians on a basis of deep agreement. On the same issues they find themselves divided from many of their fellow Christians in the profoundest way. This is bound to raise for them the question of how and why different people in the community take up different attitudes. They are bound, if they are serious, to become aware of the psychological and sociological roots of such attitudes. If they look back to the struggle of the seventeenth century they will find religious motivations omnipresent and extremely powerful. If they look at the twentieth again they will find religious motivations restricted to a minority anyway and not always very strong there. They will be forced to enquire about the nature of the change from one society to another and the nature of the society in which the contemporary church lives. Above all, they will begin to provide sociological explanations of facts which they have been brought up to hear theologically explained.

Someone is bound to say at this point that to give sociological (or biological or physical) explanations is in no way incompatible with giving theological explanations. Divine creation is not a rival explanation to natural selection, and divine vocation is not an alternative which excludes social rôle. But this is a dangerous defence for religion, if applied too generally. Upon the matter of the possible use of the H-bomb, as to whether it would ever be permissible to use it or not, one would expect a divinely inspired morality to be clear. And if it is not clear, is it sin that clouds the minds of Christians or what? Or does sin cloud the minds of those who take one view but not of those who take the other? Or what? I think asking these questions reveal very clearly that the moral situation and the motivation of Christians is the same as that of everybody else. And then what of grace and guidance?

What I am arguing is that participation in those political and social movements into which their Christianity will help to push some more radical members of the church will raise for these people just the questions which may lead them out of the church in a Marxist direction.

One additional reason for thinking that this might happen is that something not too unlike this path was taken by the founders of Marxism. Engels had a pietist evangelical background; Marx's school essays on religion still survive. They are warmly eulogistic of what Marx took to be Christianity. The secularised Christianity of Feuerbach was a bridge for both of them to their later positions. The category of 'alienation' was precisely that by which the young Marx passed from quasi-theological to quasi-sociological explanations. Its original Hegelian use in which it stands for the rupture between finite and Absolute Spirit makes it almost a pseudonym for 'original sin'. Its later Marxist use makes it descriptive of certain types of economic activity.

The religious dimension in Marxism survived to Marxism's detriment and helped to shape the forms of its corruption. Bukharin noted that: 'One of the most widespread forms of ideological class-struggle against Marxism is its treatment as an eschatological doctrine, with all its accompaniments of chiliasm, of soteriology, of myth.'[5] In fact, of course, in its attitude to heresy and orthodoxy, in its ecclesiology of the party, and in its apotheosis of Stalin, Soviet Marxism revealed the recurrence of religious patterns. (I do not mean this to be taken as an *explanation* of Stalinism.) And those Marxists who broke with Stalinism have been divided into those who retained the religious element in their Stalinism but merely changed their religion, and those who had to embark on a new criticism of a religion of which they had long thought themselves free.

---

[5] Bukharin 1935, p. 3.

It will be objected to this whole discussion that I have talked about the possible effect of Marxism on Christians but not *vice versa*. There is a good reason for this over and above my own standpoint. The history of Marxism over the past years is so defaced by crimes and betrayals that anyone who is not yet disillusioned with Marxism is unlikely to be so in the near future. Marxists will remain few in number. Christians are much more numerous and this fact alone makes it probable that the very small traffic between the two doctrines will be largely one way.

> 'Let's hope.'
> 'You might pray,' I laughed.
> 'Never does me any good. I've never gotten anything I prayed for. Have you?'
> 'Oh, yes.'
> 'Oh, rot,' said Brett. 'Maybe it works for some people, though.'
> 'You don't look very religious, Jake.'
> 'I'm pretty religious.'
> 'Oh, rot', said Brett. 'Don't start proselytising today. Today's going to be bad enough as it is.' (Ernest Hemingway)[6]

[6] Hemingway 1976, p. 174.

Chapter Nineteen

Rejoinder to Left Reformism[1]

I

It was important that the discussion on reformism should be reopened and that it should be done as well as Henry Collins has done it.[2] Collins puts the case for contemporary left reformism with all the lucidity with which Bernstein put the case for left reformism (and we forget too easily that Bernstein was a *left* reformist) in his own time. This continuing reformist argument matters for at least two reasons. First, reformism is not just a set of arguments held by political opponents; it is the ideological air we breathe. We take in the concepts of reformism in all the transactions of daily life. To combat it is to combat a tendency which constantly arises inside us as well as in our opponents. Secondly, would-be Marxist thinking on this topic is dominated by a stereotype which constantly deadens the discussion. This stereotype consists of a mock battle between an inaccurate version of Bernstein and a misleadingly selective version of Lenin. The chosen battlefield is usually 'the nature of the state' or 'the role of the party'. I shall return to this mock battle at the end of the argument in order to contrast and oppose the

---

[1] Originally published in *International Socialism*, First Series, 6, Autumn 1961, pp. 20–3.

[2] Collins 1961.

revolution which is the concern of Marxist theory with the 'revolution' which figures in this mock-battle. But for the moment I am concerned to quarrel more with what the reformism of the stereotype has in common with the revolutionism of the stereotype than with what separates them, that is with the economic basis from which they start. For this is reproduced in Collins's argument.

What is Collins's theoretical structure? Since he never states it, it has to be deduced from his arguments on particular issues and I shall risk being unfair. But, unless it is stated clearly, what is at stake will remain obscure. I want to pick out five features of his argument, which together suggest a general theory of contemporary society. First, the premises of his argument are economic. The basic diagram with which he analyses capitalism is one in which political activity may modify or check the workings of an economic system which is a law to itself unless so checked. This economic system is described in partial abstraction from the activity of and the effects upon the people whose social relations *are* capitalism. In particular, *beliefs* about the system are not pictured as playing a role inside the system. (One would never guess from Collins that Marx's starting point was the critique of bourgeois political economy or that Marx's revolutionary standpoint was advanced before the specific economic analyses of *Capital* were elaborated.)

When beliefs enter Collins's picture, whether the beliefs of capitalists about capitalism or those of Collins or those of Marxists, they appear as external to the system described. So it was with Bernstein too. The basic difference from Marx is about the relation of beliefs to social systems. Because beliefs are external to the system, the politics which impinge on the economy also appears as external to the economy, for the social link between economic activity and political action can never be brought into the picture. For Collins, Marxism is an economics and a politics, not – what it really is – a sociology of a peculiarly philosophical bent.

Secondly, in the economic diagram a key idea which Collins takes over from the Lenin v. Bernstein stereotype is that of 'the limit'. This is the notion that capitalism can survive so long as it can expand; and that it can expand so long as it can find markets. But markets are limited and when the limit is reached, capitalism must become crisis-ridden to the point of extinction. The question which reformists continually put is whether in fact Marx was not profoundly mistaken as to where the limits of capitalist expansion lie.

Monopolistic foresight and control, imperialism, technological expansion, the permanent war economy: some or all of these have at different times been offered as temporary panaceas for capitalism, means of pushing the limit back. But, in fact, this whole concept of 'the limit' is thoroughly misleading. The limitations of capitalist production are built into the system *from the outset*; they are not something which is only reached at a certain point. How those limitations appear differs with different stages of expansion. But there is no particular point fixed in advance at which capitalism must break down. This is why Marx *both* maintains the existence of long-term trends in capitalism *and* yet refuses to have iron laws or iron theories about slumps. The slump as the 'limit' of capitalism is not a concept known to Marx. This is one reason (among many others) for the quite different emphasis in the economics of Marx and the economics of Varga.

Thirdly, the state in Collins's argument is essentially the state as it appeared in the stereotype, an executive and legislative power distinct from, even if controlled by the capitalist class. So Collins can see the working class as able to exert pressure on a state which so controls the economy that the capitalists cease to dominate. Thus he is in the odd position of allowing for fundamental changes in the economic structure of capitalism (for his economic argument requires this just as much as mine does), but refusing to allow for corresponding political changes. Yet, if the role of the state in the economy is even no more extensive than Collins concedes, it needs to be argued and not just asserted that *this* type of state is amenable to pressure from the working-class and is able to control the economy.

Fourthly, there is nothing in Collins's argument about *who* will make socialism or about *why* they will make it. Trotsky's emphasis that socialism can only be built consciously and Lenin's that it cannot be built by a minority, a party, together entail that a pre-condition of socialism is a mass socialist consciousness. In Collins we find references to 'working-class pressure' and to 'constant labour and democratic pressure'.[3] Even if we overlook the imprecision of the word 'pressure', questions about the source of these pressures remain. Where are they to come from? How is the socialist consciousness behind them to be created? This void in Collins's argument is a

[3] Collins 1961, p. 19.

counterpart to his silence about what he means by 'socialism'. For the question of *how* socialism could come about cannot be derived from the question of *what* it is to be. And the revolutionary case is in part that nothing worth calling socialism *could* come into being by reformist methods. The structure of Collins's argument is then simply this. The capitalist economy in Britain can survive all purely economic strains; the bourgeois state can survive many political strains. But the pressure from without of the Communist world and from within of the labour movement will gradually ease Britain into an undefined socialism.

This brings us to the fifth feature of Collins's theoretical outlook. The C[illegible] states are for him imperfect socialist states; about this I shall want to quarrel. But much more important is not what he says about their character, but what he does not say about their external international relationships. The whole interlocking frame of world power politics with the H-bomb at the centre is replaced once more by a curious vagueness. The challenge of Communism gives ex-colonial powers (nothing about their nature either) freedom of manoeuvre and, in the end, the ruling class will 'have lost its grip'.

So much for my polemical summary of Collins. What I must next do is to set out, by contrast, the Marxist case against reformism.

2

Reformism is not just a set of theories about society. Reformist theories are themselves part of the social life which they attempt to describe. Of what kind of social life are they typically part? They arise within a capitalism which has learnt some degree of rationalisation and of control. They represent a would-be readjustment of socialist theory to social realities. The stage before reformism is the stage of capitalist expansion in which the working-class movement may preserve an outward semblance of revolutionary aims and theory, but becomes in fact directed towards the goal of securing the maximum benefits for the working-class *within* capitalism. This is the stage which German Social Democracy reached by the 1890s: Bebel was its political tactician and Kautsky its theorist. This stage cannot continue for long before someone suggests that theory should be brought into line with practice. The actual involvement with capitalist success should be linked with a confidenc[illegible] in capitalism's powers of self-regulation rather than unrealistic prophecies of doom. Kautsky gives way to Bernstein.

Thus reformist theories both express and reinforce an abandonment of revolutionary aims. They provide the justification for an adjustment to trade union goals and to bourgeois party politics. The outcome is necessarily a disintegration of the working-class movement in two directions. The leadership becomes assimilated to the parliamentary and administrative structure of the bourgeois state. The mass membership becomes sectionalised, acquires the aspirations of bourgeois society, disintegrates as a movement. The institutions of the labour movement partly become institutions of bourgeois society and partly become part of private rather than of public life.

The acceptance of gradualism is the acceptance of the viability of bourgeois institutions. The acceptance of such institutions is the acceptance – at best – of a mode of life in which reforms are offered *to* workers rather than won *by* them. The reformist's mode is one in which the self-activity of the working-class is necessarily minimised. The self-activity of the working-class is revolutionary for it marks a total break with both the economic and the political systems of capitalism which rely upon the passive acceptance of their alienated role by the workers. And socialism is self-activity as a total form of life. This is in the briefest possible compass why the expression 'revolutionary socialism' is tautologous. To accept left-reformist theories into the labour movement is to assist in turning the labour movement away from socialism itself. Reformist tactics are the most effective enemy of revolutionary strategy.

The labour movement, under the influence of reformist theories, and, more importantly, under the influence of the social order which such theories express, becomes subject to the social pattern of capitalism. It responds to the pressures of economic and political life; it is no longer itself an effective agent of change. So that there is nowhere for the 'pressures' which left reformists speak of to come from. When movements of revolt are generated inside capitalism, the labour movement in its reformist aspects is forced to reject them as decisively as any other part of the bourgeois order. It is not because the theories held by the Labour Party leaders are right rather than left reformism that such a leadership rejects CND. It is because the whole party, Left and Right, is adapted to a reformist mode of activity (or inactivity). So it is also with the youth revolt. The goals of those adolescents whose vitality feeds Young Socialist branches are incompatible with the goals of the socie to which the Labour Party is so well adapted. Thus the labour movement debilitated by reformism into playing not even a reformist role. It express no revolt of its own and it cannot accommodate other revolts.

If there is a touchstone in contemporary political life it is the question the H-Bomb. This is because the politics of the Bomb are not just one mo issue; the politics of the Bomb are the politics of our kind of society. Th Collins can discuss contemporary politics without mentioning the Bomb itself an indictment of his reformism. There is an illusion abroad, and n only among reformists, that one can characterise a contemporary state isolation from its world situation – and then later on discuss its foreign poli and its military policy as mere appendages. In fact, any state which embar on certain types of policy is bound to have a corresponding type of intern structure. Consider any policy which leans on the massive deterrence of t Bomb. To implement such a policy there must be an immense and large secret technological and military organisation. This is bound to become least semi-autonomous, determining how surplus-value is disposed of in lar part. It is bound to evade democratic control. It is thus deeply incompatib with any sort of socialist order. No state with the Bomb can be a worker state. One could only suppose otherwise if the questions of who disposes surplus-value and to whom they are answerable are regarded as irrelevant the characterisation of socialism. For no classical socialist thinker could the questions have been regarded as irrelevant; but for those who wish to tre the CP states as socialist states they must be so regarded.

Collins asserts that the 'solidifying interest of private ownership' is necessary precondition for 'the high income and privileged groups communist societies' to congeal into a class.[4] I do not understand the warra for this assertion. Feudal ownership was often corporate not private. Colli offers no arguments to show that capitalist ownership could not also corporate. What matters is whether the relationship of exploitation hol between groups in a society. Collins admits that the actual CP states have ha to practice what Preobrazhensky called 'primitive socialist accumulation What he never raises is the key Marxist question: how could, under t

[4] Collins 1961, p. 18.
[5] Preobrazhensky 1965, pp. 77–146.

objective conditions of anything worth calling primitive accumulation, non-capitalist forms of society arise? Either the answer is 'in no way at all', or not only are the closing sections of Volume 1 of *Capital* nonsense, but historical materialism itself is falsified. What property in the means of production consists in is control over the disposal of surplus-value. To separate labour from any share in this creates the social precondition of capitalism. And this is what the process of industrialisation does. Industrialisation belongs to the realm of necessity, to the formation of a social order under objective conditions which no idealism can transcend.

Thus the onus of proof should be on those who wish to maintain that the Russian and kindred bureaucracies are not a class. But since all the trappings of class privilege appear in their society there is hardly room for argument. The sole remaining props of belief in the non-exploiting nature of the bureaucracy are three-fold: nationalisation; ideology; and the bureaucracy's achievements. But nationalised property is only workers' property when the workers own the state; Soviet Marxism has all the features of a class ideology; and the achievements of the bureaucracy are typical capitalist achievements. When Collins speaks of the rate of growth of the Soviet economy, he ignores with a piece of loose rhetoric all the relevant capitalist parallels from the nineteenth century to the Common Market. One might as well conclude that because the Americans have solved the problems of rate of growth in the agricultural sector (as Russia has not) the Americans are thereby socialist. Equally it is ludicrous to see symptoms of socialism in the liberalising tendencies of the bureaucracy. It is worth protesting here at the absurdly low standards of liberality which apologists for the Soviet Union display.

The spectacle of Western scholars who could not study or publish in the Soviet Union praising its liberalism over against that of the capitalist West is a nauseating one. When, in the Soviet Union, scholars enjoy the freedom of enquiry that Marx enjoyed in Victorian England it will become clear that the Soviet Union is being praised for its likeness to bourgeois society and not for its differences. And those who praise it unconsciously render tribute to the state-capitalist nature of Soviet society.

What is missing from Collins then is *both* any appreciation of the kind of human consciousness which might build socialism *and* any criteria of the objective conditions, both social and economic, which are necessary. There is missing any clear definition of what has to be overcome, the opposition to socialism. But the contemporary ruling class and the contemporary bourgeois state both stand in crying need of analysis. Sometimes the extension of state activity into economic and social life is treated as though this were an absorption of economic and social life into a monolithic political structure. In fact, it is as much a dissipation of the old unitary state into a multifarious network of institutions. The decline of the role of parliament in the British state is one sign of this; the relation between the planning agencies of M. Monnet, the traditional French administrative bodies, and private French capitalism is another example. The result of this is that the state becomes continually less accessible to traditional forms of political activity. Within the present structure traditional methods of political attack, such as nationalisation, become more and more irrelevant. We find in every large industrialised state, whatever its official political forms, a bureaucracy whose decision-making is carried out by a series of boards which represent the conflicting interests inside the corporate structure. The room for manoeuvre left to politically appointed and elected bodies is negligible. The question thus arises for the reformist: what is he going to reform? The social pattern will more and more be that of negotiation between labour and capital within an organised framework in which the political setting is minimal. Insofar as it does become possible for reformists to acquire state power, all the old Leninist arguments about the bourgeois state still apply anyway; but the changed character of state power itself is probably more important.

I have argued against Collins that reformism offers no hope of keeping in being or creating a labour movement that could in fact bring socialism about; that reformism must see the H-Bomb as just one more issue; that in so doing as well as for other reasons it misconceives the nature of the contemporary state; and that above all it does not understand the type of coincidence between objective conditions and socialist consciousness which is necessary for the transition to socialism. To this last point I must now turn in more detail, because it is here that Collins's accusation of 'apocalyptic Marxism' must be met.

3

The transition to socialism will be political in that it will be concerned with the arrangements of power. How does the prospect of such a transition arise

It arises because of the dual character of working-class life under capitalism. To the worker the prospect of overcoming his unfreedom is presented by the very society which also keeps him unfree. The essence of working-class enslavement is not impoverishment. It is that 'be his wages high or low' the worker leads an existence which is enforced upon him.[6] The germ of his liberation lies in the twin facts that capitalism cannot prevent him from recognising that he is unfree and from combining with other workers to free himself. Indeed by its forms of work and social life it up to a point promotes such recognition and such combination.

Against the worker and against the socialist theorist, capitalism has three lines of defence. The first is its objective capacity to ride the economic, social and political crises which it continually and inevitably engenders. Its capacity to do this is by no means independent of its ability to disable working-class consciousness, and to evacuate that consciousness of political content. To do this it falls back on its second line of defence, the institutionalisation of working-class demands within the framework of bourgeois political and social life. This domestication of the working class is intensified by its third bulwark, the promotion of middle class and of sectional attitudes in working-class people. The attrition of consciousness by private ambition, by education in half-truths, by bread and circuses, this is too familiar to need emphasising. In this capitalist perspective, reformism is absurd. The left reformist perforce acts as an unwilling liberal; he would do much better to become a conscious and aware liberal. Between revolutionary socialism and liberalism there is no third way. Yet if these are the resources of capitalism, is not revolutionary socialism absurd too? Certainly the idea of the impoverished proletariat led by the élitist party cannot be introduced upon this stage without a comic opera effect. Those who identify Leninism with this do terrible injustice to Lenin's keen sense of the politically ridiculous. And it is this which enables the Bernstein v. Lenin mock battle to continue: those who accept this false revolutionism as the alternative to reformism do as much as anybody to propagate reformism.

What then is the true revolutionary perspective? It seeks to bring together three elements in our social life. The first is the deep and incurable dissatisfaction

---

6 Marx 1976, v. 1, p. 799.

with social life which capitalism breeds. The second is the recurrent state of objective crises in capitalist social order. The third is socialist theory. Without the third, the first does not necessarily come into relation with the second at all, or only in the most fortuitous way. With the third, dissatisfaction can become creative in that it is presented with a radical alternative to the present social order. But unless that alternative is radical, is the prospect of a whole new way of life, working-class consciousness is left victim to particular reformist aims. This is not apocalyptic: it is a statement of the minimum required for socialist consciousness.

To have reached this point is to have stated in the barest and most meagre outline the case *against* left reformism. The case *for* revolution begins at this point.[7]

[7] For responses to this article see Coates 1962, Oertzen 1962 and Collins 1962. A subsequent article attempted 'to take up the case against left reformism…at the point where Alasdair MacIntyre left it', and to 'fill in some of the gaps left by MacIntyre's more methodological treatment. See Kidron 1961/2, p. 15. According to Chris Harman, Kidron's article was commissioned because MacIntyre's response to Collins was considered 'inadequate' by the *IS*. Harman 2004.

Chapter Twenty

Congo, Katanga and the UNO[1]

Katanga is the heart of the Congo. When the Congo was a Belgian colony Katanga was its economic base. The export of Katangan minerals took place through Congo trade routes. The royalties and taxes which the mining company, Union Minière, paid were paid to the central government at Leopoldsville. Without them, the Congolese economy could not have survived before independence.

In the last year before Congo became independent, Union Minière paid the colonial government £21 million. The rest of the Congo appears to have few economic potentialities, Katanga supplies not only 8% of the world's copper but over 80% of the worlds' cobalt and a large percentage of the worlds' industrial diamonds, silver, zinc, cadmium and, even in small quantities, gold and uranium.

The Congolese economy was centrally administered, but with the Belgian colonial administration. What is euphemistically called the paternalism of the Belgians led them to keep the tribal structure of Congolese society as intact as possible. It is not surprising that no Congolese politicians emerged on the eve of independence who were not tribal politicians. This, though a consequence of Belgian

[1] Originally published in *Socialist Review*, First Series, January 1962, pp. 4–5.

policy, did not suit the Belgians who recognised that only a centrally organised state was possible. They therefore discouraged all separatist tribal tendencies and their political representatives, including Tshombe, and encouraged the few who appeared likely to try to transcend tribal division, such as Lumumba. When, after a week of independence, Lumumba broke off diplomatic relations with Belgium, Belgian policy reversed.

On 11 July 1960, Tshombe had proclaimed Katanga independence. Belgium was inclined to support him until its own government was reformed after the General Strike. Since then it has from behind the scenes unwaveringly supported the central Congolese government and given it large financial subsidies. In the headquarters of Union Minière in Brussels there appears to have been a division of opinion and some at least of the direction appears to show the views of the Belgian government. This raises two sharp questions. Why do the Belgians not support Tshombe? And why have most people in Britain been led to suppose that they do?

The answer to the first question is a simple one. In a wide sense Belgium has as much interest in African stability as any other power. Her quick change act from the patterns of Portuguese imperialism to those of British imperialism marks the consciousness of this in Brussels. Rwanda and Burundi, Belgium's other African possessions are now being led through a time-table towards independence in a manner worthy of Mr Macleod himself. More narrowly, Union Minière needs a strong central Congolese government for three reasons. First, they need an export route to the sea. The only alternative to Leopoldville lies through Portuguese East Africa, a territory whose future stability is unlikely. Secondly, the Tshombe government in Katanga is inherently unstable. It is a tribal government, based on a coalition of two minority tribes against the majority tribe of Katanga. Tshombe's writ does not run very far outside Elisabethville. Thirdly, one leading member of the Tshombe government, at least, has threatened to nationalise Union Minière and expropriate the Belgians.

Why then did Union Minière support Tshombe at all? It appears to have been committed by its representatives on the spot. One of the lessons the Belgians may have learnt is that you cannot administer a British-style colonial policy without strong white settler opposition. The white settlers of Katanga saw Tshombe as a puppet for them; in his need for a white mercenary military force he quickly became a puppet and remains so. But Tshombe's government would be quite capable under certain circumstances of either nationalising or simply destroying the installations of Union Minière and returning to pure tribalism. And, at this point, we can only make the support for Katanga intelligible at all if we look at the activities of another group, which is not primarily Belgian, but British.

Northern Rhodesia is British imperialism's most vulnerable point. The imposition of a new constitution and African violent and non-violent resistance have threatened both the political structure of Welensky's federation (which is gone when Northern Rhodesia is gone, because Nyasaland is as good as gone already) and the economic wealth of the British South Africa Company, a major mining company with a finger in many pies – including Katanga. The stake in Katanga is two-fold. Through Tanganyika Concessions Ltd. the BSAC is a part owner of Union Minière (14% of the shares, 20% of the voting rights). But more than this it needs a 'safe' border for Northern Rhodesia politically. So do the companies with interests in Rhodesia. Let us now list members of parliament, lords and commons, who either have or have had an interest in Rhodesia or Katanga: Julian Amery, MP, Under Secretary of state for the Colonies; C.J. Holland Martin, MP, Treasurer of the Tory Party; and Lords Salisbury, de la Warr, Selborne, Robins and Clitheroe. The annual report of Tanganyika Concessions and the speeches of Lords Robins and Selborne have made it clear that from these British interests came the powerful and unconditional support for Tshombe. British, rather than Belgian, economic interests in fact buttressed Katanga.

In August 1960 Mr. Knaba brought a Katanga delegation to London which paid an unofficial and highly secret visit to the Foreign Office. Afterwards a party was given for them by four Tory MP's, Anthony Fell, Philip Goodhart, Neil McLean and Paul Williams. The British government has been paralysed in its public acts and utterances over Katanga; it could not act against the Katanga lobby, whose interests and influence extended widely through the Tory Party. Impressive reports have come out of Rhodesia of military supplies crossing the frontier to Tshombe. The British government at a key moment threatened to withdraw financial support from UN if the operations against Katanga went on. While Katanga had air superiority, Britain held up the jets from Ethiopia by refusing permission for their necessary refuelling at

Entebbe. The British Consul in Elizabethville met Mr Tshombe secretly and sheltered him. The British delegation in New York pressed for Dr. O'Brien's dismissal.

What does it all add up to, even if nothing had been said of Mr Hammarskjold's death? That British support for Katanga was not peripheral and accidental, a blunder to be explained away. British support is the key to the Katanga problem. For it is now tolerably clear that the division between those with interests in Katanga who support the Central government and those with interests in Katanga who support Tshombe is a division between those who have no interests in Rhodesia as well and those who have. The Katanga lobby is a Northern Rhodesia white settler voice. This leaves British socialists with a peculiar responsibility. They can only discharge this responsibility if they discard two pictures of the Congolese situation which they are being offered.

The first of these is the liberal picture of the UN force as a group of knights in stainless armour fighting villainous imperialism. But this will not do, if only because the Congolese central government and the UN force which supports it is also a creature of imperialist powers.

The second dangerous picture is that which cries an equal plague on all imperialisms and looks to the African working class. For this class, in the Congo at any rate, in a social sense does not yet exist. Attempts to present Mr Gizenga as a Marxist have played into the Katanga lobby, who wish to build him into the Communist threat in terms of which they can justify their own activities in the USA. Mr Gizenga, it is quite clear, is not affiliated to the Soviet bloc (he has expelled Eastern European journalists from Orientale) and is as limited by tribal boundaries as his rivals are.

There is in the Congo no socialist alternative. Given this, the UN solution is the best solution we have. Only in the framework of a centralised Congolese state, based on the resources of Katanga, can working-class forces and institutions be built up. Only through the UN can such a state be established and, in the even shorter run, only through the UN can the worst extremes of famine and disorder be averted. Critical support for the UN in the Congo is the only realistic attitude for revolutionary socialists.[2]

[2] For two responses to this article see the letters by Tony Young in *Socialist Review*, First Series, February 1962 and John Fairhead in ibid., March 1962.

Chapter Twenty-One
Sartre as a Social Critic[1]

Both the highly general and the completely specific are deeply moving; the metaphysician who traces the ambiguities and alienation of human nature as such and the novelist who portrays this one definite individual in his particular, detailed circumstances both excite us. But, by contrast, the middle ground of sociological inquiry, occupied by statistics of occupation and mortality, by cautious and limited historical generalisations, often appears dull. It is because there is no middle ground in Sartre that he is such an exciting writer; but it is also because there is no middle ground in Sartre that his arrival as a social theorist has been at once brilliant and disastrous.

A properly philosophical approach

Sartre is important because we need urgently a properly philosophical approach to sociology. Inquiring what kinds of concepts are appropriate in the tasks of describing and explaining human life is urgent in a discipline where it is all too easy to borrow the concepts of the physical sciences uncritically. Moreover a need for conceptual awareness in the human sciences arises in a special way. The way people think about things, about the physical world, is appropriate or not,

---

[1] Originally published in *The Listener*, 22 March 1962, pp. 512–13.

depending upon the nature of the things in question. The way people think about people, about themselves, is part of the reality about which they are trying to think in appropriate ways. The concepts which I employ to grasp what I am become part of what I am.

Sartre has been aware of these matters for a long time, and the themes of his latest book on social theory are most easily made intelligible by looking back to *L'Etre et le Néant*. There the matter is put dramatically in terms of an individual psychology. We are all acting parts, said Sartre. This man, who is a waiter, is acting the part of a waiter. This other, who mourns, acts out the role of sadness.[2] It is not part of their essence to be a waiter or to be sad, for a man has no pre-existent essence determining what he must be. He constructs himself out of his choices, out of the concepts which he chooses to grasp himself with. At this point of the argument, Sartre makes a false move. He begins by connecting this feature of human life with certain kinds of anxiety and doubts about identity. So far, so good. But he then proceeds to assimilate the (conceptual and necessary) facts that everybody has to comprehend themselves under descriptions and by means of concepts which they did not make to the (psychological arid contingent) facts that some people cannot identify with their roles, others indulged in dramatisation or pretence and so on. So he concludes that we not only all are but must be in bad faith. We are all acting parts, pretending. Sometimes it seems that there is no escape, whatever this situation. Sometimes, and less coherently, at marginal chance of escape by means of an *acte gratuit* is offered.[3] But throughout Sartre's novels and plays no clear and unambiguous example of salvation from bad faith is portrayed.

This confusion involves Sartre in a contradiction in his social and moral attitudes. On the one hand, Sartre's analysis must lead him to say that we are all necessarily in bad faith all the time. 'Bad faith', that is, appears as yet another of the pseudonyms under which 'original sin' continues to make appearances. On the other hand, Sartre has always wanted to say that some people are in bad faith in a sense in which others are not. The class of people who are not has varied. The working class, the Communist Party, Jean Genet, and Sartre himself have all at one time or another either by direct statement or by implication had this status suggested for them. The class of people who are in bad faith has been unvarying: the bourgeoisie. Why Sartre hates the bourgeoisie is not

[2] Sartre 1957, pp. 59–60.
[3] Sartre 1957, pp. 69–70.

puzzling, though he hates them in a very bourgeois way: one of his defects is the shrillness of his hates. Why he has become enamoured of Marxism stands in need of more explanation.

Sartre distinguishes sharply in his latest work between Marx and Engels; his Marx is a young Hegelian rather than an old economist. He sees this Marx as a particular kind of social scientist with two enormous merits. Marx's antipathy to a mechanistic determinism, his preoccupation with human activity ('Men make their own history, but...), and his grasp of the role of concepts in that activity ('Language is practical consciousness') make Sartre see Marxian man as an earlier version of Sartrean man.[4] At the same time, Marx sees for modern proletarian man the crucial change in his history coming through an awareness of his own history. To learn what his own history has been leads the proletarian to bring that history to a culmination in which he liberates himself from the past. It is not that history has a shape and a direction 'independently of human will' (as Stalin put it). But that men, becoming conscious of what history has been, lead it to a culmination which gives shape both to their own and to past historical experience. It is not so much that history has always had a goal, but that it new becomes possible to live so that we can see it all as moving towards the goal of human liberation.

Sartre elevates Marx above all other social scientists because of two features of contemporary non-Marxist social science to which he objects. The first is its positivism, its assimilation of sociology to the natural sciences. The attempt to describe people as though they were subject to causal laws in the same way that things are omits that very consciousness which Sartre sees as transcending what it is by grasping it. It omits the very core of the human world. Moreover non-Marxist sociology tends to explain societies by looking for what holds them together, for what stabilises this or that particular social order. It is a typical achievement of such social science to have seen that often what look like conflicts and revolts are safety valves designed to relieve tension and so avoid radical change. Marx, on the contrary, was concerned with how societies change, with how a given order is broken down and transcended. This is why Sartre looks to him for explanatory models. But, in order to use Marx in this

4 Marx 1973a, p. 146; Marx and Engels 1975–2004b, p. 44: '...language is practical, real consciousness that exists for other man as well, and only therefore does it exist for me...'.

way, Sartre has to provide a view of Marx very different from that to which we are accustomed. Some of Engels and a great deal of later Marxism have to be repudiated.

Marx through the eyes of Lukács

This view of Marx (and its accompanying repudiations) is not original to Sartre. It is roughly the same as that of Lukács in *History and Class-Consciousness*, the work of 1923 which Lukács repudiated in his Stalinist phase. But the spectacle of the middle-aged Sartre seeing Marx through the eyes of the young Lukács cannot but remind us that immediately after 1945 we saw the middle-aged Lukács condemning the young Sartre. Sartre is in his latest work bitterly contemptuous about this condemnation. The bitterness indeed suggests that Lukacs's description of existentialism as a 'permanent carnival of fetishised inwardness' touched a raw nerve.[5] For, at that time, Sartre himself was defining existentialism in terms which opposed it sharply to Marxism. The sovereignty of individual, private, inner human choice was proclaimed in such a way as to exempt human beings from all causality. Sartrean existentialism was proclaimed as a self sufficient world-view. Now this perspective has been renounced.

The first volume of *Critique de la raison dialectique* falls into two parts. In the earlier Sartre tries to overthrow Raymond Aron's dictum that one cannot be the child both of Kierkegaard and of Marx.[6] He produces a view of the history of philosophy according to which philosophers fall into two classes. There are those writers who define the philosophy of an age by laying down the concepts which then limit philosophical horizons. There are also those secondary thinkers who merely vary the perspectives within the limits set to them by the great innovators. Descartes and Locke provided one set of horizons, Kant and

[5] Quoted in Sartre 1963. The English translation of Lukács's original text is less concise. See Lukács 1973, pp. 252–3: 'As long as the pillars of capitalist society seemed unshakable, say up to the first world war, the so-called *avant-garde* danced with the fetishes of their inner life.... The gaudy carnival, often with a ghastly tone from tragic incidental music, went on uninterrupted.'

[6] Sartre 1963, especially pp. 10–14, 167–81. The two parts to which MacIntyre refers are *The Problem of Method* and the remainder of the first volume of *Critique de la raison dialectique*, which was eventually published in English (minus *The Problem of Method*) as Sartre 1976. The 'real' second volume of the *Critique* remained unpublished in full until 1991. See Sartre 1991.

Hegel the next. The horizon of the present age is set by Marx. Existentialism is not as a self-sufficient philosophy; it is merely a reminder of the concreteness of individual existence to those Marxists who may generalise it away by their trust in formulae and by their mechanical application of their own method. The essence of Sartre's warning is that Marxists often confuse the task of describing the conceptual framework with which we have to describe individual events with the task of describing the individual events themselves. He is trenchantly contemptuous of the attempt to dispose of Flaubert by simply exhibiting him as a bourgeois of the Second Empire. He contrasts this sharply with Marx's concreteness in the *Eighteenth Brumaire.*

Grasping how things happen

What this adds up to is perhaps a plea for the primacy of a historical sense in grasping how things happen. Sartre wishes to be able both to situate the individual in terms of general formulae and concepts and yet to grasp that very individuality which always evades any total categorisation. Indeed we can recognise here a more neutral, objective statement of the problem of *L'Etre et le Néant*. In that work, the Sartrean individual was confronted with the problem of grasping himself without falsification. Now Sartre looks at the same individual from outside and poses the same problem. The stimulating and inconclusive discussion leads one to hope great things from the second part of the book. Such hopes disappointed.

There are many fine moments when Sartre discusses particular sociological problems. But the temptation of a metaphysical short cut to the heart of the matter is too much for Sartre. Where 'bad faith' was once omnipresent, the fate of man is now 'serialisation'. We lose our individuality and our capacity for action by being turned into merely one term in a series which could equally well be replaced by any other term. It is important not to confuse what Sartre means with the often repeated complaint that in modern society we are all treated as units. For Sartre's examples serialisation are such as to make it clear that this, as he defines it, is a necessary feature of the human condition. His examples seem to necessitate this. Yet his argument refuses to accept it. There is a kind of political group, he argues, the disciplined revolutionary, activist group whose mode of life exempts them serialisation. We gain an identity through such a group in which we renounce our (presumably spurious) individuality.

To be a member of a class is to be serialised. To be serialised be incapable of action, at least of the kind of action which can change history. So to be a member of the working class and no more is necessarily not to be a changer of history. For this one must first be a member of a highly organised group. One's first response is to think of Lenin in *What Is to Be Done?* and suppose Sartre's diagnosis of the French workers today in their politically passive state has led him to an ultra-Bolshevik position. This was Merleau-Ponty's diagnosis.[7] But Sartre's Leninism is not the Leninism of history. It is Leninism without Marxism. It is Leninism above all without any of the practical realism of Lenin. Sartre sees it as of the nature of the highly organised revolutionary group that to join it gives the group the right of death over the members. He can write that 'the basic statute of the group bound by oath is Terror'.[8] This is not Bolshevism at all. It is the anarchism and nihilism of the last century and it is that anarchy and nihilism as portrayed by its harshest critics, by Conrad for example, in *Under Western Eyes*, or by Dostoevsky.

The anarchists and nihilists were at their furthest remove from Marxism in this: they thought that they could erupt into history, as it were from outside, and storm it by violence. Why has Sartre involved himself in this? The root mistake is an odd inversion of his earlier error. Where he ought to have treated 'bad faith' as an important, but contingent, phenomenon in human life, he treated it as a necessary accompaniment of all human actions. Now, when he ought to treat serialisation and its attendant perils as a necessary and unalterable feature of social life, he wants to treat it as only contingent and alterable. The outcome of the attempt to find somewhere where serialisation does not reign entails a retreat from the realm of social reality altogether (for wherever there is social reality there is serialisation). Hence Sartre's revolutionary group is a piece of mythology. But, in as far as it misleads us as to what is and what is not possible in society it is potentially dangerous mythology.

Lack of political responsibility

What I have diagnosed at the heart of Sartre's social thought is a continuing confusion over the necessary and the contingent. I want to connect this with two

---

7 Merleau-Ponty 1974.

8 Sartre 1976, p. 433: '…the fundamental statute of the pledged group is Terror'.

other features of his work. The first is his lack of political responsibility. Sartre has been both a victim and a propagator of the myth that the present-day Soviet Union has something to do with socialism. He has romanticised the French working class about which he sometimes appears to know nothing at all. His deep ignorance, and it does appear to be almost wilful ignorance, about the facts of social life and of history seems to spring from exactly what he castigates in Marxists. He cares about the concreteness of individual events and lives only in so far as that concreteness serves *his* formulae. Sartre has *no* real sense of history. The kind of sociologist whom Sartre despises, the cautious inductivist, collects facts but has no theoretical equipment to understand them. Sartre breeds theoretical notions, capable of yielding a great deal of understanding. But he is insufficiently interested in finding out what the facts are which we need to understand. At the same time, and perhaps because of this, he has resolutely refused to put aside what is, or ought to be, the key problem of contemporary social theory.

This problem can appear in different forms. One is that of relating sociological explanations to explanations in terms of individual psychology; or, as they would have put it in the nineteen-thirties, the problem of Marx and Freud. If we start with Marx and the sociologists we find ourselves seeing the individual as formed by socially prefabricated roles into which he has to fit. His private motives are only a shadow behind his public life. If we start with Freud and the psychologists, we find public life merely a screen on to which private motives project their images. The former picture reduces Henry Ford to 'personified capital' and Lenin to 'the vanguard of the vanguard'; the latter picture reduces Ford to 'anal fixation' and Lenin to 'unconscious sibling rivalry'. Both taken by themselves are fatal to our understanding of human beings as human beings; and merely adding them together will, not solve our problems. Sartre in trying to create a more adequate conceptual framework went straight for the right problem; but his impatience with facts and with the theories of others makes his book a short cut to disaster.

An artist, not a theorist

It may well be that what makes Sartre's theoretical confusions more tolerable to him than they are to us is that he is really an artist and not a theorist. In the *Critique de la raison dialectique*, he portrays the competitive aggression, the spiritual cannibalism, of the human race in a theoretical framework. Where, in *L'Etre et le Néant*, the individual confronted an emptiness, a nothing, which was his own unmade future, in the *Critique* men confront an emptiness which is economic scarcity. In *L'Etre et le Néant*, the rival projects with which individuals fill that future draw them into cycles of sadistic and masochistic personal relationship; in the *Critique*, the projects of coping with economic scarcity lead to the social and political war of each against all.[9] The conceptual psychology of *L'Etre et le Néant* gives way to theories about the role of economic scarcity which can be tested against the facts of social life and which turn out to be simply false. Sartre's reluctance to look at the facts is his tragedy as a theorist. But the vocabulary which he elaborates in his theory of scarcity turns up again in *Les Séquestrés d'Altona*, where the cannibalism of the human race, the feeding on each other's wants and each other's guilt, becomes in concrete terms a great imagination achievement.[10] The time has come for us to say to Sartre that what we need from him are fewer theories and more plays.

---

[9] Sartre 1957, pp. 16–45, 379–412; Sartre 1976, pp. 735–54.
[10] Sartre 1962, especially Act 4, pp. 113–48.

Chapter Twenty-Two

The Sleepwalking Society: Britain in the Sixties[1]

Begin with a simple question. Aldermaston 1962 was the biggest CND demonstration so far; probably more individuals are now committed to unilateralism than ever before. Yet it made a far smaller impact on people at large than previous demonstrations. Why? The first and easy answer is the press and the television. But why can the press so safely treat CND with such contempt? The answer is that their readers are conditioned to a view of the world in which all major hopes and fears are presented within the context of the status quo. The Russians are testing H-bombs – fallout is a danger and a scandal. The Americans are testing H-bombs – a little fall-out does nobody any harm. And in any case 'Vicar elopes with fertiliser manufacturer's mistress' is so much more newsworthy. But isn't it the press then that conditions people into not thinking CND important anyway? Certainly this is partly so. But what of the press do people read? The only papers from which one can hope to get a serious amount of reliable and important information are the *Times*, the *Guardian* and the *Telegraph*. Of

---

[1] Originally published in *Socialist Review*, First Series, May 1962, pp. 4–5.

these, the last has a circulation of a million and a quarter, and the first two have a circulation of just over half a million between them.

The *Mirror* and the *Sketch* between them have a circulation of five and half million. In his new book on *Communications*, Raymond Williams has analysed the content of the press so that the difference between the news that the middle-class reader gets and the 'news' for mass-consumption stands out. On a day when the *Times* main headline was 'Emergency Action to Restore Economy', the *Mirror's* was 'Buried Alive!'. When the *Guardian* reported 'Missile Tracker in Orbit' the *Sketch* announced '1-ton Whale Amok at Kew'.[2]

What is also notable is that those papers with the least chance of economic survival are precisely those which try to be both popular and informative, the *Herald* and the *Mail*. What and who decides which papers survive? The answer, so far as the mass circulation papers are concerned, is – the advertisers. In other words, the need to sell of private industry overrides any chance of intelligent mass political education. But, it will be said, advertisers and the press alike give people what they want. Even advertisers themselves do not always say this. As one top American executive put it: 'Our job is not to give people what they want; it is to make people want what we are about to give them.' And this brings out the next point. People are not merely conditioned by the press; they come to what they read out of a whole way of life which conditions them to expect to get what they do get.

You have to be literate to read a paper. Where do people learn to read? In junior schools, where many of them are from the age of seven streamed; in schools where division into grammar and secondary modern overshadowed the division between state and public schools. Nearly 80 per cent of our children go to secondary modern schools. Of these in *Education For Tomorrow* John Vaizey writes that 'it is virtually impossible to find any middle-class child in them'.[3] At the other end of the scale, the expensive public schools have long waiting-lists for the children of the new affluent managerial class. (Many corporations pay school fees for their top executives.) So out of the schools comes a small group trained to believe that large affairs such as the H-bomb are both beyond their understanding and outside their power.

---

[2] Williams 1966, pp. 76–82.
[3] Vaizey 1966, p. 49.

Who were their teachers? Why is there a flow of money through advertising to the papers that rely on continuing to possess an uneducated public and no flow of money to pay teachers decently and train them properly? We cannot answer this without understanding the economic shape of our society. The largest and most powerful sector of our economy – the private sector – is a market economy. Where there is a profit, there flows investment. If there is profit in oil, investment flows to oil. If there is no profit in ship-building, investment flows out of ship-building. The law of a market economy is: good does better, bad does worse. The great lesson learnt by modern capitalism is that the private sector cannot survive alone. It needs not only the coordination and regulation that government agencies can supply; it needs also a public sector where those necessary services for private industry which is unprofitable in themselves (in Britain coal and rail transport, for example) and which therefore would not attract capital in the open market, can be financed. But private industry also needs a public sector to educate its labour force. At the same time, it is involved in a contradiction in its attitude to the public sector. For it must be taxed and restricted to some extent to finance the public sector; but it cannot accept taxation and restriction if it is to expand effectively in its own way. So we get a set of priorities in the economy where private investment comes a clear first (plenty of money therefore for advertising in the mass consumption newspapers) investment in nationalised industries a bad second, and expenditure on such services as health and education a very poor third indeed.

There are two political lessons to be drawn from this analysis. The first is very short and simple. It is that these attitudes to health and education are built into the whole shape of our economy. You cannot hope to preserve that shape intact and change the attitudes to health and education. But just this is what the Labour leadership hopes to do. Gaitskell should on this point at least learn a lesson from Kennedy who was elected with a similar hope. But not a single piece of Kennedy's domestic legislation on these matters has escaped mutilation or rejection by Congress. The second lesson is that the key power in our society is the power to make investment decisions. Who exercises this power in our society? Who decides, that is, what work people will do and hence what wages they will get and what sort of lives they will lead? The answer is that a large class of top managers and executives whose influence extends from the Treasury to ICI, from the National Coal Board to the insurance companies, now made these decisions. Socially, they are a class with a remarkable unity. Their children go to the same sort of schools, they lead the same type of life, they pass easily from the civil service to private industry. They are not elected, they have no public responsibility, they are mostly completely unknown to the people whose lives they shape. They are, compared with the old capitalist class, extremely well-informed and extremely able. More than this, they have an extremely docile working class to deal with. Why?

The answer is that the working class has been effectively divided into the oppressed but helpless and the strong but bribed. Workers who cannot defend themselves are simply oppressed. These include the old, the disabled, the sick, and unorganised, unskilled labour. Peter Townsend has calculated that in Britain in 1960 about six million people were living at or below subsistence level. And these are not all by any means ill or unemployed, for nearly half are persons living in households chiefly dependent on a small wage. Most of these households consist of a married couple with three, four or more children. They are the helpless and unresisting members of the working class.[4]

The working class who have the power are those whose labour and skills are vital to the economy. The techniques with them are twofold. First there is the use of the carrots of high wages and mass consumption. Here we are back again at the advertisers, whose task is to stimulate mass consumption. For the wages that are paid out by the system to skilled labour have their function as consumer power in mopping up the surplus productivity of the system. The old Marxist view that capitalism could never provide consumer power sufficient to use up all that was produced is made completely obsolescent in a capitalism of continually expanding investment and continually expanding consumption. The second technique is to institutionalise this part that the working class plays in the system by coming to terms with the trade unions: the aim is to get the workers to accept planned, limited wage increases, geared to the expansion of capitalism itself.

But more important than either of these techniques is the creation by the education of the working class in class-stratified schools, by the mass media of

---

[4] Townsend 1962, pp. 211–15. MacIntyre cited this article as appearing in the *New Statesman*, but appears to have been confusing it with another article by Townsend, 'Freedom and Equality', which appeared in the issue for 14 April 1961.

press and television, by their conditions of work, of an attitude of apathy and acceptance towards the political status quo. And this means that no isolated political question can hope to impinge greatly on working class consciousness. Not even that of the Bomb. So we come back full circle to Aldermaston '62, and the answer to our question of why demonstrations can make so little impact is that they are running counter to our whole way of life and not simply to official policy about the Bomb. The columns of the *Mirror* and of the *Sketch* and the classrooms of the secondary modern school are the first lines of defence of the men whose power is the power of the H-bomb.

Chapter Twenty-Three

Open Letter to a Right-Wing Young Socialist[1]

Dear Comrade,

You call yourself a Gaitskellite. You have rather enjoyed the tea-party intrigues of the Campaign for Democratic Socialism and you have been flattered by the suggestion that you are a hard-headed realist and not one of those impractical utopians of the Left. You are perhaps slightly disappointed to find that those who denounced Trotskyism among your friends had never actually read Trotsky and you may even have wondered why your friends campaign so much more assiduously against the Left than they do against the Tories. But now an issue has come up which ought to worry you even more. For you claim to be a democrat, and all around you in the Young Socialists a campaign is going or directed towards proscriptions and expulsions. The despicable untruths about Communist infiltration into CND have no doubt made you uneasy. But you have probably felt happier about the proscription of INDEC,[2] which proposes to run candidates against the Labour Party at elections. Certainly this makes proscription unavoidable. But the question I want you to answer is: who made INDEC or something like it inevitable?

---

1 Originally published in *Socialist Review*, First Series, June 1962, pp. 1, 7.

2 Independent Nuclear Disarmament Election Committee.

First of all, take note that the announcement that an independent committee to promote the intervention of unilateralist candidates in parliamentary elections had been formed was greeted by the more Pecksniffian members of Transport House and the Right with public horror and private glee. Surely they had now found an excuse for proscribing at least selected members of CND! It is perhaps worth asking not only you but also those more Gadarene members of the Labour Party as they rush towards disaster to pause and ask who is responsible for the birth of INDEC? The answer is clear: it is Mr. Gaitskell and his friends. For if, at a time of crisis for the Labour Party, Labour supporters are prepared to split the Labour vote in the interests of getting the unilateralist case heard, it is precisely because of Mr. Gaitskell's determination to have his private way in the party, not by answering the unilateralist case, but by preventing it being put, insofar as he can prevent that. For Mr. Gaitskell has openly declared himself against argument: 'I have always said that the one thing that prevented the Labour Party getting into power and staying in power was our inherent tendency to argue.'[3]

The case against the possession of the H-bomb by any government whose policies we can affect does not rest upon any of the three positions to which Mr. Gaitskell is presumably alluding when he tries to smear his opponents by calling them pacifists, neutralists and fellow-travellers or even Communists. Very few unilateralists in the country are pacifists. The support for pacifism is tiny compared with the support for CND. Again, only a handful of supporters of CND are neutralists (Lord Russell dealt with neutralism in the best possible way by inviting those neutral governments who have proclaimed themselves unconditionally against testing to send their navies into the area of Christmas Island tests and so prevent them – nobody responded at all. But the moral is not just that neutralism is a political non-starter! it is that it was only from Russell's position that it could possibly be exposed in this way). But, of course, the allusions to neutralism and pacifism are only window dressing for the great CP smear. On this count, either Mr. Gaitskell is ignorant or a liar. The Communist Party is not unilateralist: it could not possibly support the policy resolution passed at the CND Annual Conference in 1961, demanding the unilateral renunciation of the H-Bomb by every government which possessed it. Moreover the Communist Party on this whole issue is fundamentally in the

[3] *The Guardian*, 7 May 1962.

same position as Mr. Gaitskell: Russia must keep its H-Bomb, because it is a deterrent. Russia must test whenever 'military necessity' demands it. There is no difference between Mr. Gaitskell and Mr. Gollan about Great Power H-Bombs, about the morality of H-Bombs or the politics of H-Bombs. Nonetheless it would be wrong to use Mr. Gaitskell's own formula of Guilt by Association. What is needed is to point out the hypocrisy of Gaitskell shouting at hecklers to 'go and see Mr. Khrushchev and tell him to ban his bomb'.[4] For he knows perfectly well that this has happened. The unilateralist peace marchers went to Moscow and told Khrushchev to ban his bomb. And he didn't, because he too uses the arguments of Mr. Gaitskell. He too is a Great Power H-Bomb man, a member of Gaitskell's Club.

But the central issue is not Mr. Gaitskell's inner party McCarthyism. It is the way that this is used to observe the central arguments on which the unilateralist cause rests. For the first of these arguments raises the very simple question: why are we socialists anyway? And the inescapable answer is that we are socialists because we are against what the existing capitalist social order does to people. But there is nothing worse than what the H-Bomb does to people. Even with all their horrors, the camps of Nazi Germany are over; but in Japan they are still dying from our atomic bombs. And the bombs which Truman and Attlee dropped on Japan are only toy-weapons compared with what they can pull out of the thermo-nuclear cupboard nowadays. Just as concentration camps could not be part of a socialist policy on any pretext whatsoever, so the use of H-Bombs cannot be. Anybody who would press the button to release nuclear weapons (and I include the misnamed 'tactical' nuclear weapons) has no conceivable place in the socialist movement.

Now I am well aware of the reply at this point: 'You are utopians. We are realists. We do not want to see H-Bombs used any more than you do. But the way to stop H-Bombs being used is to have them as a deterrent and so preserve the balance of terror. If everybody has H-Bombs, no will use them – or at least this is our best chance that they will not be used. Of course, we would not in fact ever use H-Bombs, but we must make the Russians believe that we would.' This represents the one honest and decent anti-unilateralist position, but it rests upon a profound mistake. The mistake is to suppose that

[4] *The Guardian*, 7 May 1962.

the game of 'Let's pretend we'll use our H-Bomb' can remain a game. For how far does the pretending go? We know from the expressed dismay of high-ranking service officers that they have not been told that we are never in fact going to use our H-Bomb. We know that the whole strategic procedure of our services is based on the assumption that we would, in certain circumstances, use it. Our American allies are fully committed to it. The strategists of the Rand Corporation have never been told that deterrence is all a bluff, and they obviously do not believe it. In fact, nobody except the perhaps highly moral, but if so, highly confused, members of the Labour Right appear to accept this story. And the reason why they accept it is that they are less clear than anyone else about power.

In the exercise of power through vast bureaucratic structures the will of individual decision-makers can become relatively unimportant. Those at the top become increasingly dependent upon the information and advice they are given from below. Decision-making is delegated and dispersed. Those who originally made plans become the victims of their execution. What were originally means become ends. If this is true in general it is above all true of what Eisenhower called 'the military industrial complex'. The H-Bomb was originally a means to the policy of deterrence; it becomes an end which the policies are increasingly distorted to serve. And more and more of those with power become committed, whether they will or no, to the possible use of the H-Bomb. Decisions about its use become the role of the faceless men in a structure of power, largely autonomous and wholly secret, without any public responsibility, and over which little or no control appears to be exerted, above all therefore the power of the H-Bomb is anti-democratic. And this is the second great socialist reason for unilateralism. Socialists are for the dispersal of power; the H-Bomb requires its growing concentration.

This is the case against the H-Bomb which is met by Mr. Gaitskell with silence and proscriptions. It is no wonder that unilateralists in the Labour Party come to feel that it is both their duty and their right to put their case directly outside the Party and to do this on every platform they can get, including electoral ones. The decision to proscribe INDEC is not surprising. But what its creation entails is a challenge to both Right and Left in the Labour Party. The Right must either expose their total bankruptcy by continuing to substitute bans and proscriptions for argument or they must stop arguing against their own straw men and meet this case. The Left must show by their struggle that it is possible to make this case heard inside and not just outside the Labour Party. I hope that you personally will learn from the behaviour of your friends on the Right and come over to the Left. It's never too late.

Yours fraternally,
Alasdair MacIntyre

Chapter Twenty-Four

[The New Capitalism and the British Working Class][1]

I will attempt to analyse British society in terms of two kinds of capitalism – an older and a newer, the difference between them and the tensions between them. When I give this talk in International Socialism branches it is mostly in fairly general and abstract terms. Comrades discuss the difference between a capitalism in which there is, on the one hand, an owning class whose place in the economic system is determined by their legal ownership of factories, mines and capital, and, on the other hand, a working class in which unskilled and semi-skilled workers forms the centre of gravity of the labour force. The economy is essentially unplanned and therefore the patterns of the trade cycle determine changes in the level of employment, with slump and unemployment and the other characteristic phenomena of capitalism punctuating it about every decade. It is emphasised again and again that under the new capitalism we do not live with this pattern anymore. And while it is not true that the trade cycle has been entirely eliminated, it is true that capitalism no longer lurches from ten-year crisis to ten-year crisis. It is also true

1 Previously unpublished text of a talk given to an *International Socialism* Day School at Calton House Settlement, Finsbury Park, London in 1962. Transcribed and edited from a typescript in the possession of John Charlton. The title has been added by the Editors.

that the groups that are growingly important under capitalism are not those who legally own shares and the means of production, but all those who participate corporately either as owners or managers in the top decision making processes. Against this you have a capitalism which depends on continuous technological change, where profits are reinvested in modernisation and which is therefore constantly producing new leaps forward that require a newer type of labour force in which skilled workers are becoming more and more important.

I am not going to fill out this analysis any further. What I want to do instead is to talk much more specifically about Britain today, about where we are in this transition, and about the way in which both the attitudes of those dominant in the system and the attitudes of the working class are shaped by our present conditions. This talk is therefore going to be more factually based than such talks usually are. Although I am going to outline one or two general theses, I do not apologise for trying this time to put some factual flesh on the theoretical bones.

Let's begin with what is an enormous fact for management. At a time when everybody is talking about the effects that automation is going to have on British industry, there is something of a crisis in the actual automating of British industry. Everyone had predicted that in Britain the increase in automation would follow the lines taken in the United States and which are being taken in Germany – that investment in computers, for instance, would follow the same upward trend. It has not. Not only has it not, but there has been a consequent crisis in the British computer industry which was signalled by the amalgamation of ICT and Ferranti a short time ago. Certain questions have therefore to be raised. Why is it that in the move forward into the new capitalism the required investment has not been forthcoming? Why do British industries not move forward into the new capitalism in the way that some American industries did and the way that German industries are doing?

To this the standard answer given by British economists is twofold. First not only has British industry an untrained labour force over against the possibilities of automation, it has no facilities for training the people it needs but it is also involved in a bottle neck of training at every level so far as people are concerned, from programmers and mathematicians at one end of the scale to the technicians at the other. Second, it is also asserted that in Britain unlike both Germany and the United States, the employers still feel unable to create redundancies as against merely to pass them on. Let me explain what I mean.

Employers have no hesitation whatsoever in declaring Ford workers unemployed if this can be shown to be the result of not getting contracts, or the loss of contracts or similar factors. But at the moment they do not know what to do in a situation in which the deliberate modernisation of their factories would produce the need to radically lower the number of men they employ and radically change the pattern of skills in the factory. If they go about social dislocation at this moment it would entail automating at the speed at which industry was automated in the United States and they would not know how to cope. This is not to say that they are going to go on puzzling for very long or that they are not going to find a way through this. It is to say that, in this situation, in this temporary pause, it is a particularly good time to ask how strong the labour movement and the working class are in face of the impending social change.

The impression given by the employers is that the unions are very strong indeed, and that employers dare not deliberately create redundancies for fear of retaliation from the unions. If one tries to measure the strength of the unions by looking at the patterns of wage claims and achievements over the past few years, you might indeed get quite an illusory impression of strength. Perhaps the most important social fact for socialists in Britain is that the share that wages taken of the national income remained relatively constant for most of this century. It did increase slightly until the middle 1950s and then began to drop. In respect of wages today, the whole working class overall is, in relative terms, slightly worse off in relation to the rest of the economy than it has been for a long time. It is not even as strong absolutely as is thought, because although people are implicitly aware of the drop in the value of money from the effects of inflation, what they are not aware of is the extent to which their own wage increases are paid for out of inflation.

Inflation is created every time wage demands are even partially conceded and then employers pass them on in raised prices, which in turn force on the inflationary cycle. Commonplace Tory propaganda, commonplace even among official Labour Party economists, is that, from time to time, the workers should be asked to restrain themselves because otherwise there will be wage increases which cause inflation. There is no doubt at all that in the inflationary cycle there is a point in the cycle at which wage increases occur, and if you pick out this as the point at which the cycle begins you can show very nicely that at any given period all the other consequences of inflation follow from the wage increases, but the important thing is that wage increases are simply part of the cycle.

This is important for another reason. Around the middle of the late 1950s a great many trade-union leaders were worried about their standing with their members in relation to bread-and-butter demands. For a long time they found it very, very easy to put in the annual wage claim and to go to their members and to say to them: 'look how well we are doing'. If you want the most striking example of the creation of this illusion in the past, it is the record of the Communist Party leadership of the ETU.[2] The Communist Party always said in the ETU 'We may be bastards, we may be vote-riggers, but we do raise your wages.' If you drew the lines of the graph that show you the expansion of the electrical industry and the expansion of the electrical profits and at the same time you drew the line on the page that shows you the rise in wages while Haxell was General Secretary, you would discover the rise in wages was more than financed out of expansion in the industry, and then you discover something else – it is that Haxell never once refused an offer from the employers. He never had to: he was able to give apparently fantastic rises in the early 1950s to his members simply through taking what the employers offered and what the employers could well afford out of the expansion that was going on in the industry. It follows that, at the level of official negotiations the trade unions, have not been operating as groups that have been militantly pressing against the system's limits when negotiating wage increases, even in negotiating their most successful demands. They have very largely been playing a part in the capitalist system which they did not control and insofar as the patterns are now changing, their resources for standing up and fighting in a new situation are probably rather low. Why?

First, because trade-union organisation is predicated upon a pattern of working-class life that is largely out of date. It is predicated, for instance, on the assumption that there is a good deal of stability in the nature of the labour force and, of course, this is no longer true. The most striking fact is the fact of mobility: not only geographical mobility, but also job mobility. This is already well established. For instance, in the most recent year for which

[2] Electrical Trades Union.

we have Scottish figures, 49,000 workers moved out of Scotland and 31,000 moved in. In relation to Scotland's population, this represents a very sizeable change-over. You could find a lower rate of change in areas that are more developed than Scotland, but the pattern in general is maintained: workers move around a great deal more often than one has a superficial impression of them doing and this is going to increase. And why is this important for trade-union organisation? First of all, because the worker who is on the move is not usually an effective member of the trade-union branch. But, secondly, because conditions about which trade-union officials would normally negotiate are not the conditions of the worker who is just coming in or the worker who is just leaving; they are the conditions of the worker while he is there, and it is exactly at the point at which training for the job is concerned and the redundancy rate for the job is concerned that trade-union negotiation is probably at its weakest.

Secondly, a change in composition of the labour force, about which I shall have more to say later, is the fact that there are more and more white-collar jobs in proportion to other working-class jobs, and fewer and fewer jobs for unskilled workers. Where you have had successful pay claims in spite of the inflation-rate cycle, you also have striking increases in productivity and sales of the industries concerned. The picture is that, so far, the trade unions have exerted little or no pressure against the system at all and, insofar as the system is prevented from moving forward, it is due to its own stagnation, its own lack of resources and has nothing whatsoever with working-class resistance. The government says the guiding light for wages should be 3.5% measured over against a 4% increase in the whole of the economy and every single proposed wage increase is measured against this standard. Even when the workers and the trade unions reject it, this establishes the horizon and going beyond this looks very bold and bad. Take the industries in Britain which today are expanding, like chemicals.

Four years ago, chemicals expanded by 6%, three years ago they expanded 6% and the year before last they expanded 12%, last year they expanded 12%. And if you take the other end of the scale, the kind of declining industry in an underdeveloped backward area where you are not getting expansion at all, you get sporadic bursts as in shipbuilding, you see that the notion of the 3.5% limit is a notion which does not help workers in backward industries which cannot afford to pay anyway, and is the most tremendous imposition on wage claims in industries that are expanding far beyond the 4% target. The notion of the national pattern is a myth created by the employing class in relation to wage claims, which not only has the bad effect of actually hindering people in advancing their wage claims, but also of giving them a quite wrong impression of how well they have already done.

In this situation, we have also got to face some very sad facts about working-class solidarity. There are two extreme attitudes on issues such as differentials, and they are both intelligible and can both be defended in context, but they bring out one essential feature of working-class life. If you take an industry like steel, which has done quite well in recent years, and new techniques are introduced, the issue of differentials in terms of the traditional wage claim becomes an acute one and you get a dispute like the Port Talbot dispute. The dispute is one that essentially drives the workers in that industry further apart from each other and this is the product of certain workers taking advantage of their new strong position. Let me put it like this: there is a sad case for saying that being in an economically strong position today against the employers, in certain industries at least, means that the issues on which you are likely to fight and even possibly to win are just the issues that are going to divide you from the less skilled workers. Take the sort of industry where there is strong solidarity.

The London busman not so long ago refused an offer of 7/6d. for drivers and 6/6d. for conductors, and accepted 6/6d. for everybody. The garages themselves almost unanimously took the line that they did not want the differential between the drivers and conductors increased. But what would you find if you went round the cases like the busmen where solidarity has been more important than economic gains? You would find that solidarity is bred where you have an industry in which workers have continually been on the defensive in which there position has been continually worsened and which they are working under difficult conditions and which they are essentially very weak. In that situation, you find that solidarity is unfortunately bred of weakness and the fragmentation is bred of strength and it is just on the whole that there is a divisive tendency which socialists have got to find the policy and means to counteract. To get a sense of perspective it is important to see that the actual size of the wage packet has to be related to quite a lot of factors and particularly to the kind of services which the workman receives in various ways.

Begin at the bottom with education. Let's not spend too much time reiterating the very familiar facts about the 80% of our children who go to secondary modern schools about the way in which steaming continually militates against the working-class child and let's just emphasise just one thing out of those facts, namely that the expectation built into the C-stream child is that he cannot do well. The expectation built into the secondary modern child is that he cannot do any better than what actually happens to him. One of the things that the working-class child in contemporary Britain does is to breed acceptance of inequality, and that is quite important too. Inequality is something which the working-class child is experiencing all the time in the most random way. Let's take a simple little fact. At the moment in Gloucestershire, 40% of the children go to grammar school; in Oxfordshire, 15% of the children go. This means that the children who live along the Gloucestershire/Oxfordshire border have the experience of, on the one hand, large numbers of working-class children going to grammar school and, on the other hand, of large numbers failing.

This arbitrariness of inequality is related to a type of social pattern that I shall talk about later, and it is related to immediately to the role of local authorities in administering public services. Let's dwell on something more important. The numbers of school leavers who enter apprenticeship have increased over the past ten years, but the proportion of school leavers who enter apprenticeship has not. If you take the total number of children who leave school at the ages of 15, 16 and 17 together, only just over one third of these children enter any form of further training. And that means that almost two thirds, which in 1962 was 214,500 out of 336,000, have no training whatsoever. And that means that you are continually putting larger proportion of unskilled workers onto the market. At the same time, the proportion of jobs for unskilled workers is dropping in the economy all the time, with the result, as you would expect, that well over half of the unemployed in this country are unskilled and these are people who are not wanted by industry, who have no social power to exert through industrial action.

Consider what happens to the working-class boy who does succeed in terms of the present system, the working-class boy who passes the 11 plus and goes to the grammar school. All the evidence we have, such as Marsden and Jackson's book on the working-class grammar-school boy, or the scholarship papers which are written by working-class boys for Oxford and Cambridge open scholarships, shows that it in this section of the population that there are the strongest anti-trade-union and anti-working-class sentiments in any section of the population.[3] Again and again, scholarship papers written by working-class boys characterise the working classes as ignorant masses who need to be ruled for their own good. Within the British population, there is the sharpest possible division in the way one section sees the other and the pressure exerted from above on the 80% by the 20% is tremendously complete. You can see this in the irrelevance of the ideals that are officially handed out to the working-class people. Take, for instance, the issue of housing and homes: the dominant ideal which actually affects most working-class people, though it is a hopeless dream, is the idea that you can own your own house. Why don't workers own their own houses? The answer is obvious, but let's spell it out. The Co-operative Building Society last month produced some interesting figures which pointed out that the average house in London today, and the average house is pretty average on their specification, costs £4,300. The worker who is extremely well off in London earns £1,000 a year. No building society will lend you more than three times your annual income. Consequently, you could not possibly hope to begin buying your house through the facilities offered by a building society unless you had saved £1,300, and it is not only workers who find it difficult to save £1,300. What about local authorities? For reasons that should become clear when I talk about them in relation to housing, they have very little money to lend because, on the whole, they are usually over extended in order to build their own housing. Why? Because the chief charge on local authority housing is the interest rate. For a house costing £2,500, over 50% of the costs the local authority pays is repayment of interest, and a very small sum indeed is actually spent on building the house. Local authority housing is largely being financed by money that has to be borrowed on the market at the going market rates, such that a great many local authorities see no way out but to charge economic rents. What are they doing when they try to charge economic rents? They are charging a rent for the house which puts the burden of the interest payments on the shoulders of the working-class people who live in the house. Working-class people who pay economic rents in council houses are being forced to borrow money on the market in order to live in the house; the local authority is merely an

[3] Jackson and Marsden 1962.

intermediary in the process in passing the interest rates on to the person who lives in the house.

No matter how willing and how radical a local authority may be, it can in the nature of things do very little about this. The limits within which it may move are very, very narrow indeed. St. Pancras Labour Party discovered this when they came to power pledged to alter the housing situation in the borough and then found that the legal limitations on its actions were such that it could do very, very little that was different from the Tories, although it could say how much it disliked doing it, instead of being like the Tories and saying it was a very good thing. But the effect on the people who actually live in the houses is very little different; to know that your Councillors do not like passing on the interest rates to you is very small consolation. Consequently, in 1962, 2,000,000 households in England and Wales alone were looking for other accommodation. In London – and London on the whole is rather well-off compared with places like Dundee or Liverpool – 25% of the households have one bedroom and 6% have no usable living room at all. The White Paper on housing said that the Government was determined to press on with the struggle for slum clearance, except in areas where the need for a high density of population makes this impracticable in the short run. Unfortunately almost every slum in this country is in such an area. The government also pledged itself to end Britain's housing problem by building 300,000 houses a year for ten years, and this would solve the housing problem by providing the necessary stock of housing. But it also said that the gvernment refused to commit itself to any date when this process was going to start. In a way, the government was unnecessarily cautious here. The crucial fact is that slogans like '250,000 houses' or '300,000 a Year' are impossible slogans, are impractical slogans, unless you ask for whom and by whom are they going to be built? The simple fact at the moment is that of the houses that are being built, half are for middle-class buyers, and the people who need to be rehoused are not, of course, the middle-class buyers. We do not know what the stock of middle-class housing available is, because we do not have the kind of census that would tell us. What we do know, is that, in the present situation, there are large middle-class areas where there is empty housing at the same time as the local authority in the area make numerous family centres where the parents have to be separated and the children removed from their parents because there is no housing space for them.

What is the position of the builders in this? The building industry in Britain is possibly one of the most inefficient British industries, but it is also one that has the highest profit margins. It is not at all uncommon for builders to take 30% on the job. The source of this profit is not though where you might think it might be, simply in the profit made on building, it is connected with the fact that a great many of Britain's most important builders in the late 1940s and early 1950s bought up most of the available building land in Britain. There was recently a commission on building industry in Scotland, which had among its conclusions the threat to the industry that the industry is so inefficient that, in the end, the Scottish builders might be driven out by the English builders who would come in competitively and do the job. But that is not going to happen, and it is not going to happen for the very simple reason that almost all of the available building land in Scotland of the kind that builders need is already owned by Scottish building firms, and this land is not available to local authorities for rehousing, nor to rival builders who could build cheaper. It is there for the builders to go on until the point comes on the market when it is profitable for them to put up yet another estate of semi-detached or detached middle-class housing.

Why do I emphasise all this? Because the wage increases that the worker gets means very little until it is set beside what the worker is forced to spend his wages on. And if you take the essentials that the worker is forced to spend his wage on such as housing, you are at once thrown on to issues such as the way in which housing is financed through the local authorities, the way in which the local authority has to create policy about rents in relation to interest rates, the way in which the building industry is organised, who owns land and the actual individual grievance of the worker who is living with one bedroom with a lavatory that does not work with, an outmoded drainage system, in a slum which the government say they will clear when the areas cease to be a high-density area for the purposes connected with the pattern of work. But none of this is alterable except in terms of an alteration of policies which cannot be touched except by political action, and that the economic action of the workers in the factory striking for higher wages, striking for a shorter working week within the factory cannot of itself do anything to touch the factors like housing which impinge on the worker through the whole system, economic and political.

Housing is only one system of this kind; we have got also to take into account such services like transport. I want to bring out one assumption that underlies the sort of society we are living in; this is quite simply that more and more of life is centred on and financed by the private householder. I shall give two examples of this.

First, both town planning and transport schemes make the assumption that Britain is largely going to become a nation of car owners. Now you would be very silly to deny that even quite a lot of working-class people have cars today, and it would be even sillier to deny that a lot more of them are going to have to have cars in the future. But what is the crucial difference between a car and a bus? The answer is that you pay for the car out of your wage packet, and in paying for a car, even if you share a car with three other people, the sort of pattern that you get very often in transport to work today when workers do use cars, you do this, you still being forced by the system by taking away of public transport by buying a quarter of a car to replace a public-transport system, and the erosion of public services under the guise of affluence, continual back-door dropping of the level of wages.

My second example is extremely sinister but scarcely noticed as a political issue. The Mental Health Act of 1959 introduced the concept of community care. The concept of community care at its own level is an excellent concept. It is the case that there are very, very large numbers of the mental patients who today occupy a fantastic proportion of hospital beds who would be treated much better not in mental hospitals, but in their own homes, provided two things are available. First, that there are out-patient facilities so that they can get the sort of treatment they now get in hospitals by going around twice a week instead of remaining in a hospital all the time and rotting away in bed. Second, that there are continual emergency services on call so that the relatives who are looking after them know that, if things do get out of hand, they can as a matter of fact relieve the tension by calling in the emergency service and having the patient taken back into hospital for treatment. Community care therefore is theoretically the ideal. The Act says that because community care is such a good idea, what we will do in Britain is we will lower the number of hospital beds by 1970 or thereabouts to a fraction of what it is now and we will return mental patients to their homes. The mental patients are being returned to their homes. Now the majority of mental patients come from working-class homes. What the Mental Health Act of 1959 does not provide for, what nobody mentions in public defence of the Act, is that what are not being provided are either the out-patient facilities or the emergency services. The actual economic effect of the Mental Health Act of 1959 it is that the charge of keeping the majority of mental patients will be thrown back on the working-class household.

This is all part of the contemporary concept of the home; the concept which is imposed on the worker at a period in which most are better able than they were in the past to create homes, to buy furniture and to have many of the things that they did not have. This use of the concept of the home is driving workers back onto private life in which the wage packet becomes, not something to be taken alongside of the provision of various services by the state and the local authority, but itself something out of which the services are increasingly financed. The worker is increasingly the person who actually not only creates profit through his labour, but also refinances the services through the way his wage has to be spent in various ways. It follows that assessments of wage levels simply in terms of the amount taken home in the wage packet are entirely misleading.

In a situation in which the worker is privatised in this way, what happens to the work? Let us take one example; we can discuss how general it is and how important an example later on. Let's take Fords. Fords recently, having got rid of its so-called trouble makers, gave its workers very much larger wage increases than they expected. Why? Well one answer is that somebody at Fords bought a copy of Ken Weller's pamphlet *The Truth about Vauxhall*.[4] You see what in fact is happening at Fords of Dagenham at the moment is that they have looked at Vauxhall and suddenly realised that they need not be as silly as they have been. What is the fundamental fact about both Fords and Vauxhall? (And remember this is the car industry, this is one of the new industries, one which the expansion in plastics and chemicals and electronics feeds on.) It is the speed of the production line. The one thing which is not negotiable, in Vauxhall or Fords, is the speed of the assembly line. It is a simple thing to see that, if this is not negotiable, nothing really is, for no matter what privileges you win from management through strikes or negotiation, they can be nullified by simply increasing the speed of the assembly line in relation

[4] Weller 1961.

to the number of men who are present, so that fewer men do more work in order to make up for the concessions and pay for the concessions that the men have won. You could systematically show that there is not a single concession the men in the motor-car industry have won, whether in hours, wages or conditions which they themselves have not paid for in one way or another. Why has this created an intolerable situation for the management at Fords and not for the management at Vauxhall?

Vauxhall insist always on paying slightly more and giving slightly shorter hours than the surrounding factories in their area and the other parts of the same industry. For this reason, many people are inclined to describe Vauxhall as a model employer. But, at the same time, Vauxhall makes sure that their factories are located in areas where they provide the major employment, so that in Luton and Dunstable there is relatively little alternative for Vauxhall workers. At the same time, in return for the higher wages, Vauxhall insist on a clause in their agreements with the trade union, which the union has never even questioned, which gives Vauxhall the right to transfer any man at any time, not only from one part of the factory to another, but from one factory to another, so that workers in Vauxhall are continually being moved about from one place to another. You can see how difficult that makes union organisation. More than this, Vauxhall also insists on a gradation of rates of an extremely complicated and detailed kind, so that in fact it makes the most enormous difference to in what grade you are placed and workers are easily made to compete for the grades and continually having differentials emphasised by the conditions of the job. Given all this, what you get is relatively atomised, very unhappy and very hard to organise labour force, where from time to time you may get things happening, but over the long run very little. Fords are trying to reproduce this situation at Dagenham. What Fords are going to do is raise the overall level of wages, make hours negotiable, but not the speed of the assembly line. By a process of differentials and transfers, they will try to break up the workers, which is terribly easy in a situation where there are as many unions competing for membership as there are inside Fords.

This is a pattern continually emerging in the newer capitalism in which there are conflicting needs. On the one hand, capitalists are going to need a labour force which is continually being retrained with new skills, with new technologies, and which has a great deal of mobility. On the other hand, capitalists are also going to need a stable labour force that he can hold with predictable rises in wages through long-term wage contracts, through government-enforced limitations on wage rises and the like. Consequently, capitalists need the enforcement of a wages policy and the kind of educational system which will produce the sort of skills which they want. It is important to emphasise the very small number of skilled workers who are wanted. Take the top end of the scale. If you listen to Mr. Harold Wilson, you would imagine that after six years of a Labour government, Britain will be so flooded with scientists that you will scarcely able to sit down on a bus without someone talking to you about the structure of fundamental particles or entropy, or whatever. At the moment in Britain, there are different criteria for what constitutes a scientist, but on one figure there are 250,000 and on the other 300,000. When we have all we can conceivably use, we shall have about 350,000, and it may be by this time there will be unemployment in scientists if you increase the figure to 350,000. If you move down the scale to technicians and highly-skilled workers, the numbers needed will be considerably larger, but it still does not compare with the number of unskilled workers for whom there will be fewer and fewer jobs at all.

In this situation, the people capitalism needs and to who it is going to be able to pay relatively high wages are going to be a minority of the labour force, an élite, and they are the people who are going to get the whole benefit from educational expansion. This means that every time you are offered figures for education expansion do not look at them in relation to the baseline of the people who now receive the type of education in question; ask what percent of the labour force is involved. The suggestion is that the 17% or, if Robbins is implemented, something like 18% of our children will receive higher education, and that is to say, roughly speaking, those who now go to grammar school will go to university. Those who do not now go to grammar school will still be kept out of the educational process in more or less the same proportion as they are now. And that is very important. It is not that, given the new pattern of skills, what we shall need is all the people who now have grammar school education having university education, and all the people now having secondary-modern education having the equivalent of grammar-school education. It is rather that the grammar-school children will have a university education and the secondary-modern children will have no more than at present. What will appear is a huge broadening of the social gap.

What is working-class response likely to be? The first thing to stress is that there always will be a bread-and-butter response to attacks on the wage packet, rents, pensions and the like. But, when we start breaking down this bread-and-butter response, we discover that it has the character of a response that capitalism can cope with perfectly easily. Last year, 20,000 people demonstrated against the new rents policy in Portsmouth. In Glasgow there was a demonstration of the same size. What happened to the rents policies in these cases as a result of the demonstrations? They are relatively unmodified. You may win on occasions concessions from a particular council, but you cannot really win very large concessions because the council has not any money with which to make them. The council cannot have because of the structure of the local authority borrowing. The point which I am trying to make is this: if you go to your neighbours and you say, 'they are going to put up the rents, we have got to get together, we have got to organise tenant's protests', if the rent increases are sufficiently damaging, you will get your response. If you went to your neighbours on a council estate and tried to organise against the council being made to borrow money at the interest rates, to protest at the fact that the bank rate has been put up and this puts new pressure on local authorities, you would get no response at all. You would get no response at all because you would be speaking to them in a political vacuum in which they could not possibly connect what happened to them and their rents to what is happening in the economy as a whole.

Let me now try to explain what I have been trying to say more theoretically. It is of the essence of capitalism that it makes the worker, and what happens to the worker as a result of the system, occur as a result of large scale forces, large-scale working of the system, which immediate action in the immediate environment cannot touch. You can see capitalism as a large overall system which breaks down into a series of units. Each of these units can be thought of in terms of the individual factory, the individual housing estate or whatever you like. Workers can see what is happening in their factory or their housing estate, and to a point they can understand and fight against it with the only weapons available. But insofar as they fight against it within the particular unit they are in, the factory, the housing estate, whatever it is, they leave the system, must leave the system, absolutely untouched.

It is not of course that we have a working class that is raving with militancy. The vast majority of workers in Britain have never been in a long industrial dispute in their lives. The average industrial dispute in Britain lasts something under two days, and most people who are involved in industries where they say there is a great deal of trouble, or in industries where there are perpetual small troubles as in Cowley, what you actually find is that there are continuous grievances against which the very short-term action that is effective or ineffective depending on the situation, and then the thing is over. There is no kind of spontaneous growth of the working class through this kind of individual struggle, and this is connected with the depoliticisation of the working class.

One of the other important facts for socialists is the last general election, 30% of the male trade unionists voted Tory and 40% of the trade unionists' wives voted Tory. I think we all know that the other 70% were not ecstatic about Labour; some of them did not vote and of those that did vote Labour, quite a high percentage are people who have done so all their lives; in the last general election, you had a group who acquired their habit of voting Labour before the last Labour Government was elected. Insofar as workers today go on voting Labour, therefore, they do so increasingly in the way in which in the latter part of the nineteenth century workers voted Liberal; they are faced with two bourgeois parties which they recognise as bourgeois parties and they support whoever they think will give them most. They are very likely to believe that Labour will give them most, but this has got nothing whatever to do with socialism or an understanding of the system under which they live. It follows that working-class life today offers no basis at all for the theory that the origins of socialism lie in spontaneity. In fact, there is no place at all for the notion that, given the actual conditions of working-class life, workers themselves can organise to defeat the system. Anybody who says the opposite has got in fact to produce an account of where in the British working class today there is the social base for anything like spontaneity. But more than this, what would any group that wanted to turn this non-political class into a political working class have to do?

It is quite clear also to me that for one thing it would be fatal to do is to go to workers and say: 'Comrades, the trouble is that you do not have any control over the system. You will be able to do nothing until you get socialism, because socialism will be workers' control over the system, and with anything short of this you cannot possibly hope to improve your position.' There are a series of knockdown arguments that prove irrefutably that any particularly reform which one wins within the capitalist system will be nullified by the system itself, and be at best an improvement of the conditions in the short run here or there. It may even be that during a particular period of capitalist expansion it is possible for workers in certain sections to make quite large gains without this being anything to do with politics at all, certainly nothing to do with socialism. We have got to ask what are the issues on which workers can exert pressure and formulate demands, so that they are engaged in winning short-term improvements and yet at the same time are beginning to discover that what they confront are not a series of local authorities or a series of employers, but a total system in which they are raising the question of class power. Let me give you two examples.

If the argument which I have been trying to produce in a very fragmentary fashion this afternoon is correct, some of the most important social issues for the working class today are the questions of what investment is made in the building industry, what direction the investment is made in and who decides on the direction of the investment: How many houses do we need? How many hospitals? How many schools? What labour force would we need to build these? What firms would we have to employ to build them? What legal measures would we have to put through to stop the waste of the firm's equipment and its workers in building office blocks, on building for property companies, on building middle-class houses? If you ask these questions you ask questions which cannot be answered simply in terms of housing alone or the building industry alone. Because you raise the whole question of where the money in the building industry come from and how you divert investment from other sectors the building industry. The solution which a great number of left Labour people have for the housing problem is to nationalise the building industry. Certainly, nationalising the building industry might be the necessary first step to doing anything at all, but if we simply nationalise the building industry today the investment that flows into building today would flow elsewhere. What we would find on our hands was an inefficient industry which the government would have to finance in the way that it has from time to time industries like the railways and the mines. It would become one more public service paid for out of taxes and in the end very largely out of the wages packet.

Nationalisation by itself is nothing. What is something is to assert the claim that, of the total national income, a certain amount must be invested in housing. To assert that claim over investment would be to ensure that at some point the national income is viewed as a whole. The national income as it exists today is a useful economist's trick, because of course 'the nation' doesn't have an income. The national income happens to be the income of whoever happens to constitute the nation: it is not a unit that can be controlled just as investment is not a unit that can be controlled. To assert as a minimum the need for control over housing by controlling investment in housing would be to ask for a whole series of institutional changes. It would be very easy at this point to raise the slogan for the next Labour government of no limitation on wages except a minimal control in investment and investment if you like in housing to be a test case. You then have to say: to whom are you asking for this control to be given? If you asked this question at a Labour Party meeting, Mr Wilson would say that it was an absolutely excellent suggestion and would can assure you that when he comes to power there will be a subcommittee with representatives from the Treasury, the Ministry of Production and every other Ministry that has anything to do with housing, and they will keep a continuous eye on the level of housing in the country and even Mr George Brown will sit on this committee from time to time between his other jobs. This is not what we mean by control over investment. When we assert the need for control over investment, when we assert that workers should not accept control over their wages except where there is control over investment, we are asserting that the working-class movement institutions have got to be created which will be capable of exercising that control. We have got to produce trade unions which are political, not only in the sense that they have political aims, but they are prepared to envisage the creation of working-class political institutions in which there is a direct link between the worker who lives in a house and the policy which results in him having this kind of house to live in.

This would involve a programme for the remaking of the trade-union movement in a political form. It follows that, step by step back, the first simple demands about housing cannot be expressed in except in terms of an attack on the system. It does not follow from this that one ought to express demands about housing in an all-or-nothing form. The attack on the problem of housing is a political attack, taking the form of continuous pressure for improvements in the housing system which will break of the present system of investment in housing. We do not put these forward as cunning demands to lead the workers on, so that they think they are asking for housing and what they are really asking for is power then they suddenly discover this. We say: 'You want houses, but you can only have houses if you are prepared to take power. You won't believe and we don't expect you to believe it now, what we say is try to get the houses anyway and see what happens.'

This is the form in which political demands ought to be presented in the present context. The demands we are formulating therefore are not at all irrelevant to the kind of programme which is actually put forward in the name of the next Labour government. You know and I know that the next Labour government will do something against which the working class will have to contend. We ought not to conceal from the labour movement that we believe this to be the case. We also ought not to conceal the fact that it would be simply the asking for a new working class and a new trade-union movement to be dropped from heaven for us to believe that most people in the working class and the trade-union movement agree with us. What they can be expected to agree with us on is the need for a housing policy that will produce some houses in the right places and at the right rents and with right sort of accommodation, and we must say therefore what we ought to be fighting for in the labour movement is a policy of reforms which people will accept as their reform, which they believe can be achieved without necessarily raising the issue of working-class power. We ought to put them forward as reforms which are worth having in themselves and because they raise the issues of working-class power, so that in a series of actions fought by the working class over the next ten years there is a possibility of continual improvement. Earning the right to present such a programme is the role of leadership.

I said earlier that working class could not hope to do the job spontaneously because there is nothing in the social base of the working class or the conditions of the working class which will push them beyond what Lenin called trade-union demands. A lot of people worry about the concept of leadership here because they believe this means a lot of people coming down from the editorial board of *International Socialism* or whatever and telling the workers from above because the stupid lumpen people just don't know. Of course, this has nothing to do with the Marxist conception of leadership, but it has got a great deal to do with the concept of leadership current in some traditional organisations. The concept of leadership I am proposing is one from which people can hope to learn. If they do not learn then socialism will not be made, because only they can make socialism and no leadership can make socialism for them. But, if there is not an organisation at work in the labour movement propounding the sort of policies from which people will learn, then the learning process never begins.

In this situation it would be very wrong to conceal the fact that we start with a great many disadvantages given the nature of working-class life today in relation to the demands of the capitalist system. We start with the situation in which at one and the same time we have our greatest strength among workers in industries where they are unlikely to use it, because capitalism can satisfy their trade-union demands, and our greatest weakness in industries which cannot begin to satisfy trade-union demands, but that do not mind if workers go on strike or go away because all they want is for them to die quietly. In this situation, it is also true that the working class as a whole is knit together not by the conditions of the worker in the factory, but by those features of our social life which belong to the system as a whole and which are a part of the political and not just the economic life of the nation, such as services like the educational system, housing and transport. What we have to connect therefore is the struggle in the factory at the level of trade-union demands, which is the point at which the worker meets the struggle day to day, with the political struggle which the working class as a whole can carry on against the system as a whole. I have said nothing about how to do that, but I have suggested what the minimal conditions to which any realistic programme will have to conform.

Chapter Twenty-Five

C. Wright Mills[1]

The radical Left throughout the world have cause to mourn the death of C. Wright Mills, when still in his late forties with many years of creative work in front of him. This most untypical American professor of sociology would not have been sad if the chief stimulus of his work were a stimulus to disagreement. And so, for once, a death may prompt us to ask in a properly critical spirit: just what was his achievement? Where can he lead us and where may he mislead us? His earlier sociological works *White Collar* (1951) and *The Power Elite* (1956) directly underpin his later political works such as *The Causes of World War Three* (1958) and *Castro's Cuba* (1960).[2] So that it is possible to find a unity in his work, by means of which one book may throw light upon others. And the light that is thrown by *The Causes of World War Three* reveals the basic weakness of all Wright Mills's work.

The apparent contradiction of that book is that, on the one hand, we are shown a whole social and economic system (that of American capitalism) driving towards war, while, on the other hand, we are offered a solution to the problem which involves

[1] Originally published in *International Socialism*, First Series, 9, Summer 1962, pp. 21–3.

[2] Wright Mills 1951; 1956; 1958; 1960.

no change in the overall shape of that social and economic system. But this apparent contradiction is perhaps to be resolved by considering the ambiguous way in which Wright Mills describes the American social system. Wright Mills describes the behaviour of the American political, economic and military élites. But he never makes it clear whether he is describing social roles or the people who are playing out those roles. Is he describing a system which lays down roles so that the actors have no alternative but to play their prescribed parts? Or is he describing a set of actors who happen to be playing their parts in this way but to whom other interpretations of their role are open? The indecision between these alternatives or some third possibility means that Wright Mills can both use a rhetoric of inevitability about the processes of modern bureaucratic capitalism and also invoke the responsible intervention of intellectuals within the system.

The ambiguities in Wright Mills's political writings are assisted by the scarcity and selectivity of his facts. It is impossible to tell from *The Causes of World War Three* whether he would have regarded the Kennedy administration as a reversal or an endorsement of the trends which he describes; it would be equally impossible to draw from it an intelligible account of Eisenhower's role in ending the Korean War and working for a Summit. Both these gaps spring from a reluctance to be complex, which is stylistically honourable in Wright Mills the pamphleteer, but dangerous for Wright Mills the sociologist.

Yet Wright Mills's final conclusion is clear: the wrong decisions are being taken by the wrong people. It is up to the right people to intervene. Here, the political writings are backed up by the sociological analysis of *The Power Elite*. What that analysis misses is the active connivance of the ruled in the dominance of their rulers. Conservative political theorists would describe this connivance in terms of 'the consent of the governed': Marxists would describe it in terms of the ideological pervasiveness of the ideas of the ruling class. Neither would miss the existence of this social bond. It has traditionally been missed by liberal radicals, who have therefore been prone to conspiracy theories of society. And, although Wright Mills was well aware of the fallacies of such theories, there is at least a hint of conspiracy about *The Power Elite.*

This mistaken analysis is perpetuated in a version of the dichotomy between rulers and ruled which leaves the ruled necessarily for the most part helpless in the hands of the decision makers. It is characteristic of Wright Mills's work that he sees the notions of an impersonal fate and an incomprehensible destiny as essentially notions belonging to the consciousness of the ruled. They cannot make history and these notions reflect their impotence. He never follows up two key questions: are not these notions equally (in a variety of forms) part of the consciousness of the rulers? And are not both ruled and rulers impotent partly precisely because they are impotent? Wright Mills's failure here is part of the Marxism of his later years, an unfortunate episode to which I shall return.

His view of the power elite and of the centralisation of decision-making in vast bureaucracies leads him to see 'the ordinary man' as passive, a prisoner of circumstance, needing to be renewed by someone else. The ruled are, for Wright Mills, not actively part of the system in the way the rulers are, for they are not active. The labour movement he treated in an early book and then left alone; and he always seems to view the labour movement in the world at large through the image of the American labour movement rather than *vice versa*. Wright Mills's 'ordinary man' is essentially lower middle-class and he receives his classic treatment in *White Collar*. This is much the best of all Wright Mills's books. This study of a dependent class shows their abdication of decision-making and their beliefs about society as a constituent part of the social system which leaves them so helpless. The belief is one of the progenitors of the fact. Or, to put it another way, *White Collar* shows us one section of the ruled made intelligible as part of a total society, while *The Power Elite* shows us a ruling class so external to the ruled as not to be an intelligible part of a total form of social life. Ideologically, it is the transition from Weber to a crude version of Marx (and not even, as with Lukács, a Weberian version of Marx).

The path from *White Collar* to *The Power Elite* is made easy by Wright Mills's idealisation of the American past as against the American present. The eighteenth century and early nineteenth century in the United States are, for Wright Mills, a time of decentralised local, face-to-face communities in which responsible publics democratically debate the great issues and mandate their representatives. This idealised picture of the relations between rulers and ruled misses out the true social bonds just as much as the cynicism of *The Power Elite* does. He identifies the past ruling class with its own self-image just as disastrously as he misses any connection at all between the present ruling class and its self-image except the connections of self deception and of self interest.

In this sense Wright Mills is himself a victim of the American dream. Indeed, *The Power Elite* must remind us of a long tradition of specifically American radicalism, exemplified in F.D. Roosevelt's early Presidential tirades against the rich and the powerful. So the relatively complex intra-group analyses of *White Collar* in the end are not extended to the liaisons between social groups. Hence his radicalism is displaced by a view of class which leads easily into the crudest of all political analyses from the Left: the workers are passive before a ruling group which must be displaced by an élite of the right kind. Who are the élite? The intellectuals. These in both *The Causes of World War Three* and in *The Sociological Imagination* are the potential liberators, just as they were for Lenin and for Karl Mannheim.[3] There is something very piquant about the older Wright Mills's denunciation of his intellectual colleagues as individuals, while looking to them as a group for social salvation.

Wright Mills once described himself as a Leninist without being a Marxist. In this light his transition from *The Power Elite* and his appeals to the intellectuals to his uncritical support for Castro and his sympathy for the present-day Soviet Union are easily intelligible. The wrong people are taking the decisions; what matters is that the right people should take them. The only problem then is to identify the right people. What is absolutely missing from Wright Mills is the notion that the masses should cease to be masses, that decision-making should belong to everybody and not just to some people. Democracy, for Wright Mills, is at best idealised bourgeois democracy.

So Wright Mills never attended to two crucial features of contemporary society which are essential to making good the kind of analysis he was looking for. One is the managerial structure which makes decision-making the monopoly of the few, no matter who they are, and which constitutes the social identity of the Soviet Union and the United States. The other is the way in which a term like 'managerial structure' refers to the embodiment of certain attitudes and beliefs in both managers and managed. These are not two things: how society is organised and how people are conscious of and respond to this organisation. The way people think and react is the most important part of the organisation. In other words consciousness constitutes

[3] Wright Mills 1958, Part 4, 'The Role of the Intellectuals'. Compare Wright Mills 2000, Chapter 10, 'On Politics'.

base as much as superstructure. Or, rather, consciousness is the unity which makes the notions of base and superstructure false abstractions.

The latest work on which Wright Mills was engaged was a selection from and commentary upon the Marxist classics.[4] This reflects the degree to which his Leninism was finding its basis in a stereotypical Marxism which, by its concentration on the notions of private ownership as the key to capitalism and on consciousness as secondary to economic forms and forces, inhibited him at precisely the point at which he most needed insight.

The moral of Wright Mills's intellectual career is that social reality always takes its revenge on those who do not take it seriously enough. So, towards the end of his life, the Wright Mills of *The Power Elite* was apparently taken in by Khrushchevite managerialism. If Wright Mills had been more anxious to see, and less anxious to see through, he would paradoxically have been in a better position to expose contemporary capitalism. Imaginative sympathy with a social form can be among the deadliest weapons available for its destruction.

Nobody would have replied more vigorously to this criticism than Wright Mills himself, had he lived. The Left has all too few intellectuals for us to be able to spare someone as able as Wright Mills. And, if his intellectual achievement is in the end to warn us of a variety of traps which await us, then we ought all to beware. The idea which we too often inherit from Marxism is that social analysis is easy. The lesson, and too often the only lesson, to be learnt from neo-Marxist writers of recent years is that it is enormously difficult.

---

[4] Wright Mills 1963.

Chapter Twenty-Six

Going into Europe[1]

The British Left is unhappy about foreigners, partly because they theorise. The weakness of its complacent pragmatism is doubly revealed when it is confronted simultaneously with questions of theory and questions about foreigners at one and the same time, as it is over the Common Market. So with a few slick references to Gallipoli and Vimy Ridge,[2] the Labour Party constitutes itself as the party of the English-Speaking Empire, and all through the balancing of pros and cons nobody pointed out that 'Socialism in One Country' is a sad slogan for a Gaitskell to inherit from a Stalin.

What criterion should a socialist use here? It belongs both to the ends and to the means of socialism that it is international. One end is a new mass democracy in which economic and political institutions serve rather than master people; but no revolutionary changes of this kind can be insulated from the outside world. Either, as Lenin saw, they expand to an international scale, or they regress.[3] And the labour movement which brings about such

---

1 Originally published as part of 'Symposium III: Going into Europe', *Encounter*, v. 22, n. 2, February 1963, p. 65.

2 These were the sites of two First World War battles of cultural significance to Australians and New Zealanders (Gallipoli) and Canadians (Vimy Ridge) due to the massive and unnecessary loss of life.

3 See, for example, Lenin 1960–70i, p. 95: 'Regarded from the world-historical point of view, there would doubtless be no hope of the ultimate victory of our revolution if it were to remain alone, if there were no revolutionary movements in other countries.'

changes will have to be genuinely internationalised, breaking through the narrow bureaucratised national forms of the present-day labour movement. The last intention of the fathers of nineteenth-century capitalism was to lay the foundations of the labour movement; but they did. The last intention of the founders of the Common Market is to pave the way for a United Socialist States of Europe. But I am all for taking them by the hand as a preliminary to taking them by... but that would be tactless.[4]

I do not understand those socialist who are against Franco-German capitalism, but somehow prefer British capitalism. I detest the anti-German chauvinism of the anti-Common Marketeers. I can see nothing but good in an enforced dialogue with the exciting movements on the Italian Left. Labour leaders should be using the demand for equalisation upwards of welfare benefits in the Treaty of Rome to dramatise the conservative dreariness of our (false) national belief that Britain leads in welfare. CND-ers should be considering internationalised non-violent action against nuclear crimes. We should all be posing the problems of socialism as they would be, rescued from the dead clichés of our national stereotypes. But that would drive us all into socialist theory. We should have to take seriously brands of European Marxists and brands of European anti-Marxists of whom we had scarcely heard. How much nicer to use the Common Market as the one scapegoat in whom Gaitskell and Cousins and Foot and Jay can all agree to bury their hatchet. But when the scapegoat gets up and walks away, what will they do with their hatchets to each other then?

---

[4] T.A. Jackson wrote in 1921 to members of the newly-formed Communist Party of Great Britain: 'Let us take Labour leaders by the hand as a preliminary to taking them by the throat' (*The Communist*, 24 December 1921.) Jackson was paraphrasing what Lenin had written the previous year about the need for revolutionaries to offer a bloc with the Labour Party and to support its parliamentary candidates where British Communists were not standing their own: 'If I come out as a Communist and call upon [British workers] to vote for [Arthur] Henderson and against Lloyd George, they will certainly give me a hearing. And I shall be able to explain in a popular manner... that, with my vote, I want to support Henderson in the same way as a rope supports a hanged man – that the impending establishment of a government of the Hendersons will prove that I am right, will bring the masses over to my side, and will hasten the political death of the Hendersons and the [Phillip] Snowdens just as was the case with their kindred spirits in Russia and Germany.' Lenin, 1960–70j, p. 88.

Chapter Twenty-Seven

Prediction and Politics[1]

> What the bourgeoisie therefore produces is its own grave-diggers. Its fall and the victory of the proletariat are equally inevitable. (Karl Marx and Frederick Engels)[1]

> As Marxists we do not hope for this or that, we confidently predict... (Any sectarian group)

> I cannot follow your habit of regarding economic inevitables as unworthy targets for opposition. (Peter Sedgwick)[2]

> History is on our side. (Any politician when drunk)

I

From Marx and Engels to the present words such as 'inevitable', 'must', 'cannot' and their logical kith and kin have been nourished among socialists. It is perhaps worth disentangling the different strands of truth and error here in order to make sure that the maximum of sense is combined with the minimum of rhetoric. I have therefore in this article attempted to provide a revolutionary child's guide to the use of these words. The paradox for socialists is that

---

1 Marx and Engels 1973, p. 79.
2 Sedgwick 1962–3, p. 26.

whereas the socialist message began with explaining to working people that the social order under which they lived, and in which they are excluded from social and economic power is not inevitable but that their own choices and agency could begin to play a part in transforming social relations, too often socialists have ended by asserting that the overthrow of the existing social order is *inevitable*, and even mechanically inevitable. A liking for physical analogies and metaphors has not helped. 'The wheel of history is still revolving forwards' cried Dimitrov in the dock at Leipzig.[3] Trotsky in *Their Morals and Ours* could write of 'the deep conviction that the new historic flood will carry them to the other shore'.[4] But do the predictions that we make about the future history of human society ever resemble the predictions that we can make about eclipses, tides, wheels and mechanical systems? In order to answer this question we must first inquire about the nature of such predictions.

2

All systems of physical objects, larger than sub-atomic particles, are governed in their behaviour by laws such that, given an initial state of the system, we can confidently predict what future states of the system are going to be; provided, that is, that nothing interferes with the working of the system. Hence, even in nature, no future event is simply inevitable; it is at most inevitable that such and such an event should occur, if none of an indefinitely large class of other events occurs. The light put to the fuse does not make the explosion of the gunpowder inevitable, except on condition that in the intervening period rain does not extinguish the flame, Britain does not sink beneath the sea, and so on. Yet it is clear that, for many systems, we can be perfectly certain that there will be no such intervention. We do predict tides, eclipses, earthquakes and the like with perfect confidence.

Are social systems like physical systems? One central difference can be brought out as follows. If I learn what laws the particles in a physical system obey, I do not thereby affect the operation of those laws, but I may have taken a first step towards altering what happens in the system. Learning the laws of

[3] Dimitrov 1960, p. 80: '*The wheel of history moves on towards Soviet Europe, towards a world Union of Soviet Republics.*'

[4] Trotsky 1973, p. 52.

gravity was not learning that flight was impossible, but was a necessary step in the invention of the aeroplane. By learning the laws of the system I learn what events I must bring about or prevent in order to bring about or prevent other laws. For all laws are of the form 'If x, then y.' If this is true of physical systems in which human intervention is from outside the system, it is also true of social systems where the human beings who may learn what the laws of the system are and proceed from what they have learnt to alter the laws of the system may themselves be part of the system which they are altering. Physical bodies, from particles to planets, must behave as they are going to behave, could not behave other than as they do behave, unless something else interferes with them; human beings in becoming conscious of the laws which govern their behaviour sometimes learn how to emancipate themselves from the laws in question. Compare the courses of the planets with the pig cycle.

The courses of the planets are so fixed by the laws governing the movement of bodies that tides and eclipses can be confidently predicted for many years to come. Where we cannot predict as confidently as this it is often simply because of complexity, because of the number of the factors involved. So it is with the weather. And so some social scientists have supposed that it was with economic events. But the difficulty in prediction here is different in kind. Consider the pig cycle. In Britain between the wars, a great many small farmers and small-holders went in for pig-breeding. Their activities followed a periodic cycle. At a time when very few farmers were breeding pigs, the demand and consequent price for pig products would be high and the cost of pig food so low as to be negligible. Consequently large numbers of farmers would conclude that there was profit in pigs. As the numbers of pig-breeders grew the price given for pig-products would fall and the price of pig food would rise. As a result, the profit in pigs would diminish, large numbers of pig-breeders would recognise the unprofitability of the enterprise at about the same time, and the number of pig-breeders would decline sharply. Consequently the supply of pig products would fall, the price given for them would rise and the price of pig-food would fall, until once more and once more at about the same time large numbers of small farmers would conclude that there was profit in pigs, and the cycle would recommence. Given a knowledge of the number of farmers, the size of the market for pig products and so on, one could formulate the laws which governed the working of the cycle in such a way as to predict when there would be a glut and when a shortage of pig products, but the limitation on such prediction is not merely that of the complexity of the factors involved. There is also this limitation, that prediction of future events in the cycle depends on confidence in the continuance of the cycle, and the continuance of the cycle depended upon those whose activities constituted it remaining unconscious of its pattern. To become conscious of the pig-cycle or any other economic cycle is not all that is necessary to break its hold upon human behaviour; but unless men became conscious of such cycles, their hold could only be broken by other external factors impinging.

The lesson therefore may be that consciousness or the lack of it is one of the keys to historical change. But, at once, two points must be made. The first is that consciousness is never enough. We may become conscious of the laws which govern our behaviour and yet be unable to change it; for there may be no alternative to behaving in the way that we do. Or again, there may be alternatives, but not ones that enough of us would prefer to the present social system. Consciousness is a necessary, not a sufficient condition for liberating ourselves from a particular social system of whose workings we had previously been unconscious. The second is that the coming into being and passing out of existence of social systems is commonly no more a matter of conscious choices and agency than their operation while they are in being. Indeed, in the view of Marx, precisely what would differentiate socialist society from all earlier societies and more specifically from bourgeois society, is that it would be brought into being consciously and intentionally. But we cannot understand either the notion of social action for ends of which the agent is unconscious or the notion of conscious social construction unless we understand consciousness is not in this context a matter of all or nothing, but a matter of more or less.

The individuals who make up a social system describe themselves and each other in a variety of ways. The sum total of these descriptions, the vocabulary of kinship, of work, of social hierarchy, in their interrelationship make up a description of the total system. The individual may be unable to describe the whole social set-up, and even more unable to understand its workings, yet in so far as he operates within it he grasps it at least partly. And there is a crucial sense in which men cannot be mistaken about their own social system at this level. But, if this is so, then any wider consciousness of the social system and its working grows out of a consciousness which is already implicit in the activity of those who make up the system. All sorts of facts may limit social consciousness. But false consciousness essentially a matter of partial and limited insight rather than of simple mistake.

I have up to this point used the Marxist term 'consciousness' without questioning it; but, beyond this point, in order to avoid pitfalls, I shall abandon it, simply because it is too much of a portmanteau word, which carries too much around with it. Instead I shall examine the role of *beliefs* and *choices*, though very briefly. About beliefs I shall make two points.

First, they are related to actions internally and logically, rather than externally and casually. That is to say, a man's actions can be consistent or inconsistent with his beliefs, can follow or fail to follow from what he believes, just as one belief can be consistent with another. This is because what a man does is specified by his intentions and his intentions are formulated from the same stock of descriptions as his beliefs and indeed presuppose these beliefs. The possibilities of description and belief logically delimit the possibilities of action.

Second, beliefs are affected by theorising in a variety of ways, some of them unpredictable in principle. They are unpredictable first because genuinely new ideas and theories do occur; and to call them new in any radical sense is to say precisely that they break with our prior conceptions and could not have been predicted on the basis of them. And they are unpredictable secondly because a genuinely new idea may have effects which could only have been predicted if we already had experience of the effects of similar ideas; but in calling it new or original we pick it out as not resembling any other such ideas. The original invention of ideas as different as Luther's 'Justification By Faith Alone', Darwin's views of the origin of species and Keynes's general theory of money and employment was in no sense predictable or law-governed; and both because of this and because of my last point their social effect was not predictable or law-governed either. This does not mean that we cannot *after the event* set out all sorts of conditions which were favourable to their production and dissemination. But these conditions do not furnish us with *laws*.

Choices are intelligible only in terms of beliefs and therefore their predictability depends upon the predictability of beliefs. For it is in terms of beliefs that alternatives have to be formulated. But not only in terms of beliefs. For what alternatives confront a given agent or a given society depends upon historical circumstance, levels of economic and social development and so on. The beliefs of agents in a situation are partially constitutive of that situation, but only partially. Hence we can predict that some choices are doomed t frustration, simply because of uncontrollable circumstances. But of thos choices which are not doomed to frustration, which are between alternative which circumstances leave open we shall be less able to predict the outcom And since choices and beliefs are on occasion effective in altering circumstance social prediction is always in jeopardy in ways in which prediction about th natural world would never be.

But whoever thought otherwise? Is not the emphasis on the nature of huma action near the heart of Marx's criticism of the French eighteenth-centur materialists and of Feuerbach? Certainly, but the expulsion of mechanisti ideas of society from Marxism was not permanent. For these ideas recu first with Engels and then with Stalin. And with them an entirely misleadin concept of inevitability is developed.

3

This concept is familiar to the readers of the text-books. All nature is governe by laws. Darwin discovered the laws of the evolution of species, Marx the law of the evolution of societies. For Stalin, societies develop through a mechanic sequence of economic basis and social superstructure, with technologic change as the lever of development. Ideas can hasten or retard developme but cannot alter its direction.[5] [For Engels], so far as capitalism is concerne 'The forces operating in society work exactly like the forces operating i Nature...' so long as we refuse to understand them, and failure to understan is inherent in 'the capitalist mode of production and its defenders': 'Thus pa history proceeds in the manner of a natural process and is essentially subje to the same laws of motion.'[6] Socialism will be different, for then men wi understand social laws and thereby cease to be dominated by them. But u to the arrival of socialism the objective laws operate. Thus it follows that the

[5] Stalin 1938, especially pp. 113–14.

[6] Engels 1975–2004b, pp. 386, 387: 'But, what is true of nature, which is thereb recognised also as a historical process of development, is likewise true of the histor of society in all its branches and of the totality of all sciences which occupy themselve with things human (and divine).... Thus the conflicts of innumerable individual wil and individual actions in the domain of history lead to a state of affairs quite similar t that prevailing in the realm of unconscious nature.'

govern the transition to socialism. Three forms of inevitable sequence are invoked.

The first is the large-scale sequence of types of society: precapitalist, capitalist, socialist. The second is the sequence of development of a capitalist economy: primitive accumulation, investment, expansion, periodic slump, final crisis. The third is the sequence of development of the consciousness of the working class. For the workers there is a progress from peasant outlook, through misery to comprehension culminating in revolutionary consciousness. These three sequences are interrelated. The second is a stage in the first. The third is what Engels calls a 'reflex' of the second. Together they constitute the proof of the inevitability of socialism.

The belief in inevitability suited the character of German Social Democracy before 1914 extremely well. Trotsky has written of how its tradition 'bore a semi-automatic character: each day followed "naturally" from the day before and just as "naturally" prepared for the day to follow'. The inevitability of socialism in the future when capitalism has worked its way through to its final crisis provided a sanction for merely routine activity in the present when capitalism cannot as yet be overthrown. But the very features of this mechanistic version of Marxism which made it acceptable to the bureaucrats of German Social Democracy rendered it totally unacceptable to the Bolsheviks. For the stage which Russia had reached in the sequence of development was still immensely remote from socialism. The Mensheviks accepted the inevitability thesis. Russian socialists, on their view, simply had to wait for the development of Russian capitalism and its political superstructure, the bourgeois state. But both Trotsky and Lenin refused to accept this mechanical view of social development. Neither of them however produced any coherent substitute. Both, on occasion, acted as voluntarists with no eye to the actual possible alternatives open. And this in general has been the Marxist pattern: periods of acting upon the inevitability thesis leading to reactions in which the question of the objective limitations of possibility never get raised at all. So Menshevik automatism led to Bolshevik voluntarism; Stalinism's mechanistic philosophy to Trotskyism's voluntaristic talk of crises of leadership; even the orthodoxy of the British CP to the voluntarism of the New Left. The details alter, but the pattern recurs. And one very good reason for this is that the pattern did not rest upon a simple mistake. For long stretches of time Engels's description of capitalism remained true; capitalists did remain blind to the laws which governed their economic systems, boom and slump did recu workers did become socialists in increasing numbers. But the mechanisti framework in which the system was embedded led to a belief that this proces *must* inevitably continue. And yet its continuance was no more inevitabl than that of the pig-cycle. Just as pig-breeders could, by becoming consciou of the pig-cycle, cease to be dominated by its ups and downs, so surely th capitalists too could by becoming conscious of the business cycle learn how nc to be dominated by it. For Engels and for many later Marxists, this possibilit of capitalist consciousness is ruled out and just as much as the growth c proletarian consciousness is assured. The same mechanistic scheme entail both certainties. But what happened? It is vital to ask this because, from *Tribun* leftwards, the idea of the inevitability of the fall of capitalism and the rise c socialism dies hard. Sooner or later that slump will come. Yet the roots of thi idea are in Engels's version of Marxism. And what that version of Marxisn has to say about laws, prediction and inevitability is clearly incompatible wit my own earlier argument about social systems and consciousness. So wh is right? The answer can only be found by inquiry into what *did* happen t capitalist consciousness and proletarian consciousness.

4

The answer is the very opposite to what Engels had predicted. Capitalisn was transformed by conscious, intelligent innovation, while working-clas consciousness suffered diminution after diminution. And these two processe did not proceed independently of each other. Capitalist consciousness grev in three distinct ways.

The first – which perhaps came last in time – is growth in economic expertis One of the quaintest assumptions of Marxists since Engels is that capitalist could not possibly benefit from the reading of *Capital*. This assumption derive from the belief that the workings of the economic system were such that an capitalist who survived in it would have to behave in ways which promote crisis within the system; and that to understand the system therefore woul be to understand its inevitable final crisis. But, in fact, the expansion of th capitalist system was such that the search for profit and the regulation c the economy through government spending, state ownership and financi controls proved not merely compatible but essential to each other. It is nc that capitalists stood back from the system, saw what it lacked and invited the economic experts to intervene. It is, rather, that, in planning the enterprises of the individual firm, the promotion of a stable economic environment for that enterprise became apparent.

Secondly, what kind of economic expansion led to this enlarged capitalist vision? Many socialists have attacked or ignored post-Keynesian economics, almost uniformly without reading Keynes, because they have correctly understood that capitalism is an economic form in which the rule is: expand or perish. But they have wrongly supposed that the limits of capitalist expansion are fixed in advance. What they ignored, and what Marx's model in *Capital* ignores, is the role of technological innovation. This innovation, itself in part the outcome of the stimulus of competition, provides profitable new fields for investment which know no logical limit. It was this and not the permanent war economy alone which stabilised post-1945 capitalism. For example, the American economy suffered from signs of impending slump before the Korean War; but it did not, as some Russian mythology has it, avoid that slump by war production for the Korean War. For it had begun to recover quite clearly and certainly before the Korean War started. Yet it is only in the Korean-War period that the United States finally established the permanent war economy. This is not to minimise the role of so-called defence spending. For in both West and East now technological innovation is largely shaped by the needs of the armed forces. And economic expansion and defence spending consequently become so closely linked that, in the long run, problems of extreme complexity will arise – if there is a long run. But scientific education, competition in invention between Western capitalist firms and that between Western capitalism and Eastern capitalism, all boost the role of conscious technological innovation in the new capitalist economies.

Thirdly – and this came earliest in time – the rise of the trade-union movement was accompanied by a realisation by capitalists that to maximise the rate of exploitation was to create labour trouble in future. The stages by which the trade unions as institutions have been domesticated by capitalism are not fully intelligible unless we recognise the interest of the capitalists in a contented labour force. What contentment means in this context is entirely compatible with large pockets of unemployment, with low old-age pensions and with areas of poverty. What it requires is a skilled, competitive and fragmented labour force, with relatively high rewards for precisely those workers who are in a strong bargaining position. Thus the ideology of trade-union recognition, personnel management, joint productivity councils and the like is far too easily dismissed by socialists as mere bluff. It represents something very real and important for the contemporary capitalist.

Thus, economic and sociological self-consciousness did enter the system. If capitalists had behaved in the 1940s and 50s as they did in the 20s, the apparently mechanical laws of the economy would have issued in a slump. But there are no longer slumps for the same reason that the pig-cycle is no longer with us: the changed self-consciousness of the participants. More than this, however, the capitalist class have confronted a working class which has not moved in the least towards a revolutionary consciousness of the kind predicted by Marx and Engels. And this for at least two reasons.

The first is that poverty radicalised workers no more than affluence does. Workers who are *already* politically conscious will respond to economic attack as in the General Strike. But wage cuts and unemployment of themselves produce, at best, haphazard reactions and, at worst, apathy and distress. Yet, more than this, capitalism has in fact produced its own ill-distributed affluence.

The second is that the organisations of the working-class, both trade unions and social-democratic political parties, have responded to the capitalist invitation to persuade workers that it is within the capitalist framework that their hope lies. Moreover, the very form of these organisations presupposes a break between the class and the party: workers are taught to be passive and that politics is a matter of a five-yearly vote. Those who have challenged social democrats in working-class parties have usually themselves been equally guilty here, for they have conceived their task so often as one of 'changing the leadership' that the party organisation and not the working class has been the scene of struggle. This is the great mistake in the so-called tactic of 'entrism'.

5

We therefore confront a period in which the specific predictions of classical post-Engels Marxism are more of a hindrance than a help. But to say this is in no sense to abandon a Marxist analysis of society. For Marx was not a post-Engels classical Marxist, whoever else may have been. And, in his own work, particularly his historical work, we do not find this type of mechanical prediction. We find, instead, two kinds of explanation, with consequently two kinds of prediction. On the one hand there are conditional predictions, in which it is asserted that, given certain initial preconditions, certain other consequences must follow. These concern states of affairs where no matter how conscious the participants in the system might be of what was occurring, they could not substantially alter it once the system had been set in motion. So, for example, we can predict that, *if* capital accumulation is set on foot by means of an industrial revolution which begins from peasant labour, we shall get a corresponding class structure created, no matter what the private, individual wills of the participants. But, within that class structure, all kinds of alternatives will arise at various points, and here our predictions will be of a different order, just as our explanations are of a different order. For here we are predicting that, *if* the objectively available alternatives are such and such at a given time, and *if* the level of consciousness is such at a given time, then we can expect this *or* that. So Marx explains the activities of different French social groupings in the *Eighteenth Brumaire of Louis Bonaparte* in just this pattern. He does not predict the mechanical development of consciousness, but knowing how and of what people are conscious predicts what alternatives will lie before them, even sometimes, on a basis of knowledge of their past choices, predicts which alternative they will choose.

We can now see that the damage done by mechanistic error to Marxism was of two quite distinct kinds. First of all, it involved us in actually making erroneous predictions. But, secondly, because it saw all predictions as being made on basis of overall knowledge of a single mechanical system – capitalism-in-the-world-market – it blurred the variety of types of explanation and prediction to which we are committed. And this error is itself a component part in some political mistakes which socialists have made. Let us consider two of them. The argument is that, because socialists have been trapped by a single mistaken concept of inevitability, they have both erred as to what is inevitable and as to what is not. They have *either* supposed that what could not be altered could be *or* supposed that what can be altered cannot be. And both suppositions have sprung from the same picture which appears to present the alternatives of a mechanistic economism or a voluntaristic irrationalism. It is precisely those trapped by this picture who will frame charges of economism when limitations upon action are pointed out to them.

The first of the two examples concerns the development of peasant economies by industrialisation under conditions which necessarily concentrate the disposal of capital. Such a society is Cuba. It is not that there are no alternatives before Cuba; it is rather that all the available alternatives fall within the framework of state capitalism and here consciousness does not enter into the factors which are sovereign and decisive. So that those who locate Cuba's advance into state capitalism in Castro's mistaken policies, or in his union with the Communist Party miss the point. Short of a change in consciousness in some key class in Cuba, the system does evolve mechanically, as much of nineteenth-century capitalism evolved.

The second example is the Common Market issue. Here the mistake is a more complex one. For the condition of there being an alternative to *either* rationalisation of British capitalism within the Common Market *or* rationalisation outside it (EFTA and the Commonwealth) is that there should be a higher level of consciousness in both the British and the European working class. But since there is not, it is not that British entry was or was not inevitable; but that what was inevitable was some sort of capitalist rationalisation. To oppose entry therefore was mistaken precisely because the only political alternative immediately open was a capitalist alternative. This is how socialists found themselves supporting the Commonwealth. But to oppose entry was doubly mistaken for a condition for the changed working-class consciousness we need is precisely a break in the national framework which entry would have helped to bring about. Hence, the alternative for socialists was not: entry or staying out. It was: policies which are designed to create and foster class consciousness, or policies which will inhibit its growth.

The type of prediction involved here does not concern the mechanical workings of a system, but the nature of the choices which both capitalists and workers are called upon to make. What is possible is always limited both by economic circumstance and by the attitudes, beliefs and decisions of different social groups. The latter are never merely the shadow or the reflex of the former; and it is from supposing that they are that the mistake arises of thinking that our choices should be concerned with this or that economic alternative within the capitalist system, instead of with creating the kind of consciousness which will make the predictable outcomes of the system no longer predictable. The fall of capitalism is in no way inevitable; but nor is its survival. The condition of its fall is a long-term mass change in consciousness;

and there are no conditions which can make such a change either inevitable or impossible. It depends on us, but not upon us, because we are borne along by the wheel or tides of history; nor upon us, because we are leaders exempt from the workings of social systems. But upon us because with our working-class allies we may yet learn both what now makes us behave as we do, and what may transform our action until we become capable or making the transition to socialism.[7]

[7] In a subsequent issue, *International Socialism* reprinted an article by Hal Draper 'as part supplement and part reply' to this article. See Draper 1963/4. According to Ian Birchall, who was on the editorial board of *IS* at the time, the Draper piece was published 'at [Tony] Cliff's insistence' as 'represent[ing] his own position'. Birchall 2000.

Chapter Twenty-Eight

True Voice[1]

A Review of Victor Serge, Memoirs of a Revolutionary

It was in Dwight Macdonald's journal *Politics* in 1944–5 that the only extracts from these memoirs published in Victor Serge's lifetime appeared. The honour that is due to Macdonald's nonconformity in that period may be measured by the fact that the editor of one Mexican journal which was publishing Serge in the same period was summoned before the Minister of the Interior (later President) Aleman, to have passed on the request not only of the Soviet but also of the British ambassador that Serge be excluded from publication.

Whose was this voice that had to be silenced? A voice in which the unpalatable truth about the Russian Revolution was told: unpalatable in 1944 to the Western myth-makers about Stalin; unpalatable to both Stalinists and neo-Trotskyists for his testimony about the dictatorship, not of proletariat, but of the bureaucrats from 1919 onward; unpalatable to all dogmatic anti-Bolsheviks for his refusal to admit the inevitability of the Revolution's degeneration:

1 Originally published in *New Statesman*, 30 August 1963, pp. 259–60.

> It is often said that 'the germ of Stalinism' was in Bolshevism at its beginning. Well I have no objection. Only Bolshevism contained many other germs – a mass of other germs – and those who lived through the enthusiasm of the first years of the first victorious revolution ought not to forget it.[2]

Victor Serge was, in adolescence, an anarchist in Belgium and France; in adult life, a revolutionary in both Barcelona and Leningrad; a leading official of the Third International and a leading organiser of the Left Opposition; and an exile in France and Mexico pursued by the GPU. His life is as much a microcosm of revolutionary activity as Trotsky's was, but it is complementary to Trotsky's. Trotsky, at every stage, had problems of organisation in the forefront of his mind; Serge, at every stage, had problems of people. In the critical years of the Russian Revolution, Serge as an anarchist adherent to Bolshevism was trusted both by those Bolsheviks who had libertarian doubts and by those anarchists who remained outside Bolshevism. He is thus able to give a more complete portrait of many Communists than they themselves ever dared to reveal in public, among them Lukács and Gramsci.[3] It is because he brings he brings political insight to bear in drawing this fine series of private faces that he is such a fine analysts of the human substance of the revolution.

This does not make him any less tough-minded. He supported the party during the repression of the libertarian revolutionaries at Kronstadt: there was no alternative to the Party. But he never concealed his hatred of the Cheka. And he had no illusions about the cardboard character of the Third International. What is more, these were not attitudes constructed after the event: unlike so many others, Serge never had to do violence to his own memories, never had to suppress or distort. The result is a document on a level with N. Sukhanov's personal record of the Revolution, Trotsky's *History* and Alfred Rosmer's account of the Third International under Lenin. Indeed, the four comprise the essential library of the Revolution.[4]

The most original and perhaps most exciting section of Serge's memoirs is that concerning the history of the Left Opposition in the Soviet Union. All three issues on which the Opposition fought, party democracy, agriculture and China, have remained relevant. Indeed, the Chinese Communist Party

---

[2] Serge 1939, p. 54.
[3] Serge 1978, pp. 186–7.
[4] Sukhanov 1984; Trotsky 1977; Rosmer 1971.

leaders who wish to understand the Soviet Union's betrayal of its alliance with them will need to read Serge. To understand him, of course, they would have to understand what is wrong with their revolution too. On the Left Opposition in general, Serge's account is a useful corrective to a too narrowly Trotskyist perspective on its activities. Serge understood that even the Trotskyist opposition to Stalin had to be transcended to carry through a socialist critique of modern society that would not remain within dead, authoritarian categories. The pathetic history of later so-called Trotskyism bears out everything he wrote.

Yet the fate of writers like Serge is too often read for support by those who wish to be confirmed in their own complacent dislike of all revolution. To these Serge can offer no comfort. His own ten years in prisons of various sorts left him nothing in common with the defenders of established social order.

The translation is excellent, and so are the editorial footnotes. The text, however, has been shortened by about one-eighth, a practice which leaves the French original as essential reading. Why this absurd parsimony?

Chapter Twenty-Nine
Trotsky in Exile[1]

A Review of Isaac Deutscher, The Prophet Outcast

Trotsky learning to fish in the Sea of Marmora from an illiterate Greek boy; Trotsky on a ski trip in the Norwegian Arctic; Trotsky feeding the rabbits among the cacti at Coyoacan: images such as these all contribute to the violent sense of dislocation which is produced by turning from the first two volumes of Isaac Deutscher's biography to the third. But this dislocation is not, of course, merely a matter of place. Trotsky's physical remoteness from events in the years 1929–40 is only matched by his apparent political isolation. The creator of the Red Army is reduced to the leader of a scattered following of a few hundred militants; the inspirer of the soviets is a stateless exile. Exile, of course, is not necessarily impotence. But the question must be faced. Is Trotsky in exile, like Marx in the British Museum, a commentator who is also an actor, or is he, like Napoleon on St. Helena, an outcast from world of action?

What kind of answer one gives to this question will determine the whole perspective in which one sees Trotsky's last decade. To understand Deutscher's

[1] Originally published in *Encounter*, v. 21, n. 6, December 1963, pp. 73–8. Reprinted in A. MacIntyre, *Against the Self-Images of the Age: Essays on Ideology and Philosophy*, Duckworth, London 1971, pp. 52–9.

answer fully, we shall have to look back to his Stalin. Deutscher's own statement in the preface to the 1961 edition of *Stalin* of the unity of his work on Stalin and Trotsky justifies us in so doing.

'In attempting to find an historical parallel to Stalin', wrote Trotsky in 1940, 'we have to reject not only Cromwell, Robespierre, Napoleon, and Lenin, but even Mussolini and Hitler.'[2] 'What appears to be established', wrote Deutscher in his *Stalin* (1949), 'is that Stalin belongs to the breed of the great revolutionary despots, to which Cromwell, Robespierre, and Napoleon belonged.'[3]

The gap between Deutscher's judgement and Trotsky's is a first clue to Deutscher's standpoint. For Deutscher believes that there is a 'broad scheme of revolutionary development' which is 'common to all great revolutionaries so far'. The first stage is one in which 'popular energy, impatience, anger and hope' burst out, and 'the party that gives the fullest expression to the popular mood outdoes its rivals, gains the confidence of the masses and rises to power'. There follows a second heroic stage of civil war in which revolutionary party and people are so well attuned that the leaders 'are willing and even eager to submit their policies to open debate and to accept the popular verdict'. This stage is short. Weariness and ruthlessness combine to open a gap between party and people. The party cannot abdicate without sacrificing the basis the revolution has created for social advance and prosperity; but it can no longer listen to – it must indeed in time suppress – the voice of the people. At this point the revolutionary party is split between those who see government by the people as the heart of the revolution and therefore cry that the revolution is betrayed and those who justify the new antidemocratic use of power as the only way to serve the ultimate interests of the people by preserving the gains of the revolution. This story is one that Deutscher supposes can be told of any 'party of the revolution, whether it be called Independent, Jacobin or Bolshevik', whether it is English, French or Russian.[4] It is within the framework of this story that Stalin and Trotsky are made to appear as playing out necessary roles. Trotsky, the caretaker of revolutionary purity, is necessarily doomed to political isolation in the period of the anti-democratic conservation of revolutionary gains. The significance of the quotation from

[2] Trotsky 1947, p. 413.
[3] Deutscher 1966, p. 550.
[4] Deutscher 1966, pp. 180–2.

Machiavelli which stands at the head of Deutscher's first volume is now clear: the prophet must be armed precisely so that he can, when the people no longer believe in the revolution, 'make them believe by force'.[5]

This is the setting for the message that is spelled out in the concluding volume. Trotsky's ideas and methods, so Deutscher argues, belonged to classical Marxism; but the 1930s were an epoch hostile both to revolution and to Marxism. After the Second World War, revolution resumed its course – but not as Marxism had predicted. It was revolution from above, brought to Eastern Europe by a foreign army, to China by a peasant *jacquerie*, which nonetheless inaugurated a socialist revolution. The Soviet bureaucracy – so Deutscher continues – is gradually reforming itself and at some point in this process will be forced to acknowledge Trotsky's greatness.[6] Classical Marxism will then have come into its own. Trotsky is thus honoured by Deutscher on two counts: as the great dissenter whose protest was both necessary and necessarily ineffective; and as the future patron saint of post-Khrushchevite Russia. That this is the frame within which the portrait of Trotsky in his last years is painted entails that Deutscher has written both a biography and a political tract. The weakness of his book arises from the conflict between these two tasks.

The strength of the book lies in the meticulous scholarship: names, dates, places; at this level of fact, Deutscher, as always, is a model of industry. Moreover his style is as magisterial as ever. He writes with the restrained passion of the deeply committed writer, whose deepest commitment of all is to objectivity. And yet, although objectivity can rescue one from many errors, it cannot either obliterate or conceal the effects of the basic incoherence of Deutscher's perspective. To exhibit this incoherence it is enough to look at how Trotsky himself developed his own positions in the years of exile.

Trotsky between 1928 and 1940 held at least four positions on the nature of the Russian state. In 1928, he held that political power, though effectively controlled by the bureaucrats, was still in some sense in the hands of the workers, because it was still possible for them to use constitutional means to 'regain full power, renovate the bureaucracy and put it under its control by the

5 Deutscher 2003a, epigram facing p. 1. See also Machiavelli 1975, pp. 51–2.

6 Deutscher 2003c, pp. 418–24.

road of reform of the party and the Soviets'.[7] He could write, in a letter to the Sixth Congress of the Communist International, that 'the socialist character of industry is determined and secured in a decisive measure by the role of the party, the voluntary internal cohesion of the proletarian vanguard, and conscious discipline of the administrators, trade union functionaries, members of the shop nuclei, etc'.[8] What matters is the access to political institutions still available to workers.

By 1933, Trotsky believed that this access was no longer available, but that Russia was still a workers' state. The cruel repression exercised by the bureaucracy is not incompatible with their maintaining the core of revolutionary gains so long as the means of production remain nationalised; but they have been able, by reason of the backwardness of Russia, to produce a tyranny which endangers the revolution. Trotsky by now believed that, inside and outside Russia, the Left Opposition had to constitute new political parties, genuinely revolutionary in the rest of the world, genuinely reformist in Russia. Reformist, because the bureaucracy was not as yet a new ruling class in the classical-Marxist sense, and the prospect of a political strategy in which the bureaucrats could be expropriated without force in the long run was not as yet unrealistic.

By the time *The Revolution Betrayed* was written in 1935, the perspective had changed yet again. Certainly Russia is still a workers' state, even though so gravely degenerated. But the bureaucracy can only be overthrown by a political revolution. The portrait of deadening, tyrannical oppression which is painted in *The Revolution Betrayed* could not be bettered.

Why then did Trotsky continue to insist that bureaucracy was only a caste, not a class, and why did he make the preservation of nationalised property the criterion of socialism? The answer is that, up to this point, he always envisaged the bureaucracy's final goal as being the restoration of private capitalism. He supposed that socialism and private capitalism exhausted the political alternatives – wrongly. For, in the period immediately before his death Trotsky did come around to envisage, even if only as a theoretical possibility, a new kind of exploitation – the collective class rule of the bureaucracy. This he

---

[7] Trotsky 1981, p. 295.
[8] Trotsky 1974, p. 230.

did not believe to have yet occurred. But his analysis of Soviet totalitarianism became even more radical:

> 'L'état c'est moi' is almost a liberal formula by comparison with the actualities of Stalin's totalitarian regime. Louis XIV identified himself with both the state and the Church – but only during the epoch of temporal power. The totalitarian state goes far beyond Caesaro-Papism.... Stalin can justly say, unlike le Roi Soleil, 'la société c'est moi'.[9]

Although Trotsky continued to defend the view that, in some sense, the Soviet Union was a workers' state, he had committed himself to predictions about the results of the Second World War, the outcome of which would for him settle the matter. If his view were correct, the Soviet bureaucracy after a victorious war would be overthrown as a result of proletarian revolution in the advanced countries of the West. If the view of those Trotskyists who held that a kind of bureaucratic state capitalism existed in Russia were correct, they would be vindicated by the failure to occur of such a revolution and such an overthrow. It was with this question still before him that Trotsky died.

To read Trotsky's successive evaluations of the Russian state against the background of what was done to his followers, his family and himself is to understand that theory too can have a dramatic role. For it was not merely Trotsky's person but his theoretical powers that Stalin wished to condemn to death. Stalinism required the pulverisation of every independent political voice in Russia and in the international Communist movement; hence not only the Moscow trials, but the extended passion of the Trotskyists in the Siberian camps, where those who had never surrendered, but who had continued to organise strikes, protests, and political propaganda among their fellow prisoners, were in 1938 marched out in groups and shot. Leon Sedov, Trotsky's elder son, died mysteriously in Paris with the GPU not far from his bedside; Sergei, who had reacted against both his father and his father's politics, and who worked quietly as a private citizen in Moscow, died at the hands of the GPU; Zina, one of his daughters – the other was already dead – had committed suicide under intense nervous strain in Berlin some years before. Rudolf Klement, the Secretary of the Fourth International, was in 1938 murdered, mutilated, and dropped in the Seine. If Trotsky was not

---

[9] Trotsky 1947, p. 421.

utterly crushed, it was only because he was upheld by his wife Natalya and by the conviction that no one but he could carry through his task and that the importance of his work was only to be measured by the venom he aroused in Stalin.

Among the many characters with walk-on parts in this drama some are familiar. Those who in 1962 protested at the Home Secretary's inhumanity to that 'persecuted progressive', Dr. Soblen, will meet him again in Deutscher's pages as the GPU Roman Well. Mr. Kingsley Martin turns up at Coyoacan, but the meeting is not altogether pleasant, because Mr. Martin wishes to defend the honour of his friend Mr. D.N. Pritt over his defence of the Moscow trials. M. Léon Blum appears suppressing protests against the trials and purges. Theodore Dreiser, Romain Rolland, and Louis Fischer play familiar roles as Stalinist apologists. If anyone says that at that time any of them could not have known better, that the threat of fascism and the effectiveness of Stalin's propaganda exculpate these men, the answer is that many were far from Trotsky's Marxism did know better. The aged John Dewey, chairman of the committee that vindicated Trotsky against Stalin's accusations, comes out of the whole affair with immense honour. So does Charles Beard, the veteran American historian. And they were not alone.

But the dimensions of Trotsky's tragedy and the way in which reactions to it became a touchstone of honour and dishonour only make the re-evaluation of his views the more crucial. An essential piece of evidence is Trotsky's single most brilliant piece of political comment, the pamphleteering on Germany from 1930 to 1933. The diagnosis of Nazism as 'the extremism of the center' which Professor S.M. Lipset advanced in *Political Man* is already made by Trotsky.[10] His castigations of the Comintern over its attitude to the Social Democrats, to the government of Brüning, and to Hitler himself all bore fruit in verified predictions. At the centre of his analysis the stress is on the importance of the presence or absence of a politically awakened working class. (Trotsky's advice about the mobilisation of the workers was never taken by the Comintern; but a parody of his point was taken, perhaps unwittingly, by Debré and de Gaulle when the paras threatened. Was there by the remotest of chances and historical ironies a link in Malraux?) This remains at the core of

[10] Lipset 1960, pp. 131–49, 173–6.

all Trotsky's analyses. For the Trotsky of the 1930s, as for Marx, socialism can be made only by the workers and not for them.

It is in part because of this that Trotsky, had he lived, would have had to treat his predictions about the aftermath of the Second World War as falsified. He could not but have concluded from his own premises that Russia was in no sense a workers' state, but rather a grave of socialism. The liberalisation of Khrushchev would have appeared to him as parallel to the liberalisation which has developed in other capitalisms once primitive accumulation has been accomplished. He could never have accepted Deutscher's analysis, which has only one thing in common with his own: the use of nationalised property as a criterion for socialism. Trotsky never believed in the possibility of the bureaucracy's self-reformation. In *The Revolution Betrayed* Trotsky wrote of the bureaucracy that

> To the extent that, for the benefit of an upper stratum, it carries to more and more extreme expression bourgeois norms of distribution, it is preparing a capitalist restoration. This contrast between forms of property and norms of distribution cannot grow indefinitely. Either the bourgeois norms must in one form or another spread to the means of production, or the norms of distribution must be brought into correspondence with the socialist property system.[11]

According to Deutscher, it is this latter course that Stalin's successors have adopted. In what way the norms of distribution differ from bourgeois norms he never explains (in Deutscher's view Britain also has surely abandoned bourgeois norms of distribution). But what is most interesting is that both Alfred Rosmer, Trotsky's most able and trusted companion, and Natalya Trotsky herself drew the opposite conclusion. It was for this reason that Natalya Trotsky explained her break with the stunted and ingrown politics of the self-styled Trotskyists by writing:

> If this trend continues, he (Trotsky) said, the revolution will be at an end and the restoration of capitalism will be achieved. That, unfortunately, is what has happened even if in new and unexpected forms.[12]

---

11 Trotsky 1937, p. 244.
12 Sedova Trotsky 1972a, p. 9.

Almost her last political act was a letter in *Azione Comunista* in November 1961 denouncing the idea that Mao Tse-tung was in any sense Trotsky's heir, and asserting that Russia and China were as far from socialism as Franco's Spain.[13]

One has, therefore, to choose. Either one can see Leon Trotsky in Natalya's perspective or in Deutscher's, but not in both. There seems little doubt which Trotsky would have chosen. The distressing thing to him about Deutscher's biography would have been that it makes him so acceptable to those against whom he struggled for his entire life. What is more, Deutscher's adroitness will make his conclusions equally palatable on both sides of the Iron Curtain. The news that socialism is Khrushchevite liberalisation plus nationalised property will not come amiss in Moscow. Both Trotsky and classical Marxism, it turns out, have to be amended to fit in with Russian reality. Trotsky's Marxist predictions were wrong, but Marxism is somehow vindicated nonetheless and so is Trotsky. I do not understand how. In the West too the news that the Khrushchevite régime is the necessary outcome of the Russian Revolution will be welcome. For this can be thrown back at all believers in the possibility of socialism in the West. It is admirably suited for apologists of the status quo. Trotsky, the inevitable protester against the inevitable course of socialist history, can be safely received by both sides as a dead martyr, with a sigh of relief that they have not the living revolutionary to deal with.

What is most curious about Deutscher's anxiety to approve of the present developments in Russia, and of Trotsky and of the letter of classical Marxism, is that Trotsky's own attitude to Marxism was far less hagiographical. Throughout his life, Trotsky was prepared to reformulate Marxism. The theory of permanent revolution bears striking witness to this. In the 1930s, we see him trying to use the Marxist theory of classical capitalism to understand entirely new situations. In this situation, it may have been that Marxism proved a totally inadequate scheme (the orthodox sociological response) or it may have been that it provided a necessary starting-point for a new, more complex, but still Marxist, schematicism. The attempts to characterise the Russian bureaucracy pose just this question; the attempt to characterise postwar Western capitalism would have posed it even more harshly. But

[13] Sedova Trotsky 1972b, p. 15.

whatever answers Trotsky might have given, he could never have been an accomplice to Deutscher's worship of the accomplished fact. Deutscher himself sees clearly in his discussion of Trotsky's *History of the Russian Revolution* that Trotsky was no believer in Deutscherian necessity.

The Shakespearean richness of character which is among the chief glories of the *History* brings out the important difference between those actors who are essentially representatives of a social group or class, and who are therefore replaceable, and those actors who are more than this, who cannot be so replaced. Miliukov, the Russian liberal, is essentially a mirror for the Russian bourgeoisie – 'grey, self-interested, cowardly'.[14] Lenin, by contrast, was both an expression of his party and more than this. Had he been absent, the Revolution's chances, so Trotsky argued, would have been very different. Deutscher devotes several pages to trying to refute Trotsky's conclusion on this point and we can see why this is necessary for his whole argument.[15] If, from time to time, history presents us with real alternatives where my actions can make all the difference, then I am not just part of an inevitable historical progress. Deutscher invokes Plekhanov's determinism on his side and the reminiscence of Plekhanov is suggestive. Deutscher's life of Trotsky, with all its scholarship, its brilliance of style, its perversity about socialism, its service of the established fact, and its determinism, is just the biography that we can imagine a Plekhanov of the 1960s writing. But Trotsky himself evades all the categories of a Plekhanovite Marxism; his image refuses to be accommodated.

The truth of this is reflected in the way that his name continues to haunt all established powers. So-called Trotskyism has been among the most trivial of movements. It transformed into abstract dogma what Trotsky thought in concrete terms at one moment in his life and canonised this. It is inexplicable in purely political dimensions, but the history of the more eccentric religious sects provides revealing parallels. The genuine Trotskyism of Rosmer and Natalya must have at most a few hundred adherents in the entire world. Yet Trotsky's is the name which is continually invoked, at one level by employers who fear rank-and-file industrial agitation and at another by those super-

14 Trotsky 1977, p. 207.
15 Deutscher 2003c, pp. 195–204.

employers, the Russian and Chinese states, in their polemics against each other. If they were to read Deutscher and to accept his conclusions, they would wonder what the spectre could have been which haunted them. But I doubt if it is possible to lay Trotsky's ghost so easily.

Chapter Thirty

Labour Policy and Capitalist Planning[1]

> But of late, since Bismarck went in for state ownership of industrial establishments, a kind of spurious socialism has arisen, degenerating, now and again, into something of flunkeyism, that without more ado declares all state ownership, even of the Bismarckian sort, to be socialistic. Certainly if the taking over by the state of the tobacco industry is socialistic, then Napoleon and Metternich must be numbered among the founders of socialism. (Frederick Engels).[2]

> But however much they do plan, however much the capitalist magnates calculate in advance the volume of production on a national and even on an international scale, and however much they systematically regulate it, we still remain under capitalism – capitalism in its new stage, it is true, but still, undoubtedly, capitalism. (V.I. Lenin)[3]

---

[1] Originally published in *International Socialism*, First Series 15, Winter 1963/4, pp. 5–9.

[2] Engels 1975–2004a, p. 265, note.

[3] Lenin 1960–70g, p. 448.

The new capitalism

From Togliatti to Wilson the cry goes up across Western Europe that socialism is now state-sponsored planning plus automation. It is sad that neither Wilson nor Togliatti is a keen student of Engel's dialectic; for it would be a great comfort to those who believe that opposites become one in a higher synthesis to realise that, oddly enough, capitalism too is now state-sponsored planning plus automation. What is the shape and what are the needs of contemporary capitalism?

Capitalism is essentially rationalistic in its approach to means, even if absolutely irrational in regard to ends. The individual firm, at first competing blindly for a share in a market whose potential is unknown and simultaneously competing for a share in a similarly unknown potential investment, is forced into prediction. Unsuccessful prediction entails losses. Successful prediction brings with it not only profits but an identification of the factors that need to be controlled if the unknowns of investment and the market are to be replaced by what is known. The control of these factors is of course beyond the power of the individual firm, even in the end beyond the power of the large corporation. But it is not beyond the power of the state apparatus to provide the legal controls, the financial underpinning, a variety of state enterprises and bureaucratised links between state and private enterprise, and even international agreements, which enable investment, production and the market to be planned.

There is thus a natural progress from the anarchy of capitalist competition to the order of capitalist planning. Not that the progress of capitalism from anarchy to planning was in fact easy or natural. It took decades of the business cycle, crisis, stagnation and above all, war, for capitalism to make this transition. Even then, it is always made unevenly, often unwillingly, and past anarchy continually invades present planning. Nonetheless, it is this capitalism which has stabilised itself in a way that the old capitalism never could, and which has stabilised itself self-consciously. This is why the sneers made at the Labour Party conference about the Conservative Party leadership's late conversion to planning could be misleading, as misleading as Togliatti's approval for government regulation and intervention in Italy. Planning is *not* inherently alien to capitalism.

How does capitalism plan? By attempting only to control the size of the flow of credit, and through that the economy, one produces the kind of cycle of inflation and deflation which occurred in Britain in the Fifties. One has also to control the direction of investment, partly by government spending and investment in state enterprise, partly through the planned investment of the large corporations. Through international banking and tariff agreements one can, to some extent, lessen the risks of international trade. But, above all, either directly or indirectly, one has to integrate one's objectives for investment, production and profits. The concept which expresses the ideal of such an integration is that of 'overall growth'. The instruments of this concept include the French *Commission du Plan*, the secretariats of the Common Market in Brussels and the European Iron and Steel Community, and at home, NEDC. These instruments are essentially meeting-points for different capitalist interests. It is as these different interests embody the joint decisions in their own plans, those of ICI and Unilever, of Krupps and BSA, of Renault and the National Coal Board, that capitalist planning becomes a reality.

Who plans? The corporate controllers of capital, the managers of production and the managers of investment. To be a manager in this sense is not just to do a technical job for an employer; it is not to be a superior foreman executing someone else's decisions. The decisions in the board-rooms are rarely, if ever, controlled by the shareholder in any real sense. Even the decisions in the board-rooms are only part of a total process of decision-making in which the substance of power is widely shared and the title to a share is gained partly by ownership of private capital, and partly by membership of a managerial élite. What are the planner's aims and needs?

First, of course, continuous reinvestment of capital in an unbroken programme of replacement and technological modernisation. Here, everything turns on a high degree of mobility in the labour force, which must be available for hiring at points of expansion and which must be expendable in declining industries. Automation entails both the continual recurrence of redundancies and the need for ever new types of technically trained manpower. We must, in other words, have a labour force that can be continually reshaped, expanded and contracted according to the demands of technological reinvestment.

Secondly, the planners require maximum predictability in terms of availability of resources and they must therefore be able to predict costs – and especially labour costs. They require to know in advance what the wages bill will be. They require the co-operation of unions and employers in framing an agreed long-term wages policy in which a limitation is securely placed on the growth of wages. This is why, although NEDC is a model for the new bureaucratised corporate capitalism, NIC is not. For NIC cannot get the co-operation of the unions and cannot therefore produce a planned incomes policy.

It is worth pointing out that a great deal of private, old-fashioned unplanned capitalism survives alongside the new model. But it is even more important to emphasise that the new planned capitalism is still capitalism. For here we have to combat both the disciples of Crosland and the antique Left, who share the belief that the essence of capitalism resides in private ownership and control, on the one hand, and anarchic, unplanned investment and production on the other. The antique Left recognise that we still live under capitalism, and are therefore forced to deny the facts of corporate planning; Crosland has a keen eye for the facts, but is therefore forced to conclude from his premise that we no longer live under capitalism. Yet neither Crosland nor the antique-dealers were the dangerous men at the Labour Party conference. The dangerous men were found in every wing of the party and what united them was the adoption with enthusiasm of the programme of the new capitalism as Labour's aim. For, in Britain today, the principal needs of the new capitalism are clearly two-fold: an expansion of technological education and control of wages. Moreover, these must be carried through in such a way as to leave the working class as unclear as possible as to the implications of these policies. The ideal for the new capitalism is therefore precisely a Labour government with Wilson's policies. But here at once a question arises: why did a party conference which fought Gaitskell's right-wing reformist policies walk like a lamb behind Harold Wilson? The answer given by both Wilson's admirers and his enemies is that Wilson is a superb political manipulator; to this the reply must be that Wilson's record as a political manipulator up to this point makes Guy Fawkes seem a brilliant conspirator by comparison. But not only is this view of Wilson false, it is dangerously misleading. We must look not at the leader, but at the party. If we do so, it becomes clear that Wilson arrived just as the party's reformism had become finally out-dated. What Wilsonism filled was a vacuum. We must now ask how this vacuum was created. What happened to the reformism of traditional social democracy?

The end of reformism

Reformism is the conviction that socialism can be achieved by the use of and participation in the existing political institutions of the liberal-bourgeois state. It was the natural, although not the inevitable, horizon of the working class in the last decades of the last century and the early years of this. One reason for this was that the political differentiation of the working class from other classes in Western Europe entailed the creation of mass working-class parties competing for working-class allegiance with bourgeois parties; and, in a situation where successful insurrection was impossible, it was natural to conclude, as Engels concluded, that the increase in the parliamentary vote is the road to working-class power.[4] It was not, of course, originally the case that the reformist conception of socialism, of the final goals of politics, differed substantially from that of revolutionary socialists; it was primarily a difference as to the means, a difference which in time did transform the content of reformist socialist goals. Kautsky's career illustrates this transformation excellently. There are, however, three other reasons for the rise of reformism, the occurrence of each of which separately is a necessary precondition for social-democratic politics.

The first lies in the social character of the working class. A tolerably homogeneous working class, with its own institutions, and a widespread consciousness that its aims could only be achieved politically, appears in the last decades of the last century. Its life is dominated by the facts of low wages and intermittent unemployment. Poverty defines its form of life. Only very

[4] The belief that Engels came to such a conclusion is based on the version of his 1895 introduction to Marx's *The Class Struggles in France*, first published in Germany in Social Democratic Party paper *Vorwärts*. This version was still in print at the time 'Labour Policy and Capitalist Planning' was written, yet it was heavily edited by Eduard Bernstein to the point of distortion, notably by omitting the passages in which Engels argued for the continued necessity of street-fighting. Engels complained to Kautsky on the day of publication: 'I was amazed to see today in the *Vorwärts* an excerpt from my 'Introduction' that had been *printed without my prior knowledge* and tricked out in such a way as to present me as a peace-loving proponent of legality *quad meme* [i.e. come what may].' Engels 1975–2004f, p. 486. Engels had avoided revolutionary rhetoric in the introduction for two reasons. One was that that the SPD executive were worried that formulations of this sort would give ammunition to supporters of the anti-socialist laws then being debated in the German parliament. The other was that he was concerned to instruct young socialists in the need to avoid putchist emphasis on military tactics at the expense of politics. He also discussed the difficulties of barricade-based street-fighting given the greater power of the state than in 1848. See Rees 1994/5, pp. 79–81. The entire article can now be read in its original form in Engels 1975–2004d.

rarely can individuals or families hope to rise from the working class; the thesis of Victorian self-help, of the rewards of thrift and hard work, has been empirically falsified. The propagation of socialist theory has sharpened and clarified the sense that there is little or no community of interest between the working class and the rest of society. For the working class does not benefit from the unrestrained pursuit of profit; this pursuit, in fact, it is precisely in the interest of the working class to restrain. Production must be planned so that the vagaries of the trade cycle and the consequent vagaries of employment cease to occur; and it must be planned as a whole, that is there must be national ownership of the means of production.

The second precondition of social democracy is that there shall be a widespread and plausible belief that the state is, at least potentially, politically neutral as between rival classes and economic interests. The institutions of the state can be transferred from the control of the representatives of the bourgeoisie to those of the working class. It is very easy now to castigate this belief as pure and even obvious error. But it is not only a belief to which Engels late in his life seemed to have given his sanction, it is a belief which appears to find a charter in Marx's *Inaugural Address to the First International*.[5] Moreover, the working class was able to win real victories in the form of parliamentary legislation, and for a long time the nature of classical capitalism nourished this belief in the neutral state. Classical capitalism as an economic form requires of the state principally non-intervention. The state must not itself infringe and must prevent others from infringing the freedoms of the free market, and especially the freedom to recruit, exploit and fire labour. There is more than one form of state compatible with this requirement; capitalism has flourished under parliamentary democracy, Bismarckian paternalism, Japanese hierarchical government, Nazi dictatorship, and a variety of other forms. It is natural enough, therefore, to envisage state and economy as somehow independent of each other, and to miss the fact that capitalism as an economic form is tolerant only to rival and alternative political forms within strict limits, the limits being set by the relations between capital and labour which capital requires. The existence of a working class with the kind of political aims which it had acquired and of an apparently neutral and

5 Marx 1974b, p. 80: 'To conquer political power has therefore become the great duty of the working classes.'

controllable form of state in parliamentary democracies supply the obvious preconditions for a social-democratic programme in which the attempt is made to eliminate unemployment and the trade cycle by planned production on a basis of national ownership and to eliminate poverty by redistributive taxation and by planned welfare.

The third, and less obvious, precondition for social democracy is the existence of the kind of ruling class which is able and willing to accept the rules of the parliamentary game and with them the possible implementation of parts of the social democratic programme. The inducement to a ruling class to do this is two-fold. First of all, the consequences of excluding the working class from power are likely to be far more devastating to the established order than that of encouraging their parliamentary illusions. For to do this would be to assist revolutionary socialism at the expense of social democracy. Secondly, it becomes increasingly clear that many social-democratic measures coincide with the needs of capitalism as it discovers the increasingly severe defects of *laissez-faire* methods for its own purposes. There is thus a potential area of co-operation between capitalism and social democracy, which helps to assure social democracy of its parliamentary rights. Anyone who doubts this should compare Mr. Harold Macmillan's book *The Middle Way* with Lord Attlee's *The Future of the Labour Party* (sic), two statements of policy about Britain in the 1930s.[6]

Reformism then depends upon the presence of three preconditions: a certain type of working class, a certain type of view of the state (itself possible only if the state is of a certain kind) and a certain type of ruling class. But all three preconditions have in fact disappeared. We no longer have the same type of working class, the same type of state or beliefs about the state, or the same type of ruling class. The working class is far less homogeneous. The gap between workers in relatively stable employment with relatively high wages and the poor (the ill, the mentally ill, migrant labour, seasonal labour, minorities doing unskilled jobs) has enormously increased. The skilled working class is itself divided and fragmented in all sorts of ways. What is more the goals of working-class people are not now political in the sense that they were; that is they can see no connection between getting what they want and any actual political institution. Part of the reason for this lies in the

[6] Atlee 1937; Macmillan 1938.

changed character of the state, which is now so well integrated with the key institutions of the capitalist economy that it cannot any longer be conceived of as a neutral, independent source of power that could be used against that economy. Consequently, the whole reformist programme of nationalisation and planning by the use of the existing institutions of the bourgeois state has become irrelevant. The transfer of steel from 'private' to 'public' ownership would entail essentially a new set of titles for the same set of committees, the criteria of efficiency in the industry would remain the same, that is the industry would be ruled by the criteria of profitability.

Equally, as I have already argued, the ruling class has changed. They do not need to accommodate themselves to the working class now by means of parliamentary institutions. The fundamental transactions in which class meets with class are directly economic and take place in the various institutional forms of arbitration and negotiation. These institutions absorb the reformist leadership into not merely legislating for capitalism (as the reformist used to do in parliament) but actually helping to administer it. Neocapitalist bureaucracies can assimilate trade-union bureaucrats in a way that old-style capitalists never could.

In this situation, therefore, the traditional reformist programmes and attitudes become largely irrelevant, and, under the pressure of irrelevance, left and right reformism split even further apart than they had already done. What was originally a difference about the pace and degree of reformist activity becomes a difference of principle. Both sides recognise that traditional reformist means can never lead to traditional reformist ends. Right reformists preserve the means, but abandon the socialist goal and become in respect of the new capitalism not socialist, but liberal reformers. Left reformers preserve the ends of socialism, but become increasingly vague as to the means. Their key term tends to be 'pressure', which they hope to exert on a leadership that will otherwise drift to the right. For them, contemporary politics becomes a question of Harold Wilson's intentions, of how to strengthen his socialism, or of how to replace him if it flags. But, in fact, Wilson's intentions are not and cannot be sovereign. What determines the policy of the next Labour government is not primarily a matter of who leads the party. It is primarily a matter of the consciousness first of the working class and then of the party, as to how the class issues are to be defined under the new capitalism. Any policy which simply and blindly meets the needs of that capitalism, as the

Scarborough policies do, cannot but be anti-socialist, however good the private intentions of the leaders.

We can now see why Wilson could succeed where Gaitskell failed. The collapse of reformism has left a policy vacuum among the traditionalists of both Right and Left, and the new capitalism has no place in their theoretical maps. Moreover, the continuity between the work of the last Labour government and the shape of the new capitalism is sufficiently evident for reformist adherence to the new capitalism to be strongly reinforced. To this explanation of Labour's official acceptance of the new capitalism (which extends to the expressed desire to get rid of 'the dead wood in the board rooms') two footnotes must be added.

The first is that in the new situation that that we now face a good many of our old characterisation of people and groups as Left and Right may break down. It is a period of possible realignments. We ought therefore to be insistent that what matters are the issues, not the personalities. To accept Wilsonism is to have moved over to the Right at least for the moment, no matter what other professions of socialism are made; to be prepared to understand and criticise planned capitalism is the essential first stage in a move to the Left. Journals such as *Tribune*, *Keep Left* and *Union Voice* will have to decide which way they are going to move.

Secondly, just as within and alongside the new planning the old capitalist anarchy can still be found, so inside the Wilsonian Labour Party there are still footholds for the old reformism, particularly in fighting defensive actions on behalf of workers in declining industries or depressed areas. But these facts do not alter the general directions of both capitalism and the official Labour leadership.

Socialist policies

'....but still, undoubtedly, capitalism.' Lenin's words are of fundamental import. Capital's economic domination of labour, the drive to accumulate, the criteria of profitability, the subordination of consumption to production – all the cardinal characteristics of capitalism survive the transition from anarchy to planning. Poverty remains. The unbalance even between long-term and short-term projects (a decent transport system *versus* speculative property development) for growth, let alone between production for growth and production for need (almost anything *versus* nurses' pay and hospital provision) exhibits itself everywhere. The subordination of consumption to production is well-marked in the reasons given for and the priorities suggested for educational expansion. We do not produce more so that our children shall have a fuller and more human education; we need more pure and applied scientists and technicians, in order that British firms may compete in the world market, and so we devise new educational programmes. Above all, the new capitalism exhibits its continuity with the old in the two realms left untouched by conventional reformist politics: the relations of capital to labour *within* the factory at the point of production and the relations between capitalist states in which the sanction of pure force is exhibited most nakedly. It is here that the worker does continue to experience all the pressures of capitalism in relation to his actual wants and goals: the continual frustrations of being subjected to the process of production and the continual threat of nuclear annihilation. It is at these two points that the genuine politics of class must be discovered.

If this is so, the apathy towards conventional politics, broken only when scandals or personalities can turn conventional politics into an entertainment along the lines of *Z-Cars* or *Coronation Street*, is entirely intelligible. For, on the one hand, we have the fact that parliament is only legislating with one eye to needs and pressures that are determined elsewhere, either by the individual decisions of the managerial class or by the objective and impersonal development of the whole shape of the new capitalism. We have the whole process of transition from parliamentary decision to cabinet decision to premier's decision which has been traced in successive British governments by political scientists. And we have also the contentless character of a debate between parties in which each vies with the other for the possession of the slogans of neocapitalist modernisation. On the other hand, we have the exclusion from conventional politics of the substantial issues which necessarily impact on working-class experience and which necessarily define the arena of class-struggle. In this situation, the discovery that many working-class people are apathetic about politics should therefore cause us neither surprise nor alarm. It would be alarming indeed if it were otherwise.

It would, however, be a great mistake to conclude from all this that we should therefore turn away entirely from the traditional institutions of the labour movement and concentrate instead *only* upon the rank-and-file shop floor struggles in industry and the peace movement. For to do this would be to accept the class struggle on the terms in which the capitalist would wish us to accept it. It is precisely *within* the factory or *within* the particular industry that workers can be isolated and defeated; it is precisely insofar as they transcend these limitations and build institutions which express their life and struggle as a class that they escape the narrowness and isolation which bring about their defeat quite as much as the efforts of the employers do. But this is not advocate traditional policies of entrism or to combat traditional policies of non-entrism; both these alternatives die with the death of reformism. Capturing the Labour Party leadership is a pointless as well as a hopeless aim. What is neither pointless nor hopeless is the task of recreating a *political* trade unionism out of the existing links between the Labour Party and the unions. It is in building organised political support for policies for the whole class that we can do this. The policies which we need are of at least two kinds.

There are first of all the policies which are directed towards the re-organisation of the working class. Part of the urgency here derives from the fact that if the working class is often divided and weakened by the impact of the new capitalism, it is also strengthened by the new recruits whom it receives. Just as skilled technicians become the key workers, so many groups who formerly thought of themselves wholly in terms of middle-class status are reduced to the condition of skilled technicians: teachers, insurance officials, bank clerks, and nurses. Their conditions of work force them towards trade-union militancy. Their class reunion with the skilled technicians and the semi-skilled worker could mark the arrival of a more educated and aware working class than ever before, with the possibility of more sophisticated strategies of struggle to match the new capitalist sophistication.

Second, we need to provide agencies, staffed by skilled economists, which can inform the working class of the overall shape of the new capitalism and of its points of vulnerability. We need to frame wage demands based not upon what workers take home now, but upon what the industry can only just bear to give, but cannot bear not to give, in case strike action should upset its time-table of agreed objectives. The very fact that the new capitalism is planned opens up the way to new methods of disruption by an informed choice of when and where to strike. But this overall strategy for the class will only be operable if almost every worker is able to understand and assent to this strategy, if there is a national web of democratically inclusive and democratically effective trade-union institutions. And a first prerequisite for such institutions is the defence and extension of the shop stewards' movement.

We have to frame these policies with an eye to the key question of which class is to have power over planning, and it is this question which has also to inform our attitude to the by-now-probable next Labour government. Here we have three specific political demands to make us a counterpart to our trade-union programme.

The first is that in the battle between employers and workers over control of wages, the Labour government must side with the workers and against the employers. The only condition on which the workers should accept controlled and limited wages should be control by workers over profits and investment.

The second specific demand is that education shall be in the interests of equipping workers to control their own lives and to take power, not in the interests of allocating workers to subordinate positions of powerlessness. Here, we have to challenge any attempt to implement the Robbins Report at the expense of the secondary-modern schools. We have to challenge any attempt to teach technical skills without giving social consciousness. We have to attack the limitations of education and welfare in the interests of arms spending, and we can infer from all that the Labour leadership have said that they are unlikely to want to diminish arms spending.

The third specific demand is the abolition of the Bomb. The abandonment of the struggle for unilateralism by almost all the Labour Left must be underlined. The commitment of the bourgeois state to force has to be brought out in terms of the truth of the axiom of all bourgeois statesmen that they can only hope to negotiate from strength. What this means is evidenced in the fact that Kennedy could only hope to make the test-ban treaty acceptable by pledging renewed arms expenditure, including renewed expenditure on nuclear weapons, to the US Senate. Every concession of a disarming kind entails by the logic of this process a counterpart in rearmament. And this is true also of the type of concession promised by Labour's foreign policy. But we have to make the struggle against the Bomb not a series of sporadic reactions to crisis situations, but a thread which runs through all our political work. For here, in the Bomb, the irrationality of capitalism and its inability to control the technological powers it unlooses are permanently manifest and permanently manifest as the threat that they are.

For the interest in wages, the interest in their children's education, and the interest in survival are permanent interests for the working class which engage them politically as a class. A policy of trade-union activity without these objectives would be narrow and confined; with them, it becomes a policy which questions not merely the details of the new capitalism, but its deepest assumptions. This programme raises the question not of merely of the reform of the new capitalism, but of its replacement, and it raises it both for the struggle at the point of production and for the political struggle.

A case for optimism?

Every delay in breaking with and exposing Wilsonism does harm to the cause of promoting working-class consciousness. All the pressures towards party unity make it more urgent for the statement of an alternative attitude towards the new capitalism. I have had in setting out the arguments here to explain the case for a new sociology of capitalism and a new strategy towards capitalism with extreme brevity. In correcting what I have had to say, other comrades will also, I hope, expand it. But it is worth editing upon a note of optimism. Revolutions do not take place in fact against backgrounds of pauperisation and slump. They take place when in a period of rising expectations the established order cannot satisfy the expectations which it has been forced to bring into being. The new capitalism cannot avoid calling into being a new working class with large horizons so far as not merely wages but also education and welfare are concerned. It equally cannot avoid controlling incomes and allotting its educated workers frustrating positions of subordination. Whether it will or will not founder on this contradiction depends in part on the forms of our present activity. It would be silly to be over-optimistic, but it may be that we are entering the first period for a long time in which over-pessimism is a greater danger for socialists.

Chapter Thirty-One

Marx[1]

The rich complexity of Marx's thought cannot be compressed into one easy summary, in spite of the fact that, from Engels onwards, Marx has been presented as the author of a single coherent system. In fact, at different periods of his life, Marx responded to quite different pressures and any true account of Marx has to preserve both the unity and the diversity.

I shall try to divide Marx's intellectual history into three periods. The first is that in which Marx developed all his fundamental theses, and this was complete by 1846. The second centres upon the revolutionary years of 1848–9. The third is that of the years in exile in London after 1849, marked both by the mature economic writings and by the founding of the First International. The key works of the first period are the *Economic-Philosophical Manuscripts* and *The German Ideology*, of the second *The Communist Manifesto* and the *Address to the Communist League*, of the third the *Inaugural Address* to the International Working Men's Association and the first volume of *Capital*.

Marx's originality was the product of an immense capacity for both digesting all that his predecessors had written and allowing their ideas to combine in

[1] Originally published in M. Cranston (ed.) *Western Political Philosophers: A Background Book*, Bodley Head, London 1964, pp. 99–108.

new and unexpected ways. The younger and more radical of Hegel's followers, with whom Marx at first belonged, saw the growth of freedom and rationality in terms of an intellectual struggle against false beliefs and a political struggle against governmental and especially Prussian censorship and repression. Marx, as the editor of a liberal newspaper, the *Rheinische Zeitung*, not only experienced the power of the censor, but continually had his attention drawn to the conflicts between such social groups as industrialists, landowners and peasants, and to the economic issues which engendered these conflicts. An intensive reading of classical political economy from Quesnay and Adam Smith to Say and Ricardo was fused with his earlier Hegelianism to produce a critique both of political economy and of the capitalist order which it portrays.

Hegel had seen history as a series of transformations of human consciousness, logically interconnected and developing to a climax in Hegel's own philosophy, in the course of which men became alienated from themselves and each other. Part of this alienation consists in a false consciousness by which men conceive of what are, in fact, the products of human decision and purpose as impersonal forces reigning over them. Freedom consists in overcoming this alienation. This, for Hegel, is to be an achievement of philosophy.

For Marx this bondage of men to a false consciousness is real, but secondary. Their true alienation is rooted in the social organisation of work under capitalism, where the worker is treated as a mere productive unit of labour, whose products are taken away from him in return for a subsistence wage. Political economy with its abstract categories and its impersonal laws presents the capitalist economy as produced by the workings of necessary and unalterable laws. Its impersonality, which reflects the social impersonality of capitalism, both falsifies the nature of capitalism and strengthens illusions about its inevitability.

The laws which govern the production and exchange of commodities are up to a point an accurate description of the process in which labour itself becomes a commodity and in which the labourer produces an accumulated capital in which he has no share, but the power of which dominates him. Yet political economy is written as if its categories – commodities, labour, capital, rent and so on – were ultimate. In fact these categories are abstractions which disguise rather than explain the place of economic transactions in total human activity. If we look at the history of such activity we can explain how these categories came to have application, how the capitalist system came to be. If we look at the workings of the system to which they apply we can see that what these categories omit – that is, the social context of the economic system – blinds political economists to the creation within capitalism of a class whose basic human needs and demands are necessarily denied by capitalism, the industrial working class. This class is both necessarily created by and necessarily antagonistic to capitalism.

Thus classical political economy fails to understand the transitory character of capitalism, of how capitalism itself prepares the conditions which will bring about its downfall; and it fails also to understand its own role as not at all a neutral descriptive account of capitalism, but a partisan justification of it disguised as such an account. From this early analysis, Marx drew four conclusions which constitute the essential core of Marxist theory.

The first is that all social systems to date are misunderstood if we try to analyse them in terms of an actual or possible common general interest. Utilitarian slogans such as 'the greatest happiness of the greatest number' blur the conflict between social classes which is such that to realise the interests of one class is to frustrate those of another. The political, social and economic forms which constitute the unity of a society are an index of which class is dominant, of what the tensions between classes are and of what battles the ruling class has to fight. The dominant modes of thought cannot escape being those of the ruling class. By a class, Marx means a group united by their role in the processes of production and capable of a conscious unity on the basis of the common activities and aims which such a relationship affords them.

Secondly, Marx concludes that the key to political and social relationships in his own time (and, he would have said, in ours) is the relationship between bourgeoisie and working class. The strength of the bourgeoisie is, of course, dependent upon their having succeeded in abolishing the limitations on a capitalist mode of production which a feudal social order imposes and in having somehow resolved their consequent struggle with a land-owning aristocracy. The Germany of Marx's youth and the Russia of his old age both had weak bourgeoisies by this criterion; England and France therefore furnished him with his models of bourgeois societies with developed institutions. The strength of the working class is dependent upon capitalism having progressed to the point at which workers are concentrated in cities, are organised in self-consciously working-class institutions as a result of their experience of industrial life, and have learnt the inadequacy of bourgeois-liberal parliamentary democracy for remedying their conditions. The working class is the sole revolutionary class; other classes, petty bourgeoisie and peasants, for example, may suffer under capitalism, but their experience neither disciplines them nor educates them into the possibilities of a new classless society in which commodity production for profit, organised by the few, is replaced by socialist production for human need, in the control of which everyone shares. The view of the disciples of Mao Tse-tung that the peasantry can be an independent revolutionary class is entirely foreign to Marx.

Thirdly, no political theory can be understood out of its context in the struggle between classes. Of course, Marx did not deny the possibility of neutral factual description of political and economic conditions; he was an inveterate user of the reports of factory inspectors, of government blue books, and of *The Economist*. But all attempts to explain the social system either express its self-image and so serve the ruling class, as classical political economy did, or else they undermine and subvert that self-image by exposing the true nature of the system and so serve the working class. This is the function of Marx's own writings. It follows that there are no neutral standards to which appeal can be made in this conflict. Appeals to principles of morality or justice are worse than useless, for these principles as they exist to date will be well adapted to express the interests of the hitherto ruling classes. Appeals to religion are worse, since religious illusions have the two-fold function of providing justifications for a hierarchical society and false consolations for the oppressed which can only emasculate revolutionary activity. More generally, Marx refuses to detach intellectual activity from its social role. He has sometimes been depicted as arguing that ideas are essentially powerless, and that the moving force of history is economic activity. But this is a misrepresentation. Marx denies the existence of genuinely disinterested theorising, and he thinks that the social power of theories depends upon the power of the social and economic movements that they express. But he also believed that without appropriate expression in the realm of ideas, social movements could fail. Moreover, the power of reason to inform human activity so that it can master its environment more effectively increases at each stage of human history. In bourgeois society, nature no longer enslaves men; in communist society they will no longer be enslaved by social relationships. The question about beliefs and theories is always: what kind of activity do they express? 'The philosophers have hitherto interpreted the world; the point however is to change it.'[2]

Fourthly, the struggle by the working class against the bourgeoisie is a political struggle; but Marx recognised that no political struggle can transcend the limitations set by a given stage of economic development. The failure of the French Revolution to realise working-class democracy was not due to any organisational failure on the part of the revolutionaries, in the way in which Babeuf, for example, thought; it was due to the limits set on political possibility by the development of a bourgeois economy to a certain stage. Germany in Marx's youth could not hope to see a growing communist movement among the working class without further development of capitalist industrialisation. It is only when the necessary preconditions have been realised in economic growth that revolutionary possibility opens up for the new class. Until that stage is realised when workers act politically, they necessarily act as supporters of a still-rising bourgeoisie. So it was in France in 1789–93; but it was in France in 1848 that, for the first time, the working class appears as revolutionary against the bourgeoisie.

In the revolutionary years of 1848–9, Marx made a substantial transition from social theory to political programme. It is in the *Manifesto of the Communist Party*, which he and Engels wrote for the London branch of the Communist League in the closing weeks of 1847 and the early days of 1848, that this transition first becomes visible. The style of the *Manifesto* is itself a notable expression of Marx's belief in the unity of theory and practice; for it links theoretical insight to a call to action with a passion rarely encountered in the works of political theory. 'A spectre is haunting Europe – the spectre of communism.' Why? This spectre is the outcome of all previous history. 'The history of all previous society is the history of class struggles.'[3] Feudal landlord replaced slave-owner; capitalist replaced feudal landlord; now capitalism breeds its own destruction. The bourgeoisie in their time played a revolutionary part. By the untrammelled pursuit of profit and the ruthless utilisation of every conquest of nature the bourgeoisie broke the bonds of feudalism. All patriarchal ties, all the traditional links between men have

---

[2] Marx 1975c, p. 423: 'The philosophers have only *interpreted* the world, in various ways; the point is to *change* it.'

[3] Marx and Engels 1973, p. 67: 'The history of all hitherto existing society is the history of class struggle.'

yielded to the solvents of the market economy. What has replaced those ties is the cash nexus.

But the acquisitive, exploiting bourgeoisie, in carrying through its enormous transformation of both nature and human life, has overreached itself. It can no longer control the forces and processes it has called into being; the symptom of this is the recurrence of economic crises. And it cannot prevent the continual growth of the industrial working class, for a capitalist economy both requires the existence of this class and necessarily organises it in such a way that the workers eventually profit from this organisation by using it against their masters. The values which will be destroyed by a revolution which abolishes private property in the means of production will merely be the values of bourgeois life.

The claim by the defenders of property that socialism will extinguish freedom, culture and morality rests on identifying these with bourgeois freedom, culture and morality, which are all empty as far as the working-class is concerned. When that class takes power, its first measures must be to attack the anomaly of capitalist production by nationalisation of land, of credit and of transport. It will take measures to tax wealth, to increase production, to introduce both work for al and education for all and so on.

The reader cannot but be struck by the contrast between the highly specific character of this programme and the lack of any equally specific account of how the working class are to take power which will enable them to carry it out. Near the beginning of the *Manifesto,* Marx had described two alternative possible outcomes to class-struggle: the victory of one class over the other or 'the ruin of the contending classes'.[4] Why is Marx so confident that of these alternatives it will be a working-class victory which results, when he is so vague about the nature of the transition to socialism?

This very question in a number of forms preoccupied Marx for the rest of his life. In particular he gradually restated his opinions on two matters. The first was the relationship between the small number of politically conscious revolutionaries and the rest of the working class. Here, Marx came to hold that a prerequisite for revolution was a widespread consciousness of revolutionary purpose among the working class. He stood at the opposite pole from the

[4] Marx and Engels 1973, p. 68.

kind of élitism which thought that a small, disciplined party of leaders could make the revolution on behalf of the working class.

Moreover, Marx struggled with the question of the relationship between the economic difficulties and crises of capitalism and the revolutionary activity of the working class. He realised in the light of later nineteenth-century experience that capitalist breakdown does not automatically breed working-class revolution. So there is an important place for the revolutionary party which nationally and internationally brings the working class to consciousness of its revolutionary potential. Hence the most crucial later activity of Marx lay perhaps in helping to found and guiding the International Working Men's Association, to which Marx declared in the *Inaugural Address* 'That the emancipation of the working-class must be conquered by the working-class themselves'.[5] This marks a decisive opposition to Fabianism and all other doctrines of 'socialism from above'. But it still leaves the question of a working-class political growth obscure. Marx's willingness to do this has at least three sources.

The first is pure error. The early Marx differed from Hegel as to what the inevitable progress of world history consisted, but never rid himself entirely of the notion of an inevitable progress. The later Marx accepted from Engels what was essentially a mechanistic and evolutionary version of historical development, in which Marx's thought was forced into the strait-jacket of a system at once metaphysical (its laws govern numbers, chemical combinations and grains of wheat just as much as they do social classes) and optimistic. So there returns to his thought the notion of inevitable and necessary laws governing human affairs and bringing them to their goal; yet this is just the notion which the young Marx had attacked as a symptom of false consciousness and alienation.

Secondly, however, Marx certainly thought that the elucidation of the workings of the capitalist economy was the prime essential in understanding the future. Hence his own intellectual efforts were devoted for thirty years to the writing of *Capital*, of which only the first volume was completed, and published in 1867. *Capital* is classic whose arguments are uneven. On the necessary expansion of capitalism it is as illuminating as when it was written. Capitalism is an economic order for which the law is: expand or perish. The

[5] This statement in fact occurs in the 'Provisional Rules', Marx 1974c, p. 82.

market economy which capitalism creates is characterised in a permanently valuable way. In specific prediction, Marx is less happy: right about the concentration of capital and the growth of the large combine; wrong about the falling rate of profit and about the polarisation of social classes into capitalists and workers. But *Capital* is positively misleading about the possibilities of expansion which will in the future prove open to capitalists. Marx did not allow either for the role of technological innovation or for the use of welfare-state methods to avoid underconsumption. His errors here are the counterpart of his insights. He envisages capitalism on the model of a finished, closed system, a necessary first step in understanding its systematic character. He works with the categories of capital, labour and the like in terms of this model. The result is that he cannot allow for the possibility of the capitalist coming to understand the system and taking steps to prevent the system collapsing in the way that Marx predicts. Here again, Marx is the victim of an error which he himself had earlier exposed; just as the classical political economists did, he assumes the ultimacy and the sufficiency of his own abstract categories.

Third, if, however, Marx was the victim of an over-mechanical view of development in his theory, his convictions about the emancipation of the working class were not grounded solely on these views. Indeed, they could not have been, since they were developed prior to his own mature economic theory and to Engels's interpretations of their shared philosophy. Marx's experience of working-class life and achievement was always at least as important to him. What prefigured socialism to him in later years was much more the activity of workers in the Paris Commune and the rise of German Social Democracy than any pure reliance on a theory which was to prove highly vulnerable to Keynes and to others. The theoretical framework which he used to interpret working-class activity is not so much that of the particular formulations of *Capital* as that of the writings of the 1840s, whose thought he never repudiated.

Chapter Thirty-Two
The Socialism of R.H. Tawney[1]

A Review of Richard Henry Tawney, The Radical Tradition

The deaths of R.H. Tawney and Hugh Gaitskell occurred so close together that they provide an apt symbol for the end of a period in the history of the British labour movement. It was a period in which the right wing of the Labour Party was hard put to it to provide a rationale for its policies, which would both justify its opposition to Marxism and yet enable it to escape from the platitudes of merely liberal goodwill. The number of those who might have provided such a rationale was surprisingly few. The Webbs defected to Stalinism from the Fabian Society (consistent élitists who believed throughout their career in socialism imposed from above, they merely changed in their choice of élite); John Strachey only defected *to* the Fabian Society from Stalinism at the end of the 1930s; and G.D.H. Cole was always too much of a Marxist to work within the limitations that the Labour Right imposed upon itself. Tawney therefore stood almost alone.

---

[1] Originally published in *The New York Review of Books,* 30 July 1964, pp. 21–2. Reprinted in A. MacIntyre, *Against the Self-Images of the Age: Essays on Ideology and Philosophy,* Duckworth, London 1971, pp. 38–42.

The present collection of essays, written at various dates between 1914 and 1953, reiterates themes from all Tawney's major work.[2] In *The Acquisitive Society*, he criticised capitalism because it encouraged economic power without social responsibility. The right to property had become separated from any obligation to discharge a useful social function. In *Equality*, he attacked the view that the natural inequality of man in respect of ability justified inequalities of wealth and status; rather, so he argued, it would be in an egalitarian society that diversity of abilities would flourish most for the common good. In *Religion and the Rise of Capitalism*, he studied the origins of acquisitive individualism. The present collection of occasional pieces on social history, on education, and in defence of the programmes and performances of British social democracy, accompanied by a preface by Rita Hinden and by Gaitskell's address at the 1962 Memorial Service for Tawney, makes an illuminating book.

The heart of the matter for Tawney is the moral deficiency of capitalism:

> The revolt of ordinary men against Capitalism has had its source neither in its obvious deficiencies as an economic engine, nor in the conviction that it represents a stage in social evolution now outgrown, but in the straightforward hatred of a system which stunts personality and corrupts human relations by permitting the use of man by man as an instrument of pecuniary gain. . . . It is this demon – the idolatry of money and success – with whom, not in one sphere alone but in all, including our own hearts and minds, Socialists have to grapple.

Sentences like these are scattered throughout Tawney's writings. One need not be a cynic or an immoralist to find so much cliché-ridden high-mindedness suspect. The answer of his admirers may be to stress, as Gaitskell does in his address, Tawney's personal goodness: 'I think he was the best man I have ever known.'[3] The difficulty is that what both the reminiscences and Tawney's own writings communicate is a banal earnestness rather than the manifold virtues ascribed and praised. It is fairly clear what is missing. The moral denunciation of British capitalism took its content and its interest not from the morality of socialists but from the immorality and evil of capitalism. What we miss in these essays is the social context of the 1920s, of poverty, of unemployment, of suffering.

---

[2] Tawney 1964.

[3] Gaitskell 'Postscript: an Appreciation', in Tawney 1964, p. 214.

Moreover, the immediacy of these evils was linked with a hard-headed, commonsense practicality about their cure. Public ownership of the coal mines or the railways in Britain was not a radical solution; that it was the only solution, was implicitly acknowledged by the lack of Conservative opposition when the measures were finally put through Parliament in the late 1940s. But why did it take so long to achieve this solution? A government commission headed by Mr Justice Sankey and including, along with Tawney, men of widely different views had recommended the nationalisation of the mines in 1919. The reason for the delay lies in the failure of nerve in Britain's ruling class between the two wars. The politicians of the age – MacDonald, Snowden, Bonar Law, Baldwin, and Chamberlain – are, in perspective, tiny and impotent figures. No wonder that, in comparison with them, Tawney assumed the appearance of great moral stature. Yet, if he appears impressive by contrast, we must also ask whether, in many ways, he did not share many of the attitudes and indeed illusions of his contemporaries.

Tawney equated capitalism with private capitalism, and private capitalism with the effective sovereignty of the functionless shareholder. He defined socialism on at least two levels, both of which were inadequate. At one level, he meant the moral values of fraternity and equality, which are, unhappily, terms too vague and general for political guidance until they are embodied in specific social practices and institutions. At another level, he defined socialism by his concept of capitalism: the replacement of private ownership by public ownership or control and the state's acceptance of responsibility for social welfare. Thus he never took stock of the capitalism of the big corporation – the capitalism which may for its own purposes accept trade unionism, the welfare state, and even measures of state intervention and public ownership. He is, in fact, oblivious not merely of Keynes, but of the kind of capitalist ethos in which neo-Keynesian politics could be made effective.

Yet is it not perhaps absurd to criticise Tawney for being limited by the horizon of his period? Not if what we are criticising is above all lack of *political* intelligence and imagination. The lack of political imagination is notably present in his estimate of the role and achievement of the postwar Labour government.[4] He profoundly underestimates the continuity of that government with the wartime coalition government. He writes of the Labour ministers as

[4] Tawney 1964, especially pp. 145–54; 171–2.

if they were by deliberate choice implementing socialist policies, when, in fact, they were providing the necessary and inevitable solutions to the problem of laying a new basis for British capitalism. He never mentions the frustration and disillusionment that that government engendered, especially among its working-class supporters. To say this is not to underrate the achievements involved in implementing the 1944 Education Act (passing it was the work of the wartime coalition government), or of the handing over of power in India, or of the creation of the National Health Service. It is to say that any intelligent pragmatist, thoroughly but far-sightedly imbued with capitalist values, could not and would not have done otherwise. And it is not only that Tawney underrated the resources of an intelligent conservative defence of capitalism. In his statement of socialist objectives, he is curiously blind to how greatly his declared ends and his chosen means were at odds with one another. He cared passionately that workers should extend their control over the work process; and he wanted, probably more than anything else, to democratise the British educational system. Yet the kind of orthodox Labour-Party politics in which he put his hope has always been managerial and meritocratic. The Labour Party has shown immense hostility to those rank-and-file trade unionists who have been concerned with issues of workers' control; and it has shown a simple lack of interest in many less radical measures concerned with democracy in industry. In education, the Labour Party's support for comprehensive schools and for equality of opportunity did not, when it was in office, prevent it from helping to create through the 1944 Education Act a class system in education which not only favours the middle-class child, but has helped to create new class barriers. Labour is increasingly the political expression not of workers, but of managers and technocrats. It is the party of the other half of our ruling class.

Why did Tawney succeed in concealing from himself as well as from others the extent to which the British Labour Party is merely an alternative Conservative Party? One answer can be found in *The Radical Tradition*. Tawney did not lack that essentially English quality, insularity. It is no accident that there is little in his book about peace or international socialism. In his essay on 'Social Democracy in Britain' he asserts that 'it is not for a foreigner to discuss' the standing of capitalism in the United states.[5] And he appears to

[5] Tawney 1964, p. 138.

restrict himself not only geographically but theoretically. We have jibes – not arguments – against Marxism, and economic expertise is treated as a topic for a joke. The limits of theoretical inquiry appear to be those which actually exist in the House of Commons, a not very theoretical body.

Tawney thus appears to define politics itself as what might go on in a British Parliament. Since the role of Parliament, and consequently of electoral politics, in the decision-making processes of British life has steadily declined, it is not surprising that, already, his writings have a curiously antique air. He never even asks whether Parliament may not be among the institutions which need democratising. And, however radical he may be about the economic activities of private capitalism, he is a true member of the Labour Party in being completely complacent about British political institutions.

So a book of essays designed to celebrate 'the Democratic Socialist *philosopher* par excellence' is, in fact, a monument to the impotence of ideals.[6] It is not that Tawney failed to live up to his ideals or to propagate them. He succeeded admirably. Nor is it that his ideals were insufficiently high. It is simply that the Socratic question of whether one would rather have one's shoes mended by a good cobbler or a good man has relevance in politics too. Goodness is not enough.

---

6 Hinden, 'Editor's Introduction', in Tawney 1964, p. 9.

Chapter Thirty-Three

Pascal and Marx: On Lucien Goldmann's *Hidden God*[1]

A Review of Lucien Goldmann, The Hidden God

The irregular verb which many Anglo-Saxon philosophers conjugate on their way to international conferences runs: 'I am sober; you are intoxicated; he is a French philosopher.' A tradition of rhetoric and a belief that, for Frenchmen, clarity is not an achievement but a birthright have admittedly often worked havoc with analytical sobriety across the Channel. But the unfamiliar atmosphere of French philosophy has other more admirable causes. It is, in particular, more conscious of its background in intellectual and social history, and not just in the history of philosophy. It is therefore often at its best when it is self-consciously historical in its approach. And this, too, is often the best way for us to approach it. History may provide an initial common ground where philosophy itself would fail us. Metaphysical excitement may appear the more justified at the close, if the starting-point was dull and factual. What facts more dull than names and dates?

[1] Originally published in *Encounter*, Volume 23, Number 4, October 1964, pp. 69–76. Reprinted in A. MacIntyre, *Against the Self-Images of the Age: Essays on Ideology and Philosophy*, Duckworth, London 1971, pp. 76–87.

Every one of Macaulay's utopian schoolboys knows the name of René Descartes; not even they know that of Antoine Le Maître. But it was in successive years (in 1636 and in 1637) that Descartes published the account of that winter morning nearly twenty years before when he stayed in by the stove and so founded modern philosophy, and that Le Maître withdrew from the world to live in solitary penance at Port-Royal. Both Descartes and Le Maître are significant because of what the future was to make out of them, and the more significant because they came to symbolise two incompatible alternatives for the modern world. It turned out that Descartes had woven into a single rational system some of the dominant themes of the next age, in its life as well as in its thought: the isolated individual as self-sufficient in knowledge and action; the ideal of mechanical explanation; the reduction of God to the status of a guarantee that the gaps in rational argument can be filled, and the actions of individuals harmonised; the dualisms of reason and the passions, and of mind and matter. Cartesianism is the new consciousness expressed as a doctrine. From the world to which Descartes gave expression Le Maître withdrew, abandoning his already successful career as a lawyer. His spiritual director was the Abbé de Saint-Cyran, friend of Cornelius Jansen, the Bishop of Ypres, and director of the nuns of Port-Royal, then in Paris. On May 2, 1638, Saint-Cyran was arrested on Richelieu's orders, accused of depriving the state of its ablest subjects, and never left prison.

From the very first, therefore, the devotional and doctrinal movement of Jansenism was recognised by the powers that be as their enemy. Withdrawal from the modern world was challenge to it. In its withdrawal Jansenism asserts its own counter-thesis: 'It is from our separation and absence from the world that is born the presence and feeling for God' (Saint-Cyran).[2] Or again:

> We must have a low opinion not only of the truths which we discover through our own minds, but also of those which God gives us by his divine light. For this light is not the perfect gift of which the Scriptures speak... (Barcos).[3]

Most radically of all, Jansenism declared that there are divine commandments which the just man who lacks the requisite Grace – and the just man may

---

[2] Goldmann 1964, p. 40.
[3] Goldmann 1964, p. 147.

well lack the requisite Grace – cannot by his own efforts obey. So we get the paradox of the just man who is yet condemned by God, who is yet a sinner. Or at least these positions seemed to the critics of Jansenism to follow from its central thesis – the Jansenists themselves oscillated between denying that this was a correct characterisation of Jansen's theology and asserting that it was a correct characterisation not only of Jansen's views, but also of St. Augustine's, and therefore orthodox. What matters is the Jansenist assertion of an unbridgeable gap between the concepts by means of which the world understands justice and those in which God reveals his will.

God or the World? As always the choice was between a highly specific God and a highly specific world: an Augustinian God and a Cartesian world. How was one to choose? Within the Jansenist movement, there were different answers. One, that of Martin de Barcos, was a total refusal of the world. Another, that of Antoine Arnauld, involved the drawing of an almost Thomistic line between the realm in which natural reason is competent and the realm in which only faith in supernatural revelation can guide. Characteristically, Barcos wrote to advise other adherents of Jansenism on matters of faith; Arnauld, equally characteristically, was the author both of *De La Fréquente Communion* (paradoxically named, since the standards of spiritual achievement demanded prior to communion are so high that infrequent communion would have to be the rule) and of the *Logique de Port-Royal.* Arnauld tries to give unto Descartes the things that are Descartes's, and unto God the things that are God's. Unfortunately, as Barcos correctly saw, one cannot serve both God and Descartes, at least in any easy synthesising way. This becomes plainest when one considers the role of God in Cartesianism: the God whom Descartes *uses* to guarantee the existence of the external world and to give the first push to the mechanisms of the physical universe is precisely that God of the philosophers whom the Jansenists contrast with the God of Abraham and Augustine.

The question of compromise with the world arose, too, at the political level. Barcos, the consistent extremist, severed his connection with Port-Royal finally when the compromise embodied in the *Peace of Clement IX* in 1669 was accepted. That Barcos was in some sense right is shown by the fact that neither the Roman church nor the French state was able to compromise with Jansenism from their own point of view and pressed forward to its total destruction. What was it that they could not accept? The Jansenists, especially Barcos, recognised a duty of obedience to their God-given superiors. They asked only to be left alone. But, in providing a withdrawal from the world of church, state, and Cartesianism, they affronted it. To understand in what the affront consisted we must consider further *who* the Jansenists were. Yet before asking that question it is even more important to note that the possibilities of Jansenism are not exhausted by the alternatives of Barcos and Arnauld.

Suppose that, unlike Arnauld, one recognised the impossibility of a compromise between God and the contemporary world; yet, unlike Barcos, one could not deny the achievement of Descartes and wished to go beyond it by criticising it. Suppose that none the less one could not but live in the sight of the God of Abraham and Augustine. One would then have to affirm two apparently incompatible truths: 'If ever there is a time when one should make profession of opposites, it is when one is accused of omitting one of them…' (*fragment 865*).[4] It is for failing to do this that Pascal reproves the Jansenists.

Pascal aspires both to reject and to accept the world. He could thus, in one and the same period of his life, write of the vanity of scientific pursuits and set himself successfully to solve the problem of the cycloid. When Gilberte Pascal wrote her brother's biography, she explained his application to mathematics at that period as an attempt to take his mind off his toothache.[5] Léon Brunschvicg explained Pascal's denigration of science by referring to his failure to convince the Jesuit Noel and Descartes of the significance of his experiments with the vacuum. Both explanations obscure the complexity of Pascal's position: 'One does not show one's greatness by being at one extreme, but by touching both at the same time, and by filling all the space between.' This is not the position of Pascal in the *Lettres Provinciales* in which the Jesuit opponents of Jansenism are met on their own ground. But, on this interpretation, from March 1657 onward Pascal elaborated a new and paradoxical attitude of which the *Pensées* are the expression.

This interpretation of Pascal is the work of Lucien Goldmann, the Marxist editor of Barcos's correspondence, himself an original philosopher of great powers.[6] In Goldmann's view, Pascal's final position is an extreme rendering of a coherence implicit in the rest of Jansenism, but only expressed in other

---

[4] [I have numbered the fragments as in the Brunschvicg edition. – AM.] Pascal 1904.

[5] Pascal 1962, p. 53.

[6] de Barcos 1956. [Lucien Goldmann's untimely death in 1970 robbed us of the finest and most intelligent Marxist of the age – AM.]

writers in one-sided and incomplete forms. He lays great stress on the change in Pascal in 1657; the earlier crisis of 1654 when Pascal had the religious conversion, whose record was the *Mémorial,* had led Pascal into a life which only found its intellectual expression after 1657. Until then, he stood with Arnauld in dividing the provinces of faith and reason.

But, after 1657, he affirms both a philosophical view of the world which transcends Cartesianism and a view of God which makes all worldly activity worthless. Sometimes, these attitudes are combined in the same fragment:

> Descartes – We must say, approximately, 'This occurs by figure and motion', for that is true. But it is ridiculous to say which figures and motions; and try to reconstruct the machine. For it is unnecessary, uncertain, and difficult. And even if it were possible, I do not consider the whole of philosophy to be worth an hour of trouble. (*Fragment* 79.)

Sometimes, we get an acute criticism of Cartesianism of purely philosophical interest:

> If man were to begin by studying himself, he would see how incapable he is of going beyond himself. How could it be possible for a part to know the whole? But he may perhaps aspire to a knowledge of at least those parts which are on the same scale as himself. But the different parts of the world are all so closely linked and related together that I hold it to be impossible to know one without knowing the other and without knowing the whole. (*Fragment* 72.)

At other times, we find the whole of human knowledge brought under condemnation:

> Everything here on earth is partly true and partly false. But essential truth is not like this, for it is wholly pure and wholly true. The mixture that we find here on earth both dishonours and destroys this truth... (*Fragment* 385.)

Is Pascal simply inconsistent? Should his solution have been in a tough-minded way to grasp one of the horns of his dilemma and abandon the other? This would have been the Cartesian solution, as it would also have been the Augustinian. But Pascal inhabits two conceptual universes the claims of which he can neither reconcile nor abandon. Torn as he is between two realms, he can see each from the point of view of the other and his own predicament from both. Thus, from within Christianity, he sees his dilemma as itself prefigured by Christian theology. For does not Christian theology assert that we inhabit two realms, that man belongs both with the angels and the beasts, that if human nature ignores its limitations and seeks to be angelic it becomes bestial, that a hidden God has revealed himself incarnate and so on? The paradoxes of Christianity show it to be divine.

Yet, from within the world, he can see Christianity in the perspective of his own critique of Cartesianism. His scepticism about clear and distinct ideas ('Too much clarity darkens') and about any allegedly indubitable first principles, even those of scepticism, extends to any alleged arguments for Christianity, even his own. The theory of chances, which he had elaborated to assist his friend Méré at the gambling tables, encounters its limit at the point at which there are no more probabilities, but the stakes are infinite. Yet, at this very point, a wager cannot be avoided. It is only through a wager that God exists that meaning is conferred on an otherwise meaningless world. Yet it is from the standpoint of that world that we have to learn that belief in God has to accept the status of a wager.

Let Pascal abandon the world and he becomes the ancestor of Kierkegaard, of a self-contained fideism. Let him abandon Christianity and he becomes the ancestor of Hume, avoiding scepticism only by calling nature and custom to his aid. His greatness is in abandoning neither. Why? To understand Goldmann's answer to this question we must turn to his use of Marx and Lukács.

The danger is that we read what Goldmann has to say through our own preconceptions; and, where Marxism is concerned, no one is without preconceptions. Goldmann's thesis is that Pascal expressed, in one particular form, a coherent world vision which Lukács was to characterise. That world vision, the vision of tragedy, is rooted in the social history of Jansenism, expressing the attitudes implicit in the predicament of the *noblesse de robe*. Our preconceptions and prejudices might lead us to treat Goldmann's views as just one more explanation of the history of thought in terms of an economic and social basis. But, if we did, we should miss the concreteness of Goldmann's concerns. He is very far from forcing the interpretation of Jansenism and Pascal into an already existing theoretical structure. Rather, it is at least partly through his studies of Jansenism and Pascal that he gives meaning to his theoretical terms. So, one cannot fully understand the early theoretical chapters of his book until one has read the later historical and literary studies. Pascal and Jansenism are made to illuminate Marxism quite as much as Marxism is made to illuminate Pascal and Jansenism. Pascal himself would have understood this: 'The last thing one discovers when writing a book is what ought to have come first' (*Fragment* 19).

The tragic vision, which Lukács described, is the vision of a world where God is no longer present, and yet, even in his absence, life has to be lived out by the tragic hero with the eye of God upon him.[7] Because God is absent, the hero cannot succeed in the world. Because God, though absent, still regards him, he cannot abandon his task. He is the just man under condemnation, whom the critics of Jansenism saw at the heart of Jansenist doctrine. So long as he responds by refusing the world, he is Barcos. So long as he tries to live in the world and yet also to refuse it, he is Pascal himself. The Lukács of 1911 saw the tragic vision as one form of aesthetic insight; Goldmann sees it as capable of embodiment only when it expresses a form of social life which can recognise its own crisis in this vision.

The *noblesse de robe* (as contrasted with the *noblesse de cour*) was composed of those lawyers and administrators whom the French monarchy used in achieving hegemony over the rest of the nobility, strengthening itself by this alliance with the Third Estate and the townsmen. During the seventeenth century, the monarchy breaks this alliance and becomes an independent power, balancing class against class and governing through its own *corps de commissaires*. Members of the *noblesse de robe* thus find themselves on the defensive; their allegiance to the crown and to the established order is the condition of their flourishing and yet now the crown has less and less use for them. They can less and less live out the only role they know, and yet they must recognise the legitimate authority of the power that is abolishing that role. The congruence of this social experience with the tragic vision is clear. (One is reminded of Milton, who does not just have to justify the ways of God to man in general, but has to reconcile the hidden fact that God rules with the manifest fact that Charles II rules and the saints do not.) Thus the *parlement*'s manifest sympathy for Jansenism is, for Goldmann, a sign of recognition by a segment of the middle class that in Jansenism their own fragmentary attitudes receive completer expression and endorsement than elsewhere.

[7] [In *Die Seele und die Formen*, Essays Fleischel, Berlin 1911. The Lukács whom Goldmann follows is the since self-condemned Lukács of this book and of *Geschichte und Klassenbewusstsein*. Lukács has now (1971) altered his attitude to his work of this period yet once more – AM.] See Lukács 1974 and Preface to Lukács 1971.

Goldmann is at the opposite extreme from those self-styled Marxists who have tried to reduce the artist or the philosopher to a mere product of his social background. He sees that such a reduction fails to account precisely for what interests us in a writer's achievement, his distinctiveness. Goldmann's injunction is rather that we should understand the background through the writer, seeing in the coherence of great art or great philosophy something that is only implicit in the thought and action of ordinary men. So he invites us to understand Jansenism through Pascal, and the *noblesse de robe* through Jansenism. Moreover, the greatest writers both express and transcend their age. They show us the possibilities in the age of going beyond it, whereas lesser writers exhibit the limitations imposed upon them by the age.

It is not only Pascal whom Goldmann views in this light. He analyses Racine's tragedies in terms of the concept of the tragic vision, seeing a parallelism between the Jansenism of refusal of the world and the tragedies of refusal, *Andromaque* and *Britannicus*, while Pascal's attitude is paralleled in *Phèdre*. These parallelisms are brought out within a much more detailed classification of tragedy. The justification of this classification and the use of Lukács's artificial construct of the tragic vision can lie solely in whether it enables us to understand better not only the plays themselves, but also the author's relationship to them. And Goldmann follows Racine himself in seeing the heart of Jansenism in *Phèdre*. For it was in the preface to *Phèdre* that Racine hoped that his method in this play 'would perhaps be a way of reconciling with tragedy a number of persons famous for both their piety and doctrine' – although he does so ostensibly for the platitudinous reason that in his play virtue and vice receive their deserts. Whereas, in fact, if Goldmann is right, the greatness of Phèdre herself is that she cannot refuse the claims of the world as embodied in her own passion and her conception of Hippolytus but nor can she refuse to live with the eye of God upon her. Of Phèdre what Lukács wrote of the tragic hero holds:

> He hopes that a judgment by God will illuminate the different struggles which he sees in the world before him, and will reveal the ultimate truth. But the world around him still follows the same path, indifferent to both questions and answers. No word comes from either created or natural things, and the race is not to the swift nor battle to the strong. The clear voice of the judgment of God no longer sounds out above the march of human destiny, for the voice which once gave life to all has now fallen silent. Man must

> live alone and by himself. The voice of the judge has fallen silent forever, and this is why men will always be vanquished, doomed to destruction in victory even more than in defeat.[8]

Tragic thought is not simply an episode in the past. Pascal, in Goldmann's view, is not only illuminated by Marx and Lukács, he is their ancestor. He anticipates their epistemology in two crucial respects. First of all, he understands that the knowledge of man himself depends on grasping the individual as part of a totality. Yet we cannot grasp the totality except insofar as we understand the individuals who comprise it. Marx wrote:

> A loom is a machine used for weaving. It is only under certain conditions that it becomes *capital;* isolated from these conditions it is as far from being capital as gold, in its natural state, is from being coin of the realm.[9]

What are these conditions? They include both the existence of a whole system of economic activity and the informing of human activities and intentions by concepts which express the relationships characteristic of the system. We identify a loom as capital or gold as coin only when we have grasped a whole system of activities as a capitalist or monetary system. The individual object or action is identifiable only in the context of the totality; the totality is only identifiable as a set of relationships between individuals. Hence we must move from parts to whole and back from whole to parts.

Goethe, Hegel, and Marx all grasped versions of this truth about the human sciences. Pascal, as Goldmann interprets him, uses it against Descartes in the fragments about the whole and the parts and about figure and motion, which I quoted earlier. We can put the essence of his criticism by saying that, just as no amount of mechanical explanation of the working of a loom will tell us

---

[8] Quoted in Goldmann 1964, p. 377. See also Lukács 1974, p. 155: 'What he hopes to obtain from the struggle of different forces is a judgement of God, a verdict upon the ultimate truth. But the world round him goes on its way, untouched by such questions or answers. All things have become dumb, and laurels or defeats are awarded indifferently at the end of the struggle. Never again will God's judgement be heard in the workings of destiny. It was God's voice that gave life to the whole; but then that life had to go on by itself, alone, and the judging voice fell silent forever. That is why Jarl can be victorious where Macbeth was defeated; he is the victim doomed to perish, and as victor he is ever more defeated than he would be as a loser.'

[9] Marx 1975–2004a, p. 211: 'A cotton-spinning jenny is a machine for spinning cotton. It becomes *capita*l only in certain relations. Torn from these relationships it is no more capital than *gold* itself is money or sugar the *price* of sugar.'

what weaving is, or how a loom becomes capital, so no amount of mechanical explanation of reflexes will tell us what human action is or how a man becomes in his actions like an angel or a beast. For that we need to understand human action as part of a total system in which certain norms are established. The difficulty is that men have false as well as true consciousness of the systems of which they form a part. They need a criterion for discriminating true from false, and they exhibit this need especially in trying to understand the overall context of their actions. For Pascal, this context is provided by God and his will; for Hegel and Marx, by the history of society. For Pascal, the contradictions involved in the task are ultimate and irresoluble; for Hegel and Marx, they can be transcended in a future form of human community. But, if tragic thought and dialectical thought differ in these crucial respects, they also resemble each other at key points. Both know that one cannot first understand the world and only then act in it. How one understands the world will depend in part on the decision implicit in one's already taken actions. The wager of action is unavoidable. Goldmann is willing even to use the word 'faith' of the Marxist attitude, and he sees a real continuity between Augustinian theology and Marxism, despite their differences on such issues as the actual existence of God:

> Subsequently, Hegel, and especially Marx and Lukács, have been able to substitute for the wager on the paradoxical and mediatory God of Christianity the wager on a historical future and the human community. In doing so, however, they have not given up the main demands of tragic thought, that is to say a doctrine which explains the paradoxical nature of human reality, and hope in the eventual creation of values which endows this contradiction with meaning and which transforms ambiguity into a necessary element in a significant whole. Not eternity but the future provides a context which gives meaning to individual parts in the present. The future which does this is as yet unmade; we wager on it not as spectators, but as actors pledged to bring it into being.

Thus, if Goldmann presents us with a Marxist Pascal, he also offers us a Pascalian Marx. In so doing, he breaks, as the young Lukács broke before him, with the view of Marxism as a closed, mechanistic and deterministic system of thought, and he illuminates a variety of Marxist texts which both Marx's critics and his defenders too often neglect. He makes it possible to understand the horror with which the Stalinist Lukács must have come to regard his own youth.

Is what Goldmann says true? Partly this is an empirical question, to be answered by close historians of Jansenism and careful students of Pascal and Racine. Partly it is a question of how far the notion of 'the tragic vision' is a useful construct. What does it help us to see to which we should otherwise be blind? But the implications of Goldmann's work extend far more widely than do these questions. For by placing tragic thought, Cartesian rationalism and Marxism in the way that he does he commits himself to schematic interpretation of the history of modern philosophy. This schematism is made explicit at a number of points in the book, but more especially in a brilliant excursus on the Faust legend and in several discussions of Kant, to whom Goldmann devoted an earlier book.[10] To put it very crudely, Goldmann sees Kant as standing at an extreme point in the development of the related rifts between fact and value and between virtue and happiness. For Kant, the highest good is still virtue crowned with happiness; but virtue and happiness cannot be brought together within the world. It is only beyond the present world by a power outside it that they can be reconciled. Practical life is intolerable unless there is such a divine power, but theoretical inquiry cannot show either that there is or is not such a being. So, for Kant, moral rules are independent of how the world goes, to be obeyed whatever the consequences of obeying them; and yet there would be no point in obeying the rules unless the universe were of a certain kind. Thus Goldmann sees Kant, too, as holding together a tragic contradiction, and in so doing acting as Pascal's successor.

It is in his treatment of Kant that the striking differences between Goldmann and his Anglo-Saxon counterparts emerge. Moral philosophy in England is notably unhistorical. Books are too often written about 'the' moral vocabulary apparently on the assumption that there is an unchanging structure of concepts. It is too often assumed, when moral philosophers apparently disagree about 'good' and 'ought', that they are holding rival and competing views of the same concepts, rather than elucidating very different concepts from very different historical periods. Goldmann's book is, in this respect, a model of how to write moral philosophy.

---

[10] [L. Goldmann, *La communauté humaine et l'univers chez Kant*, Presses Universitaires de France, Paris 1948 – AM.]

Moreover, in bringing out the links between Augustinianism and Marxism, for example – and they go far further than I have suggested in this review – Goldmann contributes to an urgent contemporary task, that of redrawing the lines of intellectual controversy. It has been becoming increasingly plain that whether a man calls himself a Christian, a Marxist, or a liberal, may be less important than what kind of Christian, Marxist, or liberal he is. I remarked earlier that Augustinians and Marxists do differ after all about the existence of God; but they agree that whether God exists or not is a crucial question. In so doing, they unite against both Christians of the Tillich-Robinson kind and liberals of a certain kind who think religion a matter of 'private' life. Equally that both Goldmann and Sartre call themselves Marxists does not obliterate the gulf that separates their views, let alone that which separates both from M. Garaudy and the French Communist Party's intellectual enclave.[11]

Finally, it is not of course true that the tragic is a category which can finally be transcended and left behind. It remains a possibility wherever the attempt is made to live within and to transcend a society. This attempt need not be tragic in its dimensions. Stendhal's heroes make it in quite a different way. But it remains a possibility:

> There are only three kinds of person: those who, having found God, seek Him; those who, not having found Him, spend their time seeking Him; and those who live without having found Him and without seeking for Him either. The first are both blessed and reasonable, the last both mad and unhappy, and the second unhappy but reasonable. (*Fragment* 257.)

This is an age when no one is blessed and reasonable and most are mad and unhappy. The task is to be unhappy but reasonable.

[11] [In spite of Roger Garaudy's later reversal of his Stalinist positions, I see no need to change what I wrote earlier (1971) – AM.]

Chapter Thirty-Four

Marxist Mask and Romantic Face: Lukács on Thomas Mann[1]

A Review of Georg Lukács, Essays on Thomas Mann

> The dictatorship of the proletariat, the politico-economic means of salvation demanded by our age, does not mean domination for its own sake and in perpetuity; but rather in the sense of a temporary abrogation, in the Sign of the Cross, of the contradiction between spirit and force; in the sense of overcoming the world by mastering it; in a transcendental, transitional sense, in the sense of the Kingdom. The proletariat has taken up the task of Gregory the Great, his religious zeal burns within it, and, as little as he, may it withhold its hand from the shedding of blood. Its task is to strike terror into the world for the healing of the world, that man may finally achieve salvation and deliverance, and win back at length to freedom from law and from distinction of class, to his original status as child of God. (Naphta in Thomas Mann's *The Magic Mountain*)[2]

[1] Originally published in *Encounter*, Volume 24, Number 4, April 1965, pp. 64–72. Reprinted in A. MacIntyre, *Against the Self-Images of the Age: Essays on Ideology and Philosophy*, Duckworth, London 1971, pp. 60–9.

[2] Mann 1927, v. 2, p. 511.

> In *The Magic Mountain* the spokesman of the reactionary Fascist, anti-democratic *Weltanschauung*, the Jesuit Naphta...(Georg Lukács)[3]

'Lukács, who is anyhow well-disposed towards me (and who plainly has not recognized himself in Naphta)', wrote Thomas Mann in a letter in 1949.[4] That Georg Lukács's essays upon Thomas Mann form part of the elaborate defences with which Lukács buttresses his inability to recognise himself as he was in his brilliant and many-sided youth lends to these essays a poignancy and a fascination which they certainly do not provide in their role as literary criticism. The pompous, ponderous style in which they are written all too easily conveys the impression of one Grand Old Man saluting another, the Gamaliel of Central-European Communism (as a [London] *Times* leader writer once called Lukács) applauding the Nobel Prize winner. Nor is the translation to blame for this impression; the translator has rendered Lukács's professorial prose excellently. And the consequence might well be that the brief, uncomplicated, facile judgments on Lukács, which it has become fashionable to pass in the West, will not be shaken at all by these essays. Yet they are, in fact, further evidence of the enigmatic and complex quality of Lukács's achievement.

It is common knowledge that Lukács has publicly disavowed his youth. In Hungary in 1948, he was accused by György Somlyó of staging an auto-da-fé with his own early writings. Lukács replied vehemently that those works 'which I have transcended with my own development and which were moving in an improper direction' should not receive attention either from himself or from others.[5] He raged when Merleau-Ponty in 1955 discussed his *History and Class Consciousness* of 1923 and spoke of 'treachery' and of the 'falsification of a book forgotten for good reasons'.[6] This un-Marxist attempt to separate his present from his past, the self from its deeds, has so strong an emotional charge behind it that one cannot but ask, 'Why?' Unless one can answer this

[3] Lukács 1964, p. 33.

[4] [For the facts about the Mann-Lukács relationship, see the essay by K. Kerenyi, 'Zauberberg-Figuren', in *Tessiner Schreibtisch*, Stuttgart 1963. For a suggestive, but speculative interpretation see V. Zitta, *Georg Lukács' Marxism: Alienation, Dialectics, Revolution. A Study in Utopia and Ideology*, introduced by H.D. Lasswell, Humanities Press, New York – AM.]

[5] Lukács 1948, p. 179.

[6] Merleau-Ponty 1974, pp. 66–9. The letter in response from Lukács, from which these quotes are taken, is in Garaudy et al. 1956, pp. 158–9.

question posed in a very general way one is unlikely to answer satisfactorily the particular question of why Lukács, consciously or unconsciously, has refused to recognise his own features in those of Naphta. There is, of course, a strong presumption that the refusal is at least semiconscious, even though Mann himself exhibited strong anxiety that Lukács should not recognise himself in Naphta and was completely certain that he had not done so. The reason for doubting whether Mann's assurance was justified is simply that, in his references to Naphta, Lukács seems to rely upon his readers not actually having the text of *The Magic Mountain* available. How otherwise could he so confidently and without explanation characterise as fascist a character who propounds belief in Communism, the abolition of classes, the dictatorship of the proletariat, and a version of the labour theory of value? Of course, Naphta (as Thomas Mann himself insisted) differs from the young Lukács in a large number of ways. Naphta is a Jesuit; Lukács is not. But the young Lukács was deeply involved with Christianity and often writes of God with immense seriousness. The influence of Dostoevsky is strong in the years before 1914; so more surprisingly is that of Plotinus and of the German mystics Eckhart and Tauler.

The commonest explanation of Lukács' rupture with his youth assimilates it to the recantations of intellectuals in the Stalinist period in Russia. There would be some room for doubt about the explanatory value of this parallel just because it is still unclear how far we understand the psychology of these recantations. But, in any case, Lukács's behaviour since 1924 bears all the marks of being not so much a response to pressures from without as a continuous self-inspired attempt to destroy what survives in him of his youth. He has, of course, not been able to avoid a continuous return to the subject matter of his early writings. But he voluntarily and long before he went to live in the Soviet Union abjured their standpoint, as a result of the condemnation of *History and Class Consciousness*. Ernst Bloch predicted in his original review of it that the Russians would dislike it: 'Some of them will say that Marx had not placed Hegel on his feet so that Lukács can put Marx back on his head.'[7] None of the Russians was in fact as witty as this. Zinoviev nagged shrilly at the Fifth Congress of the Comintern in 1924 that 'we must not let this extreme left tendency grow up into a theoretical revisionism' and picked out

[7] Bloch 1969, p. 601.

Lukács's work in philosophy and sociology for special mention.[8] Lukács was at once confronted with a dilemma whose roots were already obvious in the text of *History and Class-Consciousness*. For there he explains Marxism as the class consciousness of the proletariat whose articulate representative is the Communist Party. Thus it is entailed by Lukács's own argument that, if the Comintern holds that Marxism is not what Lukács says it is, then Lukács must be wrong. Or, rather, either Lukács is wrong or the Comintern is not the true Communist Party. But if it is not, then Marxism is only a theory, only an idea; it lacks any material incarnation. To have grasped this horn of the dilemma would have thrown Lukács back to his starting-point in an unbearable way. And his tragedy resides in his never having been able to return to it. But what was his starting-point and why would return to it have been unbearable?

In answering this question, we can also try to answer another. It is a commonplace that, in *History and Class-Consciousness*, Lukács produced a Hegelian interpretation of Marx that set Marx's own writings in a systematic framework quite different from and incompatible with that in which Engels had set them in *Anti-Dühring*. When, in 1931–2, Marx's so-called *Economic and Philosophical Manuscripts* of 1844 became known, it was clear that Marx himself had defined his own thought near its outset in precisely the terms of that same Hegelian framework which Lukács had once more spelled out. This confirmation of Lukács's interpretation – Lukács could not possibly have known of the contents of the manuscripts in 1923 – was a brilliant literary reconstruction for which his disowning of *History and Class-Consciousness* has never allowed him to claim the credit. What, in fact, enabled Lukács to do this was the degree to which he had in his own experience recapitulated Marx's intellectual development. In order to understand this, both Marx and Lukács have to be placed – if in the briefest, most inadequate way – in relation to their own culture.

The seminal period of German culture is essentially philosophical in a way that English culture never is. It is therefore much easier to interpret it in terms of a unity of ideas and imagination, to narrate its history as a series of attempts to frame answers to pervasive questions that were at once Kantian and Faustian. The literary critic of this culture cannot evade, any more than

8 Communist Party of Great Britain 1924, p. 17. This section of Zinoviev's speech was entitled: 'The Struggle Against the "Ultra-Lefts" and Theoretical Revisionism.'

the philosopher can, the relationships and the antagonisms between value and fact, law and inclination, reason and the passions, society and the individual. But the literary critic has to deal with these not just as conceptual oppositions, but rather with embodied, imaginative resolutions of these antagonisms in the Greece of Hölderlin's poems or in Goethe's later writings. One way of recounting Lukács's career would be to set out the history of his continuous reinterpretation of the central features of German culture between 1780 and 1850. If one did this, one would discover a recurrent instability in which the would-be settled views of any one period in his life are undermined by his insights at other periods.

At his worst, in his self-willed Stalinist period before the war, he writes in terms of the crude dichotomy between idealism and materialism fathered by Engels and by Lenin's *Materialism and Empirio-Criticism*. But these concepts, as Lenin himself understood later, are chameleons of the mind, taking colour only from the examples which they are ostensibly used to explain. So, in the *Destruction of Reason*, Lukács turned instead to the conflict between reason and unreason and tried to use this as an analytical tool. In so doing, he continued his campaign against the interpretation of German romanticism as essentially irrationalist, an interpretation which he stigmatised as anticipating Nazi interpretations of German cultural history.[9] (This did not save him from being himself stigmatised as a revisionist for abandoning the cant about materialism and idealism.) The most important justification that Lukács has ever given for this view has, however, implications which he himself has never understood (or at least admitted). Discussing the romantic opposition of reason to the passions in *Goethe and His Age*, Lukács argued that this opposition depends upon a falsely partial view of both reason and passions, an opposition which had been created by the rationalists of the eighteenth century.[10] It follows that it is not reason itself, but a distorted view of reason against which the Romantic rebels. Yet, if this is so, doubt is then thrown on Lukács's own categories. For, in a culture where concepts of reason and the passions are thrown up by the very nature of its social life and its definitive ideas, the man who claims to be able to detect the distortion must warrant his claims by showing how it is

[9] See, for example, Lukács 1980, p. 89: 'The beginnings of this process may be found in the feudal, counter-reformist reactionary-romantic struggle against the French Revolution, and as we noted it reached its peak in the imperialist age of capitalism.'

[10] See, for example, Lukács 1968, pp. 14–15.

possible for him to escape the distorting influences which imprison everyone else.

Neither the young Marx in the 1840s nor the young Lukács in 1918 was able to take Hegel's way out, that of claiming that in him the Absolute has finally broken through the relativities of history so that the thoughts expressed in the *Logic* are the thoughts of God himself, thinking them through Hegel's pen.[11] But both have to try and find a vantage point outside their own society and culture. In order to explain Lukács's attempt to do this, one cannot avoid attempting to explain Marx's; and this is not quite the boring rehearsal of stock platitudes about The Young Marx that it might seem to be, since The Young Marx is a plaster figure in whose lineaments it is fairly difficult to pick out the face of the young Marx.

The myth of the plaster figure runs: once upon a time there was a young humanistic Marx who inherited from Hegel and from the Left Hegelians the notion of alienation. This Marx was not yet preoccupied with socio-economics. But as he became so pre-occupied, he discarded the notion of alienation. Indeed his break with the Left Hegelians and his discarding of the notion of alienation are sometimes seen as two aspects of the same process. The *locus classicus* for this myth is Lewis Feuer's 'What Is Alienation? The Career of a Concept', and, in order to destroy the myth, one has only to set two of Feuer's key theses beside what Marx actually says.

So Feuer writes: 'In these early writings, Marx and Engels, as Freudian forerunners, regarded love, not work, as the source of man's sense of reality', and he quotes from *The Holy Family* (published in 1845 but written in the autumn of 1844).[12] But, already in the *Economic and Philosophical Manuscripts* (written in April to August 1844), Marx had clearly argued the central relationship between work and the sense of reality. And, indeed, the quotation from *The Holy Family* does not bear an entirely clear sense when placed in its context.

Secondly, Feuer claims that 'the word "alienation" was absent from Marx's mature analysis'.[13] But in the *Grundrisse* in 1857–8 (unpublished until 1939–41) Marx is still writing:

[11] See, for example, Hegel 1969, p. 50.
[12] Feuer 1962, p. 120. See also Marx and Engels 1975–2004a, pp. 20–3.
[13] Feuer 1962, p. 125.

> The ancient conception in which man always appears (in however narrowly-rational, religious, or political a definition) as the aim of production, seems very much more exalted than the modern world, in which production is the aim of man and wealth the aim of production. In fact, however, when the narrow bourgeois form has been peeled away what is wealth, if not the universality of needs, capacities, enjoyments, productive powers, etc., of individuals produced in universal exchange? What, if not the full development of human control over the forces of nature – those of his own nature as well as those of so-called 'nature'.... In bourgeois political economy – and in the epoch to which it corresponds – this complete elaboration of what lies within man appears as total alienation.[14]

This survival of the concept of alienation into Marx's mature writings is important for my immediate purposes; for, had the concept not, as Feuer claimed, survived in them – although the word is admittedly not used in *Capital* – how could Lukács have correctly deduced the core of Marx's thought from the later writings which he knew? The survival of the concept is important for other reasons. The concepts of work and freedom in the mature Marx are in fact unintelligible unless related to the notion of alienation, and to precisely that notion of alienation set out by Lukács.

Alienation has at least four defining features. First of all, men are divided within themselves and from each other, by not being able in their work to pursue ends that are their own, by having external ends imposed upon them. Secondly, means and ends are inverted. Where men should eat and drink in order to act, they have to work in order to eat and drink. Thirdly, men reify their social relationships into alien powers which dominate them. In virtue of

---

[14] Marx 1964, pp. 84–5. See also Marx 1973, pp. 487–8. 'Thus, the old view, in which the human being appears as the aim of production, regardless of his limited national, religious, political character, seems to be very lofty when contrasted to the modern world, where production appears as the aim of mankind and wealth as the aim of production. In fact, however, when the limited bourgeois form of wealth is stripped away, what is wealth other than the universality of individual needs, capacities, pleasures, productive forces etc., created through universal exchange. The full development of human mastery over the forces of nature, those of so-called nature as well as humanity's own nature?...In bourgeois economics – and in the epoch of production to which it corresponds – this complete working-out of the human content appears as a complete emptying-out, this universal objectification as total alienation, and this tearing-own of all limited, one-sided aims as sacrifice of the human end-in-itself to an entirely external end.'

this reification they become involved in conceptual puzzles and confusions. And, finally, men find life irremediably split up into rival and competing spheres, each with its own set of norms, and each sphere claiming its own narrow and therefore deforming sovereignty. But all this makes it clear that alienation is essentially a contrast concept. We can understand what it is to be alienated only if we can also understand what it is or would be *not* to be alienated. Whence did Marx, whence did Lukács derive the notion of a form of human life in which man would create his own ends, in which conceptual confusion and contradiction would be resolved into a clarity about means and ends, so creating a human nature in which the ideal and the actual would at last coincide? The surprising answer may be that the unalienated men of the Marxist future are the artists of the German romantic ideal.[15]

'Thus man also creates according to the laws of beauty.'[16] So Marx. Marx's description of the senses of reintegrated man finding their own proper aesthetic objects, his attempt to establish a connection between freedom and aesthetic activity, and his belief that in free, aesthetic activity the contradictions of unfree existence are resolved, is a reissue of a theme in Schiller's break with Kant in the 'Kallias' letters. Even more, Schiller's concept of *Selbstbestimmung* is an important anticipation of Marx's 'self-activity'. The Hegelian concept of self-activity is not its only ancestor. It is hardly surprising that Lukács, coming across Schiller's declaration that it is man who plays (and play includes the whole realm of aesthetic activity) who is most truly man, should use this saying to interpret Marx in a sense relevant to his own problems. These were complex.

Both the energy and the 'intellectual poetry' (his own phrase) of the young Lukács arise out of the tension between the conceptual and theoretical resources available to him to interpret reality and the impact of the reality itself. In the view of the young Lukács, the poet faced with the inadequacy of the first to the second creates his own reality. But the critic cannot rest content except with a grasp of both poetry and social reality which can only

---

[15] In both the original version of this essay in *Encounter* [p. 68] and the reprint in *Against the Self-Images of the Age* (p. 66) this sentence reads: 'The surprising answer may be that the unalienated men of the Marxist feature are the artists of the German Romantic ideal.' However, this is clearly a misprint as the sentence only makes sense if 'feature' is replaced by 'future'.

[16] Marx 1975b, pp. 352–4.

come from a philosophy in which reality is disclosed. Lukács reads the history of past literature and criticism in terms of the attempted resolution of the tension between the realm of intelligibility and that of brute reality. Belief in God plays a key role here, especially in the definition of the tragic vision in which the hero who is confronted by the demands of a transcendence which he cannot discover anywhere in the empirical world must live out his tasks in conflict with a reality that never discloses the divinity he seeks.[17] The tragic vision in which meaning can only be conferred on the world from outside it, and yet the world is silent as to its own meaning, recurs in a conceptualised form in classical German philosophy. The tragic hero is transformed in turn into the epistemological subject of Kantianism whose categories can never reveal the *Ding-an-sich*, the Fichtean Ego, and the Hegelian Self. But each of these philosophies finds itself still external to the reality it seeks to comprehend, reduced to spawning metaphysical fictions on a grand scale. It was the insight of Hegel, rendered into realistic social terms by Marx (and Marx's 'materialism' consists, in really, no more than this rendering) that the escape from the contradictions and mystifications thrown up by this philosophy did not lie simply in intellectually dissipating them by greater clarity in conceptual analysis.

In the Hegelian-Marxist view, such conceptual contradictions and mystifications express the incoherences of a whole form of life. To overcome them, one does not have merely to philosophise more clearly, but to learn to act in a new way: revolutionary *praxis*, as characterised by Marx in the *Theses on Feuerbach*. Here, Lukács sees the resolution of his new problems. The *praxis* in which contradiction disappears is that of the proletarian, not just that of the actual workingman but that of the essential proletarian for whom the Hungarian Soviets of 1919 provided a spokesman. So the contradictions of tragedy are overcome; transcendence re-enters the world; the immediate ends of man become meaningful. The Kingdom of God will have been taken by storm. To read *History and Class-Consciousness* as a solution to the problems of *Soul and Form* is to read it as the work of Lukács-Naphta.

---

[17] [For the best account of this phase of Lukács's thought, see L. Goldmann, *The Hidden God: a Study of Tragic Vision in the Pensées of Pascal and the Tragedies of Racine*, translated from the French by P. Thody, Routledge and Kegan Paul, London 1964. – AM.]

Thus, Lukács staked his existence on the possibility of integrating art with social life in a *praxis* in which life should itself have the coherence and meaning of art. He analyses bourgeois social reality with the tools derived from Georg Simmel and Max Weber; he understands art and literature in terms of the romantic ideal. And he invokes Marxism to link the two analyses so that the aesthetic may be at home in the world. But, in so doing, he creates insoluble problems for his own future activities as a critic, problems that are nowhere more apparent than in his writings on Thomas Mann.

Lukács's immense sympathy for Mann derives from the fact that the externality of art to bourgeois society is itself a central imaginative theme for Mann; Lukács's difficulty in writing about Mann is that Mann was always ambivalent in his attitudes both to art and to bourgeois society. This Lukács concealed from himself by simply not seeing in Mann's work every tendency which might underline the *necessary* gap between art and social life to the possible non-existence of which Lukács's whole critical career is pledged. Thus Lukács cannot acknowledge himself in Naphta because the manifestly desperate character of Naphta's enterprise corresponds to the latently desperate character of Lukács's own enterprise. What is desperate and neurotic, of course, is not Lukács's Communism or his wish to resolve the contradictions of theory with the conceptual scheme of a new form of social life; it is his impatience with history, with the slow pace of social development. This he himself was to recognise, but his recognition of this impatience was turned into an acceptance of the subintellectual world of Stalinist materialism and thereby into a disowning of both the origin and the meaning of his own enterprise.

Lukács's arbitrary excision from Mann's work of all that does not fit into the role which he imposes on Mann – that of the bourgeois realist who disowns the decadence of modernism – is most obvious when Lukács simply writes off the opinions Mann professed in his essays. So Mann's expressed admiration for Freud is dismissed and *The Holy Sinner* read as a refutation of Freud.[18] Equally, Mann's expressed attitude to Nietzsche has to be discounted. For Lukács wants to see Adrian Leverkühn in *Dr. Faustus* as a contemporary Nietzsche. But, of course, there *is* a strong element of Lukács's antimodernism in Mann; neither Mann nor Lukács really understands Schiller's notion of art

[18] Lukács 1964, pp. 112–13.

as play, which underlies so much modern art. Both are therefore least at home with music. And Lukács's attack on Schönberg (like his distaste for Joyce) is rooted not in social perceptiveness, but in a clinging to the values of the bourgeois nineteenth century. This clinging is truer of Lukács than it is of Mann. There is in Leverkühn more of Mann than Lukács could allow and Mann's attitude to the narrator, the old-fashioned classical humanist Serenus Zeitblom, contains far more irony than Lukács can detect. This is because there is in Lukács more of Zeitblom than he realises. In an age when the formality of art and its autonomy have been among its chief safeguards from degeneration (this is what the Nazi attacks on Schönberg and Joyce signify), the attitudes of the older Lukács smack more than a little of the 'power-protected inwardness' which he condemns in Bismarckian Germany.

Yet, in the latest of these essays, on 'The Confessions of Felix Krull, Confidence Man', that Lukács is a genius still appears. The comparison of the Joseph saga with Felix Krull is full of insight into Mann's handling of character.[19] But it is, by now, genius that has paid a high price for survival. Lukács most resembles one of Stendhal's characters. Like them, he has lived in a post-revolutionary age in which the price of survival is to pay more than lip service to the values of petty, bourgeoisified despotisms. And the romantic aspiration to embody art in life itself could not have continued to inspire as it has done if Lukács had not reincarnated it so often in the Protean doctrines with which he disguises the unchanging inheritance from *Soul and Form* and *History and Class-Consciousness*.

Like Julien Sorel or Fabrice, Lukács has involved himself in countless stratagems; like Sorel, he has faced the death penalty, like Fabrice, he has avoided it. But the declining quality of his writing suggests that time has done its work, that the face behind the mask has taken on the aspect of the mask. Naphta's suicide was one way of paying the debts of romanticism to reality; the long, tortuous, intertwining of enlightenment and deception that Lukács has practised is another.

---

19 Lukács 1964, pp. 110–11, 113, 116–17, 122–6, 54–6.

Chapter Thirty-Five

Recent Political Thought[1]

Most previous writers of chapters in *Political Ideas* have been able to put a single thinker in the centre of their stage. It is one of the distinctive marks of the present age that I cannot hope to do that. Political theory has not only become too complex and varied in its subject-matter, but it has also had a tortuous history of its own. It is only a decade or so since its death was being confidently announced in some quarters, a death that was felt by those who announced it to be a welcome relief. They saw the past of political theory as a series of metaphysical confusions which positivist philosophy had now revealed to be linguistic muddles. Moreover, in practice the theories which had dominated the thirties, those of Stalinism and fascism, appeared not only to be conceptually confused but also to be dangerous and vicious in their practical consequences. How much sounder and safer it seemed to be able to welcome the end of ideology and to return to a comfortable and comforting English empiricism – to drop the theory and remain close to the facts. Henceforward, the fact-gathering discipline of political science would replace the imaginative flights of political theory.

[1] Originally published in D. Thompson (ed.), *Political Ideas*, Penguin Books, Harmondsworth 1966, pp. 189–200.

As it turned out, these obituary notices were premature. For one thing, the notion that politics could be conducted without theory was itself all too plainly a theory. But more than this, two quite independent influences combined to show how necessary political theory is. The first influence was that of empirical political science. Here, as in other sciences, fact-gathering only becomes fruitful if it is part of the process of framing hypotheses and explanations, and of testing them. All the multifarious pieces of information we now have about voting behaviour, for example, only become of use and interest in so far as they help us understand the nature and possibilities of alternative voting systems; and to understand this is to theorise. The second influence is that of political practice; politicians continue to use theories not only to understand and to explain, but also as instruments and weapons. And the way in which they use theories suggests the need for a theory about theories.

We can begin from the 'Cold War' confrontations of the Soviet Union and the West. The most familiar criticisms of the Russian social and political system have been first of all that it is inimical to freedom because it does not embody the canons of parliamentary democracy, and moreover that it could not but be inimical to freedom because it was fathered by Marxists. In other words, the Russian reality is confronted by John Stuart Mill's ideals and fails the test; while the explanation of this failure is that within Marxism the seeds of unfreedom always lay and lie. We are thus plunged straightaway into contentions about theory. Nobody could deny that John Stuart Mill would be unhappy about even post-Khrushchevite Russia; but is this the best clue we have to the nature of Russian unfreedom?

To answer this question I begin with another and ask why Marxist theory should be accused of having fathered Stalinist tyranny. Of the many arguments that have been used, two perhaps deserve special notice. The first is the accusation that Marxism is wedded to a view of history which necessarily leads to totalitarianism. The Marxist, so it is said, believes in inevitable trends in history. He believes that he and his party are the contemporary representatives of those trends and are thus justified by historical necessity in depriving their opponents of liberty and even of life. But Marxism, so it has been suggested, is mistaken simply because there are no such trends. It was Karl Popper, the philosopher of science, who named all those who believe in such unconditional and inevitable trends in history 'historicists'.

Historicists do not see, so he argued, that the existence of any historical trend depends upon initial conditions – and that these conditions may not persist, may be alterable. Not only Marx, but other nineteenth-century philosophers such as Auguste Comte, so Popper suggested, have been in danger of being the victims of confusion in ignoring the difference between absolute and unconditional *prophecies* of the future and the conditional *predictions* of the scientist – precisely because they have ignored the initial conditions of the trends they claimed to discern:

> The point is that these conditions are so easily overlooked. There is, for example, a trend towards an 'accumulation by means of production' (as Marx puts it). But we should hardly expect it to persist in a population which is rapidly decreasing; and such a decrease may in turn depend on extra-economic conditions, for example, on a chance invention, or conceivably on the direct physiological (perhaps biochemical) impact of an industrial environment.[2]

So Popper in *The Poverty of Historicism*. But did Marx in fact confuse prophecy and prediction? His use of words like 'inevitable' certainly suggests a belief in irresistible unconditional trends. Yet such a belief is, for example, incompatible with Marx's own picture of the working class intervening to put an end to the trends of capitalist development by altering the conditions on which their continuation depends. That Marx is not wholly conceptually clear seems undeniable. That he is totally and necessarily committed to what is genuinely fallacious in historicism seems less clear.

A second type of argument used by other recent critics of Marx is that Marxism is committed to the notion of a centralised, undemocratic revolutionary party with an iron inner discipline which, in the name of democracy, is to impose upon the masses not what the masses say they want, but what the party knows that they really want, irrespective of what they may say. Marxism, so it was asserted, had inherited the tradition of such a party from the Jacobins in the French Revolution, who had in turn been influenced by Rousseau. So, once again, theory was seen as lying at the root of political error.

It is therefore fascinating that when in 1956–7 there was widespread revolt against the established authorities in Eastern Europe, it was from Marxism –

---

[2] Popper 1957, p. 129.

according to its Western critics, the source of the tyranny – that many of the leaders of the revolt drew their inspiration. The mechanistic picture of historical inevitability which Western critics identified with Marxism they identified with the Stalinist corruption of Marx's thought. So too with the dogmas of the dictatorial party. Instead they stressed Marx's concern with freedom. The ambiguous formulae of traditional Marxism, which can be read in several ways, were reinterpreted in the light of the rediscovered libertarianism especially of the younger Karl Marx. The Polish philosopher, Leszek Kolakowski, argued against historicism as powerfully as Popper had done, but in the name of Marxism. The Polish sociologist, Stanislaw Ossowski, treated the Marxist theory of class structure and class struggle as a contribution to sociology to be judged by ordinary scientific standards. But, in the course of this liberation of Marxism from its own dogmatism, a new question came to be formulated.

The West had insisted that the Soviet Union failed if judged by the standards of Mill's liberalism. To some thinkers in the East, this seemed not the most relevant standard; what they urged was that the Soviet Union should be judged by the standards of its own professed doctrines. How, they inquired, would Russian society look if it was seen in the light of the Marxist perspective which the Russians themselves claimed to use to criticise the West? To American claims that America is a classless society, in spite of the wide differences in income, because there is openness of opportunity, the Russian reply was that the wide differences in income reflect wide differences in power, and that these are rooted in a class structure in which the opportunity to move from one class to another does nothing to diminish the existence of classes. But, in Soviet society, we find wide income differences too – what do these reflect? Mere functional differences in the usefulness of certain sorts of job, reply the apologists for the *status quo* in Russia. But this after all is what apologists for the American *status quo* say of inequality in the USA. Ossowski in his *Class Structure in the Social Consciousness* noted this and went on to frame an answer which he was prudent enough to put into the mouths of *émigré* anti-Soviet intellectuals. He first points out that, in general, Marxist methods – because they threaten established stereotypes and social fictions – are not used by the privileged and the established, but by the hostile outsider. Some Soviet *émigrés*, and, so he might have added, some of Trotsky's later Western followers, let alone a critic like Djilas, have tried to show how in Russia a new class structure has been formed.[3] Ossowski writes:

> ...those who like to apply Marxian methods to Soviet society in the Stalinist period stress the wide range of wage-scales and the importance of such economic privileges as were not included in the total of monetary rewards. They try to emphasize the tendency to stabilize class differences, citing such features as the great reduction in death duties and the sliding scale for income tax introduced in 1943; the reintroduction of fees for secondary and higher education in 1940, which was confirmed by the amendment of the 121st article of the Stalinist constitution in 1947; the system of rights, subsidies, privileges, and so on. In general, they attempt to apply the Marxian theory of the state to the Soviet state.[4]

Ossowski restricts his account to the Stalinist period. But for all the liberalisation of post-Stalin Russia, the critics could still point to the entrenchment of hierarchy and privilege.

It is for this reason that the very theory, which the Russians try to project outwards on to the Western world, they cannot allow to be used for the study of their own society – or else the realities of their own state capitalism and of their treatment of their own working class would stand revealed. And it is not only Marx whom they have to fear, it is Lenin too. Writing only two months before October 1917, Lenin had discussed the organisation of the early phases of the new revolutionary society, in terms of the most democratic and egalitarian strain in Marxism. He envisaged every citizen participating in the administration of the state. Capitalism, so he believed, had simplified accounting and control to the point where every literate worker could participate without difficulty in government: 'The whole of society will have become a single office and a single factory, with equality of labour and equality of pay.'[5] Lenin himself certainly never managed remotely to embody the ideals of *State and Revolution* in the young Soviet state. But, so long as his writings are canonised in the Soviet Union, there is a deep incompatibility between what the Soviet theorists are forced to admit about what ought to be

---

3 See Djilas 1957.
4 Ossowski 1963, p. 117.
5 Lenin 1960–70g, p. 479.

the case in Russia, if Marxist-Leninism really prevailed, and the way that they themselves live as part of the privileged ruling-class bureaucracy.

I have tried to bring out the contrast between the proclaimed political ideals of the Soviet Union and the truth which their own official political theory would reveal if they applied it to themselves. But we must ask if it is only of Russia that this is true? In an even sharper form, we find a similar contrast in the West, where established political theory and established political ideals contradict each other in the most violent way. Our established political ideals are those of parliamentary liberalism; we believe officially in a society in which the people choose their rulers by free and responsible majority vote after having considered the merits of the alternative policies of rival candidates on the basis of both past records and future projects. Equality of opportunity, it is asserted, although admittedly imperfectly realised, means that almost everyone has at least some chance to participate at the level he wishes to in the political process. What is interesting is that no other single theme has so engaged Western political theory as the attempt to show that this ideal is never realised, that people *cannot* rule themselves, that ruling in politics and management in industry are necessarily the specialised function of minority élites, and that inequality is a political and social necessity. 'The formula "Government of the people by the people" must be replaced by this formula: "Government of the people by an élite sprung from the people"', writes Professor Duverger, the French expert on élite theory when he comes in his great book, *Political Parties*, to express the nearest possible approximation to democracy that one might realistically aspire to.[6] But an élite sprung from the people is still an élite and an élite quickly becomes professionalised. So Schumpeter wrote cruelly and truthfully 'that democracy is the rule of the politicians'.[7]

Why must politicians and managers rule? One form of argument in élite theory would begin by trouncing what would be seen as the naïveté of Lenin's view of administration in the passage quoted earlier. Administration, man-management, involves the use of varied and difficult skills. A society or a factory can only be run along the grooves of social order. A much more interesting form of argument turns on the analysis of what any system of

[6] Duverger 1954, p. 425.
[7] Schumpeter 1950, p. 285.

parties and electors *must* become. Parties become in-groups, elections become occasions when rival minorities solicit the electorate, and the electorate plays a passive rather than an active role in its choices. This kind of theory was first formulated over half a century ago by writers such as G. Mosca and R. Michels in the light of experiences of the transformation of popular movements and working-class parties in Europe, such as the German Social Democrats, into machines dominated by full-time officials and working politicians. It has been extended by American sociologists to explain the detail of politics in a variety of situations. It is summarised in another aphorism of Schumpeter's that democracy is a system 'in which individuals acquire the power to decide by means of a competitive struggle for the people's vote'.[8] The people constitute not the sovereign power, but rather the arena in which leaderships contend. The role of ordinary citizens is to provide others with power.

Just as a Marxist analysis of the Soviet Union is more deadly than any Western critique, so to judge the West by the ideals of Mill's liberalism is likely to be more devastating than anything the Russian say. Each side in the 'Cold War' indicts the other for depriving the vast mass of ordinary working people of effective political power. Each frames its indictment in terms of a theory by the standards of which it too would stand indicted. Of course it remains true, as apologists for the West would argue, that there are alternative élites in the West, while in the Soviet Union there is only one. But this, though true, may obscure the truth that in the West rival parties within the parliamentary frame share a power of which the electorate is deprived, as effectively as it is deprived in the East, although in ways that are far more free from terror of censorship. Not that I underrate freedom from either.

The present situation in political theory presents us, therefore, both with new theoretical problems and with urgent political tasks, partly arising from questions about the role of theory itself. When we find that the two major societies in the world each tries to legitimate and justify itself by exalting a political theory the application of which would in fact show that its claims as a form of government were illegitimate and unjustified, we have to ask how in the political process itself this fact is so successfully obscured. Or is it? Does the ordinary Russian or American working man feel deprived of power by élites? If they do feel it, do they mind it? If not, how is it concealed from

[8] Schumpeter 1950, p. 269.

them? To answer these questions more fully than has yet been done would throw light on the use of theory as a weapon by government against its own citizens.

Here, too, the modern age is distinctive once more. The classical political theorists often offered advice to governments, usually critical advice. But apologists for government, such as Hobbes and Locke, wrote as private persons, almost as much as radical critics like Rousseau did. The theorist can now no longer be a private person. The light that he throws by theorising must not only alter his attitudes to, but probably his treatment by, government. The apologist for contemporary oligarchy is very likely to become – if he is not already – an oligarch. To any democrat, the situation outlined above obviously raises urgent practical political questions. But even to those satisfied with the *status quo* immediate practical questions arise in new theoretical forms.

For new spectres haunt the contemporary political world. One is that of the 'Third World', of the undeveloped Afro-Asian and Latin-American countries, which see themselves as deprived of power internationally by the Russo-American axis. The Third World has many distinctively different voices. But the one that is likely to be heard most insistently is that of the Chinese. And part of the Chinese polemic against, not the Russians explicitly, but the Yugoslavs (whom the Chinese habitually use as whipping-boys for the Russians), is that if you apply Marxist standards to Yugoslavia you must conclude that it is a state-capitalist power. In other words, the Chinese have started to develop the theme of this talk. In so doing, they are able to use Lenin himself against the Russians with great effect. When Lenin writes of the struggle between the working class and the bourgeoisie, his characteristic doctrine and his characteristic tones in *State and Revolution* are well represented by two quotations:

> The petty-bourgeois democrats, those alleged Socialists who substituted dreams of class harmony for the class struggle, even pictured the Socialist reformation in a dreamy fashion – not in the form of the overthrow of the rule of the exploiting class, but in the form of the peaceful submission of the minority to the majority which has become conscious of its aims. This petty-bourgeois Utopia, which is inseparably bound up with the idea of the state being above classes, led in practice to the betrayal of the interests of the toiling classes, as was shown, for example, by the history of the French revolutions of 1848 and 1871, and by the 'Socialists' joining bourgeois

> cabinets in England, France, Italy and other countries at the end of the nineteenth and the beginning of the twentieth centuries.[9]

> The doctrine of the class struggle, as applied by Marx to the question of the state and of the Socialist revolution, leads inevitably to the recognition of the *political rule* of the proletariat, of its dictatorship, i.e., of power shared with none and relying directly upon the armed force of the masses. The overthrow of the bourgeoisie can be achieved only by the proletariat becoming transformed into the *ruling class*, capable of crushing the inevitable and desperate resistance of the bourgeoisie, and of organising all the toiling and exploited masses for the new economic order.[10]

Lenin's doctrine is: first that there can be no truce in the war between the classes; secondly that only the working class can overthrow the bourgeoisie; and thirdly that the transition from bourgeois to working-class rule cannot be peaceful. But the voice of Khrushchev and the voices of his successors, as the Chinese and Albanians have pointed out, is not the voice of Lenin. Khrushchev was in fact not unlike the dreamy socialist reformists of whom Lenin spoke. In place of violent struggle between classes he put peaceful economic competition between states; and he did not believe in the Western working class overthrowing their own bourgeoisie, but in Soviet achievements so impressing the West that, in the end, the Western countries will make a calm and gradual transition to socialism.

The Chinese not only denounced Khrushchev for abandoning Lenin; they also thought that they knew why he was doing it. The Russians have now enriched themselves. They aspire to join the capitalist nations in peaceful harmony, just as reformist socialist leaders aspired to join bourgeois cabinets. The Russians still preserve Lenin's writings as sacred texts; but the Chinese are now able to indict the Russian ruling group of not holding the creed in which the Russian government still officially believes. We can expect much more of this. Even if the West and the Russians will not themselves face up to the discrepancy between their official theories and their actual practices, the voices of the Third World will increasingly force them to attend to it.

---

9 Lenin 1960–70g, p. 408.

10 Lenin 1960–70g, p. 409.

Obviously, even so wide a range of topics as that which I have attended to in all too short a space has still left untouched vast themes. One too important not to mention finally is that of totalitarianism. It is little more than twenty years since a hitherto apparently civilised nation was marching the Jews into the gas-chambers; and even less since Stalin's monolithic police apparatus enforced its terror. It would be absurd to suppose that totalitarianism is an episode now happily and finally over, if only because we have not yet acquired the explanatory theory which would enable us to grasp why we once so nearly all fell prey to it. Any realistic political theory about our future will have to clarify for us this danger too. But the context of all such clarifications will have to be the large present conflicts which I have described. Those conflicts make it clear that theory is once again of the greatest possible practical relevance. Carlyle in a possibly apocryphal anecdote is reputed to have said to a businessman who reproached him for merely dealing in ideas:

> There was once a man called Rousseau who wrote a book containing nothing but ideas. The second edition was bound in the skins of those who laughed at the first.

I wonder in whose skins the future editions of Marx and Mill will be bound.

Chapter Thirty-Six

Herbert Marcuse: From Marxism to Pessimism[1]

Marxism is in most of its versions an optimistic philosophy; so it is, for example, in Herbert Marcuse's earlier writings, when Hegel is castigated because his philosophy 'ends in doubt and resignation'.[2] But the later Marcuse himself ends in a state of doubt, if not one of resignation: 'Those social groups which dialectical theory identified as the forces of negation are either defeated or reconciled with the established system'.[3] This theme has been elaborated at length in *One Dimensional Man*, and it is worth enquiring whether on examination this transformation of Marxism into a pessimism does not reveal something about the character of Marxism and not just something about Marcuse's own intellectual development. To carry through this enquiry it is necessary to note certain features of Marxism.

Lukács, long ago in his essay on 'The Change in Function of Historical Materialism', argued that the time had come for historical materialism to engage in self-scrutiny.[4] The central thesis of historical materialism is that every major philosophical doctrine has features which show it to be the characteristic product of some specific form of social life. Of what

1 Originally published in *Survey* 62, January 1967, pp. 38–44.
2 Marcuse 1960, p. 248.
3 Marcuse 1960, p. xiv.
4 Lukács 1971, pp. 228–9.

specific form of social life then is Marxism itself a characteristic product? Of that nineteenth-century form of bourgeois life, in which the economic on the one hand and the political and cultural on the other were so sharply distinguished and segregated that the two could be taken to stand in an external causal relationship, such that the economic basis determined (in some sense) the political and cultural superstructure. That is to say, Marxist theory in its account of the political and the economic reflects the special relation of the non-interventionist state to the free-market economy, and in some hands (most notably those of Engels) has hypostasised certain features of that relationship into eternal characteristics of all forms of social life. But we can be rescued from this error by distinguishing those features of Marxist method which are valid only in their original nineteenth-century context from those which have validity in the present.

If Lukács is correct, a central feature of Marxism ought to be its capacity to renovate itself by self-scrutiny and self-criticism; and, equally, if Lukács is correct, we must be able to provide a criterion by which we may distinguish between those parts of Marxist theory which merely reflect the age in which it was first conceived and those parts which are more permanently valuable. In fact, no Marxist – nor anyone else – has ever produced an adequate version of such a criterion. But it is clear that, if such a criterion can be produced, it will be concerned with the relation between the empirical content of Marxism and its theoretical and conceptual form. Lukács indeed wanted to make Marxism's theoretical form entirely independent of the particular contingent empirical content which Marx gave to it; but never in his own writing did he succeed in doing this and he soon abandoned the attempt. If Marcuse perhaps resembles the younger Lukács in trying to make Marxist theory over-independent of the results of empirical enquiry, it may be that Marcuse's errors have also included the smuggling of an arbitrary empirical content into his otherwise Hegelian version of Marxism.

It is perhaps chiefly as an interpreter of Hegel that Marcuse excels. His early work, *Hegel's Ontologie und die Grundzüge einer Theorie der Geschichtlichkeit*, is a scholarly anticipation of the theories of *Reason and Revolution*, which is certainly the best statement in English and one of the best statements in any language of the connection between Hegel's logic and his social theory.[5] Yet Hegel is

---

[5] Marcuse 1932.

an essentially ambiguous author, open to interpretation in a number of ways which are all plausible, and Marcuse's interpretation of Hegel is revelatory of Marcuse as well as of Hegel. What it reveals may be most clearly shown by placing Marcuse's interpretation on a spectrum of Hegel interpretations.

At one end of this spectrum lies a Hegel for whom the world of historical experience is merely the phenomenal clothing of the timeless logical categories which constitute the successive phases of the self-development of the Absolute. The emphasis is on the gap between the partial and inarticulate gropings of those condemned to merely finite perspectives, and the total grasp of reality involved in philosophical thought, in which at its culmination the thought of the philosopher and that of the Absolute has become one.[6] This interpretation of Hegel is fundamentally a theological interpretation and although in this Hegelian scheme the metaphysical reality behind finite experience does not enjoy the independence of its this-worldly manifestations which it does in Christian theology, nonetheless it is this element in Hegel which enabled Right Hegelianism and Lutheranism to cement a relationship.

At the other end of the spectrum lies the interpretation of Hegel according to which the categories of the logic are thought of as having no more reality than that bestowed upon them by their embodiment in historical form. Each specific form of human social life is defined by a particular conceptual framework; every framework – and with it every particular set of social forms – develops incoherences which tend to force it into transformations that result in a new and more adequate conceptual scheme. The history of philosophy, of categories and concepts, and the history of social transactions are but two sides of the same coin. This interpretation emphasises the empirical aspect of Hegel's thought, and especially the fact that the logical progress in both societies and conceptual schemes is something that can be discerned only after the event. We cannot discover the patterns of development without a close study of what actually happened. The owl of Minerva flies only at dusk.[7]

Marcuse's interpretation of Hegel lies midway between these extremes. The sharp contrast which he wishes to draw between dialectical thinking and merely empirical thinking, and the way in which he presents the dialectic

---

[6] Hegel 1969, p. 50.

[7] Hegel 1952, p. 7: 'When philosophy paints its grey on grey, then has a shape of life grown old. By philosopher's grey on grey it cannot be rejuvenated but only understood. The owl of Minerva spreads its wings only after the coming of the dusk.'

as constituted by a set of laws to which all empirical reality must conform and to which we can know in advance that it must conform, separate him from the latter end of the spectrum. He treats, for example, Hegel's account of finitude and potentiality not as a conceptual analysis, but as the statement of a universal law.[8] Yet he also centrally maintains that Hegel's analysis of social life has application to actual societies, and that in this application lies its main point. The Hegel who maintained at the end of his life that philosophy entered a realm separate from and higher than that of society or politics is, on Marcuse's view (and correctly, I think), unfaithful to the core of his own thought. But, in combining these attitudes, Marcuse courts disaster. For what he desires is a theory of social life which, while it applies to actual empirical social life, is warranted not by empirical evidence, but by its conforming to the standards of something else which he calls dialectical thinking. In desiring this, he desires the logically impossible.

We can bring out the nature of the difficulties in the face of which Marcuse's enterprise founders by considering one way in which Hegel's central positions can be viewed fruitfully from the standpoint of social theory. Hegel argues that to understand any form of social life one must attend not merely to the presently existing state of affairs, but to the way in which it simultaneously opens up and inhibits certain possibilities of human development. The concept of 'the negative' in its application to social life is the concept of those forces at once incompatible with and destructive of a given form of social life which are nonetheless inevitably bred out of that form. This Hegelian view of societies as necessarily transforming themselves out of existence can be illuminatingly compared and contrasted with the Parsonian view of social orders as necessarily self-maintaining. Both Hegel and Talcott Parsons have written as if their type of analysis necessarily applied to all societies, and both obviously cannot be right. It may well be the case that some types of society are best analysed in terms of a Parsonian, others in terms of a Hegelian scheme. But whether this is so or not cannot be settled independently of empirical investigation, and this latter point would never have been denied by Marx. It is effectively denied by Marcuse.

It has to be so denied because of Marcuse's attitude to science. Marcuse inherits from Hegel the view that there is the sharpest possible distinction

[8] Marcuse 1960, p. 137.

between the study of human life and the natural sciences. His attacks on Saint-Simon and Comte in *Reason and Revolution* centre upon the charge that they assimilate sociology to physics – as indeed they do. He interprets Marx as holding that society cannot be understood in the way that nature is:

> Marx considered society to be irrational and hence evil, so long as it continued to be governed by unbreakable objective laws. Progress to him was equivalent to upsetting those laws, an act that was to be consummated by man in his free development.[9]

Free development is then sharply contrasted with law-governed development. It follows that although the development of capitalism, an unfree form of economy, may be law-governed, the transition to socialism cannot be, and Marcuse therefore consistently affirms that, although classical capitalism is necessarily self-destructive, there is no necessity about its replacement by socialism. Moreover, sociology is not an empirical discipline in the sense that the natural sciences are. But here he diverges most sharply from Marx. Marx uses both deterministic and non-deterministic language and does not commit himself on the philosophical issues about freedom and causality; but he does ground his beliefs about the transition to socialism not only on general truths about human nature and society as Marcuse does, but upon the actual character of the working-class and the labour movement as he discussed it empirically. (It is as impossible to imagine Marx writing, as Marcuse does, that 'the transition from capitalism's inevitable death to socialism is necessary, but only in the sense that the full development of the individual is necessary', as it is to understand what this sense is.[10])

What Marx believed on these points may of course have been false; but it is a question of empirical fact whether it was true or false, while Marcuse, by ignoring the empirical basis of the Marxism he uses, renders it unfalsifiable and unrevisable from an empirical point of view. This has dangerous consequences. For his presentation of Marxism, although unfalsifiable, is not empty of consequences for his beliefs about society. Marcuse identifies the Hegelian negative with the industrial working class; he feeds Marx's empirical findings about that class into his own metaphysical machine in

---

[9] Marcuse 1960, p. 332.
[10] Marcuse 1960, p. 317.

such a way that he is bound to conclude that, if the capitalist form of life is to be replaced by another, only the industrial working class can replace it. What constitutes the working class as a revolutionary force for Marcuse is not so much empirical evidence of their 'historical' role, as the fact that they live outside the schematism of the civil order of middle-class society as Hegel defined it. It follows that, if the working class were to be domesticated within that order, then there would be lacking any negative forms to transcend and destroy that order. In other words, a particular social order would have become invulnerable; that our own social order has in large part done so is the message of *One Dimensional Man* (1964).[11]

Marcuse's position in *One Dimensional Man* is, so I am committed to arguing, in part a consequence of his having failed to distinguish, as Lukács urged that we must distinguish, between those elements in Marxism which are always essential to it and those which have application only at a certain period. But it is important to note that, in *One Dimensional Man*, he not only clings to the unessential, he abandons the essential. For, in spite of all his scorn for contemporary sociology, his own account of contemporary society is, in many ways, very like that of those Parsonians or others who see it as a well-integrated and self-maintaining social order. In his analysis of contemporary society, he nowhere seeks for specifically contemporary negative forces, as on his own Hegelian terms he ought to, and his abandonment of this search is reminiscent of Hegel's own belief in the stability he had been prepared to concede to no previous age. But I cannot discuss the analysis in *One Dimensional Man* properly unless I first consider some of the content of *Eros and Civilization* (1955).[12]

In this book, Marcuse supplemented his Marxism by an adherence to Freudian theory of a largely uncritical kind. He does revise Freud in order to use him; but he does, for example, also appear to accept much Freudian apparatus (including the belief in a death instinct) which most Freudians reject. Here, once again, Marcuse's resolute stance against investigating what empirical confirmation his beliefs might have makes criticism difficult. His chief revision of Freud concerns the role of sublimation. Freud saw sublimation as both an agency repressing fundamental human desire and

---

[11] Marcuse 1968b.
[12] Marcuse 1969.

a necessity for cultural achievement; Marcuse envisages the possibility of a society in which sublimation can cease to be repressive, and the sexual desires are at once sublimated *and* realised. But, according to *One Dimensional Man*, social development has moved not in this direction, but rather in the direction of what Marcuse sees as a controlled and repressive desublimation. Modern Western culture, by its greater permissiveness towards sexual desires, enables these desires to be spent on transient satisfaction instead of informing an attitude of revolt towards the established order.

This psychoanalytic thesis is used by Marcuse in partial explanation of what has happened to the working class. The working class represented for him the forces of negation which might transcend and overcome capitalism. Their motivation, according to Marcuse, in performing this task is revealed by his remark on the subject of the welfare state that 'there is no reason to insist on self-determination if the administered life is the comfortable and even the "good" life'.[13] That is to say, the thesis that the welfare state, by raising levels of consumption, and a culture of permissive sexuality, by raising levels of satisfaction, have deprived the working class of motives for revolutionary action, shows that Marcuse embraces that crude theory of revolutionary motives according to which only the absolute deprivation of material comfort radicalises workers or anyone else. Why he should believe this proposition is unclear; but it is perhaps part of the penalty paid by those who believe that 'this power of facts is an oppressive power', that they should find themselves believing what is not the case.[14] Of course, the belief that only absolute deprivation radicalises is widely shared by Marxists. Baran and Sweezy's pro-communist position in their *Monopoly Capitalism* (1966), and Deutscher's view of the West in *The Great Contest* (1960), both presuppose that the working class has now been permanently domesticated, and that, until a desire to emulate the achievements of the Soviet bloc excites a desire for socialism in the West (a fantasy that scarcely deserves comment), the West will remain, just as Marcuse supposes, secure in its self-development.[15]

The lacuna in *One Dimensional Man* that makes it at once too easy and more difficult to criticise, is the total absence of any account of contemporary social

[13] Marcuse 1968b, p. 53.
[14] Marcuse 1960, p. xiv.
[15] Baran and Sweezy 1968, pp. 348–53; Deutscher 1960, pp. 66–72, 78–82.

structure. If we try to reconstruct one from what Marcuse says on other topics, we encounter another difficulty, namely that Marcuse says that:

> My analysis is focused on tendencies in the most highly developed contemporary societies. There are large areas within and without these societies where the described tendencies do not prevail – I would say: not yet prevail.[16]

This reservation constitutes a difficulty, because, in the picture he actually constructs, Marcuse depicts a totally homogeneous society in which even those elements from whom Marcuse does acquire a minuscule hope of revolutionary action – 'the substratum of the outcasts and outsiders, the exploited and persecuted of other races and other colours, the unemployed and the unemployable' – have no real place.[17] The homogeneous social structure presupposed by his analysis appears to contain only two social groups, the manipulators and the manipulated. The first includes government, private management, and their intellectual allies, the latter everyone else. Characteristically, Marcuse discusses the consequences of a decision by the managing groups to automate the whole economy, rather than the type of decision to automate this or that feature of production taken by a particular management in particular circumstances. From this standpoint, then, there disappear from view all those phenomena of complex, uneven, and fragmented development which are so fundamental to advanced industrial life.

If we try to understand the welfare state in the context of such development, then we have to bring in the fact that it had and has to be politically achieved by the struggles of the labour movement – the notion of it as simply handed down from above, as nothing but an administrative device of the rulers to subordinate the ruled, is historically absurd – and that it is not necessarily a source of political or social stability. For the institutionalisation of welfare, like all other rises in the standard of living, alters the horizons of possibility for different social groups and alters too the standards by which they assess their deserts and their rights. Not absolute but relative deprivation becomes crucially important. The varying pace of technological development, the varying institutional responses to that development and the changing

[16] Marcuse 1968b, p. 15.
[17] Marcuse 1968b, p. 200.

character of the labour force combine to create in advanced industrial societies all sorts of possibilities of conflict. It does not follow of course that one should expect social disorder.

That is to say, the stability of an advanced industrial order, which is genuine enough in the short run, may depend not, as Marcuse supposes, upon its homogeneity, but upon the very variety of stresses it generates, and it follows from this that the possibility of its revolutionary transformation would then have to be set in a very different perspective. Marcuse sees correctly that the type of relationship which once existed between the industrial working class on the one hand and capitalist employers and the nineteenth-century state on the other, exists nowhere in modern society – a single line or cleavage upon which many conflicts focus. He infers incorrectly that society is therefore becoming homogeneous.

The counterpart to his view of society is his view of contemporary ideology as single and all pervasive. Linguistic analysis in philosophy, behaviourism in psychology, operationalism in the natural sciences, the activities of the Rand Corporation, the language of *Time* magazine, and modern American social science are all linked manifestations of that one-dimensional thought in which the possibility of critical opposition to the established order is obliterated. What is wrong with this is of course partly just a matter of the large, crude mistakes about contemporary philosophy and science made by Marcuse and partly a matter of the same pattern of overall homogeneity being imposed upon the material.[18] But it also misses, and most strikingly, the contemporary debate about theory in the social sciences. Works like those of Goldschmidt and Lévi-Strauss in anthropology, Blau and Homans and Dahrendorf in sociology, reveal a remarkable absence of theoretical consensus. It is not indeed that we have too few theories, as Marcuse suggests, but too many. This richness will not of course last, for some perspectives will prove fruitful and others barren. But it is therefore peculiarly regrettable that, at this particular point, what Hegelianism and a Marxism that has learnt from Hegel have to contribute to the theoretical debate should appear in the disguised and disconcerting form which Marcuse gives to it.

[18] [On philosophy see A. MacIntyre, 'Modern Society: an End to Revolt?', *Dissent*, Volume 12, Number 2, Spring 1965, and on natural science Peter Sedgwick's brilliant critique of Marcuse, 'Natural Science and Human Theory: a Critique of Herbert Marcuse', in R. Miliband and J. Saville (eds.) *The Socialist Register* 1966. – AM.]

The Hegelian account of societies as developing, through their own schemes of thought, points of conflict which become points of transformation, is, at the very least, an important corrective to other current modes. But it is only a schematism, a set of directives for developing theoretical explanations of actual social phenomena. It is not itself a substantive theory. Marcuse, like some other Marxists, moves from the level of a schematism for constructing theories to that of substantive theory without distinguishing the two, or even being aware that there are two levels. This leads him to suppose that if contemporary society does not exhibit the type of conflict laid down in Marx's theory of classical capitalism, conflict as such must be absent. Because his hope was pinned on that single type of conflict, despair or something very like it therefore ensues, as well as intellectual confusion. But, if Hegelianism has anything to teach us, it is that different forms of society will each have their specific form of conflict. It is the very philosophy which Marcuse professes that could have rescued him from his errors.

Chapter Thirty-Seven

How Not to Write About Stalin[1]

A Review of Svetlana Alliluyeva, Twenty Letters to a Friend

Miss Stalin both demonstrates and helps to perpetuate one of the myths of the modern world: the belief that the explanation of what is puzzling on the public stage lies in the realm of private life. There is a small grain of truth here. Sometimes a man's relations with his wife or friends may suggest a new light in which to see his actions as a revolutionary or a statesman. But, in general, what is crucial in the relationship of private to public life is the irrelevance of the one to the other. That Himmler detested cruelty to animals does nothing to explain the politics of the Final Solution. Miss Stalin's revelation that her father was exceptionally good at handling domestic servants is quite as uninteresting, and obviously so. Less obvious and therefore more dangerous is the suggestion that two of Stalin's personal relationships may explain at least in part the development and character of his tyranny.

---

1 Originally published as an untitled review in *Yale Law Journal*, 77, 1967/1968, pp. 1032–6. Reprinted as 'How Not to Write about Stalin' in A. MacIntyre, *Against the Self-Images of the Age: Essays on Ideology and Philosophy*, Duckworth, London 1971, pp. 48–51.

The first of Miss Stalin's suggestions is that her mother's suicide may hav played a decisive role in Stalin's development.

> What was the effect of my mother's death? Did it simply leave my father free to do what he would have done in any case? Or was it that her suicide broke his spirit and made him lose his faith in all his old friends?[2]

The second suggestion is that the author of the essential evil in Stalin's care was Beria. Kirov's murder, for example, so Miss Stalin says, was far mo probably the work of Beria than of Stalin. The two suggestions are linke for Beria's ascendancy followed, on Miss Stalin's interpretation, the death her mother. It is true that she claims that she is not trying to shift blame fro Stalin to Beria: none the less she writes that 'the spell cast on my father by th terrifying evil genius was extremely powerful, and it never failed to work'.[3]

Her metaphor is at once revealing and inapposite. Everything we kno about Stalin makes the notion of him as somehow spell-bound extreme unconvincing. But Miss Stalin has no other terms in which to think of h father. In particular, she seems incapable of thinking in political terms. Hen those of Stalin's political actions which impinged upon her – the imprisonme of Alexander Svanidze or that of Polina Molotov – appear in her narrative arbitrary and unrelated actions. This appearance of arbitrariness infects eve her account of her mother's suicide. She says of her mother's suicide no that she has been told by those who saw it that 'it was a terrible letter, full reproaches and accusations: It wasn't purely personal; it was partly politic as well'.[4] But, either she does not know, or she is unwilling to say what th political content of the note was. Her comments are as follows:

> People shot themselves fairly often in those days. Trotskyism had been defeated. Collectivization of the farms had just gotten under way. The Party was torn by opposition and factional strife. One leading Party member after another did away with himself. Mayakovsky had shot himself only a short time before. People couldn't make sense of this, and the memory was still very fresh. I think all this couldn't fail to have had its effect on my mother,

[2] Alliluyeva 1968, p. 125.
[3] Alliluyeva 1968, pp. 122–3.
[4] Alliluyeva 1968, p. 102.

> impulsive and susceptible as she was. The Alliluyevas were all sensitive and high-strung…[5]

In other words, suicide was breaking out all over and her mother was peculiarly liable to contagion. But there is, in fact, no reason for believing that Nadezhda Alliluyeva was peculiarly vulnerable to suicide, except that she did in fact kill herself; and suicide was relatively frequent at that period for highly specific reasons, on which her remarks about Party strife throw no light. Party strife had been bitter for many years without bringing comrades to self-destruction.

The hypothesis I would advance about Nadezhda Alliluyeva's suicide is suggested partly by its date, November 1932. It occurred, that is, when the consequences of Stalin's politics of forced collectivisation and speeded-up industrialisation had already become clear, but when the repression and the purges in the Party had yet to begin. Terror in the countryside and increased exploitation of the working class had become central facts of Soviet social life, but the mass killing of Communists would still have seemed novel and horrific even to those who were about to carry it out. Stalinism had laid its economic foundation, to use a different idiom, but it had not yet erected its political superstructure. What was the relationship between these two periods?

The key lies in the nexus between Stalin's economic policies – which were directed toward problems for which, as Trotsky never fully understood, there were no *socialist* solutions – and the political need for purges created by the failure to acknowledge that socialist theory had perforce been left behind when these policies were adopted. In the final analysis, Stalin succeeded, not so much because of the ruthlessness of his tactical manoeuvres, as because there was no alternative to the substance of the economic policies he pursued during both periods. Certainly, there was a gratuitous inhumanity in the implementation of those policies. But the capitulation of so many principled and tough Old Bolsheviks cannot be explained in terms only of weakness, torture, or bribery. It *is* explicable in terms of the incoherence of Stalin's adversaries who could not by applying their socialist and democratic principles frame any more adequate solution. Moreover, many of Stalin's supporters were sufficiently principled to discover in time the gap between their socialist desires and ideals and the

[5] Alliluyeva 1968, p. 103.

form of state which Stalin was actually bringing to birth. Indeed, when th purges came, Stalin's own earlier supporters were decimated as much as we the ranks of the old Trotskyists and Bukharinists.

But though there may have been no alternative of substance to the econom policy which Stalin had pursued since before 1932, what could have bee admitted was that what was being built was not socialism. One can imagin that, if Lenin had survived to 1930, he would have pursued in a more radic way the approach he followed when he defended the NEP not as socialist, bu as necessary. What led to the corruption of socialism was Stalin's insisten that what he was doing was socialist. A whole redefinition of Marxis thereby became necessary. To secure that redefinition, a whole generatio of Marxists was to be obliterated. Briefly and perhaps cryptically, it is ofte supposed that Bolshevik history has had to be rewritten in Russia becaus the purges and the trials made unpersons of so many Old Bolsheviks. Th truth is, I suggest, that the purges and the trials were necessary because th history of the Bolsheviks, including the history of their theoretical position had to be rewritten so that the true nature of socialism could be forgotten an the Stalinist redefinition could reign unchallenged in society where not th working class but the bureaucracy ruled.

In 1932, the task of ideological redefinition was only beginning, and th gap between Stalinist deeds and Marxist words was at its most obvious. was at this point that Syrtsov, Lominadze and Riutin, all of them Stalinist hoped to depose Stalin; all were imprisoned. In this year, Skrypnik, also Stalinist, committed suicide when Stalin discovered the opposition to him i the Ukrainian government, in which Skrypnik was Commissar for Educatio Suicide is, indeed, a much more intelligible reaction among the disillusione Stalinists than it would have been then among the adherents of Trotsky c those of Bukharin, who must for some years have lost most, if not all, of thei illusions. Thus, Nadezhda Alliluyeva's suicide falls into its tragic place i the historical sequence. Miss Stalin, who sees only the sequences of person biography, thus deprives her mother's action of one possible meaning it ma have held. Equally, she sees Beria as a private author of evil; she does not se that the unfolding of Stalinism created a role for Beria and those like him. Th role and not the man determined the scale of the evil.

Nonetheless, to treat the weaknesses of Miss Stalin's memoirs as simpl symptoms of a defective point of view, without inquiring about the soci roots of that point of view, would merely duplicate her error. Miss Stalin has a religious perspective upon the world, albeit a rather indefinite one, and her devotion to Russia has religious overtones. Indeed, when she wrote her memoir she believed that she would never be capable of leaving Russia. One can understand why the Russia Miss Stalin confronts, the Russia which she claims that her father always loved, was an abstract mystical entity; privilege and wealth have always separated her from social reality. The most characteristic Soviet experience is to stand in a queue for bread; this does not seem to be a thought that Miss Stalin has ever had. It would be too prosaic for her.

There remains one aspect of her book which is of real value. She does reveal in how impossible a position we put the children of major figures. They lead private and not public lives, but their private lives are distorted by the way in which they are exposed to the public gaze. Of Stalin's children, one became a drunkard and one has now written memoirs; but one became a hero. Yakov, the son of Stalin's first marriage, who was largely disowned by his father, seems to have been, and not only from this account, a straightforwardly moral and finally heroic figure who defied the Germans in his prison camp and was murdered by them. Miss Stalin when speaking on the power of Truth and Goodness to survive falls victim to her own rhetoric; on her half-brother's simple nobility of character, she sounds more truthful than at any other point in her unattractive book.[6]

---

6 Alliluyeva 1968, pp. 139–44.

Chapter Thirty-Eight

How to Write About Lenin – and How Not to[1]

A Review of Leonard Schapiro and Peter Reddaway (eds.), Lenin: The Man, the Theorist, the Leader

Discussions of historical method rarely illuminate one crucial point: what kind of *rapport* must the historian have with his subject if he is to write about it successfully? Clearly, it is not just a matter of a certain sympathy to be felt by the historian for his subject. A certain lack of sympathy may indeed be necessary. But it must be a lack of sympathy of the right kind. For those who intend to write about Lenin there are at least two prerequisites. The first is a sense of scale. One dare not approach greatness of a certain dimension (and what holds of Lenin would hold equally of Robespierre or of Napoleon) without a sense of one's own limitations. A Lilliputian who sets out to write Gulliver's biography had best take care. Above all, he dare not be patronising. This danger is not entirely avoided by all the contributors to a new set of essays about Lenin.

The second prerequisite is a sense of tragedy which will enable the historian to feel both the greatness

[1] Originally published in *Encounter*, Volume 30, Number 5, May 1968, pp. 71–4. Reprinted as 'How Not to Write About Lenin', in A. MacIntyre, *Against the Self-Images of the Age: Essays on Ideology and Philosophy*, Duckworth, London 1971, pp. 43–7.

and the failure of the October Revolution. Those for whom the whole project of the revolutionary liberation of mankind from exploitation and alienation is an absurd fantasy disqualify themselves from writing about communism in the same way that those who find the notion of the supernatural redemption of the world from sin an outmoded superstition disqualify themselves from writing ecclesiastical history? How much can be achieved nonetheless is witnessed to by Gibbon and by Hume, as well as by their successors; and how much is necessarily missed out is witnessed to at the same time. So far as the October Revolution is concerned, a sense of tragedy is as likely to be obliterated as effectively by the spirit of orthodox hagiography as it is by the philistinism so characteristic of much anti-communism. Indeed, orthodox hagiography has had to ignore entirely the truth about Lenin's last days.

Among Lenin's likes were cats, hunting, tidiness, and Pushkin; among his dislikes bohemianism, religion, and Mayakovsky. He once found himself unable to shoot a fox because 'really she was so beautiful'.[2] He feared the power of great music to distract his energies and emotions from revolutionary ends. These and other opaque facts about his complex and subtle character are brought out in an excellent essay by Peter Reddaway entitled 'Literature, the Arts and the Personality of Lenin'. Reddaway also notes the traits singled out by commentators as different as Trotsky, Lunacharsky, and Berdyaev, an overriding simplicity and certainty of revolutionary purpose. 'Purity of heart', wrote Kierkegaard, 'is to will one thing'.[3] It was Lenin's purity of heart that his opponents could not and his critics cannot bear. This trait has been subject of much misunderstanding. It is often treated as a personal characteristic which Lenin simply happened to have, and so it will appear if it is detached from the theoretical judgements which informed it.

Professor Leonard Schapiro, Mr. Reddaway's co-editor, stresses Lenin's 'fear that the revolution might be "missed"'.[4] As he saw it, compromises, reforms, concessions by the government, a rise in living standards, could all easily operate to postpone or even render impossible or very difficult the revolution predicted by Marx. What Schapiro does not discuss is the question of the source of this fear. To this question there may be a surprising answer.

---

2 Reddaway 1967, p. 62. See also Krupskaya 1970, p. 38.
3 Kierkegaard 1948, pp. 32, 219.
4 Schapiro 1967, p. 13.

Lenin shared the views of those Marxists whom he was shortly to denounce as 'economists' apparently up to his receiving in his Siberian exile in 1899 Eduard Bernstein's *Die Voraussetzungen des Sozialismus und die Aufgabe der Sozialdemokratie*. That he then proceeded to refute and denounce Bernstein is well known; in this, he was at one with every orthodox Marxist, including his future bitter enemy Kautsky. But, in this denunciation, he did not continue to believe, as Kautsky believed, that the history of capitalism was moving forward in a law-governed way so that even if the transformation of the labour movement into a revolutionary-socialist movement and the subsequent victory of socialism was not quite an automatic process, it was in some sense inevitable. It is difficult to see that Lenin took anywhere but from Bernstein his new belief that, in the course of capitalism's development, the working class might be domesticated and the trade unions become the instrument of that domestication. Certainly, even on this point, Lenin did not agree with Bernstein. What Bernstein thought was in fact going to happen, Lenin took to represent only one possibility, but it was the possibility which would be realised unless positive countervailing action were taken. In the very act of attempting to refute revisionism, Lenin seems to have learnt from it.

The socialist revolution is, then, from 1899 onward, an urgent matter of will, organisation, and an eye for opportunity. Any road is permissible which runs more nearly toward the goal than any other road perceived at the same moment. This single criterion allows for a combination of undeviating purpose and flexibility of both tactics and doctrine. The flexibility of Lenin's doctrine has also another source. Lenin saw threats to the revolution from a number of directions quite as if not more, clearly than he envisaged the road forward. Consequently, he rarely devoted himself to expounding doctrine except in the context of polemic. Since he polemicised from time to time on several fronts and tended to allow his project of the moment to be aimed at defeating one particular enemy once and for all, it is not surprising that the key texts are not merely inconsistent with each other, but form, in some way, a collection of fragments. Out of these fragments a monument has been built – and admiration and enmity have both contributed to it – called 'Leninism'. But 'Leninism' has a purely factitious unity. The doctrines of *State and Revolution* (1917), for example, contain elements which are found nowhere else in Lenin. Among these is a strongly stated belief in the possibility of the radical democratisation of society immediately after the socialist revolution. This belief is not only at odds with Lenin's general attitude to the working class; it is one that he never seems to have taken seriously when within a year the revolution had occurred and he was proceeding to construct the socialist order. Again if we compare his attitude to the working class under capitalism in *What Is to Be Done?* (1902) with that in *Imperialism: the Highest Stage of Capitalism* (1916) there is at least a crucial difference of emphasis. In the former, he sees the natural trend in the development of the working class as being non-revolutionary; in the latter he sees the non-revolutionary character of the working class as having to be explained by the use of the superprofits of imperialism to buy off the aristocracy of labour.[5] It is not that these two theses could not, under certain conditions, be reconciled. It is rather that Lenin tends to confront problems in isolation from each other.

Nor is this surprising. Lenin poses the problem of the transition to socialism. About this Marx said very little, Engels only slightly more, and Engels's remarks on victory through parliamentary elections and the outdatedness of military insurrections were scarcely likely to be appreciated by Lenin.[6] Classical Marxism is a doctrine in which insight into the bourgeois societies of the mid- and late nineteenth century was bought at the price of all too close a reflection of the categories of that society in its own theories. In consequence, when Marxism came to be applied to new situations at the end of the nineteenth century and the beginning of the twentieth century, would-be Marxists were left with a good deal of freedom, both theoretical and practical. The phenomena of imperialism, for example, evoked quite different response from Rosa Luxemburg, from Lenin in 1899, and from Lenin in 1916. In *The Development of Capitalism in Russia* (1899), as Professor Alec Nove points out in his outstanding essay, 'Lenin as Economist', Lenin argued against Struve's view that foreign trade can be a means by which capitalism can rid itself of surpluses which it cannot sell on the home market. According to *Imperialism* – and Lenin makes no reference to his own past views – such surpluses *can* at least for a time be exported.[7] But this very inconsistency is a sign of degree of freedom which Marxist theorists possessed at this period.

---

[5] Lenin 1960–70b, pp. 373–8; 1960–70e, pp. 193–4, 282–5.

[6] See Chapter 30, note ?, above.

[7] Nove 1967, pp. 198, 201. See also, Lenin 1960–70a, pp. 43–7, 64–7 and Lenin 1960–70e, pp. 240–5. In the latter work, Lenin refers to the export of capital, rather than the export of commodities.

This freedom to theorise within a framework which was a good deal less constraining than even the Marxist theorists themselves believed and liked to believe makes the old question of whether Lenin was or was not a genuine and orthodox Marxist one to which rival answers can with equal plausibility be given. Some of these rival answers are discussed by Professor J.C. Rees, who points out acutely how one can frame an impressive case – as Sukhanov and other Mensheviks did – for saying that on Marxist grounds Russia was in 1917 far from ready for a proletarian revolution; but that one could also in 1917 have framed an impressive case for saying that Marxist theory supplied no ready-made recipes for application to Russia and that what was required was a creative remaking of the Marxist categories.[8]

Not all the contributors to this volume are as clear as Professor Rees is about the kind of advantage that we have over Lenin in being able to view his actions as he could not, just because we know what happened next. The shadow of what happened next can far too easily be allowed to obscure what in fact happened. It ought also to be remarked that Mensheviks have been better at writing memoirs since 1917 than they were at making political decisions at the time. For when the worst has been said about Lenin it is clear that there was *no* possibility of Marxist revolution except for that which Lenin seized upon and indeed partly created. We ought not to confuse a proper grasp of the tragic dimensions of the October Revolution with the sentimentality that actually prefers tragic failures of integrity to any substantial achievement and so idolises Martov and even finds it far easier to come to terms with Trotsky or Rosa Luxemburg than with Lenin, just because, in the end, they were losers. But, of course, nonetheless Lenin lost too. His late protests against bureaucracy, against the low level of Soviet culture and more specifically against Stalin – those protests which the hagiographers cannot take seriously – in no way amount to any kind of renunciation of the revolution, but Lenin did none the less acknowledge some of his responsibility for some of the negative sides of the Soviet Revolution. Yet Stalinism was not in any sense the legitimate successor even of the negative sides of Lenin's work. The claim that Stalin's work continued Lenin's is familiar not only from Stalinist pens, but also in the writings of those critics of Lenin who wish to fasten on him responsibility

[8] Rees 1967, pp. 90–3, 103–5.

for a variety of policies which he never envisaged. To those critics one must concede at least two points.

The first is that Lenin, of course, was always prepared for tactical retreats from socialist principles and was prepared to be almost indefinitely flexible and adaptive; but, where Lenin recognised such retreats for what they were, Stalin presented them as advances toward socialism and in the course of doing so redefined socialism away into tyranny.

The second is that it is certainly true that underlying such Leninist retreats was a crude utilitarianism: the end of socialism justifies any necessary means. But the key word here is 'necessary'. The memoirs of Victor Serge, for example, witness to Lenin's personal humanity in 1917–18.[9] There was never in Lenin the sense of pleasure in terror or the sense of gratuitous *personal* hostility so evident in Stalin. It remains true that such utilitarianism corrupts and corrupted, that it formed the moral link between Lenin and Stalin.

Lenin's was a heroic attempt to force a social situation unforeseen by Marx into the categories of Marxist theory, and to do this not merely, in theory but in deed. The future as Lenin envisaged it was the same future which Marx had envisaged. The past which Lenin viewed was the past which Marx had depicted. Lenin's task was to remake the present so that it might be a bridge between that past and that future. The intractability of that present, its refusal to be moulded in Leninist ways, teaches the moral that Leninism provides us with few, if any, specific political recipes; what Lenin achieved, in spite of that intractability, carries the moral that this may not be as important as Lenin's detractors have thought.

---

[9] Serge 1978, especially pp. 101–2, 110, 134.

Chapter Thirty-Nine

The Strange Death of Social-Democratic England[1]

The most striking piece of news about Britain recently has aroused practically no comment. There are now over half a million unemployed, more than there have been in any June since the war, and since March the average increase in the number of unemployed each month has been 20,000. These facts are surely striking enough in themselves, but, when we add to them another fact, that this unemployment has been deliberately created by the government, we ought all of us surely to be a little more astonished and appalled than we are. Every previous Labour government regarded rising unemployment as a defeat, as a sign that its policy was not working or that it has chosen the wrong policy. This is the first Labour government which must regard rising unemployment as a victory for its policies, as a sign that they are working in the way that the Chancellor predicted that they would work. Left-wing critics of Labour governments have often felt able to accuse them of pursuing not socialist but Keynesian economic policy – a criticism which pays a quite undeserved compliment to former Labour Chancellors and at the same time quite gratuitously

[1] Originally broadcast on 'Personal View' on the BBC Third Programme, 20 June 1968 and published in *The Listener*, 4 July 1968, pp. 7–8. Reprinted in David Widgery (ed.), *The Left in Britain 1956–68*, Penguin Books, Harmondsworth 1976, pp. 235–40.

insults Keynes. But Mr Jenkins is our first Labour Chancellor whose policies would even have been intelligible and acceptable to those as yet untouched by the Keynesian revolution, and it is well worth asking why Labour has made, and has felt able to make, this total change of attitude. If we are to do so, however, we must remember that a political change on this scale never occurs in isolation. Indeed, I want to go so far as to suggest that what we are seeing is a major change in the social scene, a change which might well be called 'The Strange Death of Social-Democratic England'.

It is now over thirty years since George Dangerfield published a book called *The Strange Death of Liberal England*, in which he diagnosed in the years 1910–13 a fundamental change in the assumptions which defined British politics.[2] One can summarise an important part of Dangerfield's thesis by remembering that, in the decades before 1910, politics had been played according to Liberal rules, even by the opponents of Liberalism. And then those whom Liberalism excluded or pretended did not exist suddenly rose around it on all sides: trade unionists in militant strike action, suffragettes, Irish nationalists, Irish Unionists. What would have happened if the German Emperor had not rescued England from internal strife by kindly invading Belgium is a great unanswerable question. But the central moral is clear. When the parliamentary system cannot express the major social conflicts of an age, then those conflicts will be expressed not only outside but against that system. It is some of the consequences of this truth that I want to explore now.

I have suggested that if the years from 1910 to 1913 witnessed the strange death of Liberal England, then the years which we are living through now are witnessing the strange death of social democracy. The basic premises of social democracy were twofold. The first was that class conflict was genuine, that in the market economy of classical capitalism the interests of the working class ran clean counter to those interests which relied upon the smooth working of the economic system. This premise social democrats shared with a variety of revolutionary socialists, whether communists, syndicalists or anarchists. But they differed from all varieties of revolutionary socialist in holding that a second premise was true, namely that the political system of parliamentary democracy can at once contain and express that conflict. The classical social-democratic belief is that the interests of the working class can be expressed by

[2] Dangerfield 1936.

a political party which would both adhere to the conventions of parliamentary democracy and also accept the fact that the interests of the working class must conflict with the goals which dominate the economic system.

This belief was strongly expressed, for example, in the policies of the Labour government of 1945–51; the goal of full employment was taken to have overriding importance, and so firmly was the importance of this goal imprinted that, in the immediately succeeding years of Conservative rule, the impossibility of not pursuing the goal of full employment was taken for granted. The Conservative claim even became that they too could achieve some of the basic goals of social democracy; the political game was being played according to social-democratic rules. The contrast between Conservative government in 1951–5 and Labour government now could scarcely be sharper, for we are in a situation in which full employment, the level of spending in the welfare state and the growth of wages are all being sacrificed to those traditional gods of the British economic and commercial system, the exchange-value of the pound sterling and the achievement of a surplus on our external trading figures. The political cost of this economic policy is the gradual disenfranchisement of the working class, resulting from the insistence that the working class have no specific and special interests in conflict with the interests of others. Consider, in this respect, the operation of the prices and incomes policy.

The background to any consideration of this policy must be the grotesque degree of inequality which still exists in England. About 7 per cent of the population owns over 80 per cent of all private wealth. The richest 1 per cent of those receiving incomes receives over 12 per cent of the total incomes received. Furthermore, there has been remarkably little change in recent decades in relative incomes as between different social classes. Middle-class people still often believe in the myth of a period of radical income redistribution during the war and the 1945–51 Labour government. But no such redistribution occurred. We remain very much where we were in the 1930s, and what John Strachey wrote in 1956 has been true for the whole of this century:

> Capitalism, it has turned out, is a Red Queen's sort of country from the wage earner's point of view. They have run very fast for a long time to keep in the same place relative to other classes.[3]

[3] Strachey 1956, p. 150.

What the so-called prices and incomes policy does is at least to freeze and maintain this situation of inequality and perhaps to accentuate it. For, because of a variety of fringe benefits, of salary scales with automatic increments and the like, middle-class incomes simply are not subject to the same degree of restraint that working-class incomes are. Now, in this situation of gross inequality, the only institutions which are available to the working class to express their special and conflicting interests turn out to be part of that trade-union and Labour-Party network in which power is held by those operating the very policies which ignore their interests. The Labour Party and the Labour government have accepted definitions of political reality and political possibility according to which social democracy can no longer exist. And this is something genuinely new.

I am not saying, what some Marxists used to argue, that social democracy must be ineffective in all circumstances in a capitalist society. I am, instead, saying that we must recognise this in the period from 1900 to 1955 in Britain, and in differing degrees elsewhere, social democracy could provide a viable expression for interests that the working class were able to recognise as their own. Where Communists have seen social democracy as betraying the interests of the workers, I am asserting that social democracy was often their authentic representative and voice. But the acceptance of the assumptions of the new technocratic growth-oriented capitalism by the British Labour Party has necessarily severed this link. For, in the perspective of that capitalism, no allowance can be made for the special interests of the working class. It follows that the electoral prospects of the Labour Party must be in graver doubt than they already appear to be. For, if I am right, what we are experiencing in the present run of by-elections is, in some part, not just another swing of the pendulum, a temporary dissatisfaction, but a permanent shift of the working class, perhaps not merely away from the Labour Party but even from the electoral system.

Yet, radical as this is, it still remains at the political level: it scarcely merits the title 'The Strange Death of Social-Democratic England', with its strong suggestion of the death of an entire social order. To justify that title, I shall have to ask what it was about the social-democratic period in our history which marked its entire social order. And the answer goes far beyond any merely political argument and concerns large changes in the values of society. During the social-democratic period, a new set of answers was given to the questions of what rights individuals have, of how they may legitimately claim their rights, and of what responsibilities the community has for the fate of individuals.

The particular institutions of the welfare state, from Lloyd George's social insurance scheme to Aneurin Bevan's National Health Service, were the embodiment of a whole new social climate. For the first time, the poor, the unemployed, the ill and the old were recognised as having equality of citizenship at an economic as well as at a political level. The consensus as to these new values was always very far from complete and it was the outcome of continuous struggle by radicals and socialists inside and outside the trade unions. But it was a consensus in striking contrast to the values of Victorian society, being a repudiation both of private paternalism and of the extension of the values of the market into social life. Social democrats may, and often do, overrate the achievements of social democracy, but the rest of us ought not to underrate them. One way not to do this is to realise how the values of social democracy contrast not only with the values of the society that preceded it, but also with the values which have become established now.

I remarked at the outset that what is surprising is not merely the fact that the government has been actively promoting the growth of unemployment, but also and above all that fact of the astonishing lack of response to its policies. This is important, for it is in the degree of response to political facts of this sort that we find one important clue to the values of a society; and silence may be the most significant response of all. What else are we silent and unresponsive about? Well-grounded predictions which have in fact been made that the collapse of the National Health Service is imminent would, one might have expected, have brought questions about the nature of that service to the centre of national discussions of social questions. They have not. We no longer treat welfare questions as important questions compared with questions about productivity. 'Production for what?' – the old social-democratic inquiry, voiced for example by R.H. Tawney – is not heard.

A social order in which the values of welfare have been removed from those which the established consensus maintains, and in which the working class have been disenfranchised from the political system, is one in which an increase in conflict has become inevitable. That increase is made all the more likely by two other facts. The first is a matter of the way in which political agreement over central goals among those within the established parliamentary system may leave those who cannot articulate their dissent, even on marginal issues, with no alternative but to break with that system; and this may be as true of those who are not radicals as it is of the radical.

The strange death of Liberal England was the outcome of a system that could neither accommodate nor come to terms with the trade unions, the Irish or the suffragettes, conservative as many of the leaders of these in fact were. The strange death of social democracy has been accompanied by an unwillingness even to admit the existence of demands for local and regional self-government and of the degree of support which has emerged for Welsh and Scots nationalism. Moreover, the equivalent to the old hysteria about trade unionism is the new hysteria about unofficial strikes. The Prime Minister and Mr Ray Gunter have been all too willing to see strikes as led by, indeed devised by, Communists or Trotskyists or whatever. In fact, of course, what they see and what they fear in unofficial strikes is the resurgence of an independent working-class leadership. The most dangerous single threat to freedom in our society is the will to prevent unofficial strikes – that is, to prevent any direct expression of their interests by working-class people which goes beyond the limits set by established institutions.

A second factor which will exacerbate conflict is this. All government depends on the tacit consent of the governed. But it is characteristic of our present-day society, in Britain at least, that government has continuously to appeal in a self-conscious and visible way to the governed, inviting them to collaborate in the operation of those very same social structures in which they are excluded from power. And, in the course of doing this, government continuously promises what it cannot in fact perform. Government legitimates itself not merely through parliamentary elections, but through continuous assurance by every political party, in power and out of power, of rights to employment, to education, to material prosperity, and so on. This deeply embedded appeal to and promise of rights has to coexist, not just with the present facts of inequality which I have described, but with a future in which inequalities of income and status must be maintained, if the economy is to flourish at least in terms that would be recognised by this Labour government, or any feasible alternative in the parliamentary system. What people are promised as their rights will therefore not be performed. And working-class people will gradually learn that they are still to be excluded, and that in streamed comprehensive schools and expanded universities, it will still be the case that all the advantages lie with the children of middle-class parents. If they learn also that no conventional political remedy can help them, then they will have the choice between a kind of non-political subservience that has been alien to them even at their most apathetic and a new politics of conflict. For my part, I hope that they learn both lessons fast, and if it is said that I have been presenting something akin not so much to a personal view as to a partisan political broadcast, let me point out that I am talking for and of a group that has no party, the British working class.

Chapter Forty

In Place of Harold Wilson?[1]

A Review of Paul Foot, The Politics of Harold Wilson, *and Tyrrell Burgess et al.,* Matters of Principle: Labour's Last Chance

Nobody will be able to accuse Paul Foot of having understated the case against the Prime Minister. For well over 300 pages, he relentlessly documents that tortuous career. It is often on quite small matters that Paul Foot is most effective: when he quotes the Prime Minister as deprecating appeals to the Dunkirk spirit in 1961 and then appealing to it in 1964, he brings out the way in which the man will trim his utterances to his circumstances.[2] This kind of behaviour has been essential to Wilson's career, for at the core of that career has been an attempt to achieve the policies of the right while posing as the leader of the Left. In policy Wilson has always been a Gaitskellite, even if a Gaitskellite with a difference. On matters such as race relations, Gaitskell himself at least was quite prepared to put liberal – not socialist – principle before political calculation; how wicked by contrast has been the genteel racism of the Wilson government. But, like Gaitskell, Wilson is a technocratic believer in a mixed economy; and, like all such believers, he has become bemused by the

---

1 Originally published in *The Listener*, 10 October 1968, p. 476.

2 Foot 1968, pp. 155, 159–60.

fetishism of the Gross National Product. Growth is all; and even the deliberate creation of unemployment is a legitimate means of fostering growth.

Yet precisely what is Paul Foot indicting? Certainly not only Harold Wilson as a person, but the substance and style of pragmatist and opportunist politics. Yet, in his chapters on Harold Wilson and the Labour Left and on the futility of Wilsonian pragmatism, Foot's argument becomes unfortunately cloudy. He situates Wilsonian politics in the wider context of Labour parliamentarism and of the bureaucratic neocapitalism of the 1950s and 1960s without ever making it clear what he thinks the basic causal connections are. But this question of the causal relationships between the larger social and economic system and the political system and the particular acts of the Prime Minister is crucial. If we criticise Wilson in the way that Foot does, it implies that the Prime Minister, or at least someone else, could have done better; but, if Wilsonian politics is the inevitable outcome of the social environment, and only a revolutionary transformation of that environment could win us a new and better politics, then the criticism of particular Labour failures is almost beside the point. If, on the other hand, we believe that even with the existing context, the Prime Minister and his colleagues could have done very much better, then Paul Foot's root-and-branch diagnosis becomes irrelevant to the explanation of why they failed.

The political importance of this point is underlined by the essays in *Matters of Principle: Labour's Last Chance*. Tyrrell Burgess on education, John Rex on race relations and Michael Lipton on the confusions in the government's whole perspective have written three outstanding essays all of which suggest ways in which the present government could have acted creatively, and failed so to act.[3] If they are right, there are policies which it would still make sense to press upon the Labour government; if Paul Foot is right, not merely this government, but the whole political system, is beyond redemption. Paul Foot's book thus invites the type of rejoinder which it has received from Michael Foot and Raymond Fletcher: you are, they say in effect, crying for the moon, you are failing to recognise that politics is the art of the possible. To them, one must reply that the definition of politics as the art of the possible is a conservative definition: socialist politics is concerned with altering the limits of the possible. But even so, we can only do this by starting with what

[3] Burgess 1968; Rex 1969.

is. Paul Foot's faith in rank-and-file militancy is never spelt out in terms of the specific goals which militancy should urge upon government, and so his argument appears needlessly utopian.

Had he spelt out these goals, he would inevitably have had to involve himself in the reformist aims which he castigates in the Labour Left. In race relations in particular, the urgency of the struggle to free immigrants from discrimination means that immediate concrete issues of housing, education and employment have to be faced; and they cannot be pursued without pursuing government intervention. Time is short, particularly because of the increasing corruption of the Conservative Party on this issue. The unfortunately unrecognised political function of Mr Enoch Powell on the issue is to make Mr Heath appear reasonable and humane by comparison. But Mr Heath is merely more subtly odious than Mr Powell. His latest proposals amount to a new form of discrimination: black men have to be of good character to be Britons (we did not ask for evidence of good character when Indians, Pakistanis and West Indians fought to save us from National Socialism), while white men can still be old-fashioned British scoundrels.

Paul Foot and John Rex both set out clearly the ways in which the Prime Minister and his government have steadily retreated into Conservative positions on race.[4] It would be a great pity if Paul Foot's arguments had the unintended effect of presenting Wilsonism as an unalterable part of the political scene, or at least as one that can only be removed by altering the entire social order. One of the true lessons to be learnt from his narrative is the law of diminishing socialist returns, a little-known law which states that in the normal conditions of capitalist society everyone's actions tend to be to the right of their principles. From liberals one gets mildly conservative actions, from right social democrats liberal actions, from left social democrats right-wing social-democrat actions, and so on. From this law it follows that only those with a revolutionary perspective are likely to promote genuine left-wing reforms. If revolutionary critics of society neglect their responsibility here, no one else is likely to assume it.

---

[4] Foot 1968; Rex 1969.

Chapter Forty-One

Marxism of the Will[1]

A Review of Che Guevara, Venceremos! The Speeches and Writings of Che Guevara; *Che Guevara,* Reminiscences of the Cuban Revolutionary War; *Che Guevara,* The Complete Bolivian Diaries of Che Guevara and Other Captured Documents; *Ricardo Rojo,* My Friend Che; Régis Debray, Revolution in the Revolution?; *and Jean-Paul Sartre,* The Communists and Peace

Of these books, the two most important are Gerassi's collection of Che Guevara's writings and Rojo's brilliant biography. Guevara's own reminiscences of the Cuban revolutionary war are interesting, but the reader needs to be well informed already to make much use of them. Debray's theorising is perhaps only interesting for the contrast between the Debray version of Che and Che as he was, and the Sartre is worth noticing in this context because it helps us to judge how much of Debray is Paris academicism. Finally, I notice the American version of Che's diaries merely to note that it differs in important ways from the Cuban version. The publishers on their dust jacket say their edition 'was authenticated not by Cubans or Bolivians but by Americans'; here's news

---

[1] Originally published in *Partisan Review*, Volume 36, Number 1, Winter 1969, pp. 128–33. Reprinted in A. MacIntyre, *Against the Self-Images of the Age: Essays on Ideology and Philosophy*, Duckworth, London 1971, pp. 70–5.

for you, Stein and Day – I still do not trust it. James accuses Che of 'person pique'; his publishers join with him in entertaining the suggestion that Castr was jealous of Che, deliberately denied the help he could have given, and s betrayed him.[2] This obscene suggestion does not come well from American who ought at least to realise that the death of Guevara may well cost them a much as his life did.

The death of Che had – and it is difficult to use the word after it has been s cheaply misused – tragic quality. To use a dramatic metaphor is not to sugge anything histrionic about Che's actions or passions; it is to indicate that thos actions and passions are an appropriate subject for poetry as well as fc history, because, as Aristotle said, poetry is 'more universal' than history. Ch was not just an individual, but a representative figure, who lived out a tragi action. A tragic action is one in which a hero encounters a catastrophe as result of a flaw in his character. By character I do not mean a mere assemblag of psychological traits, I mean rather the incarnation of a role. (What poetr was for Aristotle, sociology is for us.) What was Che's flaw?

To ask this question, I have suggested, is to ask about a role and not abou an assemblage of personal traits. That personal traits can explain little i political or social action is made clear once again in reading reminiscence of Che by those who knew him well. He was an asthmatic who develope a will strong enough to take him onto the athletic field and through medic school. He was an ascetic who did not undervalue sex or alcohol. He was a altruist, but without any signs of that self-contempt which so often underpin altruism. I shall suggest later that these traits were not entirely unimportar in relation to some key positions that Che took up; but there are no splendi psychological generalisations to be constructed which will demonstrate tha asthmatic, ascetic altruism is the seedbed of revolution. As so often, what i impressive is not the connection, but the relative lack of connection betwee individual personality and social role. The need to reminisce about Che has i any case obviously little to do with any task of explanation; it is much mor as though his friends still have to reassure themselves that it all really di happen, that this living out of one of our political dreams was not in fact onl a dream.

2 James 1969, pp. 13–14.

The search for such reassurance is perhaps connected with the extent to which the Cuban Revolution was an accidental happening. By this I mean much more than that it did not follow out the patterns of previous revolutions. Régis Debray is able to emphasise that and yet to insist that the Cuban Revolution embodied an experience from which more generally applicable laws and maxims can be extracted. In this, he follows Che faithfully and yet there is an important difference in tone between what Huberman and Sweezy call Debray's 'comprehensive and authoritative presentation of the revolutionary thought of Fidel Castro and Che Guevara' and what we actually encounter in Che's writings.[3] This difference arises from the stale, academic atmosphere of Debray's arguments. For however authentically Debray may reproduce what is new and Cuban, he does so in a setting and a style which is old and French. So that, while in Guevara's own narratives the Marxism-Leninism somehow coexists with a sense of the Cuban Revolution as a chain of improvisations and coincidences, in Debray's writing revolutionary action becomes nothing but matter for theoretical formulae counterposed to other theoretical formulae. Accident has disappeared and with it truth.

We find in Debray a constant reiteration of Sartrean themes. There are the same strange attempts to unite historical necessity and absolute freedom, to dissent from Stalinism and yet to count Stalin among the revolutionary ancestors, and to portray Trotskyism as the villain of the piece; indeed, Debray explicitly refers back to Sartre's fifteen-year-old anti-Trotskyist polemic in *The Communists and Peace*.[4] One can well understand why Trotsky's ghost haunts Sartre and Debray. For both Sartre and Debray have a peculiar conception – far more élitist than that of Leninism – of an inert mass of be it workers, be it peasants, who need a leadership of particular gifts to rouse them to revolutionary activity. Sartre in 1952 and 1954 was equally contemptuous of those sociologists who declared that the French working classes were not revolutionary and those Trotskyists who declared that they were revolutionary – but that their revolutionary tendencies were suppressed or inhibited by their reaction to the Stalinist leadership of the Communist Party of France.[5] In Sartre's view, the working masses are not, but will become,

---

[3] Huberman and Sweezy 'Foreword', in Debray 1968, p. 9.

[4] Debray 1968, p. 39, footnote: 'For a good description of the Trotskyist position, See Sartre: *Les communistes et la paix*.'

[5] Sartre 1969, pp. 91–119, 120–4.

a revolutionary class precisely because the Communist Party presents ther with goals which transcend their immediate needs; so, for Debray, the guerril army is to present the peasants with goals which transcend their immedia needs. It is a doctrine which enables Sartre and Debray to set on one sid in the most arbitrary way the question of what workers or peasants do i fact want now. It also enables Sartre to disregard the theoretical positions o Stalinist bureaucrats; his understanding of the falsity of Stalinism seems i his writings of the early 1950s only marginal to his evaluation of Stalinism political function. So Debray too exalts questions of organisation ove questions of political goals and programmes and sneers at the Trotskyists fo their emphasis upon fundamental theory.

In his intellectual style, then, Debray is unlike Che; but Che himself could no avoid facing dilemmas which in other contexts were responsible for creatin Trotskyism, and he could not avoid making choices which were incompatib with Trotskyism. This is because Trotsky himself had had to face at successiv points in his career all the dilemmas of those who wish to make a Marxis revolution in an underdeveloped country and because, too, the failure o Trotskyism to provide a recipe for successful revolutionary practice in th face of those dilemmas is an inescapable fact.

What is the part of the peasantry in the making of a socialist revolution? Mar could see no part for them, Mao invented one *ex nihilo* and called it Marxis and every position intermediate between Marx's and Mao's has been take up by some Marxist theorist at some time. Trotskyism, at the very leas represents the thesis of the ineliminable necessity of the participation of a industrial working class in revolution-making.

Can there be socialism in one country? One paradox of post-Stalin Stalinism i that it may be those who are most repelled by the surviving Stalinist feature of the Soviet Union who therefore try to build a socialist revolution in isolatio from the Soviet camp or at least in the minimum of contact with it. But, i so doing, they revive the very thesis of 'socialism in one country' on whic Stalinism was founded and in this way reject Trotskyism.

What is the place of the revolutionary party? The orthodox Communist Partie in Latin America are obviously not revolutionary parties; their weakness an their reformism are notorious. But in the struggle waged by peasant guerrilla there is little room for a party at all. Hence Trotskyism once more appears a the ghost of orthodox Bolshevism, repudiating militantly the only militant strategies apparently open in Latin America.

Guevara's position is thus easily defined by contrast with that of Trotskyism, and in this, at least, Debray is perceptive. But if Guevara offered us a revolution made by peasants, a revolution which creates socialism in one country, and a revolution with a revolutionary army rather than a revolutionary party, he aspired to do so as a Marxist-Leninist, and here is the crux. For, if Bolshevism can only appear in the modern world in ghostly form, Trotskyism is indeed its authentic ghost. How then can an anti-Trotskyist position be grafted on to Marxism-Leninism? To answer this question will return us to my initial inquiry as to the tragic flaw in the role acted out by Che. For what Che uses to close the gap between what the Marxist-Leninist must hold on an objective analysis to be a situation in which the socialist revolution cannot yet be made and the revolutionary aspirations of the selfsame Marxist-Leninist who confronts himself with this, as it must seem, defeatist analysis, is an appeal to pure will. Lenin too was confronted with this gap and at every stage wrestled to link the present and the future by means of a consciousness nurtured by the organisational forms of the party. In Guevara, although questions of organisation are treated with intellectual respect, it is the voluntarist component of Leninism which is appealed to as never before.

Consider, for example, the question of planning. Guevara conducted a polemic against the French Communist expert on *planification*, Charles Bettelheim, in which he argued that, because of the level that consciousness (in the Marxist sense) had reached in the world at large, the social and political consciousness of Marxists in a country where the objective conditions for a socialist revolution had not yet been reached could nonetheless enable them to transcend those limitations and to do what seemed objectively impossible. From this premise, Che argued further in more general terms for a relative independence of cultural superstructure from the economic base. This led him to quarrel with Bettelheim and other Marxists on economic policy. Material incentives, such as may be provided by a wages structure may be appropriate as the mainspring of a market economy, but are inappropriate to socialism.[6] Centralised planning demands the centralisation of major economic decision-making, but it does not require centralised management.

---

6 See Guevara 1969b.

What is to take the place of material incentives and of the dictates centralised management? A new motivation springing from the new natu of socialist man. Moral incentives must be the mainspring; material incentiv must be subordinate. The word 'moral' recurs throughout Che's writing He was the minister who awarded the title 'Hero of Labour' to worke who excelled. In his speeches to workers, he constantly urged sacrifice ar hard work. His personal asceticism put his right to make such calls beyor question. But their theoretical justification is quite another matter.

Behind the Leninist voluntarism we see in Che the revival of an older answ to the Marxist dilemma about morality. Marx himself never raises explicit the question of the motives of those who seek to achieve socialism. At th turn of the century, Bernstein raised the question of the moral foundations socialism and turned back to Kant's invocation of duty in order to answer i Kautsky replied to him with a crude invocation of utilitarianism which relie on an underlying appeal to material self-interest; and Rosa Luxemburg in h polemics against Bernstein avoided coming to grips with this question at al Bernstein's Kantian answer was in fact more influential than we sometim realise; and to be Kantian was not necessarily to be a right-wing soci democrat. After 1914, Kautsky the orthodox Marxist was far to the right Karl Liebknecht, the Kantian and Spartacist. Guevara was Karl Liebknecht spiritual heir; like Liebknecht, he in the end bore witness to the fact that mor heroism is not enough. In the improbable environment of Cuba, Kantia moral theory was reborn as revolutionary.

Che's moral heroism, his attempt to transcend the material environmen was the tragic flaw which finally destroyed him in Bolivia. When he left Cub he wrote to his children:

> Above all, always be able to feel deeply any injustice committed against anyone in any part of the world. It's a revolutionary's most beautiful quality.[9]

---

[7] Bernstein 1993, pp. 209–10.

[8] Kautsky 1983, pp. 43–5. Kautsky's most sustained discussion of neo-Kantia positions within the SPD was in fact written in response to Otto Bauer, rather tha Bernstein. See Kautsky 1983, pp. 46–52.

[9] Rojo 1968, p. 182.

And to his parents: 'Essentially, nothing has changed, except that I am much more conscientious, my Marxism has struck deep roots and is purified.'[10] Again, the Kantian note is struck. Conscientiousness took him to his death, because it led him to ignore political and military facts, and especially Barrientos's ability to mobilise peasant support.

When I stress Che's moralism, I do not want to underestimate his intellectual qualities. Americans in particular should read the speech rejecting the Alliance for Progress made at the Punta del Este Conference of the OAS in 1961; about that particular Kennedy cloud-cuckoo project Guevara has proved alarmingly right.[11] But when Guevara is not being critical of imperialism, he is all too apt to substitute invocations of honour or of the spirit of sacrifice for intellectual analysis. Guevara's student admirers are indeed moved precisely by this and so is John Gerassi who has done scholarship a service by his collection of Guevara's speeches and writings. Yet what they admire is just that abstract moralism which Marx himself ought to have taught us to suspect. Che's last letter to his parents begins with an allusion to Cervantes: 'Once more I feel Rocinante's ribs under my heels; I'm taking to the road again with my shield on my arm.'[12] Perhaps as he wrote this he should have remembered that other reminiscence of Cervantes in a footnote in *Capital* which ends by Marx remarking that: 'Don Quixote long ago paid the penalty for wrongly imagining that knight errantry was compatible with all economic forms of society.'[13]

---

[10] Rojo 1968, p. 181. See also Guevara 1969c, p. 568.
[11] See Guevara 1969a.
[12] Rojo 1968, p. 181; Guevara 1969c, p. 568.
[13] Marx 1976, p. 176, note 35.

Chapter Forty-Two
Mr Wilson's Pragmatism[1]

A Review of Harold Wilson, The Labour Government, 1966–70

Suppose that, late in the year 1969, someone was still able to believe about 'the alleged atrocities at My Lai' that it was open to argument 'whether it was an incident – an aberration, an obscene incident – or whether it was endemic in this kind of war'.[2] What kind of person could this be? It would have to be someone who had read none of the countless reports of the air war, of the numerous strafings of unidentified South-Vietnamese peasants, none of the anguished accounts brought back by disillusioned veterans of casual killings on the ground, someone simply ignorant of the effects of modern fire-power often used not even on the enemy but on ostensible allies. That is to say, it would presumably be someone who had no access to the best American or European newspapers, let alone to the writings of I.F. Stone. We can now picture him, perhaps an untravelled inhabitant of a small Kansas town, sheltered from reality by a local Republican newspaper, authentically upset at last by the news of My Lai. But, alas, this was not who it was who went on record in the words

[1] Originally published in *The Listener*, 29 July 1971, pp. 150–1. Reprinted in K. Miller (ed.), *A Second Listener Anthology*, BBC, London 1973.
[2] Wilson 1971, p. 730.

quoted above. It was in fact the Right Honourable J.H. Wilson, then Prir Minister of Great Britain.

How had *he* come to be sheltered from reality so successfully? A great part the importance of Mr Wilson's memoirs lies in the extent to which they enal us to answer this question. We get one clue in his discussion of the proble of the Kenya Asians. Mr Wilson represents the moral dimensions of th problem as being simply a matter of balancing a humanitarian regard for t Kenya Asians against the political costs of a breach in his own governmen immigration policy.[3] It does not seem to occur to him either more particula that this was a question of Britain dishonourably reneging on her pledg word, or more generally that the importance of the strong and the power keeping their promises to the weak and powerless was what was at stak That Mr Wilson should fail even to recognise the character of the moral iss is less surprising, however, when we come to consider his account of t moral issues involved in the Vietnamese and the Biafran conflicts:

> Peace, freedom and self-determination are all ends in themselves. But they are ends that conflict with one another; where judgment is necessary, but where there can be no certainty of finality of judgment.[4]

So, considerations are weighed in some arbitrary utilitarian scale: how ma millions of Biafrans have to die before the need to preserve Nigerian uni (unargued by Mr Wilson except for a reference to the dangers of tribalis in Africa, a danger which he never shows would have been increased an independent Biafra), and the fact that the Russians would have sold t Nigerians the arms if we had not done so, are outweighed? This appea to be Mr Wilson's view of how moral problems are to be posed. Now, t most obvious aspect of this view of morals is that it proposes to weigh mo incommensurables in the balance and hence every outcome is arbitrary; a this leaves the agent subject to any and every pressure of power and intere This particular moral outlook is therefore peculiarly well-designed to decei oneself and others about the way in which such pressures operate.

Are we then to discern behind Wilson the moralist, whose pompous se adulatory manner in these memoirs is reminiscent of Gladstone, although on

[3] Wilson 1971, pp. 504–5.
[4] Wilson 1971, p. 729.

at his worst, Wilson the Machiavellian, the smooth manipulator of power and interest? Tempting as this suggestion is, it must immediately be discarded. The self-revealed Wilson of the memoirs is as uncomprehending about power and interest as he is about morality. (And this ought not to surprise us, for a true understanding of the place of power and interest in human life is inseparable from a true understanding of the place of morality.) Consider, for example, the Wilsonian account of the Labour Government's first brawl with Lord Cromer.

During the sterling crisis of November 1964, Lord Cromer, the Governor of the Bank of England, demanded 'all-round cuts in expenditure, regardless of social or even economic priorities' and was asked by Mr Wilson

> ...if this meant that it was impossible for any Government to continue, unless it immediately reverted to full-scale Tory policies. He had to admit that that was what his argument meant.[5]

Mr Wilson then threatened to go to the country on the issue of parliamentary democracy versus the power of the international bankers and financiers, or at the very least to let the pound sterling float. Faced with the threat of a devalued pound, Lord Cromer raised a loan of $3,000 million from the same bankers. Now Mr Wilson records this as a victory: but it was, of course, the moment at which the Labour government was essentially defeated. For, first of all, we were now in pawn in an unprecedented way to the international bankers, who are transformed in two pages of his narrative from the enemies of socialism and democracy to their saviours, a transformation scene equalled in few pantomimes.

Moreover, the willingness of the Labour government to collaborate in saving sterling had been made clear. Hence followed many evil consequences including the later devaluation and the crude deflationary policies which resulted in such high unemployment. What would the Labour government have challenged if it had challenged the sacred cow of sterling? It would have challenged the power of the City. But such established powers were seen by Mr Wilson's government as part of the given political and economic environment with which they had to come to terms, and not as powers that might be challenged. The true reason why Conservative policies were pursued

5 Wilson 1971, p. 37.

is that the Labour government's vision of the limits of political possibility w a Conservative vision. The key concept which determined what was perceiv was that of 'the national interest': the national interest, thus understood, served by collaboration between a Labour government and the City and is endangered by strikes. Hence the Labour government's continuous atta on the only weapon available to the working class in its struggle with risi prices and unemployment – the strike.

Mr Wilson's attempt to rewrite the record on the Industrial Relatio Bill is so blatant that it underlines this point very well. He claims that t sentences from his speech to the Parliamentary Labour Party on 17 April 19 in which he asserted that the passing of the Bill was essential for the Labo government's economic policy and its continuance in office, only give t impression that they mean what they seem to mean when they are quoted o of context as part of a legend 'unscrupulously fostered by Opposition leade and Opposition press' and helped on by at least one television interviewe In fact, a reading of Mr Wilson's actual words makes it plain that what is taking on is not the Conservative Party or Mr Robert Kee, but the Engli language. The only unscrupulously fostered legend is Mr Wilson's ow designed to conceal the fact that the Labour government attacked the trad union movement and was defeated by it, in the process rendering the tra unions much more vulnerable to subsequent Conservative legislation.

What this brings out is that a perspective dominated by the concept of 't national interest' is one in which the continuing facts of the class strugg almost disappear from view. That the working class achieved such rights a such power as they have only through struggle is not a fact which Briti social history has now left behind. But, in the Wilsonian perspective, th fact is concealed from view by the narrowness of the vision. Hence, in t memoirs, so many features of the social landscape never come into sight all, and so many others appear in truncated form. There is no serious attem to identify the malaise of British industry; no discussion of the peculiar ki of importance that welfare had in the Sixties or how welfare priorities oug to have been identified; no recognition of the way in which in the Sixties t political self-identification of the working class began to change, and t struggle for wages became successful in a quite new way. Since these omissio

[6] Wilson 1971, p. 643.

also disfigured the work of the Labour government, it can perhaps be claimed that Mr Wilson's memoirs are at least a truthful rendering of what happened. But, in not considering these topics now as part of the essential background to what happened, we can see a deep incapacity to learn anything fundamental from the Labour government's experiences and this incapacity springs from that same ideology that deformed the government's actions.

I have suggested that the interest of these memoirs lies in the exceptional clarity with which they reveal the contours of that ideology so misleadingly called 'pragmatism' by its adherents. Two other features characteristic of ideology reinforce this point.

The first is the way in which form and style match content. The chronicle running from day to day allows for a highly disjointed and breathless narrative in which the real interconnections between different actions and policies easily disappear from view. The turgid and vapid style, in which an occasional inept use of literary allusion ('February 1967 was the re-enactment, in our time, of the Sibylline books'[7]) combines with that classical trap for the writer of memoirs, a passion for the word 'I', and a philistine disregard for the whole English tradition of political prose, is so boring that it tends to disable any reflection on the memoirs as a whole: and this too has a political function.

A second ideological feature of Mr Wilson's memoirs is his inability to recognise or to portray his various opponents and critics as anything but straw men. The Conservative Party in his memoirs appears as an entirely abstract object of abuse: it seems to represent nothing, to have no social or economic roots, and to be motivated, except on rare occasions, by little more than a mixture of incompetence and malice. Rank-and-file militants in the labour movement appear only as irresponsible trouble-makers. Politics is thus abstracted entirely from the social forces which underlie it. Mr. Wilson once boasted that he had tried to read Marx, but had not succeeded in getting beyond the opening pages of *Capital*. I would recommend him to try *The 18th Brumaire of Louis Bonaparte* instead: for not only does Marx lay bare in that work the type of key relationship between politics and social forces which Mr Wilson ignores, but he also explains why it is the petty-bourgeois politician who may well prove unable to understand the point that he is making.[8]

---

[7] Wilson 1971, p. 366.
[8] Marx 1973a.

Chapter Forty-Three

Tell Me Where You Stand on Kronstadt[1]

A Review of Paul Avrich, Kronstadt 1921

Twenty miles to the west of Leningrad, there is an island in the Gulf of Finland on which stands the naval base and city of Kronstadt. But Kronstadt is not only the name of a place; it is also a symbol of that moment when, in February and March 1921, the Bolshevik régime faced for the first time the enmity of its own working class in the rebellion of the sailors and other workers of Kronstadt against Lenin's government. They were suppressed by the Red Army. Everybody who takes an attitude toward communism and Marxism has been forced to try to settle accounts with what happened at Kronstadt when the sailors revolted: Russian *émigrés*, Lenin, Trotsky, Stalin, anarchists, later historians of the revolution, each has given his account.

Paul Avrich's excellent and magisterial book is a work of non-partisan scholarship that illustrates how partisan in the best possible way non-partisan scholarship can be. He gives us the closest examination of all the available evidence that we are likely to have for some time and he uses his evidence to construct a narrative that, in its most brilliant passages, matches the power of Deutscher's

---

[1] Originally published in *New York Review of Books*, 12 August 1971, pp. 24–5.

The Prophet Armed and Moshe Lewin's *Lenin's Last Struggle*.[2] But, by so doin he strengthens rather than weakens the case for the maxim: Tell me wher you stand on Kronstadt and I will tell you who and what you are.

There are three main positions that have been taken on the Kronstadt risin of 1921 and they are all untenable. The first was that of the *émigré* group associated with the National Centre in Paris, a group founded by forme leaders of the Kadet party. Avrich prints for the first time (in English) memorandum of the National Centre written in expectation of a rising a Kronstadt, and containing plans for it, only a few weeks before the actu rising took place.[3] But, in fact all those who aspired to aid the Kronstadt rebel in order to bring about the overthrow of the October revolution failed even t make contact with the rebels. There is no evidence to show that the Kronstac rising was not entirely independent of outside assistance.

Moreover the Kronstadt rebels would not have been likely to make commo cause with the emissaries of the Kadets. Their revolutionary tradition place them far closer to the Bolsheviks. In 1905, the sailors of Kronstadt had revolte and rioted. In 1906, they mutinied again. In May, 1917, the Kronstadt Sovie declared itself the sole power in Kronstadt. In October, 1917, it was sailor from Kronstadt that stormed the Winter Palace and, three years later, wer among the crowds who cheered the re-enactment of that storming on the thir anniversary of the Revolution, only six months before they rebelled agains the Soviet government. Why did they rebel?

Avrich places the Kronstadt rising where it belongs, in the crisis of sc called 'war communism'. At the very moment when the sailors rose, Leni was carrying out at the Tenth Communist Party Congress policies designe to moderate the rigours of earlier ones which had called for confiscation c the peasants' produce on the one hand and regimentation of industrial labou on the other. These policies, combined with the shortages and the destructio caused by war and civil war, had finally brought many workers and peasant to the point of despair.

For both peasants and workers, there was a bitter contrast between th initial stages of the Revolution, in which the old owners and managers ha

[2] Deutscher 2003a; Lewin 1975.

[3] 'Memorandum on the Question of Organising an Uprising in Kronstadt reproduced in Avrich 1971, pp. 235–40. The activities of the National Centre ar discussed on pp. 102–23.

been removed from the factories and the land was distributed among the peasants, and the following stages, in which one-man management was finally re-established in the factories, and state farms were organised in the countryside; the peasants regarded the new state farms with suspicion and hated the continuous requisitioning. The grass-roots political reaction to this change was not, as is sometimes said, a demand for the 'Soviets without the Communist Party', but the belief that the Communists should and must share their power with other groups within the Soviets.

Within the Communist Party itself, the same tensions were expressed in the program of the faction of Shliapnikov and Kollontai, called the Workers' Opposition. The Workers' Opposition wished to hand over the conduct of the economy to the Soviets, the trade unions, and a national congress of producers. In his speech at the Tenth Congress, Shliapnikov cited Engels's thesis that a communist society would organise industry on the basis of a free and equal association of all producers.[4]

But, although most delegates to the Tenth Congress rejected Trotsky's call for even stricter control of the labour force in favour of Lenin's mixed policy, which included the relaxation of economic life in the NEP, they would have endorsed Trotsky's characterisation of the Workers' Opposition:

> The Workers' Opposition has come out with dangerous slogans. They have made a fetish of democratic principles. They have placed the workers' right to elect representatives above the party, as it were, as if the party were not entitled to assert its dictatorship even if that dictatorship temporarily clashed with the passing moods of the workers' democracy.[5]

The sailors of Kronstadt were right therefore in supposing that the cry 'All Power to the Soviets', which the Bolsheviks themselves had formerly used, was now an anti-Bolshevik cry.

The rebels saw the Bolsheviks as asserting the dictatorship of the party over the proletariat, and, in fact, the Bolsheviks themselves agreed that they were doing just this. Of the Workers' Opposition proposal for a national congress of producers, Zinoviev complained that 'the majority of them at this grave moment will be non-party people, a good many of them SRs [Social

4 Shliapnikov 1921, pp. 789–93.
5 Quoted in Deutscher 2003a, p. 424 and in Kollontai n.d., p. 33, Solidarity note.

Revolutionaries] and Mensheviks'. But the National Centre in Paris cou scarcely have relished the cry 'All Power to the Soviets'. Had the so-calle moderates who ran it come to power, they would have had to crush the pow of the sailors of Kronstadt and they would have crushed that power as fierce as the Bolsheviks did.

Even the Left SRs, who claimed to support the October Revolution and 1921 tried to organise support for the rising, ought to have remembered th in the July days in 1917, it was sailors from Kronstadt that would have lynche the Left SR leader Victor Chernov had Trotsky not intervened, and that sailo from Kronstadt at Lenin's bidding dispersed the Constituent Assembly which the SRs had a majority.

So, in one central aspect, the Kronstadters represent October 1917, again March 1921, the October Revolution against the Tenth Congress, and identify them with their self-appointed *émigré* friends is absurd. Just suc an identification, of course, constituted the official Soviet government vie of the rising. When Lenin reported on the Kronstadt affair, he treated th activities of the Kadets, of the SRs, and of the Kronstadt sailors as parts a single tendency of antagonism to Bolshevism. He never actually said th White Guards and generals participated in the rising itself, but an incautiou reader would certainly have supposed him to be asserting this. Later Trotsk was to make the same assertion but dropped it.[6]

What the Bolshevik case amounted to at its most cogent was twofold. Firs the Kronstadt sailors of 1921 were not the sailors of 1917; the social compositic of the fleet had changed. The sailors of 1921 were unwilling, so the Bolshevik asserted, to endure the hardships of the revolutionary régime. Secondly, successful rising at Kronstadt and its extension to the mainland would once have led to further White intervention. The latter claim is obvious convincing: it was clearly urgent that revolt had to be put down.

---

[6] Avrich 1971, p. 96. See Lenin 1960–70k, pp. 183–6. Trotsky in fact made his clain about the supposed White Guard inspiration for the rising at the time. In an intervie with foreign reporters conducted on 16 March, he laid the blame for the rising the external plotting of Russian counter-revolutionaries and agents of imperialis See 'Comments to the Foreign Press', in Lenin and Trotsky 1979, pp. 68–70. By 193 8, when the subject was again raised, Trotsky had modified his position to one claiming that counter-revolutionaries had simply been involved. See Trotsky 197 p. 748 and 1976, p. 141. In his posthumously published biography of Stalin, Trotsk makes no reference to White Guards or counter-revolutionaries, but only to anarchis and Social Revolutionaries 'sponsoring' the rebellion. See Trotsky 1947, p. 337.

But the true character of the revolt the Bolsheviks were unwilling or unable to admit. The Revolutionary Committee that led the uprising was composed of a clerk, a telephone operator, two machinists, two electricians, a medical assistant, an ordinary seaman, two factory workers, a watchman, the principal of the Third Workers' School, a sawmill worker, the head of transport in the fortress construction department, and a navigator: a large majority of proletarians.[7] After two thousand rebels were captured by the Soviet government, thirteen alleged ringleaders were singled out and tried behind closed doors before being executed: five were ex-naval officers of aristocratic origin, seven were peasants, and one had been a priest. None had in fact played any leading part in the revolt, but the emphasis of the Soviet press on their social origins makes it clear that the Soviet government wished to lie from the first about the social composition of the revolt's leadership, and was not merely mistaken.

There had, of course, been some changes in the composition of the fleet since 1917. There were a somewhat higher proportion of former peasants, but most of the sailors had always been former peasants. In fact, there is no good reason for accepting any of the Bolshevik theses about the sailors, as for example the claim that unlike the workers of Petrograd they were not prepared to tolerate hardship. The workers of Petrograd launched a wave of strikes *before* the Kronstadt rising and they, too, had had to be suppressed by force.

The question thus arises: since the Bolsheviks had an excellent military case for putting down the Kronstadt rising at once (not only was outside aid a danger, but in a few weeks the ice would have melted, making an assault on the rebels much more difficult), why did they invent an additional bad case? The excellence of the military case was universally recognised. When news of the rising reached the Tenth Congress, the delegates who volunteered to join the assault included Workers' Opposition delegates, whose own leaders condemned the rising as violently as any others. Victor Serge, the most perceptive of the anarchist supporters of the régime, understood the strength of this case, too.[8]

---

[7] Avrich 1971, p. 92.

[8] Serge 1978, pp. 128–9.

But the Bolsheviks could not remain content with it, for had they done so, they would have had to allow the truth of the separation between their party, on the one hand, and the workers and peasants, on the other, to be demonstrated much more convincingly than even Trotsky's speech allowed. A year later at the Eleventh Congress Shliapnikov was able to retort to a speech of Lenin:

> Vladimir Ilyich said yesterday that the proletariat as a class, in the Marxian sense, did not exist [in Russia]. Permit me to congratulate you on being the vanguard of a nonexistent class.[9]

For the Bolshevik Party to have admitted that it was separate from the proletariat would have been to destroy its own basis. Hence, it fed on myths and sophistries from then on. Marxism had for many years so successfully isolated itself from moral self-questioning that the question that the Bolshevik position ought to have raised about the political value, indeed the indispensability, of truthfulness was not in fact raised until fifteen years later, by Trotsky in *Their Morals and Ours*.[10]

It is tempting at this point in the argument to accept a third view of Kronstadt which may appear to gain its support from what has gone before. This is the anarchist view, held at the time by, for example, Alexander Berkman and presented in Ida Mett's *La Commune de Cronstadt: Crépuscule sanglant des Soviets* in 1949.[11]

In this view the Kronstadt rising represented genuine grass-roots democracy, 'the second Paris Commune', and it was simply wrong to put it down. Right was on the side of the sailors in every way. Now, the virtues of the sailors were clearly great: they carefully refrained from ill-treating the Communists whom they had taken prisoner; they fought assaults on Kronstadt with immense courage; and they fought solely for ideals, in no way for their own sectional interest. A large number of those who were captured were shot at once or later, and others were condemned to the slow death of the labour camp (not a Stalinist invention). They were genuine martyrs. But, in at least two ways, they are an inadequate symbol of non-Bolshevik socialist democracy.

---

[9] Quoted in Deutscher 2003b, p. 398, note 10.
[10] Trotsky 1973, p. 51.
[11] Berkman 1925, pp. 291–7; Mett 1967.

Avrich characterises the attitude of the sailors as anarcho-populist; and there is some evidence of the worst as well as the best of populism in their attitudes. While the Kronstadt Revolutionary Committee disclaimed anti-Semitism, they attacked Trotsky for causing in the Civil War the deaths of thousands of innocent people 'of a nationality different from his own', a clear attempt to appeal to anti-Semitism.[12] A Soviet military cadet in the detachment which captured Vershinin, a member of the Revolutionary Committee, when he came out to parley with them early in the rising, reported that he shouted:

> Enough of your 'hoorahs' and join with us to beat the Jews. It's their cursed domination that we workers and peasants have had to endure.[13]

Moreover, as both Avrich and Ida Mett note, the Kronstadt revolutionaries themselves wished to restrict freedom to workers and peasants.[14] They opposed any generally elected assembly, arguing that the form of such an assembly would always allow it to be controlled by a minority. Their attitude was thus in sharp contrast to Rosa Luxemburg's when she argued in 1918 against *any* restriction of freedom and in favour of such an assembly.[15] The libertarian socialist cannot follow *both* the Kronstadt sailors *and* Luxemburg, any more than he can follow both Lenin and Luxemburg.[16]

Trotsky, in his very last reference to the Kronstadt rising in *Stalin*, speaks of the putting down of the rising as a 'tragic necessity' and his reference to tragedy is to the point.[17] The collision of the Bolsheviks with the workers and peasants whom they ostensibly represented was the first staging of the internal tragedy of socialism. The central question about socialism is whether that tragedy sprang merely from local circumstances – the backwardness of Russia, the destruction of resources in war and civil war – or from deeper and more permanent factors in the life of the working class and of socialist parties and groups. As such parties and groups lurch on between heroic tragedy and unheroic farce, they should remember that Kronstadt poses a permanent question for them, even if it does not answer it.

---

[12] Avrich 1971, pp. 178–9

[13] Avrich 1971, p. 180.

[14] Serge 1978, p. 126; Mett 1967, pp. 37–41.

[15] Luxemburg 1970, pp. 389–90.

[16] For an attempt to argue that Luxemburg and the Kronstadt sailors did in fact share the same attitude to democracy, see Mett 1967, pp. 78–9.

[17] Trotsky 1947, p. 337.

Chapter Fourty-Four

Irish Mythologies[1]

A Review of Eamonn McCann, War and an Irish Town

Eamonn McCann has written a fine, argumentative book, a blend of autobiography and of political analysis, in which he continuously relates his own experience of grassroots politics to Ireland's recent history. The merits of the book are uneven; the sections of autobiographical narrative are first-rate, the political history is good in parts, but only in parts, and the application of what Mr McCann takes to be Marxism leads to a final substitution of fiction for fact.[1] Nonetheless, Mr McCann's book could play an important part in destroying the current English mythology about the North of Ireland.

The current English mythology runs like this. There were, indeed, until 1968 grave abuses in Northern Ireland which somehow English liberalism had just not got around to reforming. Then, a civil-rights movement arose and would have moved toward its goals, but for the fact that it was too influenced by – O, horror! – dangerous extremists. These extremists

[1] Part 4 of the original edition of *War and an Irish Town* (Penguin Books, Harmondsworth 1974), which dealt with the development of the state in the North from the formation of the Unionist Party in 1886, was 'reluctantly' dropped from the second edition of the book (Pluto Press, London 1981), but reinstated in an expanded third edition (Pluto Press, London 1993). References which MacIntyre makes are from these deleted sections of the 1974 edition. The footnotes indicate where these references also occur in the 1981 edition.

aroused a Protestant backlash and so that nice fellow Lord O'Neill of the Maine, who was about to solve all the problems, fell from power. That almost as nice fellow Major Chichester-Clark then came to power, but was too reform-minded to satisfy the Protestant extremists, who finally in August 1969 rioted against the Catholics so that the British Army had to be brought in to protect them. The Provisional IRA then prevented the problems being solved by attacking the British Army and cunningly winning considerable Catholic support. The British Army, of course, behaved with marvellous restraint, just as it did in Cyprus and Aden. So bad did things get that even that perhaps not-so-nice fellow, Brian Faulkner (but then, he was not an Old Etonian) could not solve the problems and the Stormont Parliament had to be suspended. Finally, that nicest of all possible fellows Mr Whitelaw came in and he solved the problem, by putting in power again that nice Mr Faulkner along with that nice Mr Fitt, who turned out only to have been pretending to be each others' mortal enemies before (how *very* Irish!). Unfortunately, so malignant are the Irish that not only have the Provisional IRA wantonly refused to go home (they are after all – O horror! – fanatics); but the entire Protestant community in the North refuses to believe what the British House of Commons has told them again and again, that the constitutional problems have now been solved (with the aid of that awfully nice fellow, Mr Cosgrave). If the Irish are not careful, the supply of Old Etonians available to solve their problems may well run out.

The fact is that Mr Whitelaw's policy was fraudulent and the Sunningdale Agreement represents the culmination of a series of conjuring tricks, exercises in political illusion. What made the former constitution of Northern Ireland unworkable was the fact that it had to be imposed by force on a substantial proportion of the population; what makes the present constitution unworkable is the same fact. Too large a part of the Catholic community could not consent in the past; too large a part of the Protestant community cannot consent now. An imposed solution is no solution. Indeed, no solution is possible, unless it wins the minds and hearts of a majority of the Protestant community. Mr Whitelaw does not betray the shadow of an understanding of that community. Here, Mr McCann also fails (I shall return to this), but on a number of other points his book is a splendid correction to the mythology.

First of all, as to the civil-rights movement. Let us be clear about it. In that movement, as so often before, not only did much of the dynamism come from the so-called extremists, but the moderates were listened to, in so far as they were listened to, in substantial part because it was the only alternative to listening to the extremists. Does anyone imagine that Mr John Hume's enlightened message of non-violence would have been accorded the respect that it has been, even by his political enemies, if they had not feared that otherwise less non-violent figures would take the centre of the stage? Mr McCann laments periodically in his narrative how, both in the early stages of the civil-rights movement and later on, the Left at key points lost out to voices of centrist moderation.[2] He ought also to reflect how different what those voices said would have been, if it had not been for the achievements of himself and his political friends. Consider, by contrast, the sad case of the Northern Ireland Labour Party, which takes care to weed out extremists. They refused to allow Mr McCann to be their parliamentary candidate in 1970, for example, because he had 'too violent an image'.[3] The result is that nobody listens to their high-minded but impotent preaching.

But Mr McCann's narrative is not, of course, a generalised account of the conflict and struggles between and within movements in the North. It is a highly specific account of what happened in Derry at particular times and places, and it helps to underline how different in some ways the events in Derry have been from those in Belfast. The fact that 'the Derry Provos, under Martin McGuinness, had managed to bomb the city centre until it looked as if it had been hit from the air without causing any civilian casualties', while the British army was killing such unarmed civilians as Seamus Cusack, Desmond Beattie and Kathleen Thompson, put events in a quite different perspective for the people of the Bogside from that which obtained in those British newspapers which would hasten to report a tarring and feathering but omit altogether such a death as Mrs Thompson's.[4]

McCann's narrative gift is exhibited powerfully in his account of the day-to-day shifting of public and individual attitudes and of the strong but often formless reactions to such events to which rival political factions aspired to give their own particular form. What is conveyed most of all, perhaps unintentionally, is a sense of ordinary people as often shocked, often desperate,

---

[2] See, for example, McCann 1974, pp. 44–8, 57–8; 1981, pp. 44–8, 57–8; 1993, pp. 101–104; 113–14.

[3] McCann 1974, p. 78; 1981, p. 78; 1993, p. 134.

[4] McCann 1974, p. 106; 1981, p. 106; 1993, p. 162.

immensely resourceful, but fundamentally not knowing where to turn, their trust in any leadership being at best fragile.

In his scourging of the rival political analyses of different factions in Derry and in the North at large, Mr McCann is merciless. No one is spared, least of all his own past self. But when Mr McCann comes to replace his past errors – he finally exhibits a certain comic magnanimity towards error, allowing that 'Even Trotsky made mistakes' – we move into the realm of fantasy. 'Only the revolutionary Left could offer the programme which is needed.'[5] What is the programme? It involves attacking the government in Dublin, as well as those in Belfast and London, uniting the working class by delivering the Protestant working class from its belief in Orangeism and the Catholic working class from its allegiance to the Church and to such bodies as Fianna Fail and the Irish Labour Party. Mr McCann sounds like a man who proposes to prevent tornadoes by resiting major mountain ranges. Such a man might well feel able to point out, as Mr McCann does, that everyone else has failed to provide a solution to the problem of preventing tornadoes.

Why does Mr McCann believe what he does? Mr McCann himself ascribes the source of his views to Marxism. His is, of course, not the erroneous Marxism of Betty Sinclair of the Communist Party or of Dr Roy Johnston of Official Sinn Fein, whose theories Mr McCann feels able to call 'crazy', but a Marxism purified of their errors.[6] Yet, to state his position, is to become clear that it is neither Marxist nor true.

Mr McCann's position involves four theses. The first is that 'the motivation of the Orange leaders was and is economic self-interest'.[7] The second is that the Protestant working masses have been duped by the Unionist machine. The leaders have, according to this account, a true but evil view of what they are doing; the led have a false but excusable view. The third thesis is that if the economic interests of the workers were only appealed to, sectarianism could be overcome: 'In terms of strict economics the only programme with any potential to undercut sectarianism would have been . . . a comprehensive anti-capitalist, not just anti-Unionist, programme.'[8] Mr McCann's fourth thesis holds that the cause of the present troubles is that the economic requirements

---

[5] McCann 1974, p. 255; 1993, p. 311.
[6] McCann 1974, pp. 239–40; 1993, p. 296.
[7] McCann 1974, p. 127; 1993, p. 183.
[8] McCann 1974, 241–2; 1993, p. 298.

of contemporary capitalism in the North of Ireland, and more generally in Ireland, became discrepant with the prevailing ideologies, more especially of Orangeism. The new capitalism was represented by the liberal Unionism of O'Neill, or by the Fianna Fail of Lemass and Lynch. This new liberalism unleashed forces and enmities that it could not control.[9] But, in this context, Mr McCann emphasises how independent ideology can be of economics: 'There is more to Irish politics than economics and reason.'[10] Against Mr McCann, let me make three points.

The first is that the Orange leaders have not duped the Protestant masses; both masses and leaders share a vision of the world which is to those who inhabit it remarkably compelling. At one point, indeed, it closely resembles Mr McCann's own: both see the Catholic Church as a nest of superstition and priestcraft. In the embodiment of that Northern-Protestant vision in the world, fear has been a stronger element than hope. Those fears will not be met by any economic programme. For economic programmes offered from outside will be interpreted by the Protestant community of the North as the mask worn by some new threat to their religious and social integrity, to their heritage of liberty, until their deepest fears have been laid to rest.

Secondly, it is no part of Marxism to believe that we are generally moved by individual economic self-interest. Marx's thesis was that men are moved by their membership of some class which constitutes itself as an agency by the kind of consciousness it comes to have of its own role. It is only those who are able to embody the ideology of a given class in their actions who are able to be its leaders. An ideology can never be simply imposed; it imposes itself alike on leaders and led, and it determines in part who is able to lead. This is why Craig and Paisley have replaced Faulkner, Chichester-Clark and O'Neill as Protestant leaders.

It follows, thirdly, that a necessary preliminary to the building of any non-sectarian working-class movement in Ireland, North or South (and it is because this is the only possible socialist goal that I value as well as quarrel with Mr McCann's arguments) must be the removal of the context in which fear and ideology do and must reinforce each other. What could achieve this? The requirement for Catholic fears to be quieted is their citizenship in a state whose

9 McCann 1974, pp. 123–7, 203–9; 1993, pp. 179–82; 259–65.
10 McCann 1974, p. 209; 1993, p. 265.

constitutional guarantees they can rely on; the requirement for Protestant fears to be quieted is the restoration of autonomy. Both requirements would be met by the restoration of a parliament with substantial powers at Stormont within a United Ireland. The danger at the moment is that proposals of this kind are seen as coming only from those in each community most mistrusted in the other, Provisional Sinn Fein and the UVF. This danger could be avoided if only the present Irish government could learn to understand why in consenting to the Sunningdale Agreement it did nothing to produce a solution in the North. For, if a government in Dublin were to offer the Protestant community in the North a serious constitution, it would now have a good chance of being heard. It is Mr Craig and Mr Paisley who should be invited to Dublin, and not Mr Faulkner or Mr Rees; and if Mr Cosgrave will not invite them, Mr Lynch should.

Of course, the United Ireland thus created will be a bourgeois state, dominated by the interests of Irish capital, and, in Mr McCann's perspective, this must be an unworthy bourgeois aim. But the Ireland thus created will be a place where the facts of class will have much more chance of being central in political consciousness than they have today. Politics needs some framework. The Provisional IRA has decisively destroyed the old framework, but since the ending of the truce their violence has become from every standpoint but their own an aimless terror with no political end. The Protestant community has learned the lesson that the British Government's last gift to its colonial dependents is always an unworkable constitution. No one else is offering the North a viable politics; do they really feel in Dublin that agreement with London is more important than peace in Derry and Belfast?

Chapter Forty-Five

Sunningdale: A 'Colonial' Solution[1]

There is one small fragment of hope to be found among the wreckage of policies produced by the Protestant general strike in the Six Counties. At long last, it may be realised that the intransigence of the Protestant community in the North, and more especially of the working-class element in that community, cannot be made to vanish by constitutional conjuring tricks.

It is almost a tradition by now for British governments to try to make their exit from a finally untenable colonial situation by offering 'the natives' as a last imperialist gift an unworkable constitution. When ''the natives', whether they are Africans or Irishmen, refuse to work the unworkable, the cry goes up at Westminster: 'You see, they are not fit for democracy'. That is essentially what Mr Harold Wilson is now saying about the Northern Protestants and those of us who have in the past had least sympathy for the politics of Unionism and the Orange Order ought to recognise that they are now sharing a very old Irish experience.

Of course, the British do really and genuinely want to get out. But, because they will not take the Protestant community's stances with seriousness –

---

[1] Originally published in *The Irish Press*, 5 June 1974.

the world view of the Northern Protestant, with its intensity of commitment, with its vision of a small beleaguered community defending truth and freedom against a hostile world, is far more incomprehensible to the secular English liberals both the Conservative and Labour parties than it ought to be to an Irish Catholic – the British have believed that a combination of liberal rhetoric and political manipulation, whether provided by the weak, but principled Terence O'Neill or by a Brian Faulkner, who is seen in the North as Mr. Facing-Both-Ways, could alter the whole historical course of the Northern Protestant community. What, in fact, they have done is to increase the fear and anxieties of a community already all too dominated by fear and anxiety.

Of course, any Irish government would want to give as much aid and comfort as possible to the SDLP. Of course, the SDLP was bound to try the road of coalition. But we ought now to be able to see that the policies which led to the Sunningdale Agreement were policies which led nowhere. The old Northern-Irish constitution was unworkable because it attempted to govern the vast majority of the Catholic community without their fundamental consent; the new Northern-Irish constitution is unworkable because it attempts to govern the majority of the Protestant community without their fundamental consent.

One set of constitutional illusions has been changed for another. To have advocated the policies embodied in the Sunningdale Agreement up till now was entirely honourable, even if an attempt to allow hope to prevail over reality. To continue to advocate them, whether in Dublin or in London, can only be seen as an obstinate preference for make-believe.

What policies then ought to be adopted? Only policies which will lessen the fears, and hence in time, antagonism of both communities. The Catholic community needs assurance of civil rights, of rights in housing, employment and in voting. The Protestant community needs to be assured that its autonomy will not be wantonly infringed – now is the time to remember Eamon de Valera's recognition of this need during the Treaty Debates in 1922. There is only one constitutional framework that can meet both needs: the restoration of the powers of the parliament at Stormont within the framework of a United Ireland. What the Protestant community has demanded and failed to receive from London ought to be substantially conceded to it by Dublin. But is this not a utopian dream? Do not the Protestant community regard any government in Dublin as their natural enemy?

First, let us remember how desperate for *some* solution the Protestant community is becoming. The only solutions considered hitherto are all barred to them. The British have decisively refused to reinstate the old Northern Irish constitution. Full integration with Britain, as advocated by Ian Paisley, has no support in Britain either. And even Mr Paisley and Mr Craig know that the Six Counties cannot go it alone, that they cannot declare independence unilaterally, if only for economic reasons.

The Protestant leadership are therefore trapped into taking desperate measures that lead nowhere. Lack of a solution reinforces fear; fear reinforces antagonism; antagonism substitutes for a sense of reality. In this situation, Dublin must do what London has failed to do: offer the Protestant leadership an honourable way out, a way of moving towards what they and their followers will see as victory; even if qualified victory, rather than as defeat.

This cannot be done, for example, by inviting Mr Paisley and Mr Craig to an all-party Eireann conference. The Protestant leadership must be approached as a high contracting party which enters negotiations on an equal footing with the representatives of the Irish government. The perfunctory invitation that was extended to Mr Paisley and Mr Craig invited the rejection that it received. Indeed, the first step should be to ask Mr Paisley and Mr Craig to receive unofficial emissaries for informal exploratory talks. From the very beginning, there must be no reliance on ambiguity and imprecision, as there was at Sunningdale.

But, if Mr Paisley and Mr Craig were to achieve a large part of what they want, would not this involve the betrayal of the SDLP and of the Catholic community? Everything turns here not only on the kind of constitutional guarantees that are written into the peace treaty, but on the way that they are to be enforced. It might be useful to provide some form of internationally sanctioned Court of Arbitration in disputed areas. At the same time, it would be essential that one criminal law – suppressing partisan violence – operated in the whole of Ireland and that there were unified forms of economic development. For, in fact, nothing feeds the communal fears of the North in the way that unemployment does. The necessary counterpart to political peace is a massive programme for economic growth.

It is here that the United States could play a much greater part. So much American aid has been wasted or is even counter-productive from an American point of view, that an invitation to participate in a programme with a positive political outcome ought not to go unanswered. Britain ought to b happy to spend a fraction of what she now spends on military operations o economic aid. A prosperous North would be much less prone to fear than poverty-stricken North.

But none of this can happen without an initiative from Dublin. Hitherto the only proposals for Northern autonomy within a United Ireland have com from Provisional Sinn Fein and the only response has been from the UVF But any proposals from those quarters will be rejected with suspicion an mistrust by the large majority in both of the Northern communities. Sinn Fei and the UVF now represent nothing and they can promise nothing credibly.

By contrast, if an Irish government were to make such proposals, it woul mark a great step forward whereas persistence in the Sunningdale policie can lead only towards disaster. There is a great opportunity for Fianna Fail, i it dares to take it. For, if the Coalition government will not talk directly to th Protestant leadership, then the Opposition should itself undertake that task A creative policy would evoke a strong response in the country.

Chapter Forty-Six

Irish Conflicts and British Illusions[1]

What does a British politician do when he finds himself responsible for a social order divided by fundamental conflict? He writes a new political constitution for it. When the results of this faith in constitution-writing turn out to be oppression, war and suffering – as in South Africa, Nigeria, the Indian subcontinent, the Sudan and Ireland – he is apt to blame the natives for their lack of the Westminster spirit and to suggest that what they need are some even more ingenious constitutional arrangements, perhaps ones which they should frame for themselves. The illusions of constitutionalism have great staying power among those who never have to pay the costs of their own illusions.

Just such illusions dominate the British government's White Paper proposing a constitutional convention for Northern Ireland.[2] They are of three kinds. There are the relatively superficial and unimportant absurdities of detail, which need to be mentioned only because they are symptomatic of the cloud-cuckoo-land thinking of the House of Commons whenever it approaches Irish questions. There is secondly the question of what sort of response the White Paper is to the events which

---

[1] Originally published in *New Statesman*, 19 July 1974, pp. 75–6.
[2] Northern Ireland Constitution 1974, Cmnd. 5675, paras 44–58.

made it necessary. Most important of all, there is the question of who will b elected to the convention.

Begin from the symptomatic trivia then. Mr Rees felt able to compare h proposal to Attlee's proposal for a constitutional convention in Newfoundlan in 1945. But Attlee was not faced with the total collapse of his own previou policies. Nor did he face any prospect of armed resistance to any decisio that the Newfoundland convention might make. Mr Rees has told us th the convention will have as its chairman 'a person of high standing an impartiality from Northern Ireland'.[3] Anyone from Northern Ireland who in fact impartial would have to be an idiot. What the British government mea by 'impartial' is, I suspect, 'sharing the attitudes of the Alliance Party or th Northern Ireland Labour Party', parties extremely popular at Westminste but not very popular in Northern Ireland. However, since it will also b necessary that the chairman should have successfully concealed his particula partisanship, perhaps this does not matter. Yet Mr William Beattie, the deput leader of Mr Paisley's Democratic Unionists, has already expressed a stron preference for a chairman elected by a two-thirds majority at the conventior

To turn to matters of substance, the White Paper blandly ignores th events that produced it. What brought about Mr Faulkner's fall? His asse to power-sharing and to the special relationship with Dublin, written into th Sunningdale Agreement. What does the White Paper require of the conventio dominated as it will be by those who helped to contrive Mr Faulkner's fal Assent to power-sharing and to a special relationship with Dublin. The Socia Democratic Labour Party welcomed the White Paper precisely because contained these elements; the Unionist response to the White Paper resolutel ignored what it actually says on these matters. Thus, what Mr Rees is proposin is that the failure of the Assembly should duly be re-enacted at the convention unless some dramatic change for the better should occur in the intervenin period. Unfortunately, the signs are that change may be for the worse. Wh when the time comes, will dominate the convention?

The most sinister force in the North of Ireland is the Official Unionist Party This is concealed by thinking in terms of 'moderates' (good) and 'extremists (bad), a habit of mind which leads Dublin and London to react more strongl against Mr Paisley than against Mr Harry West. But it is the Official Unionist

---

[3] *The Times*, 5 July 1974.

who have rebuilt a Protestant united front, which was victorious in the last British general election and which will dominate the convention. One of their central concerns has been to discourage all rational dialogue. Mr William Craig is reported to have threatened Vanguard members with expulsion if they attended this month's Oxford conference. The Official Unionists boycotted the conference. But their success in remaking Unionist unity has been immeasurably aided by the failures of the governments in London and Dublin to recognise the nature of grass-roots Protestantism, its strengths and its divisions, and to speak to it as directly as possible.

It has been widely believed that the Protestant masses were being duped by their leaders. But there has never been any attempt to talk directly to these masses. The leaders of the Ulster Workers' Council should have been involved in negotiation at the highest level at the earliest opportunity. Doubtless, this could not have been expected of Mr Heath whose horror of 'industrial action for political ends' determines his attitude to all working classes, Protestant or whatever; but Mr Wilson once made a point of talking to the Provisional IRA, yet did not think it worthwhile to talk to the Ulster workers' leaders. The result has been that the Ulster Workers' Council has been persuaded back into the orthodox Unionist fold. Mr Harry Murray, chairman of the Council during the strike, was repudiated by it for his attendance at and statement after the Oxford conference, and has resigned. The contempt for all politicians, Unionists included, so evident during the strike, is no longer expressed. At the same time, those officers in the UDA who wanted to have talks with the IRA bombers have been muzzled. The Protestant majority is, if the Official Unionists have their way, to be a monolithic majority.

But it is not only the fact that the United Unionists will have a clear majority in the proposed convention, and will speak there in a way that will suppress the divisions of opinion within the Protestant community, that constitutes a threat. In addition the British political situation may well favour the United Unionists. After a general election which may be as inconclusive as its predecessor, the temptation for the Conservative Party to recover its old lost unity with the Unionist Party may be too strong to withstand. It is in fact true that there is no conceivable political profit in continuing to support Mr Faulkner; and a growing minority of Conservative MPs has been working hard to throw their party's support to Mr West.

Even the prospect of their being successful will strengthen the most intransigent elements in Unionism. This will, in turn, produce one other outcome. There is no doubt that the vast majority of the Catholic community will continue to support the SDLP so long as they see any hope of it realising its objectives. But Provisional Sinn Fein represents the fall-back position for many Catholics. Nothing could be more calculated to drive the Catholic community into an uneasy blend of active and passive support for the Provisionals than the strategies now being pursued by the United Unionists, who in their attitudes to the Catholic community have forgotten nothing and learnt nothing. If Mr West did not exist, Provisional Sinn Fein would surely have asked God to create him.

Moreover, the policies of the British government ensure that Sinn Fein will take no part in the crucial discussion, if only because Mr Rees's policy of 'phasing out' detention has already been understood as the tokenism that it is. The army – whose record in Northern Ireland shows that it is indeed the military equivalent of British industry – opposed any relaxation of the detention policy; Sinn Fein, the SDLP and many others demanded an ending to internment without trial and Mr Rees has ineptly managed to satisfy nobody, contributing once again to the coming polarisation.

There is another cause of confusion in the present situation which ought to be noted. The Dublin government may have tried sincerely to assuage Northern Protestant fears, but they have made two great errors. The first is that they have made no real effort to talk to the genuine Protestant leaders or rank-and-file directly. This has not been their fault entirely. They were partly deceived by the discussions which they had with Northern-Irish supporters of the Executive, including that plausible turncoat Mr Roy Bradford. Their second error is that they have allowed the attitude of the Dublin Government to the Six Counties to become so ambiguous that it is easy for the Unionist leaders to exploit Protestant fears. On the one hand, Dr Garret Fitz-Gerald has declared the constitutional claim to the Six Counties 'a technicality' and Dr Conor Cruise O'Brien has announced that he is not working for Irish unity 'at this time'.[4] On the other hand, the unified approach of government and Fianna Fail leadership depends on maintaining the claim that Ireland is one and belongs to one Irish nation. It is quite clear that no Irish government today

[4] *The Times*, 7 July 1974.

could abandon this claim. Hence, there appears in government utterances what to their friends appears ambiguous, to their enemies deceitful. What they should do instead is to allow that for an indefinite future there are two Irish states, regrettable though this may be.

Why might this be important? I have been arguing that the project of a constitutional convention is probably going to lead to intensified division and polarisation in the North. Could this be avoided? There is at least one possibility that ought now to be explored. This is that Britain should impose independence on Northern Ireland, setting a date for total British withdrawal. What it should offer the convention is a continuance of the subsidy from the British Exchequer, if – and only if – the new state accepts first an internal tribunal with powers to investigate, and sanctions to deal with, cases of religious discrimination or constitutional abuse; secondly, a number of practical forms of co-operation with Dublin in such areas as economic development, transport and the enforcement of law and order; and thirdly, a pledge not to restore the B-Specials in any form.

It is clear that what underpins those Protestant fears on which official Unionism relies is the loss of any control over their own destiny. In his perceptive study of the Ulster Unionist Party, Mr John Harbinson noted two central attitudes in those whose support for Mr Paisley led them to defect to the Democratic Unionist Party. They distrusted the traditional, economically advantaged leaders of Unionism, fearing that those leaders would be willing to sell out the Protestant cause, if the price was right; and they feared the centralisation of power in modern government.[5] There is no doubt that these attitudes are basic to many sections of the Protestant community and that the fear and distrust which inspire them can only be overcome if they are given autonomy. Such power and influence for good as Britain has it will wield more effectively from without.

But if the British depart, will not the consequence be a bloodbath? It is not only Mr Frank McManus who thinks that is not in prospect. If Britain left, then a major demand of Provisional Sinn Fein would have been met, and the continuance of armed struggle would indeed become pointless. At the very least, there seems less chance of conflict after a negotiated British withdrawal than after the kind of convention now envisaged by the White Paper. It is

[5] Harbinson 1974, pp. 223–5.

unlikely, unless there is Sinn Fein representation at the convention, that anyon there will speak up for a British withdrawal. The Unionists, because they hop to manipulate the British convention once more, have ceased to speak of UD the SDLP rely all too heavily on Britain. Any radical initiative must come fro outside and preferably from Dublin, as well as from London.

What the Dublin government should offer is a largely autonomous sta within an Irish federal framework; but they should acknowledge that the onl possible first stage may be a largely autonomous state which is independent both Britain and the Irish Republic. Constitution-making only solves politic problems when a consensus exists of a kind that is not present in Norther Ireland. It cannot create such a consensus. All that Britain can now hope do is to provide the most hopeful – or, to be realistic, the least hopeless conditions for the Protestant and Catholic communities to work at their ow destinies. The White Paper gives little ground for hoping that this will b recognised at Westminster.

Epilogue
1953, 1968, 1995: Three Perspectives[1]

1. 1953 from the standpoint of 1995

When the first version of *Marxism and Christianity* was published in 1953, under the title *Marxism: An Interpretation,* Stalin was not yet dead and the Cold War had already taken determinate form.[2] In February 1953, NATO created a unified military command. In June, the Soviet suppression of a workers' rising in East Berlin exemplified the ruthless subordination of the whole of Eastern Europe to Soviet interests. It had already long been part of the stock-in-trade of many Western apologists to accept at its face-value the Soviet Union's claim that its social, political and economic practice embodied Marxist theory, in order to justify their own root-and-branch rejection of Marxism. And it was generally, if not universally, taken for granted among both theologians and ordinary church-goers that, because Marxism was an atheistic materialism, and because persecution by Soviet power was designed to deny, so far as it could, any independence to the lives of the churches, Christianity had to identify itself with the cause of the anti-Communist West. It was,

[1] Originally published as 'Introduction: 1953 1968 1995: Three Perspectives', in A. MacIntyre, *Marxism and Christianity*, Second Edition, Duckworth, London 1995, pp. v–xxxi.

[2] MacIntyre 1953.

of course, true that some parts of Marxist theory and some Marxist predictions had genuinely been discredited. It was also true that Christian orthodoxy could not but oppose that in Marxism which was either a ground for, or a consequence of its atheism. But the simple-minded wholesale anti-communist rejection of Marxism and the equally simple-minded understanding of the relationship between Marxism and Christianity as one of unqualified antagonism exaggerated and distorted these truths in the interests of the then dominant Western ideology.

It was against what I took in 1953 and still take in 1995 to be these distortions that I asserted the central thesis of this book: that Marxism does not stand to Christianity in any relationship of straightforward antagonism, but rather, just because it is a transformation of Hegel's secularised version of Christian theology, has many of the characteristics of a Christian heresy rather than of non-Christian unbelief. Marxism is, in consequence, a doctrine with the same metaphysical and moral scope as Christianity and it is the only secular post-Enlightenment doctrine to have such a scope. It proposes a mode of understanding nature and human nature, an account of the direction and meaning of history and of the standards by which right action is to be judged, and an explanation of error and of evil, each of these integrated into an overall worldview, a worldview that can only be made fully intelligible by understanding it as a transformation of Christianity. More than that, Marxism was and is a transformation of Christianity which, like some other heresies, provided grounds for reasserting elements in Christianity which had been ignored and obscured by many Christians. What elements are these? They are most aptly and relevantly identified by asking what attitude Christians ought to take to capitalism and then noting how that attitude relates to the Marxist analysis of capitalism.

What, on a Christian understanding of human and social relationships, does God require of us in those relationships? That we love our neighbours and that we recognise that charity towards them goes beyond, but always includes justice. An adequate regard for justice always involves not only a concern that justice be done and injustice prevented or remedied on any particular occasion, but also resistance to and, where possible, the abolition of institutions that systematically generate injustice. Christians have far too often behaved badly – thereby confirming what Christianity teaches about sinfulness – in failing to recognise soon enough and to respond to the evils of such institutions. Long after the evils of North-American and Latin-American slavery and the possibility of abolishing it should have been plain to them, too many Christians remained blind to those evils. And when the wickedness of fascism and that of national socialism were all too apparent, too many Christians refused to acknowledge them, let alone to engage in resistance. We therefore do well to honour those who did understand what charity and justice required: such Christians as the Dominican, Bartolomé de Las Casas, the evangelical Anglicans, John Newton and William Wilberforce, the Lutheran, Dietrich Bonhoeffer, the Catholics, Edith Stein and Maximilian Kolbe and Franz Jägerstetter.

For the same reasons, we ought also to honour those Christian laity and clergy, a very small minority, who recognized relatively early the systematic injustices generated by nascent and developed commercial and industrial capitalism. Those evils were and are of two kinds. There is on the one hand the large range of particular injustices perpetrated against individuals and groups on this or that particular occasion, where those other individuals who committed the injustices could have done otherwise consistently with conformity to the standards of profit and loss, of commercial and industrial success and failure, enforced by and in a capitalist economic and social order. The immediate cause of such injustices lies in the character of those individuals who commit them. But there is on the other hand a type of injustice which is not the work of a particular person on a particular occasion, but is instead perpetrated institutionally.

Such injustice has a number of distinct, if closely related aspects. There is the source of injustice that confronts every individual or group at the point at which they first encountered the capitalist system, usually by entering the labour market, from the period of nascent capitalism onwards. This source of injustice arises from the gross inequalities in the initial appropriation of capital – whatever point in time is taken to be the initial point – an appropriation that was in significant part the outcome of acts of force and fraud by the appropriators. This inequality in the relationship of those with capital to those without it is much more than the inequality between rich and poor that is to be found in the vast majority of societies. In many premodern social orders, just because the poor provide products and services that the rich need, there is still something of a reciprocal relationship between rich and poor, governed by customary standards. And, in such societies, characteristically the poor will have, and be recognised as entitled to, their own resources: a share of the product of the land they work, customary rights over common land, and the like. But the relationship of capital to labour is such that it inescapably involves an entirely one-sided dependence, except insofar as labour rebels against its conditions of work. The more effective the employment of capital the more labour becomes no more than an instrument of capital's purposes and an instrument whose treatment is a function of the needs of long-term profit maximisation and capital formation.

The relationships which result are the impersonal relationships imposed by capitalist markets upon all those who participate in them. What is necessarily absent in such markets is any justice of desert. Concepts of a just wage and a just price necessarily have no application to transactions within those markets. Hard, skilled and conscientious work, if it does not generate sufficient profit, something that it is not in the power of the worker to determine, will always be apt to be rewarded by unemployment. It becomes impossible for workers to understand their work as a contribution to the common good of a society which at the economic level no longer has a common good, because of the different and conflicting interests of different classes. The needs of capital formation impose upon capitalists and upon those who manage their enterprises a need to extract from the work of their employees a surplus which is at the future disposal of capital and not of labour. It is, of course, true that the fact that the profitability of an enterprise in the longer run requires a relatively stable and, so far as possible, satisfied labour force means that such exploitation must sometimes, to be effective over time, be tempered and assume a relatively benign face. And it is clearly much, much better that capitalism should provide a rising standard of living for large numbers of people than that it should not. But no amount of a rise in the standard of living by itself alters the injustice of exploitation. And the same is true of two other aspects of injustice.

Relationships of justice between individuals and groups require that the terms of their relationship be such that it is reasonable for those individuals and groups to consent to those terms. Contractual relationships imposed by duress are not genuinely contractual. So freedom to accept or reject particular terms of employment and freedom to accept or reject particular terms of exchange in free markets are crucial elements in those markets being in fact free. When, in premodern societies, markets are auxiliary to production that is not primarily for the market, but for local need, so that markets provide a useful means of exchange for what is surplus to local need, a means whereby all those who participate in them benefit, then the conditions of such freedom may be satisfied. And, in a society of small productive units, in which everyone has an opportunity to own (and not indirectly through shareholdings) the means of production – the type of economy envisaged by Chesterton and other distributists – free markets will be a necessary counterpart to freedom of ownership and freedom of labour. (This is a type of economy which does in fact give expression to the understanding of human freedom of the encyclical *Centesimus Annus*, an encyclical whose exaggerated optimism about the actualities of contemporary capitalism, both in Eastern Europe and in the United States, has led to unfortunate misconstruals of its doctrine.) But, in the markets of modern capitalism prices are often imposed by factors external to a particular market: those, for example, whose livelihood has been made subject to international market forces by their becoming exclusively producers for some product for which there was, but is no longer, international demand, will find themselves compelled to accept imposed low prices or even the bankruptcy of their economy. Market relationships in contemporary capitalism are, for the most part, relations imposed, both on labour and on small producers, rather than in any sense freely chosen.

I have tried so far in this account of the injustice characteristic of capitalism to make it clear that, when apologists for capitalism point out quite correctly that capitalism has been able to generate material prosperity at a higher level and for more people than any other economic system in human history, what they say is irrelevant as a rebuttal of these charges of injustice. But the rising standard of material prosperity in capitalist economies is itself closely related to another aspect of their failure in respect of justice. It is not only that individuals and groups do not receive what they deserve, it is also that they are educated or rather miseducated to believe that what they should aim at and hope for is not what they deserve, but whatever they may happen to want. They are, in the vast majority of cases, to regard themselves primarily as consumers whose practical and productive activities are no more than a means to consumption. What constitutes success in life becomes a matter of the successful acquisition of consumer goods, and thereby that acquisitiveness which is so often a character trait necessary for success in capital accumulation is further sanctioned. Unsurprisingly *pleonexia*, the drive to have more and more, becomes treated as a central virtue. But Christian theologians in the middle ages had learned from Aristotle that *pleonexia* is the vice that is the counterpa to the virtue of justice. And they had understood, as later theologians hav failed to do, the close connection between developing capitalism and the s of usury. So, it is not after all just general human sinfulness that generat particular individual acts of injustice over and above the institutional injusti of capitalism itself. Capitalism also provides systematic incentives to develo a type of character that has a propensity to injustice.

Finally, we do well to note that, although Christian indictments capitalism have justly focused attention upon the wrongs done to the po and the exploited, Christianity has to view any social and economic ord that treats being or becoming rich as highly desirable as doing wrong to tho who must not only accept its goals, but succeed in achieving them. Rich are, from a biblical point of view, an affliction, an almost insuperable obstac to entering the kingdom of heaven. Capitalism is bad for those who succe by its standards as well as for those who fail by them, something that ma preachers and theologians have failed to recognise. And those Christians wh have recognised it have often enough been at odds with ecclesiastical as we as political and economic authorities.

Notice now that this Christian critique of capitalism relied and relies key part, even if only in part, upon concepts and theses drawn from Marxi theory. Just as Marxism learned certain truths from Christianity, so Christiani in turn needed and needs to learn certain truths from Marxism. But wh does this mean for practice in general and for political practice in particula When I posed this question in 1953, I was able to find no satisfactory answe Partly, this was because I then aspired to an impossible condition: that being genuinely and systematically a Christian, who was also genuinely an systematically a Marxist. I therefore tried to integrate elements of Christiani with elements of Marxism in the wrong way. But, in so doing, I was also error in another respect. Among my as yet unquestioned assumptions wa a belief that the only possible politics that could effectively respond to th injustices of a capitalist economic and social order was a politics that too for granted the institutional forms of the modern state and that had as i goal the conquest of state power, whether by electoral or by other means, s that I could not as yet recognise that those who make the conquest of sta power their aim are always, in the end, conquered by it and, in becoming th instruments of the state, themselves become in time the instruments of one the several versions of modern capitalism.

2. 1968 from the standpoint of 1995

Large as these errors were, they were not the matters on which I was in 1953 most fundamentally at a loss. In the first version of this book, there was a chapter on philosophy and practice that was omitted when I revised it in 1968. That chapter was originally included because it attempted to pose what I had rightly recognised as the fundamental problem. It was later omitted because I had by then learnt that I did not know how to pose that problem adequately, let alone how to resolve it. So, in 1968, I mistakenly attempted to bypass it. But it cannot be avoided. What is that problem?

Any adequate account of the relationship between Marxism and Christianity would have to embody and be justified in terms of some systematic standpoint on the major issues of moral and political philosophy and of related philosophical disciplines. By 1953, I had acquired not only from my Marxist teachers, both in and outside the Communist Party, but also from the writings of R.G. Collingwood, a conception of philosophy as a form of social practice embedded in and reflective upon other forms of social practice. What I did not then fully understand was that philosophy needs to be conceived as having at least a fourfold subject-matter and a fourfold task. There is first of all that which has to be learned empirically: the rules and standards, concepts, judgments, and modes of argumentative justification, actually embodied in or presupposed by the modes of activity which constitute the life of the social order in which one is participating. Secondly, there are the ways of understanding or misunderstanding those activities and the relevant rules and standards, concepts, judgments, and modes of argumentative justification that are dominant in that particular social order. Thirdly, there is the relationship between these two in respect of how far the second is an adequate, and how far an inadequate and distorting representation of the first. And, finally, there is that of which a philosopher must give an account, if she or he is to vindicate the claim to have been able to transcend whatever limitations may have been imposed by her or his historical and social circumstances, at least to a sufficient extent to represent truly the first three and so to show not just how things appear to be from this or that historical and social point of view, but how things are.

Philosophy thus understood includes, but also extends a good deal beyond, what is taken to be philosophy on a conventional academic view of the disciplines. It is crucial to the whole philosophical enterprise, on any view of it, that its enquiries should be designed to yield a rationally justifiable set of theses concerning such familiar and central philosophical topics as perception and identity, essence and existence, the nature of goods, what is involved in rule-following and the like. But, from the standpoint towards which Marx and Collingwood had directed me, the discovery of such theses was valuable not only for its own sake, but was also needed to serve the further purpose of enabling us to understand about particular forms of social life what it is that, in some cases, enables those who participate in them to understand their own activities, so that the goods which they pursue are genuine goods, and, in others, generates systematic types of misunderstanding, so that those who participate in them by and large misconceive their good and are frustrated in its achievement.

Marx, for example, in his analysis of *bürgerlich* society, had shown how the characteristic forms of thought of that society at once articulate and disguise its underlying structure, and some of his heirs both within and outside Marxism – I think especially of both Karl Mannheim and Karl Polanyi – have since developed his insights further. But Marx and Engels were both blind to the extent to which their own thought not only has the marks characteristic of *bürgerlich* theorising, but was distorted in a characteristically *bürgerlich* manner, notably in their treatment of *the* economic, *the* political, and *the* ideological as distinct and separate, albeit causally interrelated areas of human activity, a treatment whose effect was to transform contingent characteristics of mid- and late nineteenth-century capitalist societies into analytical categories purporting to provide the key to human history and social structure in general.

By 1968, my reading of Lukács had taught me to recognise this fact and, with it, the general form of a central problem for any philosophical enquiry conceived as I was beginning to conceive it: how is it possible to identify in the case of other and rival theses and arguments a variety of distortions and limitations deriving from their authors' historical and social context, while at the same time being able to exhibit one's own theses and arguments, including one's theses and arguments about their theses and arguments, as exempt from such distortion and limitation? This was a question that had of course already been asked and answered by Hegel, by Marx and by numerous others. But, by 1968, I knew that not only their answers, but also their detailed formulations of the questions were vulnerable to insuperable objections.

Because I did not as yet know how to formulate this question adequately enough even to know where to look for an answer to it, I found myself distanced from identification with any substantive point of view. Whereas, in 1953, I had, doubtless naively, supposed it possible to be in some significant way both a Christian and a Marxist, I was, by 1968, able to be neither, while acknowledging in both standpoints a set of truths with which I did not know how to come to terms. In the case of Marxism, my reaction to recurrent attempts to reinstate Marxism as both economic and political theory and as *Weltanschauung* had led me for a considerable time to reject more than I should have done; for redirecting my thought I am much indebted to conversations with George Lichtheim, Heinz Lubasz, Linda Nicholson, Marx Wartofsky and Cheney Ryan, who provided a variety of illuminating perspectives on the problems of Marxism. One result is that I would not now endorse what I wrote dismissively about the labour theory of value in 1953 and I would want to say considerably more on a number of topics, including the theory of value, than I did in 1968.

Christianity had become problematic for me as a consequence of my having supposed that the theology in terms of which its claims had to be understood was that of Karl Barth. But what Barth's theology proved unable to provide was any practically adequate account of the moral life, and, although I should have known better, I mistakenly took what is a defect in Barth's theology to be a defect of Christianity as such. This judgement seemed to be confirmed by the platitudinous emptiness of liberal Christian moralising, whether Protestant or Catholic, a type of moralising in which the positions of secular liberalism reappeared in various religious guises. And this liberalism, the moral and political counterpart and expression of developing capitalism, I rejected just as I had done in 1953 and for the same reasons.

Why is political liberalism to be rejected? The self-image of the liberal is, after all, that of a protagonist of human rights and liberties. Those liberals who are social democrats aspire to construct institutions in the trade-union movement and the welfare state that will enable workers to participate in capitalist prosperity. And it would be absurd to deny that the achievement of pensions, health services and unemployment benefits for workers under capitalism has always been a great and incontrovertible good. Why then did and do I reject liberal social democracy? For at least three reasons.

First, Marxist theorists had predicted that, if trade unions made it their only goal to work for betterment within the confines imposed by capitalism and parliamentary democracy, the outcome would be a movement towards first the domestication and then the destruction of effective trade union power. Workers would, so far as possible, be returned to the condition of mere instruments of capital formation. In both 1953 and 1968, I took this prediction to be warranted, although it was then treated with great contempt by the theorists of liberal social democracy. Since then, it has, of course, turned out to be true.

Secondly, liberalism is the politics of a set of élites, whose members, through their control of party machines and of the media, predetermine for the most part the range of political choices open to the vast mass of ordinary voters. Of those voters, apart from the making of electoral choices, passivity is required. Politics and their cultural ambiance have become areas of professionalised life, and among the most important of the relevant professionals are the professional manipulators of mass opinion. Moreover entry into and success in the arenas of liberal politics has increasingly required financial resources that only corporate capitalism can supply, resources that secure in return privileged access to those able to influence political decisions. Liberalism thus ensures for the most part the exclusion of most people from any possibility of active and rational participation in determining the form of community in which they live.

Thirdly, the moral individualism of liberalism is itself a solvent of participatory community. For liberalism, in its practice as well as in much of its theory, promotes a vision of the social world as an arena in which each individual, in pursuit of the achievement of whatever she or he takes to be her or his good, needs to be protected from other such individuals by the enforcement of individual rights. Moral argument within liberalism cannot therefore begin from some conception of a genuinely common good that is more and other than the sum of the preferences of individuals. But argument to, from and about such a conception of the common good is integral to the practice of participatory community. Hence, if one holds that both justice as understood by St Paul and that justice which aspires to move from the maxim 'From each according to her or his ability, to each according to her or his contribution' to 'From each according to her or his ability, to each according to her or his need' can be embodied only in the internal and external relationships of participatory community, then liberalism will be incompatible with justice thus understood and will have to invent its own conceptions of justice, as it has indeed done.[3]

When my grounds for rejecting liberalism are expressed in this way, it is evident that they presuppose a commitment to some set of positive affirmations. But these I did not, in 1968, know how to formulate, in part because I did not know how to come to terms with either Marxism or Christianity and in part because I still lacked an adequate philosophical idiom for the statement, let alone the resolution of the relevant issues. So, it was natural that for a considerable period I found it relatively easy to say what I was against, rather than what, if anything, I was for. Perceptive critics recognised some of my underlying commitments – hostile critics saw them as underlying credulities – better than I myself did.

Marxism and Christianity were themselves in continuing and striking transformation. The debates and the documents of the Second Vatican Council, which had met from 1962 to 1965, had, by their definitive restatement of Christian doctrine, provided resources for identifying both the negative legalism of theological conservatives and the vacuous moralism of theological liberals as twin distortions of faith and practice. But ,since the discussion and evaluation of the Council was all too often framed in terms of a set of conservative-liberal antitheses and so distorted by the very errors from which the Council should have delivered us and will perhaps in time deliver us, the immediate effect was one of apparent theological confusion. For Marxists, many events of the late 1960s – the beginning of the Brezhnev era in the Soviet Union, the crushing by Soviet troops of the Czech project for socialism with a human face, the student uprisings, and the variously ineffective responses to those events of Communist parties in France and Italy and of small sectarian Marxist groups – should have given further evidence of the systematic failure of Marxism as politics. Where Marxists were to be politically effective – as in the Communist Party of South Africa – it was always because they had adopted programmes and forms of action only connected with Marxism in the loosest and most indirect ways.

---

[3] Marx 1974b, pp. 245–8.

3. 1995

As I write, capitalism, taking a variety of forms that range from the corporate capitalism of the United States to the state capitalism of China, seems to be almost unchallenged worldwide – except, of course, by its own self-destructive and disillusioning tendencies. In the United States, during a decade in which productivity has continually risen, the real wages of many types of worker have declined. The gap between richer and poorer has widened. When unemployment falls, this is treated as bad news on the stock market. Larger sections of the workforce have become aware of their job insecurity, since profitability and capital formation require an ability to fire and to hire at will. In service industries, many employees face continuing low-wage drudgery. Growth in technological expertise and in productive power have as their outcome societies of recurrently disappointed expectations, in which electorates, not knowing where to turn, exchange one set of political charlatans for another. In the world at large, the crucial gap is that between the wealthy capitalist nations and their immediate satellites on the one hand and those now condemned to the poverty of exclusion and marginality in respect of international markets on the other.

In this situation, what is most urgently needed is a politics of self-defence for all those local societies that aspire to achieve some relatively self-sufficient and independent form of participatory practice-based community and that therefore need to protect themselves from the corrosive effects of capitalism and the depredations of state power. And, in the end, the relevance of theorising to practice is to be tested by what theorising can contribute, indirectly or directly, to such a politics. At the very least, we can hope for this from sound theoretical enquiry: that we become able to approach the political tasks of the present freed in some significant measure from some of the major errors that so often undermined anticapitalist politics in the past, in the hope that reopening enquiry and debate on issues and questions whose final resolution is widely supposed to have been achieved long since may turn out to be of a good deal more than academic interest. And so I have found it.

As early as the 1970s, I had begun to formulate positions that would enable me to understand somewhat better not only what it was that had to be rejected in the moral, social and economic theory and practice of liberalism and individualism, but also how to evaluate in a more searching way the claims of Christian orthodoxy and the critique of Marxism. I came to recognise that the competing moral idioms in which contemporary ideological claims, whether liberal or conservative, are framed – the praise of Victorian values, various theories of natural rights, Kantian universalism, contractarianism, utilitarianism – were the result of a fragmentation of practical and evaluative discourse. Those competing moral idioms were to be understood as the outcome of a history in which different aspects of the life of practice had first been abstracted from the practical and theoretical contexts in which they were at home and then transformed into a set of rival theories, available for ideological deployment. What needed to be recovered, in order both to understand this and to correct it, was some reconstructed version of Aristotle's view of social and moral theory and practice. I also understood better what type of community it was by contrast with which I had rightly found the social relationships of both capitalist individualism and Soviet command economies, very different as they were, deformed and inadequate. The modes of social practice in some relatively small-scale and local communities – examples range from some kinds of ancient city and some kinds of medieval commune to some kinds of modern co-operative farming and fishing enterprises – in which social relationships are informed by a shared allegiance to the goods internal to communal practices, so that the uses of power and wealth are subordinated to the achievement of those goods, make possible a form of life in which participants pursue their own goods rationally and critically, rather than having continually to struggle, with greater or lesser success, against being reduced to the status of instruments of this or that type of capital formation.

These were not two discoveries, but one, since what Aristotelian theory articulates are in fact the concepts embodied in and presupposed by such modes of practice, and such concepts themselves need to be understood in terms of their functioning within just those same modes of practice. Aristotle's statement of his own positions is of course at some points in need of greater or less revision and at others – in, for example, his treatment of women, productive workers and slavery – requires outright rejection. But the fruitful correction of these inadequacies and mistakes turned out to be best achieved by a better understanding of Aristotelian theory and practice. My realisation that this was so was only one of several large consequences of my finally adopting what was a basically Aristotelian standpoint and then developing it in relation to contemporary issues inside and outside philosophy.

Having done so, I discovered that I had thereby discarded philosophical assumptions that had been at the root of my difficulties with substantive Christian orthodoxy. And the removal of these barriers was one, even if only one, necessary stage in my coming to acknowledge the truth of the biblical Christianity of the Catholic Church. But I also understood better than I had done earlier not only what had been right in official Catholic condemnations of Marxism, but also how much had been mistaken and rooted in obfuscating and reactionary social attitudes. Part of what Catholic theologians – and more generally Christian theologians – had failed to focus upon sufficiently was the insistence by both Marx and Marxists on the close relationships of theory to practice, on how all theory, including all theology, is the theory of some mode or modes of practice. Just as the propositions of scientific theorising are not to be either understood or evaluated in abstraction from their relationships to the practices of scientific enquiry within which they are proposed, revised and accepted or rejected, so it is too with other bodies of propositions. Detach any type of theorising from the practical contexts in which it is legitimately at home, whether scientific, theological or political, and let it become a free-floating body of thought and it will be all too apt to be transformed into an ideology. So, when Catholic theology is in good order, its peculiar work is to assist in making intelligible in a variety of contexts of practice what the church teaches authoritatively as the Word of God revealed to it and to the world. When and insofar as theology does not subordinate itself to that teaching, but claims independence of it, it becomes no more than one more set of competing religious opinions, sometimes perhaps opinions of great interest, but functioning very differently from theology in the service of the teaching church.

Marxism was proposed by its founders as a body of theory designed to inform, direct and provide self-understanding in the practice of working-class and intellectual struggle against capitalism. It, too, has recurrently become detached from such contexts of practice. When and insofar as it does so, it too becomes no more than a set of competing political, economic and social opinions. And, of course, its tendency towards degeneration into this condition is one of the marks of its failure. The errors and distortions that have afflicted Marxism are, of course, various and have a range of different causes, some of them deriving from the vicissitudes of its later history. But if we are now to learn how to criticise Marxism, not in order to separate ourselves from its errors and distortions – that phase should be long over – but in order once again to become able to learn from it, then we shall need once more to re-examine Marx's thought in the 1840s and above all the changes in his conception of the relationship of theory to practice. If we do so, we will have to recognise that Marxism was not so much defeated by criticisms from external standpoints, important as these certainly were, so much as it was self-defeated, defeated that is by the failures of both Marx and his successors to provide a resolution of key difficulties internal to Marxism.

Central among these was Marx's refusal or inability to press further some of the questions posed in and by the 'Theses on Feuerbach'.[4] And we need answers to these questions, if we are to be able to construct and sustain practice-based forms of local participatory community that will be able to survive the insidious and destructive pressures of contemporary capitalism and of the modern state. The politics of such communities and of the struggles to construct and sustain them will be much more effective if it is conducted by those able to understand and to learn from both Christianity and Marxism and to understand their relationship. If, even in a small way, this book contributes to such understanding and learning, then putting it into circulation for a third time will have been worthwhile.

[4] Marx 1975c. [For a first attempt to reopen such questions, even if only in a preliminary way, see my 'The *Theses on Feuerbach*: A Road Not Taken' in R.S. Cohen and C.C. Gould (eds.), *Artifacts, Representations and Social Practice: Essays for Marx Wartofsky*, Kluwer, Dordrecht 1994. – AM.] Reprinted in Knight (ed.) 1998.

References

Ali, Tariq 1972, *The Coming British Revolution*, London: Jonathan Cape.

Alliluyeva, Svetlana 1968, *Twenty Letters to a Friend*, Harmondsworth: Penguin.

Amis, Kingsley 1957, *Socialism and the Intellectuals*, London: Fabian Society.

Anderson, Perry 1980, *Arguments Within English Marxism*, London: Verso.

Anderson, Perry 1990, 'A Culture in Contraflow – II', *New Left Review*, I, 182: 85–137.

Atlee, Clement 1937, *The Labour Party in Perspective*, London: Victor Gollancz.

Avrich, Paul 1971, *Kronstadt 1921*, Princeton: Princeton University Press.

Baker, James 1962, 'The Need for Developing Revolutionary Theory: the Case of Alasdair MacIntyre', *Labour Review*, 7, 2: 55–56 & 65–73.

Balogh, Thomas 1962, 'The Apotheosis of the Dilettante: the Establishment of Mandarins', in *The Establishment: a Symposium*, edited by Hugh Thomas, London: Ace Books.

Baran, Paul and Paul Sweezy 1968, *Monopoly Capital*, Harmondsworth: Penguin.

Barcos, Martin de 1956, *Correspondance de M. de Barcos, Abbé de Saint Cyran avec les Abbés de Port Royal et les Principaux Personages du Groupe Janseniste*, Paris: Press Universtaires de France.

Barratt-Brown, Michael 1958a, 'The Controllers I', *Universities and Left Review*, 5: 53–61.

Barratt-Brown, Michael 1959b, The Controllers II', *Universities and Left Review*, 6: 38–41.

Barratt-Brown, Michael 1959c, 'The Controllers III', *Universities and Left Review*, 7: 43–49.

Berelson, Bernard 1956, 'The Study of Public Opinion', in *The State of the Social Sciences: Papers Presented at the 25th Anniversary of the Social Sciences Research Building, University of Chicago, November 10–12, 1955*, edited by Leonard White, Chicago: University of Chicago Press.

Berkman, Alexander 1925, *The Bolshevik Myth (Diary 1920–22)*, New York: Boni and Liveright.

Bernstein, Eduard 1993 [1899], *The Preconditions of Socialism*, Cambridge: Cambridge University Press.

Birchall, Ian 2000, Personal communication, Birchall to Neil Davidson, 24 August.

Blackburn, Robin 1970, 'MacIntyre, the Game Is Up', *Black Dwarf*, 16 January 1970: 11.

Blackledge, Paul 2004a, *Perry Anderson, Marxism and the New Left*, London: Merlin Press.

Blackledge, Paul 2004b, 'Reform, Revolution and the Question of Organisation in the First New Left', *Contemporary Politics*, 10, 1: 21–36.

Blackledge, Paul 2005a, '"Anti-Leninist" Anti-Capitalism: A Critique', *Contemporary Politics*, 11, 2/3: 99–116.

Blackledge, Paul 2005b, 'Freedom, Desire and Revolution: Alasdair MacIntyre's Marxist Ethics', *History of Political Thought*, 26, 4: 696–720.

Blackledge, Paul 2006a, *Reflections on the Marxist Theory of History*, Manchester: Manchester University Press.

Blackledge, Paul 2006b, 'The New Left and Renewal of Marxism', *International Socialism*, 112: 125–53.

Blackledge, Paul 2007a, 'Marx and Intellectuals' in, *Marxism, Intellectuals and Politics*, edited by David Bates, London: Palgrave.

Blackledge, Paul 2007b, 'Alasdair MacIntyre: Marxism and Politics', *Studies in Marxism*, 11: 95–116.

Blackledge, Paul 2007c, 'Morality and Revolution: Ethical Debates in the British New Left', *Critique*, 35:2, 211–228.

Bloch, Ernst 1969 [1923–4], 'Aktualitat und Utopie: Zu Lukács' *Geschichte und Klassenbewusstsein*', in *Philosophische Aufsatze zur objektiven Phantasie*, Frankfurt-am-Main: Suhrkamp.

Bonhoeffer, Dietrich 2001 [1943–4], *Letters and Papers from Prison: An Abridged Edition*, London: Student Christian Movement Press.

Bornstein, Sam and Al Richardson 1986, *War and the International*, London: Socialist Platform.

Bukharin, Nikolai 1935, 'Marx's Teaching and Its Historical Importance', in *Marxism and Modern Thought*, edited by Nikolai Bukharin et al., London: George Routledge and Sons.

Burgess, Timothy 1969, 'Education: Optimism is Not Enough', in *Matters of Principle: Labour's Last Chance*, edited by Timothy Burgess et al., Harmondsworth: Penguin.

Callaghan, John 1984, *British Trotskyism: Theory and Practice*, London: Blackwell.

Callinicos, Alex 1983, *Marxism and Philosophy*, Oxford: Oxford University Press.

Callinicos, Alex 1990, *Trotskyism*, Buckingham: Open University Press.

Callinicos, Alex 1991, *The Revenge of History*, Cambridge: Polity.

Castoriadis, Cornelius 1988 [1959], 'The Proletariat and Organisation I', in *Cornelius Castoriadis: Political and Social Writing II*, edited by David Ames Curtis, Minneapolis: University of Minnesota Press.

Cliff, Tony 2001a [1959], 'Rosa Luxemburg', in *International Struggle and the Marxist Tradition*, London: Bookmarks.

Cliff, Tony 2001b [1960], 'Trotsky on Substitutionism', in *International Struggle and the Marxist Tradition*, London: Bookmarks.

Cliff, Tony 2003 [1948], 'The Nature of Stalinist Russia' in *Marxist Theory After Trotsky*, London: Bookmarks.

Coates, Ken 1962, 'Reform and Revolution: Rejoinders 1' International Socialism, 8: 22–24.

Collins, Henry 1961, 'The Case for Left Reformism', *International Socialism*, 6: 15–19.

Collins, Henry 1962, 'Left Reformism Revisited' International Socialism, 9: 24–28.

Communist Party of Great Britain 1924, *Fifth Congress of the Communist International: Abridged Report*, London: Communist Party of Great Britain.

Connolly, James 1987 [1897], 'Socialism and Nationalism', in *Collected Works*, Volume 1, Dublin: New Books Publications.

Crankshaw, Edward 1959, *Khrushchev's Russia*, Harmondsworth: Penguin.

D'Andrea, Thomas 2006, *Tradition, Rationality and Virtue: The Thought of Alasdair MacIntyre*, Aldershot: Ashgate.

Dangerfield, George 1936, *The Strange Death of Liberal England*, London: Constable and Company.

Debray, Régis 1968, *Revolution in the Revolution? Armed Struggle and Political Struggle in Latin America*, Harmondsworth: Penguin.

Desmond Greaves, Charles 1976 [1961], *The Life and Times of James Connolly*, London: Lawrence and Wishart.

Deutscher Isaac 2003a [1954], *The Prophet Armed: Trotsky, 1879–1921*, London: Verso.

Deutscher, Isaac 1960, *The Great Contest: Russia and the West*, Oxford: Oxford University Press.

Deutscher, Isaac 1966 [1949], *Stalin: a Political Biography*, revised edition, Harmondsworth: Penguin Books.

Deutscher, Isaac 2003b [1959], *The Prophet Unarmed: Trotsky, 1921–1929*, London: Verso.

Deutscher, Isaac 2003c [1963], *The Prophet Outcast: Trotsky, 1929–1940*, London: Verso.

Dickens, Charles 1969 [1854], *Hard Times*, Harmondsworth: Penguin.

Diderot, Denis 1897 [1762], *Rameau's Nephew*, London: Green and Company.

Diderot, Denis 1992a [1773], 'The Supplement au Voyage de Bougainville', in *Political Writings*, edited by John Mason and Robert Wokler, Cambridge: Cambridge University Press.

Diderot, Denis 1992b [1780], 'Extracts from the *Histoire des Deux Indes*', in *Political Writings*, edited by John Mason and Robert Wokler, Cambridge: Cambridge University Press.
Dimitrov, George 1960 [1933], 'Minutes of the Speech before the Court, Delivered on 16 December, 1933', in *Selected Works*, Sofia: Foreign Languages Press.
Djilas, Milovan 1957, *The New Class: An Analysis of the Communist System*, London: George Allen and Unwin.
Dolci, Daniel 1965, *A New World in the Making*, London: Macgibbon and Kee.
Draper, Hal 1963/4 [1949], 'The "Inevitability of Socialism"', *International Socialism*, 15: 21–8.
Dudinstev, Vladimir 1957, *Not by Bread Alone*, New York: E.P. Dutton.
Dunayevskaya, Raya 1971 [1958], *Marxism and Freedom*, London: Pluto Press.
Duverger, Maurice 1954, *Political Parties: Their Organisation and Activity in the Modern State*, London: Methuen and Company.
Emmet, Dorothy 1996, *Philosophers and Friends: Reminiscences of Seventy Years in Philosophy*, London: Macmillan.
Engels, Frederick 1975–2004a [1878], *Anti-Duhring (Herr Eugen Duhring's Revolution in Science)*, in *Collected Works*, Volume 25, London: Lawrence and Wishart.
Engels, Frederick 1975–2004b [1886], *Ludwig Feuerbach and the End of Classical German Philosophy*, in *Collected Works*, Volume 26, London: Lawrence and Wishart.
Engels, Frederick 1975–2004c [1892], 'Preface to the 1892 English Edition of *The Condition of the Working Class in England 1844*', in *Collected Works*, Volume 27, London: Lawrence and Wishart.
Engels, Frederick 1975–2004d [1895], 'Introduction [to Karl Marx's *The Class Struggles in France, 1848–1850*] [1895]', in *Collected Works*, Volume 27, London: Lawrence and Wishart.
Engels, Frederick 1975–2004e [1895], 'On the History of Early Christianity', in *Collected Works* Volumes 27, London: Lawrence and Wishart.
Engels, Frederick 1975–2004f [1895], 'Letter to Kautsky', in *Collected Works*, Volume 50, London: Lawrence and Wishart.
Fairlie, Henry 1962, 'The BBC', in *The Establishment: a Symposium*, edited by Hugh Thomas, London: Ace Books.
Feuer, Lewis 1962, 'What is Alienation? The Career of a Concept', *New Politics*, 1: 116–34.
Fisher, Herbert Albert Laurens 1935, *A History of Europe*, Volume 1, London: Arnold.
Foot, Paul 1968, *The Politics of Harold Wilson*, Harmondsworth: Penguin.
Forster, Edward 1910, *Howard's End*, London: Edward Arnold.
Freud, Sigmund 1922, 'Twenty-First Lecture', in *Introductory Lectures on Psycho-Analysis: Course of Twenty-Eight Lectures Delivered at the University of Vienna*, London: George Allen and Unwin.
Garaudy, Roger et al. 1956, *Mésaventure de l'anti-marxisme*, Paris: Editions Sociales.
Gellner, Ernest 1958a, 'Logical Positivism and the Spurious Fox', *Universities and Left Review*, 3: 67–73.
Gellner, Ernest 1958b, 'Reply to Mr MacIntyre', *Universities and Left Review*, 4: 73–4.
Goldmann, Lucien 1964, *The Hidden God: a Study of Tragic Vision in the Pensees of Pascal and the Tragedies of Racine*, London: Routledge and Kegan Paul.
Guevara, Che 1969a [1961], 'On Growth and Imperialism', in *Venceremos! The Speeches and Writings of Che Guevara*, edited by John Verassi, London: Weidenfeld and Nicolson.
Guevara, Che 1969b [1965], 'Socialist Planning', in *Venceremos! The Speeches and Writings of Che Guevara*, edited by John Verassi, London: Weidenfeld and Nicolson.
Guevara, Che 1969c [1965], 'Letter to his Family', in *Venceremos! The Speeches and Writings of Che Guevara*, edited by John Verassi, London: Weidenfeld and Nicolson.
Hall, Stuart et al. 1957–8, 'The Insiders', *Universities and Left Review*, 3: 23–64.
Hallas, Duncan 1969, 'Building the Leadership', *International Socialism*, 40: 25–32.
Hallas, Duncan 1979, *Trotsky's Marxism*, London: Pluto Press.

Hampshire, Stuart 1958, 'Doctor Zhivago: as from a Lost Culture', *Encounter*, 11, 5: 3–5.
Hanson, Harry 1957, 'An Open Letter to Edward Thompson', *The New Reasoner*, 2: 79–91.
Hanson, Harry 1959, 'How Wild Is My Wilderness?', *The New Reasoner*, 9: 98–107.
Harbinson, John 1974, *The Ulster Unionist Party, 1882–1973: Its Development and Organisation*, revised edition, Belfast: Blackstaff Press.
Harman, Chris 1983, 'Philosophy and Revolution', *International Socialism*, 21: 58–87.
Harman, Chris 1998, *The Fire Last Time: 1968 and After*, London: Bookmarks.
Harman, Chris 2004, Personal Communication to Paul Blackledge, 26th October 2004.
Hegel, Georg W.F. 1894 [1830], *Hegel's Philosophy of Mind*, Oxford: Oxford University Press.
Hegel, Georg W.F. 1952 [1821], 'Preface', in *The Philosophy of Right*, Chicago: University of Chicago.
Hegel, Georg W.F. 1956 [1830–1], 'Introduction', in *The Philosophy of History*, New York: Dover Publications.
Hegel, Georg W.F. 1969 [1812–16], *Hegel's Science of Logic*, translated by A.V. Miller, foreword by J.N. Finlay, London: George Allen and Unwin.
Hegel, Georg W.F. 1985 [1821–31], *Lectures on the Philosophy of Religion*, Berkeley: University of California Press, 1985.
Hemingway, Ernest 1976 [1927], *Fiesta (The Sun Also Rises)*, London: Panther.
Herzen, Alexander 1974 [1924], *My Past and Thoughts: the Memoirs of Alexander Herzen*, London: Chatto and Windus.
Hoggart, Richard 1958, *The Uses of Literacy: Aspects of Working-Class Life with Special Reference to Publications and Entertainments*, Harmondsworth: Penguin.
Hollis, Christopher 1962, 'Parliament and the Establishment', in *The Establishment: A Symposium*, edited by Hugh Thomas, London: Ace Books.
Horton, John and Sue Mendus (eds.) 1994, *After MacIntyre*, Cambridge: Polity.
Huberman, Leo and Paul Sweezy 1968, 'Foreword', in Régis Debray, *Revolution in the Revolution? Armed Struggle and Political Struggle in Latin America*, Harmondsworth: Penguin.
Hume, David 1999 [1748], *An Inquiry Concerning Human Understanding*, Oxford: Oxford University Press.
Jackson, Brian and Dennis Marsden 1962, *Education and the Working Class: Some General Themes Raised by a Study of 88 Working-Class Children in a Northern Industrial City*, London: Routledge and Kegan Paul.
James, Daniel 1969, 'Introduction', in Che Guevara, *The Complete Bolivian Diaries and Other Captured Documents*, London: Allen & Unwin.
Jay, Douglas 1959, 'Are We Downhearted? Yes! But We'll Win Back', *Forward*, 53, 42, 16 October: 1, 12.
Jones, Mervyn 1959, 'The Moral Wilderness', *The New Reasoner*, 9: 107–10.
Kautsky, Karl 1983 [1906], 'Marxism and Ethics', in *Karl Kautsky: Selected Political Writings*, edited by Patrick Goode, London: Macmillan.
Kautsky, Karl n.d. [1908], *Foundations of Christianity: A Study in Christian Origins*, London: Orbach and Chambers.
Kidron, Michael 1961, 'Reform or Revolution' *International Socialism*, 7: 15–21.
Kidron, Michael 1961/2, 'Reform and Revolution: Rejoinder to Left Reformism II', *International Socialism*, 7: 15–21.
Kierkegaard, Soren 1948 [1847], *Purity of Heart is to Will One Thing: Spiritual Preparation for the Office of Confession*, New York: Harpers and Brothers Publishers.
Klugman, Jack 1951, *From Trotsky to Tito*, London: Lawrence and Wishart.
Knight, Kelvin 1996, 'Revolutionary Aristotelianism', in *Contemporary Political Studies*, edited by Ian Hampsher-Monk and Jeffrey Stanyer, Political Studies Association of the United Kingdom.
Knight, Kelvin 2007, *Aristotelian Philosophy: Ethics and Politics from Aristotle to MacIntyre*, Cambridge: Polity.
Knight, Kelvin (ed.) 1998, *The MacIntyre Reader*, Cambridge: Polity.

Koestler, Arthur 1943, *Arrival and Departure*, London: Jonathan Cape.

Koestler, Arthur 1947, *Darkness at Noon*, Harmondsworth: Penguin Books in association with Jonathan Cape.

Koestler, Arthur 1950, in *The God That Failed: Six Studies in Communism*, London: The Right Book Club.

Kolakowski, Leszek 1971 [1958], 'Determinism and Responsibility', in *Marxism and Beyond: On Historical Understanding and Individual Responsibility*, London: Paladin Books.

Kollontai, Alexandra 1970 [1921], *The Workers' Opposition*, London: Solidarity.

Krupskaya, Nadezhda 1970 [1930], *Memories of Lenin*, London: Panther.

Kuper, Richard 1970, 'Marxism and Christianity', *International Socialism*, 42: 35.

Lawrence, David 1950 [1936], 'Democracy', in *Selected Essays*, Harmondsworth: Penguin.

Lenin, Vladimir 1960–70a [1899], *The Development of Capitalism in Russia, Collected Works*, Volume 3, Moscow: Progress Publishers.

Lenin, Vladimir 1960–70b [1902], *What Is to Be Done?: Burning Issues for Our Movement*, in *Collected Works*, Volume 5, Moscow: Progress Publishers.

Lenin, Vladimir 1960–70c [1908], *Materialism and Empirio-Criticism: Critical Comments on a Reactionary Philosophy*, in *Collected Works*, Volume 14, Moscow: Progress Publishers.

Lenin, Vladimir 1960–70d [1914–15], *Philosophical Notebooks, Collected Works*, Volume 38, Moscow: Progress Publishers.

Lenin, Vladimir 1960–70e [1916], *Imperialism, the Highest Stage of Capitalism: a Popular Outline*, in *Collected Works*, Volume 22, Moscow: Progress Publishers.

Lenin, Vladimir 1960–70f [1916], 'The Discussion on Self-Determination Summed-Up', *Collected Works*, Volume 22, Moscow: Progress Publishers.

Lenin, Vladimir 1960–70g [1917], *The State and Revolution: the Marxist Theory of the State and the Tasks of the Proletariat in the Revolution*, in *Collected Works*, Volume 25, Moscow: Progress Publishers.

Lenin, Vladimir 1960–70h [1918], 'Extraordinary Seventh Congress of the R.C.P.(B): Political Report to the Central Committee, 7 March [1918]', in *Collected Works*, Volume 27, Moscow: Progress Publishers.

Lenin, Vladimir 1960–70i [1918], 'Political Report to the Central Committee, 7 March [1918]', in *Collected Works*, Volume 27, Moscow: Progress Publishers.

Lenin, Vladimir 1960–70j [1920], *"Left Wing" Communism – An Infantile Disorder*, in *Collected Works*, Volume 31, Moscow: Progress Publishers.

Lenin, Vladimir 1960–70k [1921], 'Tenth Congress of the R.C.P.(B) – Report on the Political Work of the Central Committee of the R.C.P.(B)', 8 March 1921, *Collected Works*, Volume 32, Moscow: Progress Publishers.

Lenin, Vladimir and Leon Trotsky 1979, *Kronstadt*, New York: Monad Press.

Lewin, Moshe 1975 [1969], *Lenin's Last Struggle*, London: Pluto Press.

Lewis, John 1954, *Introduction to Philosophy*, London: Watts and Company.

Lipset, Seymour Martin 1960, *Political Man*, London: William Heinemann.

Lipton, Michael 1969, 'The Competence Mandate: Labour's Record, 1964–8', in, *Matters of Principle: Labour's Last Chance*, edited by Tyrell Burgess et al., Harmondsworth: Penguin.

Liu Shao-Chi 1952, *How to be a Good Communist*, Peking: Foreign Languages Press.

Lukács, Georg 1948, *Uj Magyar Kulturaert*, Budapest: Szikra Kiado.

Lukács, Georg 1962 [1957], *The Meaning of Contemporary Realism*, London: Merlin Press.

Lukács, Georg 1964, *Essays on Thomas Mann*, London: Merlin Press.

Lukács, Georg 1968, *Goethe and His Age*, London: Merlin Press.

Lukács, Georg 1971 [1967], 'Preface to the New Edition', in *History and Class Consciousness: Studies in Marxist Dialectics*, London: Merlin Press.

Lukács, Georg 1972 [1950], *Studies in European Realism*, London: Merlin Press.

Lukács, Georg 1973 [1949], 'Existentialism', in *Marxism and Human Liberation: Essays on History, Culture and Revolution*, New York: Dell Publishing.

Lukács, Georg 1974 [1913], *Soul and Form*, London: Merlin Press.
Lukács, Georg 1980 [1949], *The Destruction of Reason*, London: Merlin Press.
Lutz, Christopher 2004, *Tradition in the Ethics of Alasdair MacIntyre*, Oxford: Lexington Books.
Luxemburg, Rosa 1970, [1918], 'The Russian Revolution', in, *Rosa Luxemburg Speaks*, edited by Mary-Alice Waters, New York: Pathfinder Press.
MacDonald, Ramsay 1908, *Socialism and Government*, London: Independent Labour Party.
Machiavelli, Nicolo 1975 [1505], *The Prince*, Harmondsworth: Penguin.
MacIntyre, Alasdair 1953, *Marxism: An Interpretation*, London: SCM Press.
MacIntyre, Alasdair 1959, 'The Politics of the Belfast Airport Strike' Newsletter, Vol. 3, No. 115, 29th August: 239.
MacIntyre, Alasdair 1960, 'Letter', in *The Listener*, 17 March 1960: 500.
MacIntyre, Alasdair 1962, 'Ireland Whose Own?' Socialist Review, First Series, February: 2–3.
MacIntyre, Alasdair 1965, 'Behan's Book' International Socialism, 21, Summer: 29.
MacIntyre, Alasdair 1966, *A Short History of Ethics*, London: Routledge.
MacIntyre, Alasdair 1967, *Secularization and Moral Change*, Oxford: Oxford University Press.
MacIntyre, Alasdair 1968, 'Le Rouge et Noir', *New Statesman*, 22 November 1968: 713–14.
MacIntyre, Alasdair 1970, *Marcuse*, London: Fontana Press.
MacIntyre, Alasdair 1971, 'Introduction', *Against the Self-Images of the Age: Essays on Ideology and Philosophy*, London: Duckworth.
MacIntyre, Alasdair 1971a [1959], 'Hume on "Is" and "Ought"', in MacIntyre 1971.
MacIntyre, Alasdair 1971b, '"Ought"', in MacIntyre 1971.
MacIntyre, Alasdair 1973, 'Ideology, Social Science and Revolution', *Comparative Politics*, 5: 321–42.
MacIntyre, Alasdair 1985 [1981], *After Virtue: A Study in Moral Theory*, Second Edition, London: Duckworth.
MacIntyre, Alasdair 1988, *Whose Justice? Which Rationality?*, London: Duckworth.
MacIntyre, Alasdair 1990, *Three Rival Versions of Moral Enquiry: Encyclopaedia, Genealogy, and Tradition*, London: Duckworth.
MacIntyre, Alasdair 1995 [1968], *Marxism and Christianity*, London: Duckworth.
MacIntyre, Alasdair 1998a, 'An Interview with Giovanna Borradori', in Knight, (ed.) 1998.
MacIntyre, Alasdair 1998b, 'An Interview for Cogito', in Knight, (ed.) 1998.
MacIntyre, Alasdair 1998c, 'The *Theses on Feuerbach*: A Road Not Taken', in Knight, (ed.) 1998.
MacIntyre, Alasdair 1998d, 'Politics Philosophy and the Common Good', in Knight, (ed.) 1998.
MacIntyre, Alasdair 1999, *Dependent Rational Animals*, London: Duckworth.
MacIntyre, Alasdair 2006a, *The Tasks of Philosophy: Selected Essays, Volume I*, Cambridge: Cambridge University Press.
MacIntyre, Alasdair 2006b, *Ethics and Politics: Selected Essays, Volume II*, Cambridge: Cambridge University Press.
Macmillan, Harold 1938, *The Middle Way: A Study of the Problem of Economic and Social Progress in a Free and Democratic Society*, London: Macmillan.
Malcolm, Norman 1954, 'Wittgenstein's *Philosophical Investigations*', *Philosophical Review*, 63, 4: 530–59.
Mann, Thomas 1927, *The Magic Mountain*, London: Martin Secker.
Marcuse, Herbert 1932, *Hegel's Ontologie und die Grundzüge einer Theorie der Geschichtlichkeit*, Frankfurt au Main: V. Klostermann Verlag.
Marcuse, Herbert 1960, *Reason and Revolution: Hegel and the Rise of Social Theory*, second American edition with a new Preface, Boston: Beacon Press.
Marcuse, Herbert 1968a [1958], *Soviet Marxism: A Critical Analysis*, Harmondsworth: Penguin.

Marcuse, Herbert 1968b [1964], *One Dimensional Man*, London: Sphere.
Marcuse, Herbert 1969 [1955], *Eros and Civilization*, London: Sphere.
Marx, Karl 1964 [1857–8], *Pre-Capitalist Economic Formations*, London: Lawrence and Wishart.
Marx, Karl 1973a [1852], *The Eighteenth Brumaire of Louis Bonaparte*, in *Surveys from Exile*, edited by David Fernbach, Harmondsworth: Penguin/*New Left Review*.
Marx, Karl 1973b [1857–8], *Grundrisse: Foundations of the Critique of Political Economy (Rough Draft)*, Harmondsworth: Penguin Books/*New Left Review*.
Marx, Karl 1974a [1864], 'Inaugural Address of the International Working Men's Association', in *The First International and After*, edited by David Fernbach, Harmondsworth: Penguin/*New Left Review*.
Marx, Karl 1974b [1875], 'Critique of the Gotha Programme', in *The First International and After*, edited by David Fernbach, Harmondsworth: Penguin/*New Left Review*.
Marx, Karl 1974c [1864], 'Provisional Rules of the International Working Men's Association', in *The First International and After*, edited by David Fernbach, Harmondsworth: Penguin/*New Left Review*.
Marx, Karl 1975–2004a [1847–9], 'Wage Labour and Capital', in *Collected Works*, Volume 9, London: Lawrence and Wishart.
Marx, Karl 1975–2004b [1859], *A Contribution to the Critique of Political Economy*, in *Collected Works*, Volume 29, London: Lawrence and Wishart.
Marx, Karl 1975a [1843–4], 'Critique of Hegel's Philosophy of Right. Introduction', in *Early Writings*, edited by Lucio Colletti Harmondsworth: Penguin/*New Left Review*.
Marx, Karl 1975b [1844], 'Economic and Philosophical Manuscripts', in *Early Writings*, edited by Lucio Colletti, Harmondsworth: Penguin/*New Left Review*.
Marx, Karl 1975c [1845], 'Concerning Feuerbach', in *Early Writings*, edited by Lucio Colletti, Harmondsworth: Penguin/*New Left Review*.
Marx, Karl 1975d [1859], 'Preface to *A Contribution to a Critique of Political Economy*', in *Early Writings*, Harmondsworth: Penguin/*New Left Review*.
Marx, Karl 1976 [1867], *Capital: A Critique of Political Economy*, Volume 1, edited by Ernest Mandel, Harmondsworth: Penguin/*New Left Review*.
Marx, Karl 1978 [1885], *Capital: A Critique of Political Economy*, Volume 2, edited by Ernest Mandel, Harmondsworth: Penguin/*New Left Review*.
Marx, Karl 1981 [1894], *Capital: A Critique of Political Economy*, Volume 3, edited by Ernest Mandel, Harmondsworth: Penguin/*New Left Review*.
Marx, Karl and Frederick Engels 1973 [1848], 'Manifesto of the Communist Party', in *The Revolutions of 1848*, edited by David Fernbach, Harmondsworth: Penguin/*New Left Review*.
Marx, Karl and Frederick Engels 1975–2004a [1844], *The Holy Family*, in *Collected Works*, Volume 4, London: Lawrence and Wishart.
Marx, Karl and Frederick Engels 1975–2004b [1845–6], *The German Ideology*, in *Collected Works*, Volume 5, London: Lawrence and Wishart.
McCann, Eamonn 1974, *War and an Irish Town*, Harmondsworth: Penguin.
McMylor, Peter 1994, *Alasdair MacIntyre: Critic of Modernity*, London: Routledge.
Merleau-Ponty, Maurice 1974 [1955], 'Sartre and Ultrabolshevism', in *Adventures in the Dialectic*, London: Heinemann.
Mett, Ida 1967 [1938], *The Kronstadt Uprising 1921*, London: Solidarity .
Molyneux, John 1981, *Leon Trotsky's Theory of Revolution*, London: Harvester.
Murphy, Mark (ed.) 2003, *Alasdair MacIntyre*, Cambridge: Cambridge University Press.
Northern Ireland Constitution 1974, Presented to Parliament by the Secretary of state for Northern Ireland by Command of Her Majesty, July, London: Her Majesty's Stationery Office, Cmnd. 5675.
Nove, Alex 1967, 'Lenin as Economist', in Schapiro and Reddaway (eds.) 1967.
O'Hagan, Timothy 1990, 'Searching for Ancestors', *Radical Philosophy*, 54: 19–22.
Oakeshott, Michael 1962 [1947], 'Rationalism in Politics', in *Rationalism in Politics and Other Essays*, London: Methuen.
Observer Magazine 1989, 'The Expert's Expert: Philosophers', 8 January 1989: 10–11.

Oertzen, Peter Von 1962, Reform and Revolution: Rejoinders 2, International Socialism, 8: 24–28.
Ossowski, Stanislaw 1963, *Class Structure in the Social Consciousness*, London: Routledge and Kegan Paul.
Paine, Thomas 1970 [1791–2], *Rights of Man*, Harmondsworth: Penguin.
Parsons, Talcott 1952, *The Social System*, London: Tavistock Publications in collaboration with Routledge and Kegan Paul.
Pascal, Blaise 1904 [?1657–62], *Pensées*, nouvelle edition, Paris: Librairie Hachette et cie.
Pascal, Gilberte 1962, 'The Life of Monsieur Pascal, written by Madame Perier, His Sister, Wife of Monsieur Perier, Counsellor at the Cour des Audes at Clairmont', in Blaise Pascal, *Pascal's Pensees*, London: Harvill Press.
Pasternak, Boris 1958, *Doctor Zhivago*, London: Collins and Harvill Press.
Popper, Karl 1957, *The Poverty of Historicism*, London: Routledge and Kegan Paul.
Preobrazhensky, Evgeny 1965 [1924/1926], *The New Economics*, Oxford: Clarendon Press.
Raven, Simon 1962, 'Perish by the Sword', in *The Establishment: a Symposium*, edited by Hugh Thomas, London: Ace Books.
Read, David 1958, *Peterloo: the 'Massacre' and Its Background*, Manchester: Manchester University Press.
Reddaway, Peter 1967, 'Literature, the Arts and the Personality of Lenin', in Schapiro and Reddaway (eds.) 1967.
Rees, John C. 1967, 'Lenin and Marxism', in Schapiro and Reddaway (eds.) 1967.
Rees, John 1994/5, 'Engel's Marxism', in *The Revolutionary Ideas of Frederick Engels*, Special Issue, *International Socialism*, 65: 47–82.
Rex, John 1960, *Britain without the Bomb*, London: New Left Pamphlets.
Rex, John 1969, 'The Race Relations Catastrophe', in *Matters of Principle: Labour's Last Chance*, edited by Tyrell Burgess et al., Harmondsworth: Penguin.
Rojo, Ricardo 1968, *My Friend Che*, New York: The Dial Press.
Rosmer, Albert 1971 [1953], *Lenin's Moscow*, London: Pluto Press.
Sandelson, Victor 1962, 'The Confidence Trick: Sir Norman Tullis and Partners', in *The Establishment: a Symposium*, edited by Hugh Thomas, London: Ace Books.
Sartre, Jean-Paul 1957, *Being and Nothingness: an Essay on Phenomenological Ontology*, London: Methuen.
Sartre, Jean-Paul 1962 [1960], 'Altona', in *Altona, Men Without Shadows* and *The Flies*, Harmondsworth: Penguin in association with Hamish Hamilton.
Sartre, Jean-Paul 1963a [1949], *Iron in the Soul*, Harmondsworth: Penguin.
Sartre, Jean-Paul 1963b [1957], *The Problem of Method*, London: Methuen.
Sartre, Jean-Paul 1969 [1952–4], *The Communists and Peace, with an Answer to Claude Lefort*, London: Hamish Hamilton.
Sartre, Jean-Paul 1976 [1960], *Critique of Dialectical Reason* Volume 1: *Theory of Practical Ensembles*, London: New Left Books.
Sartre, Jean-Paul 1991 [1985], *Critique of Dialectical Reason* Volume 2: *The Intelligibility of History*, London: Verso.
Schapiro, Leonard 1967, 'Lenin after Fifty Years', in Schapiro and Reddaway (eds.) 1967.
Schapiro, Leonard and Peter Reddaway (eds.) 1967, *Lenin: the Man, the Theorist, the Leader. A Reappraisal*, London: Pall Mall Press.
Schumpeter, Joseph 1950, *Capitalism, Socialism and Democracy*, third edition, London: Routledge and Kegan Paul.
Sedgwick, Peter 1962–3, 'Letter to the Editors', *International Socialism*, 11: 26.
Sedgwick, Peter 1964, 'The New Left', *International Socialism*, 17: 15–23, reprinted as 'The Two New Lefts', in Widgery (ed.) 1976.
Sedgwick, Peter 1982, 'The Ethical Dance: a Review of Alasdair MacIntyre's *After Virtue*', *The Socialist Register 1982*: 259–67.
Sedova Trotsky, Natalia 1972a [1951], 'Letter to the Executive Committee of the Fourth International and the Political Committee of the Socialist Workers Party, 9 May 1951', in *Natalia Trotsky and the Fourth International*, London: Pluto Press.

Sedova Trotsky, Natalia 1972b [1961], 'Last Statement of Natalia Sedova Trotsky', 9 November 1961, in *Natalia Trotsky and the Fourth International*, London: Pluto Press.
Serge, Victor 1939, 'A Letter and Some Notes: Reply to Ciliga', *New International*, February: 54.
Serge, Victor 1978 [1945], *Memoirs of a Revolutionary, 1901–1941*, edited by Peter Sedgwick, Oxford: Oxford University Press.
Shaw, Martin 1974, *Marxism Versus Sociology: A Guide to Reading*, London: Pluto Press.
Shaw, Martin 1978, 'The Making of a Party?', *The Socialist Register 1978*: 100–45.
Shils, Edward 1972 [1955], 'British Intellectuals in the Mid-Twentieth Century', in *The Intellectuals and the Powers and Other Essays*, London: University of Chicago Press.
Shliapnikov, Alexander 1921, 'Organizatsiya Narodnogo Khozyaistva i Zadachi Soyuzov' ('The Organisation of the Economy and the Tasks of the Unions'), speech of 30 December 1920, Records of the Tenth Party Congress, Moscow: Foreign Language Publications.
Silone, Ignazio 1936, *Bread and Wine*, London: Methuen and Company.
Slaughter, Cliff 1956, 'Modern Marriage and the Roles of Sexes', *Sociological Review*, New Series, 4, 2: 213–21
Slaughter, Cliff 1959, 'The "New Left" and the Working Class', *Labour Review*, 4, 2: 49–54.
Slaughter, Cliff 1960, 'What is Revolutionary Leadership?', *Labour Review*, 5, 3: 93–110.
Solidarity 1965, 'Cardan Debate', *Solidarity*, 3, 10: 22–5.
[Stalin, Joseph] 1938, 'Dialectical and Historical Materialism', in *History of the Communist Part of the Soviet Union (Bolsheviks): Short Course*, Moscow: Foreign Languages Publishing House.
Strachey, John 1956, *Contemporary Capitalism*, London: Victor Gollancz.
Strawson, Peter Frederick 1954, 'Critical Notice of *Philosophical Investigations* by Ludwig Wittgenstein', *Mind*, new series, 63, 249: 70–99.
Sukhanov, Nikolai 1984 [1922], *The Russian Revolution 1917: A Personal Record*, edited by Joel Carmichael, Princeton: Princeton University Press.
Tawney, Richard 1964, *The Radical Tradition: Twelve Essays on Politics, Education and Literature*, London: George Allen and Unwin.
Taylor, Charles 1957a, 'Marxism and Humanism', *The New Reasoner*, 2: 92–8.
Taylor, Charles 1957b, 'Socialism and Intellectuals – Three', *Universities and Left Review*, 2: 18–19.
Thomas, Hugh 1962, 'The Establishment and Society', in *The Establishment: A Symposium*, edited by Hugh Thomas, London: Ace Books.
Thompson, Dorothy 1996, 'On the Trail of the New Left', *New Left Review*, I, 215: 93–100.
Thompson, Edward 1957, 'Socialism and the Intellectuals', *Universities and Left Review*, 1: 31–6.
Thompson, Edward 1957, 'Socialist Humanism', *The New Reasoner*, 1: 105–143.
Thompson, Edward 1958, 'NATO, Neutralism and Survival', *Universities and Left Review*, 4: 49–51.
Thompson, Edward 1960, 'The Point of Production', *New Left Review*, I, 1: 68–70.
Thompson, Edward 1960a, 'The Point of Production', *New Left Review*, I, 1: 68–70.
Thompson, Edward 1960b, 'Revolution Again!', *New Left Review*, I, 6: 18–31.
Thompson, Edward 1978, *The Poverty of Theory and Other Essays*, London: Merlin Press.
Thompson, Willie 1992, *The Good Old Cause*, London: Pluto Press.
Thompson, Willie 1993, *The Long Death of British Labourism*, London: Pluto Press.
Townsend, Peter 1961, 'Freedom and Equality', *New Statesman*, 14 April: 573–5.
Townsend, Peter 1962, 'The Meaning of Poverty', *British Journal of Sociology*, 13, 3: 210–27.
Trotsky, Leon 1937, *The Revolution Betrayed: What is the Soviet Union and Where is it Going?*, New York: Pathfinder Press.
Trotsky, Leon 1947, *Stalin: an Appraisal of the Man and His Influence*, London: Hollis and Carter.

Trotsky, Leon 1970 [1938], 'Art and Politics in Our Epoch', in *Leon Trotsky on Literature and Art*, edited by Paul Siegel, New York: Pathfinder Press.
Trotsky, Leon 1971 [1939], 'Again and Once More Again on the Nature of the USSR', in *In Defence of Marxism*, London: New Park Publications.
Trotsky, Leon 1973 [1938], 'Their Morals and Ours', in Leon Trotsky, John Dewey and George Novack, *Their Morals and Ours: Marxist versus Liberal Views on Morality*, New York: Pathfinder Press.
Trotsky, Leon 1974 [1928], 'What Now?', in *The Third International After Lenin*, London: New Park Publications.
Trotsky, Leon 1976 [1938], 'Hue and Cry over Kronstadt', in *Writings of Leon Trotsky [1937–38]*, New York: Pathfinder Press.
Trotsky, Leon 1977 [1932–3], *The History of the Russian Revolution*, London: Pluto Press.
Trotsky, Leon 1979 [1937], 'Suggestions for a Pamphlet on Kronstadt', in *Writings of Leon Trotsky: Supplement (1934–40)*, New York: Pathfinder Press.
Trotsky, Leon 1981 [1928], 'Our Differences with the Democratic Centralists' (Trotsky to Borodai, 11 November 1928), in *The Challenge of the Left Opposition (1928–29)*, New York: Pathfinder Press.
Trotsky, Leon 1991 [1924], *Literature and Revolution*, London: Redwords.
Trotsky, Leon n.d. [1903], *Our Political Tasks*, London: New Park Publications.
Trotsky, Natalia 1972 [1951], 'Letter to the Executive Committee of the Fourth International/Political Committee of the Socialist Workers Party', 9 May 1951, in *Natalia Trotsky and the Fourth International*, London: Pluto Press.
Vaizey, John 1966 [1962], *Education for Tomorrow*, revised edition, Harmondsworth: Penguin.
Varga, Eugene 1935, *The Great Crisis and Its Political Consequences: Economics and Politics, 1928–1934*, London: Modern Books.
Weller, Ken 1961, *The Truth About Vauxhall*, Dunstable: Solidarity.
Wells, Herbert 1905, *A Modern Utopia*, London: Chapman and Hall.
Who's Who 2004, London: A & C Black.
Widgery, David (ed.) 1976, *The Left in Britain, 1956–1968*, Harmondsworth: Penguin.
Williams, Raymond 1960, *Border Country*, London: Chatto and Windus.
Williams, Raymond 1961 [1959], *Culture and Society*, Harmondsworth: Penguin.
Williams, Raymond 1965 [1961], *The Long Revolution*, Harmondsworth: Penguin.
Williams, Raymond 1966 [1962], *Communications*, revised edition, London: Chatto and Windus.
Williams, Raymond 1979, *Politics and Letters*, London: Verso.
Wilson, Harold 1971, *The Labour Government, 1966–70: A Personal Record*, London: Weidenfeld with Joseph and Michael Joseph.
Wittgenstein, Ludwig 1922, *Tractatus Logico-Philosophicus*, London: Kegan Paul, Trench, Tribner and Company.
Wittgenstein, Ludwig 1968 [1953], *Philosophical Investigations*, third edition, Oxford: Blackwell Publishers.
Wood, Neal 1958, *Communism and British Intellectuals*, London: Victor Gollancz.
Wright Mills, Charles 1951, *White Collar: the American Middle Classes*, Oxford: Oxford University Press.
Wright Mills, Charles 1956, *The Power Elite*, Oxford: Oxford University Press.
Wright Mills, Charles 1958, *The Causes of World War Three*, New York: Simon and Schuster.
Wright Mills, Charles 1960, *Listen Yankee! The Revolution in Cuba*, New York: McGraw Hill Book Company.
Wright Mills, Charles 1963, *The Marxists*, Harmondsworth: Penguin.
Wright Mills, Charles 2000 [1959], *The Sociological Imagination*, Oxford: Oxford University Press.
Yeats, William Butler 1986 [1913], 'September 1913', in *The Faber Book of Political Verse*, edited by Tom Paulin, London: Faber and Faber.
Zhdanov, Andrei 1950 [1947], 'On Philosophy: Speech at a Conference of Soviet Philosophical Workers, 1947', in *On Literature, Music and Philosophy*, London: Lawrence and Wishart.

Index